The Adolescent and Young Adult Self-Harming Treatment Manual

A Collaborative Strengths-Based Brief Therapy Approach

The Adolescent and Young Adult Self-Harming Treatment Manual

A Collaborative Strengths-Based Brief Therapy Approach

MATTHEW D. SELEKMAN

W. W. NORTON & COMPANY

New York • London

For information about permission to reproduce selections from this book, write to Permissions, W. W. Norton & Company, Inc., 500 Fifth Avenue, New York, NY 10110

For information about special discounts for bulk purchases, please contact W. W. Norton Special Sales at specialsales@wwnorton.com or 800-233-4830

Manufacturing by Hamilton Printing
Book design by Gilda Hannah
Production manager: Leeann Graham

Library of Congress Cataloging-in-Publication Data

Selekman, Matthew D., 1957-
    The adolescent & young adult self-harming treatment manual : a collaborative strengths-based brief therapy approach / Matthew D.Selekman. — 1st ed.
        p. cm.
    Includes bibliographical references and index.
    ISBN 978-0-393-70567-6 (pbk.)
        1. Self-injurious behavior. 2. Adolescent psychotherapy. 3. Brief psychotherapy.
I. Title. II. Title: The adolescent and young adult self-harming treatment manual.
    RJ506.S44S447 2009
    616.89'1470835—dc22

                        2008049953

ISBN: 978-0-393-70567-6 (pbk.)

W. W. Norton & Company, Inc., 500 Fifth Avenue, New York, N.Y. 10110
    www.wwnorton.com
W.W. Norton & Company Ltd., Castle House, 75/76 Wells Street, London W1T 3QT

1 2 3 4 5 6 7 8 9 0

CONTENTS

ACKNOWLEDGMENTS

There are several people I wish to thank for greatly contributing to the ideas discussed in this treatment manual. First and foremost, I want to thank Michele Weiner-Davis for showing me a variety of shortcuts for empowering clients and rapidly co-creating with them a therapeutic context ripe for change. From "down under," I would like to thank the late and brilliant Michael White for first introducing me to the creative therapeutic pathway of externalizing clients' oppressive problems. A special thanks goes to Harry Goolishian and Harlene Anderson for teaching me the importance of honoring therapy veterans' long problem-saturated stories and how to collaborate respectfully and effectively with all of the larger systems professionals often involved in these families' lives. I would like to thank my late colleague and researcher Haim Shulem for his excellent and insightful qualitative research work on our *Self-Harming Adolescents and Their Families Expert Consultants' Project.* I would like to thank my friend and colleague Scott Miller for introducing me to the groundbreaking research and therapeutic ideas he and his colleagues are responsible for. A special thanks to Martin Seligman and his colleagues for expanding my therapeutic horizons to the world of positive psychology research and empirically validated interventions. I would like to thank Janis Whitlock at Cornell University for exposing me to her groundbreaking research with self-harming young adult college students. Finally, I would like to thank my Navajo First Nation colleagues Darlene Begay and Lori Arviso-Alvord for exposing me to their important teachings, customs, stories, and healing practices.

There are a few important people I would like to thank for paving the way to the creation of this treatment manual. A big thank you goes to Deborah Malmud at Norton, for giving me the green light to write this treatment manual. Thank you, Kim Johancen-Walt, for contributing a chapter to this treatment manual on your innovative school-based Summit Program for suicidal and self-harming adolescents. A very special thanks goes to Elizabeth B. for contributing her wonderful poem and to all of the other clients who wished to share their artwork and self-harming stories for this treatment manual. I would like to thank Wendy Skotnikov for her thoughtful ideas and assistance with the figures in this volume. Finally, I would like to thank my loving and supportive wife Asa, and Hanna, my angel and other love.

Writing Out Loud

My life writes a book
My heart sings a song
My cuts tell my story
My scars aren't gone
Forever they remain
Forever my shame

I shouldn't be proud
I'm crying out loud
Yelling for help
Screaming in pain
I'm crying to be heard
Cutting for strength
Desperately trying to hold on

—Elizabeth B.

CHAPTER ONE

Introduction: Understanding the Territory of Young Adult and Adolescent Self-Harm

Prevalence of Self-Harming Behavior Among College Students and Adolescents

Since only a small percentage of self-harming individuals seek medical or mental health treatment, it is difficult to assess accurately in the wider population how many people are engaging in this behavior. In the mental health field, self-harming behavior may or may not accompany a constellation of symptoms and behaviors exhibited by individuals diagnosed with borderline personality disorder, posttraumatic stress disorder, and eating and substance abuse disorders. No national or international large-scale research studies to date have kept track of the number of clients diagnosed with these disorders who are self-harming as well. The limited research reports from school and community studies estimates that 10–15% of the general adolescent population has in the past and continues to self-harm (Heath, Schaub, Holly, & Nixon, 2008; Hawton & Rodham, 2006; Lay-Gindhu & Schonert-Reichl, 2005; Muehlenkamp & Gutierrez, 2004; Ross & Heath, 2002). However, Lloyd-Richardson and her colleagues (2007) found in their community study with adolescents a prevalence rate as high as 46.5%. A total of 40%–60% of adolescents who have been psychiatrically hospitalized report self-harming (Hollander, 2008). College students involved in the largest multi-college/university study to date reported self-harming behavior rates ranging from 18%–38%. Some 71% of the researchers' sample reported having self-harmed multiple times in their lifetimes (Whitlock, 2008; Whitlock, Muehlenkamp, & Eckenrode, 2008). Whitlock, Eells, Cummings, and Purington (2007) found in their survey of 290 directors of university-based student mental health centers across the country that 77.9% felt that self-harming behavior has dramatically increased over the last 5 years. In an earlier university study, Gratz (2001) found that 35% of her college sample self-harmed at least once.

Some argue that self-harming behavior is like a highly contagious disease that has spread throughout virtual communities and has lately received a lot of media attention, which may be contributing greatly to the increase of and the fadlike popularity of self-harming behavior today. For adolescents, this tumultuous developmental phase is like one big emotional roller-coaster ride, and in a defying and shocking way some of these youth are dramatizing their inexpressible pain through their self-harming behavior (Plante, 2007; Selekman, 2004). Self-harming behavior has become an emotional outlet that young adults and adolescents can perform in isolation while also connecting on the Internet with others who regularly engage in this behavior and may be experiencing difficulties with it (Whitlock et al., 2008).

Self-harming behavior and the contagion effect run rampant in confined spaces like residential treatment centers, halfway houses, boarding schools, regular schools, college campuses, adult and juvenile detention centers, and some inpatient psychiatric units of hospitals. Some young adults and adolescents are emotionally vulnerable and are easily influenced by their peers to engage in this behavior due to impulsivity and lack of mood management skills. Self-harming behavior can be a way to connect with more powerful and dominant peers in the milieu. For some institutionalized and incarcerated young adults and adolescents, self-harming behavior is a way to rebel against authority, feel powerful, and attempt to regain control over one's life (Favazza & Selekman, 2003; Selekman, 2004, 2006a, 2006b). I would argue that the social contagion effect plays a major role in why we are seeing rashes of and budding epidemics of self-harming behavior occurring more in our schools and on college campuses today. All it takes is one or two powerful and popular peers in the school to endorse this behavior and an epidemic can be set in motion (Selekman, 2006a, 2006b; Gladwell, 2002).

Most Common Reasons Why Young Adults and Adolescents Self-Harm

There are many reasons why young adults and adolescents have gravitated toward self-harming behavior. Each self-harming client's story is unique. Many young adults and adolescents indicate that the major reason why they self-harm is that it is an effective coping strategy for getting quick relief from emotional pain and distress (Hawton & Rodham, 2006; Levine, 2006; McVey-Noble, Khemlani-Patel, & Neziroglu, 2006; Ross & Heath, 2002; Selekman, 2006a, 2006b; Whitlock, Eells, et al., 2007; Whitlock et al., 2008). One study found that only 4% of the general adolescent population self-harms for attention (Hollander, 2008). Most self-harming clients fall into one of two categories: pleasure-seekers or thrill-seekers. The pleasure-seekers are the most common type and the majority of these self-harming clients are trying to quickly make themselves feel better through whatever means: cutting themselves, burning themselves, alcohol or drug use, bingeing and purging, overeating, and engaging in sexually risky behavior. The thrill-seekers tend to be adolescent and young adult males who report getting "a rush" effect from engaging in risky behaviors like pouring lighter fuel on one's arm and setting it on fire, carving symbols/objects on one's body with unsterilized equipment, placing oneself in dangerous situations that do harm to their bodies like daredevil acts, continuing to engage in these behaviors despite incurring deep bruising, broken bones, and serious cuts and abrasions, and having peers repeatedly restricting one's breathing through strangulation holds and mock hangings. Whitlock et al. (2008) and Muehlenkamp, Yates, and Alberts (2004) have identified a small subcategory of self-harming male college students whose main form of self-injury is self-battery. The thrill-seekers may feel emotionally dead inside and are activated by their provocative and forbidden daredevil behaviors. Some self-harming clients fit into both categories, particularly those individuals who engage in extremely risky self-injurious acts to feel something.

More recently, Sharples (2008) reported on a new form of teen self-harming called *self-embedding.* This consists of inserting objects directly underneath the skin or deeper into one's body. This new form of teen self-harming was discovered by a team of radiologists from Nationwide Children's Hospital; they identified 11 out of 505 adolescent patients who had inserted chunks of crayons and paper clips into their bodies. One radiologist indicated he had discovered a 6.3-inch-long unfolded paper clip in one youth's bicep on an X-ray. Upon further investigation, it was determined that the 11 adolescent patients had mental health histories and on the average had self-harmed three times before in the past.

Other reasons why young adults and adolescents say they self-harm are as follows:

- "To be less stressed out"
- "To relieve pain"
- To have control
- "As an escape from my problems"
- To stop bad thoughts
- "To numb out"
- "To feel something"
- To vent anger
- To show desperation
- "To convince others you need help"
- "To feel connected to friends"
- "It's a popular thing to do"
- "It's my drug"
- To purge bad feelings
- To reassociate
- To calm oneself
- The scars represent personal victories
- For self-punishment
- To control or hurt others

Plante (2007) contends that it is important to view the adolescent's self-harming behavior as a healthy striving toward mastering challenging developmental tasks. The self-harming and other self-destructive behaviors are all attempted solutions in the service of the adolescent's emerging sense of self. According to Plante, self-harming adolescents are "doing all the wrong things for the right reasons. Self-injury is the wrong way to cope with all the right strivings related to independence, intimacy, and identity formation" (2007, pp. 3–4).

Many college students and adolescents today complain about experiencing high levels of stress due to massive amounts of homework and excessive parental pressures to succeed academically. They are being bombarded with too many choices, have many concerns about their future careers and our unstable economy, and report that they are struggling to stay afloat (Levine, 2006; Selekman, 2006b; Selekman & Shulman, 2007; Whitlock, Eells, et al., 2007). For adolescents, if the parents are high-achievement oriented, they may be putting a lot of pressure on their kids to achieve nothing short of 'A' grades and to take Advanced Placement (AP) and honors classes so they are highly marketable to the finest universities in the country. It does not stop here for these parents in their efforts to make their kids look as attractive as possible to the top universities and colleges. They also tend to further overload their kids' circuits by overscheduling them in too many extracurricular activities (Selekman, 2006b). Pope and Simon (2005) and Pope (2001) contend that the desperation to succeed at all costs has resulted in the explosion in high rates of anxiety and depression, eating disorders, self-harming, sleep disorders, and somatic complaints among adolescents. In addition, many youths abuse drugs for attention deficit disorder like Ritalin and Adderall, and they drink large quantities of heavily caffeinated coffee and popular drinks like Red Bull to get quick energy boosts, combat depressed feelings and teen angst, and, for the dedicated student, to be able stay up all night to complete their homework.

Methods of Self-Harm

The most popular methods of self-harm are cutting, gouging and carving into the skin, scratching, sticking oneself with needles and pins, pinching oneself to the point of bleeding, inserting unsterilized objects underneath the skin (a popular new fad among teens), and burning oneself. Some self-harming adolescents cut words and symbols into their arms, legs, and abdomens (Levine, 2006; Selekman, 2004, 2006a; Selekman & Shulem, 2007; Walsh, 2006). Self-harming young adults and adolescents burn themselves in the following ways: burning themselves with lit cigarettes, pouring lighter fluid on their arms and setting themselves on fire, using lit matches, rubbing an eraser on their arms to produce a burning sensation with the friction, and pouring hot water and/or chemical substances onto their hands and arms to burn themselves. Many self-harmers pick at their scabs to prevent the healing process. This is another way to trigger the release of endorphins for relief from emotion, emotional distress, and tension. Other methods used for tension relief are hair-pulling, biting oneself (nail-biting or biting one's arms), and hitting oneself to the point of bruising. Less common methods of self-harm are head-banging, bone-breaking, and ingesting harmful chemical substances or objects (such as glass). I have worked with some aggressive young adult and adolescent males who punch their fists into walls when frustrated or angry at others to numb away emotional distress, and continue to do it despite fracturing their bones and causing serious tendon and nerve damage. In a similar fashion, some of my aggressive and gang-involved young adult and adolescent clients engage in this behavior to feel something because they have felt emotionally dead inside. Muehlenkamp et al., 2008 found that males were more likely to hit themselves, whereas females tended to rely on cutting and severe scratching. In the previously mentioned multi-college/university college study, females reported multiple acts of self-harming behavior more often than male students. Many self-harming clients use multiple methods for relieving tension and emotional distress. Whitlock and her colleagues (2008) also found that 71% of their college samples employed multiple methods.

Symptom Switching

Both young adult and adolescent self-harmers may symptom switch back and forth from cutting to bulimia, substance abuse, and unsafe unprotected sex with multiple partners. Bulimia is the most common behavior that both adult and adolescent females turn to as an alternative to self-harming or in conjunction with it, particularly if they are struggling with body-image issues and their peers are engaging in this behavior for weight control. Research indicates that between 35%–60% of female self-harming young adults and adolescents have concurrent bulimia difficulties (Conterio & Lader, 1998; Dohm, Striegel-Moore, Wilfrey, Pike, Hook, & Fairburn, 2002; Favaro, Ferrara, & Santonastaso, 2004; Favazza & Selekman, 2003; Hawton & Rodham, 2006; Paul, Schroeter, Dahmes, & Nutzinger, 2002; Whitlock et al., 2008). It is believed that self-harming females who have concurrent difficulties with bulimia are turning their pain on themselves and are so emotionally distressed and disorganized by their lack of sense of self-control that cutting emerges as another form of self-punishment and desperation (Plante, 2007). Although bulimia is the most common concurrent type of eating disorder self-harming females tend to report, I have worked with some self-harming adolescent and young adult females and males who were obese or anorexic.

The bulimic, substance-abusing, and sexually risky behaviors of self-harmers are all closely related to the self-harming behavior in that they are attempted solutions to cope with emotional distress and overwhelming stressors in their lives; these self-harmers are seeking immediate pleasure, to comfort and soothe themselves and to take back control of their lives (Selekman, 2004, 2006b; Selekman & Shulem, 2007). This view is supported by Miller (2005) and Favazza & Selekman (2003), who contend that the bulimia, substance abuse, and sexually risky behaviors are behavioral equivalents. Hilt and Nolen-Hoeksema (2008) found that 94% of their research sample of mostly Latino and African-American self-harming adolescent girls reported actively abusing substances. Joiner (2005) and Langbehn and Pfohl (1993) have found that substance abuse is a major risk factor for self-harming. In the multi-college/university study, 20% of the participants who reported self-harming also indicated that they were using alcohol and illicit drugs (Whitlock, 2008; Whitlock et al., 2008). The symptom-switching behavior of self-harming young adults and adolescents can present a real challenge and liability for treatment providers, not only because these closely related behaviors provide similar pleasurable effects as self-harming behavior does, making it difficult to stabilize any one or all of these behaviors at the same time, but they can produce serious health consequences or potential death, particularly in those individuals with impaired judgment who are cutting and gouging themselves and abusing substances at the same time.

The Biochemical Dimensions to Self-Harm

According to Favazza (1998), self-harming young adults and adolescents have lower levels of serotonin than the average person, which can cause difficulties with depressed mood, anxiety, rumination, obsessive thoughts, and problems with impulse control. Using a high dosage of Prozac or Zoloft and an antianxiety medication to take the edge off of the antidepressant selected increases the individual's serotonin level to a normal range, which can help balance his or her moods and stabilize the self-harming behavior. Favazza (1998) does not embrace the widely believed endorphin hypothesis for being the driving force for self-harming behavior.

Sachsse, Von Der Heyde, and Huether (2002) found in their research with self-harming individuals that they may have lower levels of cortisol (secreted by adrenal glands when experiencing higher levels of stress), which make them much more emotionally and biologically reactive to environmental stressors than the average person. They may react more intensely to these stressors and may tend to be more impulsive and aggressive, self-harming to regulate their intense emotional states. Chronic overstimulation of the limbic hypothalamo-pituitary-adrenal axis (LHPA) by the cortisol has been linked to depression (Plante, 2007). These researchers also found that self-harming clients have increased levels of norepinephrine (bodily stress chemical secreted during the fight-or-flight response), which also triggers impulsivity and more emotional reactivity.

Research indicates that individuals who self-harm multiple times per day and who have been self-harming for many years have an unusually high tolerance for bodily pain. One study found that 60% of their self-harming research subjects reported never experiencing any pain or bodily discomfort after self-harming (Bohus, Limberger, Ebner, Glocker, Schwarz, Wernz, et al., 2000). It is believed that heavy to long-standing self-harming clients over time may develop problems with the biological regulation of endorphins, which can lead to an increased pain threshold. Many of these self-harming clients have much higher levels of endorphins in their bloodstreams than the average person. This increases the likelihood of experiencing numbness and dissociation when experiencing negative mood states. Furthermore, heavy and longstanding self-harming clients often report "zoning out" while they cut or gouge deeply into their bodies.

Plante (2007) put it best: "The brain serves as a 24-hour pharmacy" (2007, p. 104).The endorphins are natural opiates that quickly numb away emotional pain and distress and produce pleasure and, in some cases, a rush sensation. For self-harming individuals this is a form of self-medicating. They learn how to use their self-harming behavior to regulate their neurochemistry.

Self-Harming Behavior as an Addiction

Many believe that self-harming behavior, when done regularly and over a long period of time, is similar to a drug addiction (D'Amore & Lloyd-Richardson, 2008; Selekman, 2006b; Selekman & Shulem, 2007; Miller, 2005; Joiner, 2005; Walsh, 2006; Whitlock, 2008; Whitlock et al., 2008). It is a form of self-medicating by triggering multiple neurochemical responses that produce numbing and soothing effects (Selekman, 2006b; Schroeder, Oster-Granite, & Thompson, 2002; Walsh, 2006). According to Miller (2005), self-harming behavior follows the same predictable route in behavior, thinking, and conducting relationships as addictions do. It succeeds for the self-harming individual, albeit temporarily obliterating emotional pain and distress quickly. Similar to substance dependency, we see the compulsion to self-harm, loss of control, and continued self-harming behavior despite serious consequences, such as severe physical damage and infections, family and/or relationship difficulties, loss of friends, occupational and/or school difficulties, and poor choice-making in all areas of these individuals' lives. The self-harming individual is willing to endure serious bodily disfigurement and more severe deep tissue damage to his or her body to obtain the reward, which is all endogenous opiate (Osuch & Payne, 2008). Once habituation or dependency occurs with the self-harming behavior, it is very common for these young adults and adolescents to become cross-dependent on bulimia, binge-drinking, and other substances of abuse, and they may engage in unsafe, unprotected sex with multiple partners to elevate their moods, obliterate unpleasant thoughts and feelings, or soothe themselves when experiencing emotional distress. In some cases, they are engaging in these behaviors concurrently, particularly combining bulimia with self-harming behavior often seen with young adult and adolescent females. Once the analgesic properties of the endorphins wear off a few hours later, moderate to severe self-harming individuals often experience withdrawal symptoms like irritability, emotional distress, and cravings, They are highly reactive to stressors in their home and occupational and/or school environments. Overstimulation of the endogenous opioid system can lead to actual withdrawal symptoms (Osuch & Payne, 2008).

Similar to the chemical tolerance or dependence seen with alcohol- and drug-dependent individuals, many self-harming clients report that, over time, they need to cut themselves more frequently and deeper and/or they begin to experiment with a variety of new methods to produce the same pleasurable and/or numbing sensations they were getting from this behavior in earlier periods of their self-harming practices. In the multi-college/university study, 21% of the participants indicated that they had injured themselves more severely than expected at least once (Whitlock, 2008; Whitlock et al., 2008). Michel and Nock (2008) found in their research sample a subset of self-harming adolescents who had a significantly higher tolerance for physical pain and were using multiple methods for inflicting self-harm. In fact, this subset of 23% of the self-harming subjects in the study not only were much more open to submitting themselves to the physical pain tolerance task procedure but were willing to continue engaging in this procedure for the maximum amount of time—183 seconds! The non-self-harming control group of adolescents in the study requested to stop at 61 seconds.

Finally, similar to individuals attempting to abstain from their former drugs of choice who are exposed to powerful negative triggers that may result in a relapse, the same is true for self-harming clients who get derailed from the recovery track once they are exposed to certain objects, places, music, friends who continue to self-harm, or movies and Web sites that feature graphic art or writing involving self-harming themes and behavior. The latest neuroscience research on *mirror neurons* provides a good explanation for why people who are trying to abstain from self-harming, substance abuse, and other addictive habits have a slip or prolonged relapse situation occur when exposed to friends or others who are engaging in this behavior. The activation of one's mirror neurons also activates the association of the motor plans required to grab whatever object used for self-harming and using it on oneself. Higher mirror neuron activity leads to more craving and a slip or prolonged relapsing situation. The more residual craving self-harming clients experience during treatment, the more likely they will experience posttreatment slips and prolonged relapsing situations. Higher mirror neuron activity leads to more craving and more slips (Iacoboni, 2008). D'Amore and Lloyd-Richardson (2008) found in their qualitative study with self-harming college students that they were not only feeling addicted to this behavior but that it was extremely difficult for them to kick their self-harming habits. Whitlock (2008) and Whitlock et al. (2008) found in their multi-college/university study that one-third of their research sample reporting self-harming indicated that it was difficult to control the urge to self-injure, and nothing else worked as well as self-harming to calm them.

Joiner (2005) contended that self-harming behavior has both negative and positive reinforcement dimensions to it, which is similar to substance abuse behavior. The behavior is reinforcing because it quickly gets rid of negative thoughts and feelings, and positive reinforcing because after self-harming it induces positive feelings. Kemperman, Russ, and Shearin (1997) found in their study with adults diagnosed with borderline personality disorder that the clients reported significant mood elevation after self-harming. It is believed that when individuals self-harm the body rapidly secretes endorphins, which act like a fast-acting analgesic to protect us from experiencing bodily pain and triggers a pleasurable sense of well-being and euphoria. Thus, self-harming behavior is a legal "high"; increasingly it is becoming one of the most popular drugs of the 21st century.

For some self-harming clients, pain can even become something desired, and the act of pursuing this bodily sensation takes on an addictive quality. The physical pain feels like relief compared to the overwhelming psychic pain some of these clients are experiencing (Blakeslee & Blakeslee, 2007). However, clients with moderate to heavy self-harming practices, just by thinking about engaging in this behavior and having the expectation of quickly getting immediate relief from emotional pain, based on many past positive experiences, will release endorphins that block agony and produce pleasure and intoxicating highs. Thus, familiarity breeds positive expectations (Ariely, 2008).

Another important dimension of the addictive quality of self-harming behavior is emotional arousal. Research indicates that when we are in an emotionally aroused state, we are twice as likely to engage in more high-risk behaviors. Furthermore, once we experience pleasure from engaging in a particular behavior, no matter how risky or self-destructive, it will imprint in our memory as a pleasurable experience that will help determine whether we pursue this experience when distressed or in need of pleasure (Ariel, 2008).

As accurately portrayed in the movie *Thirteen*, self-harming behavior combined with substance abuse and listening to your favorite tunes with your friends is becoming an increasingly popular recreational activity today among some adolescents. One former adolescent client of mine claimed, regarding this popular recreational activity, "Cutting connects us." Favazza and Selekman (2003), Favazza (1998), and Selekman (2004) have written about how cutting and other forms of body modification historically have been employed as symbols of tribal connection around the world.

Age of Onset

Some research studies have indicated that self-harming individuals first began this behavior around 12 to 15 years of age (Muelenkamp & Gutierrez, 2007; Ross & Heath, 2002; Sourander et al., 2006; Yates, 2004). However, a large multi-college/university study found that 41% of the students began self-harming somewhere between 17 and 20 years of age and a smaller percentage of these students started self-harming between the ages of 21 and 24 (Whitlock et al., 2008).

More recently, mental health professionals, myself included, and school professionals in their practice settings in the United States and abroad are reporting seeing more children 10 to 12 years of age who are exhibiting self-harming, bulimia, and other risky behavior such as substance abuse. One large study in Canada with high school students found that 25% began self-harming around ages 11 to 12. Fifty-nine percent began between the ages of 14 and 15 (Ross & Heath, 2002). Through increased exposure on the Internet and other forms of the media and, in some cases, their older siblings having engaged in self-harming behavior, preadolescents and older children are beginning to experiment with this behavior increasingly more. Recently, I have treated a few 10-year-olds who were experimenting with both cutting and burning themselves. One of these children was dealing drugs for a local street gang.

By Gender

By gender, research indicates that 65% of the self-harming young adult and adolescent population are female and 35% are males. Adolescent females are 4 times more likely to self-harm than males (Hawton & Rodham, 2006). Whitlock, Eells, et al., 2007) in their survey conducted with 290 directors of university-based student mental health centers across the United States, found that 87.9% reported that the majority of the self-harming students seen in their clinics were females. Recently, however, mental health, health care, and school professionals are reporting an increase in the number of self-harming young adult and adolescent males being referred to treatment (Selekman & Shulem, 2007). Gratz, Conrad, and Roemar (2002) and Gratz (2001) found with their samples of college students that just as many males were self-harming as females. The male self-harming numbers also would probably be much larger if it were not due to traditional male socialization practices that stress the importance of men being strong, not displaying publicly their emotions or any signs of weakness, and not going for counseling to talk about their feelings and problems (Benton, Robertson, Tseng, Newton, & Benton, 2003; Gallagher, Zhang, & Taylor, 2003; Selekman, 2006b; Selekman & Shulem, 2007).

For many adolescent girls, all of the physiological changes they are experiencing with their bodies as they enter pubescence is quite emotionally overwhelming and they may struggle to cope with weight gain, menstruation, sexual physical development, libidinal changes, and acne. There is often an increase in interpersonal sensitivity and concerns about being teased by their peers due to their bodily changes. For many young adolescent females, they may lack adequate skills to cope with peer harassment and rejection, which can contribute to the development of depressive symptoms and/or engaging in risky behaviors. Some adolescent girls are forced to grow up too fast through premature sexual activity and at the same time cope with all of their bodily changes and social pressures to fit in, which makes them emotionally vulnerable for psychological and behavioral difficulties. They may be pressured into making unhealthy choices about sex, drugs, and hanging out with older female and male peers who may expose them to additional unhealthy habits like bulimia, sexually risky behavior, and self-harming (Levine, 2006; Plante, 2007; Selekman, 2005; 2006b). According to Hartman-McGilley, "Women operate under constant scrutiny, embattled within and between themselves, their bodies host and hostages to self-harming dynamics. They are in a prison, which is a patriarchal culture, perpetuating an oppressive, violating disregard for women's bodies" (2004, p. 83). As therapists, we need to empower young women to authorize their bodies as sites of power and knowledge and not as battlefields for their self-harming practices (Hartman-McGilley, 2004; Piran, 1998, 2001).

I have worked with a number of self-harming preadolescent, adolescent, and young adult women who had been diagnosed with multiple sexually transmitted diseases (STDs), such as the Human Papillomavirus (HPV), which can cause cervical cancerous conditions in adolescent girls and women. Heterosexual males can be carriers of the virus and not have any symptoms. However, through rectal means, bisexual and gay adolescent males and adults can develop rectal cancerous conditions and transmit this disease to their partners.

Like females going through pubescence, young male adolescents may be experiencing feelings of inadequacy and have difficulty coping with their physiological changes, masculinity, the new world of intimate relationships, and fitting in with popular males. This can make them vulnerable prey for depression and anxiety difficulties and getting in with the wrong crowd of peers who may expose them to drugs, self-harming, and delinquent behaviors (Levine, 2006; Plante, 2007; Selekman, 2006b; Selekman & Shulem, 2007).

Heath, Toste, Nedecheva, and Charlebois (2008) and Whitlock et al. (2008) in their multi-college/university study, found that males tended to employ more extreme methods of self-harm, such as self-battery, for shorter periods of time, or infrequently engaged in this behavior over a longer period of time than females. Over twice as many females in the study fell into the most severe category group of self-harming students, reporting past suicidal thoughts and attempts, serious physical consequences due to their self-harming behavior (significant tissue damage), emotional, sexual, and/or physical abuse, and having been in treatment in the past. This group of females also reported that self-harming behavior was and continues to be a problem in their lives. In this same study, some of the self-harming males tended to use many different and more extreme methods of self-harming than their female counterparts.

Socioeconomic, Racial, and Ethnic Backgrounds of Self-Harming Individuals

Clearly, self-harming behavior cuts across all socioeconomic, racial, and ethnic backgrounds. In a multi-college/university study of 2,877 college students, the researchers based socioeconomic status on the father's highest educational level. A total of 4.1% of the students had fathers with less than a high school education, 7.2% completed high school, 10.7% had some college, 19.7% had completed college, and 58.4% possessed some post-graduate education. One of the most significant findings from the multi-college/university study was that there were no detectable class differences among self-harming students in socioeconomic backgrounds, race, ethnicity, and age (Whitlock, 2008; Whitlock et al., 2008). With large sample sizes, socioeconomic, racial, and ethnic group differences tend to be minimal. Studies involving a smaller sample size in specific urban neighborhoods or communities with larger populations of specific racial and ethnic groups will clearly indicate higher rates of self-harm among these particular groups. Hilt and Nolen-Hoeksema (2008) found in their study of mostly Latino and African-American adolescent girls from low socioeconomic family backgrounds that 56.4% of their sample reported currently self-harming. Twenty-two percent reported engaging in severe forms of self-inflicted violence. Lloyd-Richardson and her colleagues (2007) found in their community study that Caucasian adolescents were more likely to engage in cutting, burning and self-battery than African-American youth. Native American youth have extremely high rates of suicide, self-harm, and substance abuse (Miller, Rathus, & Linehan, 2007; White, 2008). In Indian and Muslim cultures, rituals of self-punishment through body beating, self-whipping, and bloodletting rituals are viewed as a way to transcend one's flesh and elevate the soul (Nasser, 2004). Historically, flagellation has been a way to repent.

"Not fitting in" is a common theme among new immigrant ethnic groups who may turn to their bodies to voice their emotional distress, which symbolizes their marginalization as a cultural group, feeling oppressed, and experiences of social injustice (Nasser, 1997). It is important to carefully determine the unique meaning of self-harming behavior with clients from different cultural and ethnic groups.

Sexual Orientation and Self-Harming

According to Hawton and Rodham (2006), female adolescents who had concerns about their sexual orientation were 4 times more likely to self-harm than boys and girls who did not have these concerns. Ross and Heath (2002) found in their sample of 440 high school students that the gay and bisexual males were much more likely to self-harm than heterosexual males. Research indicates that individuals who identify themselves as gay, lesbian, bisexual, transgendered, or questioning their gender, are strongly associated with self-harming behavior (Whitlock, 2008; Whitlock et al., 2008; Gratz, 2006; Skegg, Nada-Raja, Dickson, Paul, & Williams, 2003). We do know from research on gay, lesbian, and bisexual adolescents that many of these youths had made at least one suicide attempt in the past and, in some cases, multiple attempts. The suicide attempts often coincided with the adolescents trying to come out to their parents (Garofalo, Wolf, Wissow, Woods, & Goodman, 1999; Remafedi, French, Story, Resnick, & Blum, 1998). In the multi-college/university study, 26.2% of the gay and lesbian participant subset of the research sample self-harmed, and 24.5% had had suicidal ideation at some point or had made a suicide attempt in the past (Whitlock, 2008).

Underlying Psychological Issues

Although many self-harming adults and adolescents have had high scores on the Beck Depression and Anxiety Inventories, very little research has supported the notion that an underlying personality disorder is the main cause of self-harming individuals' behavior (Whitlock, 2008; Lofthouse, Muehlenkamp, & Adler, 2008; Michel & Nock, 2008; Ross & Heath, 2002; Selekman, 2006a; Selekman, 2006b; Walsh, 2006). Three-fourths of the sample of self-harming youth felt "lonely" and "alone" with their personal issues. This is a common theme I have heard from self-harming clients in my clinical practice and Whitlock, Eells, et al. (2007) found the same in their multi-college/university study with self-harming college students. Hawton and Rodham (2006) found that adolescent girls self-harming had high rates of depressive and anxiety symptoms. These adolescents reported feelings of hopelessness, low self-esteem, and body-image issues. Hilt and Nolen-Hoeksema (2008) found in their study with self-harming adolescent girls high rates of depressive symptoms and rumination difficulties. D'Amore and Lloyd-Richardson (2008) found in their research with self-harming college students high rates of depressive and anxiety symptoms. Klonsky (2007), however, found in his study that anxiety symptoms had a stronger relationship to self-harming behavior than depression did. Gratz (2006) contends that self-harming individuals often have more difficulty identifying and expressing their emotions than non-self-harming individuals.

Because of the intimidating and challenging nature of the self-harming behavior and many treatment providers lacking the experience, knowledge, and skills to treat these young adults and adolescents, the borderline personality disorder is frequently given to self-harming clients. According to the *Diagnostic and Statistical Manual of Mental Disorders (DSM-IV)*, in order to use the borderline personality disorder diagnosis with adolescents who are self-harming, they must have had pervasive borderline symptoms throughout their childhoods or be at least 18 years old (American Psychiatric Association, 1994). Since self-harming behavior is one of the most common symptoms of individuals diagnosed with borderline personality disorder, often mental health professionals will take this symptom out of context and make the borderline personality disorder diagnosis at intake, even before getting to know the clients, and conducting a comprehensive psychosocial history with the clients' past treatment history, psychological, family, social, and school/occupational functioning. Jerome Groopman, M.D. (2007) has pointed out, in his thought-provoking and best-selling book *How Doctors Think,* that it is not uncommon for some doctors to arrive at their diagnoses in 18 seconds. Having consulted for many treatment programs worldwide and frequently hearing the borderline label used by frustrated clinicians who found their self-destructive clients highly intimidating, difficult to work with, or unlikeable, I can attest to the fact that there are many mental health professionals out there who are as quick to diagnose as the doctors Groopman is referring to. Thus, many self-harming young adults and adolescents are misdiagnosed, needlessly psychiatrically hospitalized, and medicated well before the therapy process begins. Worse yet, they have little or no say in the treatment planning and final decision-making with treatment modality selection and goal-setting (Selekman, 2006a, 2006b; Selekman & Shulem, 2007).

With clinical populations, self-harming behavior is often viewed as a secondary behavioral characteristic of depression and anxiety, posttraumatic stress disorder, or borderline personality disorder (Skegg, 2005; Yates, 2004). However, others argue that some self-harming individuals' symptoms may not meet the criterion for a major DSM-IV disorder and should be conceptualized as a risk behavior (Kessler, Costello, Merikangas, & Ustun, 2001; Michel & Nock, 2008; Selekman, 2006b; Whitlock, 2008).

Emotional, Sexual, and Physical Abuse Background

The research findings are quite mixed about most self-harming young adults and adolescents having been sexually or physically abused in their pasts. No research to date has demonstrated a neurological mechanism by which childhood abuse leads to self-harm (Osuch & Payne, 2008). One study found that adolescents who had been physically abused were 4 times more likely to self-harm (Hawton & Rodham, 2006). Whitlock et al. (2008) found in their multi-college/university study that class 3 category students who regularly and heavily self-harming were 3.5 times likely to report family backgrounds of emotional and/or physical or sexual abuse. Selekman (2006a,b) and other specialists working with self-harming clients have reported emotional neglect and invalidation and disconnection as common features in the families of self-harming adolescents (Miller, et al., 2007; Levine, 2006; Miller, 2005; Plante, 2007). Longstanding experiences with parental invalidation can be traumatizing (van der Kolk, Roth, Pelcovitz, Sunday, & Spinazzola, 2005; Yates, 2004). Not only can this lead to serious attachment and trust issues in both parental and significant relationships outside the home, but the client may be unable to really know what they are feeling, or feel emotionally dead inside and experience de-realization. A 14-year-old former client of mine had reported that she had been invalidated by her parents repeatedly for several years and described herself as both "feeling nothing inside" and being "invisible" in her relationships with each of her parents.

According to Nasser (2004), self-harming behavior functions as a language that articulates past trauma by repeating it in the present as pain. Miller (2005) contended that the self-harming behavior and possible concurrent eating disorder and substance abuse were the physical and psychological reenactment of childhood trauma.

Many clinical specialists working with young adult and adolescent self-harming clients contended that a very small percentage of these individuals had been sexually or physically abused. Similar to the borderline personality disorder label, many mental health professionals, once they learn that their new clients are self-harming, will leap to the conclusion that they are suffering from posttraumatic stress disorder and must have experienced some form of abuse (Selekman, 2006a; Selekman & Shulem, 2007). The self-harming behavior is taken out of context.

Some individuals who had been sexually or physically abused have relied on self-harming behavior to get out of dissociative states, stop flashback activity, and for disrupting unpleasant thoughts and painful feelings that may have been triggered by intruding memories and environmental triggers. The following case example illustrates how self-harming behavior can aid an adolescent girl in re-associating.

> Cindy, a 15-year-old self-harming and substance-abusing adolescent, used cutting as a way of getting herself out of dissociative states when she would "zone out" in one of her classes. She would carve lines on her arms as a way to both get out of her dissociative state (reassociate) and to create natural boundaries between the internal conflicts about allowing herself to be emotionally vulnerable with a new boy she liked in this class and the threat he posed if he got too close and pursued her for a date. In Cindy's mind, her distorted thinking and catastrophic fear was that this boy was no different from her paternal grandfather (the perpetrator) in trying to take advantage of her if she would allow herself to be vulnerable with him. For Cindy, her cutting behavior proved to be an effective attempted solution to cope with this dilemma.

Sexually and physically abused self-harming young adults and adolescents may be seeking mastery over pain and past trauma (Miller, 2005). Yates (2004) contended that self-harming individuals who had been severely traumatized in childhood undermine their normal developmental process regarding establishing a cohesive sense of self, regulating affect, controling impulsivity, and establishing healthy relationships with others. Some of these individuals struggle with *alexithymia*, which is impairment in the ability to recognize, label, and verbalize their feelings. These individuals often have difficulties with affect tolerance, anhedonia, and self-care, and they experience psychosomatic complaints (Krystal, 1982). Self-harming can become an ideal coping strategy for regulating one's feelings or for just feeling something.

Self-Harming Versus Suicidal Behavior

Research indicates that the majority of infrequent to regular self-harming young adults and adolescents will either have never had suicidal ideation or may have thought about it at some time in their lives but had never made an attempt (Muehlenkamp & Gutierrez, 2004; Nock, Joiner, Gordon, Lloyd-Richardson, & Prinstein, 2006; Selekman, 2006a; Selekman & Shulem, 2007; Walsh, 2006; Whitlock & Knox, 2007; Whitlock, 2008). Cutting is rarely associated with completed suicide in young people and also tends to be less lethal than other forms of self-harm (Walsh, 2006). A very small percentage of self-harming individuals will have made one or more attempts to take their lives in the past and are actively suicidal prior to or while in treatment. These are individuals who are usually grappling with multiple stressors and intense emotional pain, and they have no support system (Miller et al., 2007). Favazza made the following distinction between self-harming and suicidal individuals: "Self-mutilation is distinct from suicide behavior. Major reviews have upheld this distinction. A person who truly attempts suicide, seeks to end all feelings whereas a person who self-mutilates seeks to feel better" (1998, p. 262). Similarly, the suicide pioneer Shneidman (1985) contended that the intent of a suicidal person is to "terminate consciousness" and stop the emotional pain permanently. Assessing clients' intent and the unique meanings of their self-harming behavior for them is critical. According to Nasser, "self-harming individuals do not pursue death through attacking their bodies, they attempt to defy it. They attempt to alter the deadness they feel inside and hope to expand consciousness through their acts so as to free themselves from their voiceless, yet enveloping internal anguish" (2004, p.19).

However, with longtime and heavy self-harming clients (multiple daily acts and inflicting deep and serious tissue damage), it may be a different story. Joiner contended that the "habituation and practice effects of repeated self-injury may be implicated in the escalating trajectory toward serious suicidality" (2005, p. 84). He further added that "as individuals continue to self-injury it loses its painful and fear-inducing properties and as this occurs, the main barrier to suicide erodes" (2005, p. 85). Therefore, according to Joiner's theory, once clients have self-harmed for a long period of time, they have acquired the ability and fearlessness about confronting pain, serious self-harm, and indeed death. Death may come to be viewed as a positive or beautiful thing. O'Connor, Sheehy, and O'Connor (2000) found in their study that long-standing hospitalized self-harming clients tended to report that their most current method of self-harming behavior was much more aggressive and potentially more lethal than those used by clients who self-harmed infrequently.

Another important distinction between nonlethal self-harming and serious at-risk suicidal clients is the *perceived burdensomeness to others* risk factor (Brown, Cortois, & Linehan, 2002; Joiner, Petit, Walker, Voelz, Cruz, Rudd, et al., 2002). According to Brown et al., (2002), non-lethal self-harming clients in their study reported engaging in self-harming behavior to either express their anger or to inflict self-punishment, whereas perceived burdensomeness was reported by the truly suicidal clients. Research indicates a strong association between strong desires to make others better off or burdensomeness and severe suicide attempts and completions (Joiner, 2005). Other important differentiating features between self-harming and truly suicidal individuals to assess for are: expressed intent, level of physical damage and potential lethality; intensity and chronicity of psychological pain, presence of cognitive constriction; and hopelessness and helpnessness (Whitlock, 2008).

Nock et al. (2006) and Whitlock and Knox (2007) found that individuals that have attempted suicide were more likely to have longer histories of, and use of a greater number of methods of self-harm than those without a suicide attempt. These researchers also found that individuals who do not experience any physical pain when they self-harm are also at higher risk for a future suicide attempt. Longitudinal studies are necessary with self-harming adolescents to see if continuing this behavior over time will inevitably lead to suicidal behavior.

Family Dynamics and Characteristics

There is limited research on the families of self-harming young adults and adolescents. One of the most common family dynamics often observed in families with self-harming young adults and adolescents is emotionally invalidating family interactions (Hollander, 2008; Linehan, 1993a; Miller et al., 2007; Selekman, 2006b; Selekman & Shulem, 2007). This ranges from parents or key caretakers not listening to and responding with empathic attunement to the self-harming young person, to responding in a negative, emotionally reactive manner with anger, a high level of anxiety, or criticism, or viewing the behavior as "manipulative," to emotionally disconnecting from the self-harming young person, or, in extreme situations, responding with disconfirmation (Harrington, Kerfoot, Dyer, McNiven, Gill, & Harrington, 1998; Linehan, 1993; Miller, 2005; Miller et al., 2007; Selekman, 2005; 2006a, 2006b). Selekman (2006a, 2006b) and Selekman and Shulem (2007) have observed the following types of parent-adolescent interactions in families with self-harming adolescents: Parents in the throes of their emotional reactivity to their son or daughter's repeated self-harming episodes make threats of psychiatrically hospitalizing or placing him or her in a boarding school or residential treatment center; they may greatly increase their parental overprotectiveness and squelch their adolescent's strivings for more autonomy; or constantly and critically compare the adolescent to their model sibling that has been a success story and placing undue pressure on him or her to achieve at a high level academically and in all of their extracurricular pursuits. The following case example illustrates how extreme parental overprotectiveness and the blurring of generational boundaries can get.

> Katy had been psychiatrically hospitalized for cutting due to her school's and the district psychiatrist's concern that she was suicidal. Upon being discharged from the hospital, Katy's psychiatrist strongly recommended that her mother closely monitor her to make sure she was not smuggling sharp objects into her bedroom. Katy's mother was naturally a very anxious person and had decided to move into Katy's bedroom for a month so that she could tightly monitor her. Needless to say, this not only thwarted Katy's developmental need for more freedom but further fueled the preexisting conflicts in the relationship.

Levine (2006) has found in her clinical work with upper-middle-class and affluent self-harming adolescents similar family dynamics, and she contends that many of these youth lack or have very poor self-management skills, such as self-regulation, impulse control, frustration tolerance, and the ability to delay gratification. She believes this is due to the fact that many of these adolescents have never been allowed to experience emotional discomfort, sit with and learn how to tolerate frustration, and work for what they need and really want. For some of these parents, it is about status and their love is conditional and manifests itself in the form of expensive gift-giving. The adolescents are seen as extensions of them, not separate individuals with unique needs and goals. Finally, she has found that some of these parents can be extremely critical of their adolescents, which can fuel self-hatred and self-harming behavior. Parent-adolescent conflict, arguing, emotional disconnection,and parental divorces and separations, have been identified as a risk factor for adolescent self-harm (Harrington et al.,1998; Reinhurz, Giaconia, & Silverman, 1995; Tulloch, Whitbeck, Hoyt, & Johnson, 1997). Conversely, good family communications, family harmony and cohesion, and the adolescent feeling validated and understood served a protective function against self-harming and other self-destructive behaviors (Rubenstein, Hafton, Kasten, Rubin, & Stechler, 1998; Selekman, 2006b; Selekman & Shulem, 2007; Wagner, Aiken, Mullaley, & Tobin, 2000; Wagner, Cole, & Schwartzman, 1995).

Another family risk factor for adolescent self-harming behavior is when a parent or sibling currently or in the past engaged in this behavior (Eskin, 1995; Rey Gex, Narring, Ferron, & Michaud, 1998). Similarly, adolescents who come from families where one or more family members or extended family members had made a suicide attempt or completion can be at risk for future suicide attempts (Miller et al., 2007).

With some families, the self-harming adolescents are "parentified" or "adultified"; that is, they may have to take care of their younger siblings. or serve as a junior individual and marital therapist to one or both parents (Selekman, 2006; Selekman & Shulem, 2007). Fourteen-year-old Mary's family situation illustrates her dilemma as a parentified child.

> Mary was elevated to mother status by her single-parent father who nearly died from cancer twice. Her younger brothers, 12 and 10 years of age, refused to accept her authority and constantly would rebel against her directives and argue with her. This in turn would upset her father and she would end up feeling guilty and frustrated for not doing her job well enough. Raised in a traditional way, Mary felt that it was her "duty as good daughter" not to complain about feeling overburdened by her stressful role and not to complain to and further stress out her father. Her attempted solution was to cut herself as both a coping strategy and as a way to release her unpleasant feelings in the privacy of her bedroom. This way she remained loyal to her father and got some temporary relief from her emotional distress from being overburdened by her parentified role.

Some of these parentified adolescents and young adults often end up getting involved in relationships outside the home where they play the caretaking role in certain peer and intimate relationships. They may become other-centered where their personal needs do not get met or become less significant in these unhealthy relationships. This can further perpetuate the self-harming behavior and other self-destructive behaviors.

Claes, Vandereycken, and Vertommen (2004) found in their family research with families of clients where the identified client had an eating disorder and either self-harmed or did not engage in this behavior, the families where both problems occurred had less cohesive and expressive family environments than the families where the eating disorder was the main problem and self-harming behavior was absent. Of the 131 families with an eating-disordered identified client, 47% had a concurrent self-harming problem.

In some cases, the self-harming young adults and adolescents are like *family saviors*, in that the timing of severe cutting episodes coincides with increased parental arguing, recent separations, or the threat of divorce (Selekman, 2006b; Selekman & Shulem, 2007). With noble intent, they will go to great lengths to keep their parents together, such as self-inflicting deep tissue damage to themselves with sharp objects, ending up in the emergency room of a hospital after mixing and ingesting large quantities of alcohol and other substances, or getting arrested. The following case example illustrates dramatically how far an adolescent is willing to go to prevent the demise of her parents' marital relationship.

> Carmelita, a 15-year-old female adolescent, carved deeply into both of her arms with a razor blade at school several times the morning after her father had threatened to "move out" and "divorce" her mother. Our first official family therapy session was conducted in her high school dean's office with her extremely worried parents. She not only succeeded at keeping her father in the home but the parents contracted to work on their serious marital problems with me as well. Lucinda also had reported that the frequency of her cutting episodes had increased and paralleled the frequency and intensity of her parents' arguments.

Finally, Whitlock, Eells, et al. (2007) found in their multi-college/university study that college students' concerns about the current national economic difficulties and the impact of this on their families' finances and college costs have been reported as an external stressor that they worry about. Similarly, Reinhurz et al. (1995) found that self-harming females, more so than males, worried a great deal about family finances.

Peer Contributions

According to Hawton and Rodham (2006), adolescent males who have friends who are self-harming are 7 times more likely to engage in this behavior. Adolescent girls are four and a half times more likely to engage in this behavior if their friends do as well. The researchers also found that the adolescent girls in their study tended to become much more emotionally vulnerable to self-harming and other risky behaviors following a relationship breakup than boys. Peer risk factors for self-harming behavior were arguing with friends, making and sustaining friendships, bullying, and not feeling accepted because of sexual orientation. Nock and Prinstein (2005) found in their study that 82% of the adolescents in psychiatric inpatient programs had a self-harming friend whom they admired, and that the contagion effect played a role in their decision to engage in self-harming behavior.

Clearly, peer group life is a lot tougher for adolescents today. Not being able to fit in and be accepted by one's peers is the equivalent to social death! Plante (2007) believed that pain and struggle are powerful sources of connection and identification among peers. "We are in this together, you are not alone" is the mantra. Hollander (2008) reported that peers often get a bad rap and are blamed by parents and other adults for why adolescents choose to self-harm. Hollander contended that "change comes from inside out," and that once adolescents stop self-harming, they are more likely to establish new and healthier friendships.

A self-harming peer contagion effect tends to occur a great deal in confined spaces, such as some inpatient psychiatric programs, residential treatment centers, and juvenile detention centers. This may be due to the social phenomenon of *progressive conformity:* following the lead of powerful and popular peers that are endorsing this behavior and imitation (Moos, 1979).

Since most self-harming young adults and adolescents tend to talk to their friends about their difficulties, rather than their parents and mental health and health care professionals, prevention-wise and clinically it makes a great deal of sense to involve the self-harming individuals' friends in both early intervention efforts and in the treatment process once they make it to a mental health provider. Selekman & Shulem (2007) and Selekman (1995, 2004, 2005, 2006a, 2006b) have found that peer involvement in the treatment process has helped with alliance-building, in generating creative solutions, and in preventing relapses of both young adult and adolescent self-harming clients.

Media and Internet Usage and Contribution to Self-Harming Behavior

Whitlock, Purington, and Gershkovich (2009) contended that self-injury is now firmly a part of the media landscape. Since the popular movie *Thirteen* was first shown in theaters, self-harming behavior has been featured as the "hot societal issue of the day" on talk shows and popular TV shows watched by millions, like *Seventh Heaven*, *House*, *Grey's Anatomy*, *Nip/Tuck*, and *Will & Grace*. As of spring 2007, there were 47 movies that featured self-harming behavior, among them *Thirteen*; *Secretary*; *Sid and Nancy*; and *Girl, Interrupted*, just to name a few. Most of these movies portrayed the self-harming character as being a white female "cutter." Many famous celebrities have been coming out to the public to disclose their self-harming behavior in an attempt to increase the public's awareness of how they employed this behavior to cope with personal difficulties and stressors. A few self-harmers are the late Princess Diana, Johnny Depp, Angelina Jolie, Christina Ricci, Courtney Love, Marilyn Manson, and Pink, to name a few. Pink has been quoted as saying how body modification helps her: "I like putting holes in my body. It's addictive; it's a pain to know you're alive" (Joiner, 2005, p. 85). There is a danger in popular talk show hosts inviting their current and reformed self-harming guests and celebrities to disseminate to millions their ideas, reflections, and detailed stories about how and why they self-harmed, and possibly continue to: it can set in motion a mass contagion effect. Research indicates that 52% of adolescents who self-harm learned about this behavior from both the media and friends (Hollander, 2008).

There are now 89 songs making reference to self-harming behavior. Some 87% are classified as alternative, emo, goth, heavy metal, or punk. Six percent were classified as rap and 4.8% pop, respectively (Whitlock, Powers, & Eckenrode, 2006). Some of the emo, goth, and punk performers regularly demonstrate onstage how to carve oneself up with broken bottles and other sharp objects, as well as a variety of ways to burn oneself. Selekman and Shulem (2007) and Selekman (2006b) found that a number of self-harming adolescents first got the idea to self-harm from their favorite emo, goth, or punk performers they had witnessed engaging in this behavior on concert stages.

Selekman (2006b) has had self-harming adolescents share with him that movies like *Thirteen* and certain self-harming-focused Web sites or sites where one can access self-harming thematic material like Blood Red, The Cutting World, Razor Blade Kisses, Xanga, and YouTube, to name just a few, act as a powerful trigger for a self-harming episode. In fact, some of these Web sites have live-action cams where visitors can witness individuals carving up or burning themselves. On YouTube there are hundreds of video clips and other graphic self-harming images. Some self-harming young adults and adolescents have reported that their friends have posted on their MySpace and Facebook pages photos of places on their bodies where they have self-harmed.

The popularity of MySpace and Facebook among college students and adolescents today has made this one of the most frequently used modes to communicate with friends. As one self-harming adolescent client put it to me and to her father, who had voiced his concerns about her excessive use of the Internet, "Just if you old folks don't know, this is how we communicate. It's like therapy for me." In fact, the Internet is now the number one social meeting place today. MySpace and Facebook have overtaken malls as the primary socializing venue for teens (Gross, 2004; Roberts, Foehr, & Rideout, 2005). Eighty-seven percent of teens use the Internet regularly, and 70% of adults use the Internet daily (Lenhart, Madden, & Hitlin, 2005).

However, both college students and adolescents have exploited more emotionally vulnerable peers on their MySpace and Facebook pages by posting terrible rumors, character assaults, manipulation, and inappropriate pictures, which can cause serious psychological and social harm and, in worst case scenarios, lead to a suicide attempt and possible completion (Levine, 2006; Selekman, 2006b; Simmons, 2002). Some adolescents I have worked with have referred to MySpace as "Mean-Space" after they were dropped off one or more friends' friendship lists or had typed into their Honesty Boxes on their MySpace page friends' critical comments about their bodily shapes, facial blemishes, and other things they and others do not like about them as a person. It is devastating enough for an adolescent to receive this bad news from their so-called friends but to have it posted on his or her webpage for the whole world to see can really push him or her over the edge and feel like the equivalent of social death, particularly with their social status among their peers.

Another common practice and closely related sadistic use of the Internet employed by more vicious and psychologically abusive college students and adolescents is posting on newly created webpages slanderous rumors and photographs taken by cell phones capturing fellow students and former friends they wish to scapegoat or tarnish their reputations in awkward moments or private situations, such as nude in the locker room, biting their nails, and so forth (Selekman, 2006a; Selekman & Shulem, 2007; Simmons, 2002). JuicyCampus.com is a rapidly growing and popular gossip site on college campuses that solicits content with the promise of anonymity. Unfortunately, what began as fun and games has now turned ugly, with vicious postings of rumors and lies, finger-pointing, accusations of students being racists, drug dealers, and offering sex to interested parties. The Web site allows "anyone with a grudge to maliciously attack students," as an interviewed Duke University student had reported about this site in his school newspaper (Bennett, 2007).

Some of the positive aspects of Internet usage by self-harming young adults and adolescents are the special chat room-based support groups they can access to combat social isolation and connect with others struggling with similar difficulties. In my private practice and in recent research studies, many self-harming young adults and adolescents have reported feeling "alone" and not fitting in well socially with their peers (Selekman, 2006b; Selekman & Shulem, 2007; Whitlock, Muehlenkamp & Eckenrode, 2008). Some of these chat room support groups are run by skilled therapists and are regularly monitored, while others are too loosely monitored. For some self-harming young adults and adolescents, virtual self-harming communities have been a gift (D'Onofrio, 2007). Internet groups and friends become like family, and meaningful relationships are established with others who are similar to them. Murray and Fox (2006) found that 37% of their sample indicated that self-harming discussion groups on the Internet had a positive effect on their behavior through support of their efforts to cease self-harming and/or through enhancement of self-acceptance. Only 7% of their research subjects had felt that their participation in these groups had led to an increase in self-harm.

There are close to 500 message boards on the Internet that can bring young adult and self-harming individuals together worldwide. Although designed to combat isolation and shame, they may reinforce self-harming behavior and help individuals become better at doing it by learning new methods. On the upside, Whitlock, Powers, and Eckenrode (2006) contended that the message boards provide a positive environment for self-harming adolescents, since healthy social and emotional development hinges on adolescents' ability to establish caring and meaningful relationships, to be accepted, and to feel connected to their peers. The Internet makes it possible for adolescents to find other youth similar to them 24/7, and the parents are not even aware of this immediate level of access for support.

The disadvantages of young adult and adolescent self-harming individuals mainly relying on these online chat room support groups is that they don't model or teach healthy coping and problem-solving tools and strategies, relationship skills, or how to resolve family and relationship conflicts directly. At any given time, they can reinforce an emotionally focused coping style that supports conflict avoidance. Hawton and Rodham (2006) found in their large sample of self-harming adolescents that the majority of their subjects employed an emotionally focused coping style characterized by conflict avoidance and isolation. Whitlock, Lader, and Conterio (2007) contended that another danger of these online chat room groups is *narrative reinforcement*, that is, sharing similar life stories can justify the use of self-harming as a coping strategy. This may block self-harming adolescents from looking at their triggers, taking steps to abstain from this behavior, and learning more adaptive coping strategies. They may learn better ways to self-harm from a virtual community that supports this behavior. Finally, for more emotionally vulnerable adolescents, it can become a toxic virtual environment that young people are stumbling into in the same way kids stumble into finding people who are predatory (Whitlock, Powers, et al., 2006).

Siegel (2008) contended that all of the hype that the Internet is about "connectivity" is, in fact, completely wrong. Instead, it encourages disconnection, isolation, and conflict avoidance. Spending long stretches of time in front of a computer screen communicating with faceless others does not strengthen one's peer and family relationships or develop one's social skills, such as knowing how to resolve interpersonal conflicts, tolerate frustration and delay gratification, and combat social isolation. It does not strengthen one's capacity for self-efficacy or build one's self-esteem. The following case example illustrates the extremely harmful effects of parents allowing their at-risk adolescent to be left completely unmonitored on the Internet for excessive periods of time.

> Ted, a 15-year-old self-harming adolescent I worked with, was allowed by his parents to spend close to 48 hours every weekend playing violent online computer games and visiting unhealthy chat rooms and Web sites that endorsed self-harming behavior. Whenever the parents would try and communicate with him or attempt to get him to join them on a family outing, he would become verbally abusive, punch his bedroom wall and kick in his door, and threaten to hurt them. One time he struck his father and the police had to be called to restrain him. During the school week, Ted would fall asleep in class, and would be verbally abusive toward his teachers when they confronted him about his behavior. He had a hard time concentrating in class and completing his homework, and he was failing some of his major subject classes.

According to Thomas and Watzman (1999) and Kraut, Patterson, Lundmark, Kiesler, Mukophadhyay, and Scherlis (1998), high school students who engaged in regular Internet usage over an extended amount of time tended to report spending less time talking with family members, reduced the amount of time they went out and socialized with longtime friends, and felt increases in loneliness and depression.

It is important to mention that there are some very positive Web sites that offer a great deal of individual and group support and valuable resources for both young adult and adolescent self-harming individuals. These Web sites are American Self-Harm Information Clearinghouse, SIARI, S.A.F.E. Alternatives, WebMD, and Life-Signs.

Treatment Outcome Studies

There are very few well-controlled treatment outcome research studies on young adult and adolescent self-harming clients. The limited number of treatment outcome studies that have been conducted have had small sample sizes, and have lacked samples where the main presenting problem was just self-harming behavior. Both adults and adolescents were combined in the studies, the studies are lacking balanced heterogeneous samples across genders, socioeconomic levels, and cultural groups, and there are serious research methodological problems. Couple and family treatment outcome studies with only self-harming young adult and adolescent clients are lacking as well. Most of the treatment outcome studies of clients that are self-harming assigned diagnoses of borderline personality disorder. One of the most clinically promising empirically validated treatment approaches that has shown good outcomes with self-harming adult clients diagnosed with borderline personality disorder is the dialectical behavior therapy approach of Marsha Linehan (Linehan, 1993a, 2000; Linehan, Heard, & Armstrong, 1993; Shearin & Linehan, 1994). More recently, Miller et al. (2007) and Santisteban, Muir, Mena, and Mitrani (2003) have utilized an expanded and integrative dialectical behavior therapy approach with self-harming and suicidal adolescents and their families.

Whitlock, Eells, et al. (2007) found in their survey with 290 directors of university-based student mental health centers that cognitive-behavioral therapy and dialectical behavioral therapy employed by their clinical staffs were the choice treatment methods for self-harming students. They felt that both of these models address three of the core issues that self-harming clients struggle with: poor mood management skills, distress tolerance, and self-regulation.

Evans, Tyrer, Catalan, Schmidt, Devidson, & Dent (1999) in using a manual-assisted cognitive-behavioral therapy (MACT) to treat 34 adults with repetitive acts of self-harming behavior found that the MACT experimental group, compared to the control group who received treatment-as-usual, had lower rates of self-harm as well as a longer time delay between self-harming episodes. The MACT treatment is a short-term six-session problem-solving and cognitive-behavioral intervention that teaches clients skills to manage emotions and negative thinking. Unlike in many of the other studies conducted with suicidal and self-harming clients, these researchers used a random sampling procedure where 18 of the subjects had been assigned to the MACT treatment and 16 to the treatment-as-usual group.

There are no couple or family treatment outcome studies that have been conducted that were scientifically sound and had only self-harming young adults and adolescents. Miller et al. (2007) have developed a family-based adaptation of the basic dialectical behavior therapy model, which they conduct in a concurrent parent and adolescent group format. The parent group component meets for 6–7 weeks and the adolescent group component lasts for 12–14 weeks. Family therapy sessions are only used with more resistant and stuck families. Although the authors report a great deal of success with their concurrent parent and adolescent group approach with self-harming and suicidal adolescents, they have not conducted a formal scientific treatment outcome study to date. However, a multisite study using their concurrent family and adolescent group therapy approach with suicidal adolescents and their parents is currently under way in Norway.

Santisteban and his colleagues have developed an integrative family therapy approach for at-risk borderline adolescents that they call the integrative borderline family therapy model, which incorporates the best elements from structural family therapy (Minuchin, 1974; Minuchin & Fishman, 1981), brief strategic family therapy (Santisteban, Coatsworth, Perez-Vidal, Kurtines, Schwartz, LaPerriere, et al., 2003; Szapocznik & Kurtines, 1989), multidimensional family therapy (Liddle, Rowe, Diamond, Sessa, Schmidt, & Ettinger, 2000), motivational-enhancement therapy (Miller & Rollnick, 2002), dialectical behavior therapy (Linehan, 1993a), and therapeutic ideas from the Oregon Social Learning Research Center (Chamberlain, & Rosicky, 1995; Patterson, Reid, & Dishion, 1992). In addition to substance-abusing, many of these diagnosed borderline adolescents had histories of self-harming and suicide attempts. The researchers' comprehensive family therapy approach addresses the individual needs of the borderline adolescent and intervenes at both the family and larger systems levels. Santisteban and his colleagues conducted a small pilot family treatment outcome study with 13 borderline adolescents and their families and found that their Integrative Borderline Family Therapy approach with 10 adolescents and their families reported having had strong working alliances with their therapists (70% engaged and were retained in treatment) and high satisfaction with their overall treatment experiences. Three of the families had dropped out of the family therapy experimental group after two sessions. The other three families had been randomly assigned to a treatment-as-usual individual therapy with only the adolescents. To my knowledge, this is the first family treatment outcome study with self-harming adolescents and their families. Another bonus with this small-scale study is the heterogeneous sample. However, the small sample size makes it difficult to generalize the treatment results.

Selekman & Shulem (2007) conducted a qualitative exploratory study with 20 self-harming high school–aged male and female adolescents and their families.

Each one of these youth were presenting with concurrent difficulties with bulimia, substance abuse, sexually risky behaviors, family conflict, school behavior and/or academic performance decline, and multiple treatment failures. The adolescents' self-harming behavior was the major concern of the referral source, parents, and most of the adolescents themselves, who felt they had "lost control of" this behavior. All the families had received collaborative strengths-based brief therapy (Selekman, 1997, 2004, 2005, 2006a, 2006b, 2008a, 2008b). The collaborative strengths-based brief therapy model integrates the best elements of solution-focused therapy (de Shazer, 1988, 1991; de Shaver, Dolan, Korman, Trepper, McCollum, & Berg, 2007), client-directed outcome-informed therapy (Duncan, Hubble, & Miller, 1997; Duncan & Miller, 2000; Hubble, Duncan, & Miller, 1999), MRI (Mental Research Institute) brief problem-focused therapy (Fisch & Schlanger, 1999; Fisch, Weakland, & Segal, 1982; Watzlawick, Weakland, & Fisch, 1974), brief strategic therapy (Nardone & Salvini, 2007; Nardone & Watzlawick, 2005), strategic therapy (Haley, 1980), motivational-enhancement interviewing (Arkowitz, Westra, Miller, & Rollnick, 2007; Miller & Rollnick, 2002; Rollnick, Mason, & Butler, 1999), narrative therapy (Epston, 1998, 2000; Freeman, Epston, & Lobovits, 1997; Maisel, Epston, & Borden, 2004; White, 2007), postmodern systemic therapy (Andersen, 1991; Anderson, 1997; Anderson & Gehart, 2007; Boscolo, Cecchin, Hoffman, & Penn, 1987; Friedman, 1995; Goolishian & Anderson, 1988; Hoffman 2002, 1988; Papp, 1983), positive psychology approaches (Csikszentmihalyi, 1997, 1990; Csikszentmihalyi & Csikszentmihalyi, 2006; Diener & Biswas-Diener, 2008; Emmons, 2007; Fredrickson, 2002, 2003; Keyes & Haidt, 2003; Lyubomirsky, 2007; Peterson, 2006; Peterson & Seligman, 2004; Seligman, 2002, 2003; Snyder & Lopez, 2007), Buddhist mindfulness meditation practices and teachings (Hanh, 1997, 1998, 2001, 2003; Lowenstein, 2005; Surya Das, 2007), Navajo Indian healing practices and teachings (Arviso-Alvord, 2008; Arviso-Alvord & Cohen-Van Pelt, 2000; Jim, 2008; Stone, 2008; White, 2008), and art and expressive writing therapies (Malchiodi, 2003, 2008; Pennebaker, 2004).

The research format consisted of the researcher randomly interviewing the parents and the adolescents separately throughout the course of treatment about their perceptions of the therapeutic alliance and the change process. The research interviews were conducted by an independent researcher who had had no prior contact with the families in the project after the initial family therapy session, at session 3 or 4, at the end of treatment, and at 6 months, 1 year, and 2 years after treatment. Following the research interviews with the families, their feedback about the nature of the therapeutic alliance and perceptions of the change process was fed back to the therapists in order for them to adjust their therapeutic stances and to find a better fit with the unique needs of the family members. In addition, the researcher inquired with the adolescents why they think more adolescents self-harm today, what they recommended how parents should respond after their adolescents have a self-harming episode, what parental behaviors can contribute to and maintain the self-harming behavior, what they recommended therapists should do with other adolescent self-harming clients and their families that helped them, and what therapists should avoid doing that upset them and their parents and made their situations worse. For the sake of brevity, I will limit the research project discussion to the subjects' positive treatment-related factors.

As far as important positive treatment-related factors go, we learned a lot about the participants' perceptions of the therapeutic relationship, not only important relationship skills like being "funny," "caring," and "felt understood" but why *structuring skills* (Alexander, Pugh, & Parsons, 1998) were so important to many of the families in the project. They reported that they liked when the therapists "took charge when things got out of hand" in sessions with intense blaming and arguing. Both the parents and the adolescents appreciated having their own special subsystem time alone with the therapists, particularly the therapists' "good timing" of deciding when to "break us up." There were lots of references to the use of major categories of therapeutic questions and experiments such as the *miracle question* (de Shazer, 1988, 1991), *future-oriented questions* (Selekman, 2005, 2006b, 2008b), and *scaling questions* (de Shazer 1988, 1991) as being instrumental in instilling hope, increasing their expectations for change, and, as one father put it best who had been involved in numerous outpatient counseling sessions with his daughter, "to know where we were going and where we stood at any given time" in the counseling process. Being an engineer, he found scaling questions to be very helpful. According to this father, previous counseling experiences "just drifted without a direction."

The adolescents in the project reported that the use of *art therapy* methods, expressive writing experiments, *visualization, mindfulness meditation*, and the multisensory *chilling-out room* (Selekman & Shulem, 2007; Selekman, 2005, 2006b, see Chapter 3) were most helpful to them: "it made it easier to express myself," "relaxed my mind," "were fun and easy to do," and "really helped me to stop cutting." Many of the adolescents liked the *adolescents mentoring their parents*, the *secret surprise, my favorite author re-writes my story*, and *my positive trigger log* experiments (see the therapeutic experiments section of Chapter 3 and Selekman, 2006a). The majority of the adolescents felt that the positive trigger log helped them to stay on track and reduced the likelihood of having slips. The adolescents also appreciated the main therapeutic focus being on "what's right with me" and "making kids aware of the tools built into them." (One adolescent felt that she had become much more aware in the treatment process of her key strengths and how she could use them more in all areas of her life to further improve her relationships with her parents, siblings, and peers.) Finally, the adolescents greatly appreciated having their voices heard in sessions in terms of being asked about their goals, preferences, expectations, and the specific changes they wanted to see happen with their parents' challenging behaviors. For many of these adolescents, this was a novel experience in treatment because they had felt that former therapists and treatment program staff "sided with" their parents against them.

The parents in the project also liked the treatment focus on family members' strengths and appreciated learning tools and strategies for constructively managing their adolescents' self-harming and other self-destructive behaviors. Most of the parents found it beneficial to learn what their adolescents' triggers were and the same coping tools and strategies their kids were learning in treatment. Some of the parents reported using the *chilling-out room* when they were stressed out as a way "to avoid yelling" and caving in to other unproductive parental behaviors. One common theme with all of the adolescents' stories is that they "wanted to grow into" their relationships with their parents. The parents discovered that by regularly inquiring with their adolescents about specific adjustments they could make to strengthen their relationships with them and committing to making the recommended changes, they helped pave the way for this "growing into" the relationship process. Parents also found the use of *positive consequences* as a "much more positive and effective way to discipline your kids." This consisted of parents abandoning unproductive consequences like taking important items and privileges away and grounding for lengthy periods of time and, instead, having their kids perform good deeds in the community, such as working in a homeless shelter, as their consequences. All 20 families reported being highly satisfied with their treatment experiences and at the 2-year follow-up did not report a reoccurrence of any of their original presenting problems.

Although this research project produced clinically relevant data that can inform us about *what works* and what specifically we need to do therapeutically differently with self-harming adolescents and their families, the lack of a control group and the small sample size make it difficult to generalize the treatment results. However, much of the valuable data the families provided us has been supported by 40 years of psychotherapy research on *what works*, particularly the therapists in the project making maximum use of client *extra-therapeutic factors* such as utilizing their key strengths and resiliencies in their problem areas, building on their past successes and self-generated pretreatment changes, matching therapeutic interventions with the unique stages of readiness for change of each family member, and sensitivity to family members' preferences and theories of change. In addition, the therapists worked hard session by session to strengthen their therapeutic alliances with both the parents and the adolescents. There were many references in our research project to the importance of *therapeutic relationship factors* playing an important role in creating a therapeutic context ripe for change for the clients (Assay & Lambert, 1999; Friedlander, Escudero, & Heatherington, 2006; Hubble et al., 1999; Lambert & Bergin, 1994; Norcross, 2008). Furthermore, in the self-harming behavior clinical area where there is a lack of empirically validated couple and family treatment models, and for that matter, individual therapy approaches specifically designed for self-harming young adults and adolescents, we need to rely on the practice evidence-based experience and wisdom of self-harming clinical specialists regarding what seems to work therapeutically as a starting place for the development of effective treatment approaches that can be compared with existing empirically-validated therapy models that are effective with other treatment populations.

Practice Evidence-Based Knowledge and Wisdom Gained from Existing Treatment Outcome Studies

In her critical analysis of the existing treatment outcome research literature, Muehlenkamp (2006) contends that comprehensive and integrative therapy approaches that targets interventions at the cognitive, behavioral, and interpersonal levels are a necessity when working with self-harming clients. Clearly, Linehan's (1993a) dialectical behavior therapy was the first groundbreaking integrative psychotherapy approach for clients engaging in self-harming behavior. Selekman (2005, 2006a, 2006b, 2008b), Miller et al. (2007), and Santisteban et al. (2003) are all examples of comprehensive and integrative family therapy approaches that show promising results with self-harming adolescents and their families. Many researchers and specialists working with self-harming clients would agree that the formula for treatment success with self-harming clients is the following:

1. Establish a strong therapeutic alliance and collaborative relationship.
2. Teach concrete distress management skills for tolerating strong negative emotions and for better coping with frustration and delaying gratification and disputation skills for challenging self-defeating and oppressive thoughts.
3. Teach relationship-effectiveness skills, such as communications, problem-solving, conflict-resolution, assertiveness, and resisting peer pressure.
4. Disrupt destructive couple relationship and family patterns that maintain the self-harming and other self-destructive behaviors and establish more adaptive and positive couple and family communication patterns, conflict resolution, and problem-solving skills.
5. Encourage social connection-building in healthy contexts.
6. Teach effective goal-maintenance and relapse prevention tools and strategies.

Since many self-harming clients are experiencing underlying difficulties with depression, anxiety, and managing frustration, clearly using strengths-based approaches that trigger positive emotion, raise happiness and life-satisfaction levels, instill hope and optimism, and foster resilience like solution-focused brief therapy (de Shazer et al., 2007), positive psychology (Diener & Biswas-Diener, 2008; Fredrickson, 2003, 2002; Peterson, 2006; Peterson & Seligman, 2004; Snyder & Lopez, 2007), and collaborative strengths-based brief therapy (Selekman, 2004, 2005, 2006a, 2006b, 2008b), which integrates the best elements of both of these competency-based approaches, can be quite effective with engaging reluctant self-harming individuals who rarely seek treatment by providing them with a non-threatening and positive context ripe for change. All of these therapeutic approaches can effectively counter and help stabilize their painful and overwhelming depresssive and anxiety feelings. As Klonsky, Ottmans, and Turkheimer (2003) found in their research, individuals who experience negative emotions less intensely and less often are least likely to self-harm.

The Use of Psychiatric Medications

To date, there is not one psychiatric medication approved by the Food and Drug Administration for self-harming clients (Lofthouse, 2008; Sansone, Levitt, & Sansone, 2004). The most popular administered medications used with self-harming clients are selective serotonin reuptake inhibitors (SSRIs). It is believed that SSRIs like Prozac, Zoloft, and Celexa, to name a few, will address self-harming clients' possible low levels of serotonin, which has to do with impulse control. In addition to decreasing the clients' self-harming and other concurrent self-destructive behaviors, these medications will also help eliminate their depressive symptoms (Hollander, 2008). However, Hawton, Townsend, Avensman, Gunnel, Hazell, and House (2006) found, in their intensive review of the medication research literature and in their own clinical practices on the use of antidepressants with self-harming adolescents, that in the long run they had not benefited from the use of this class of psychiatric medications. Prozac has been found to increase self-harming behaviors with clients diagnosed with obsessive-compulsive disorder and bulimia. Effexor has been found to reduce self-harming behavior in clients diagnosed with borderline personality disorder (Sansone et al., 2004). Since we know that self-harming clients learn how to manipulate their endogenous opioid systems to release endorphins for self-medication purposes when experiencing emotional distress, some psychiatric researchers are beginning to explore the use of Naltrexone to decrease self-harming behavior (Osuch & Payne, 2008). This medication is often used with heroin abusers and other opiate abusers to help them to remain abstinent in the addiction field. It is believed that by blocking the opioid receptors and preventing the euphoric or numbing effects produced by the endorphins, the clients will experience pain instead of pleasure, and thus stop their self-harming behavior. However, there is limited scientific evidence to support the efficacy of Naltrexone with non-developmentally delayed clients or clients with diagnoses other than borderline personality disorder (Osuch & Payne, 2008; Sansone et al., 2004).

A Classification System of Self-Harming Practices and Matching Treatment Recommendations

Favazza (Favazza, 1998; Favazza and Selekman, 2003) was the first pioneer in the area of self-harming behavior to attempt to identify categories of self-harming clients. His four categories are *major*, *stereotypic*, *compulsive*, and *impulsive*. The first two types of self-harming clients are rare and occur with clients with severe psychiatric disorders. The compulsive and impulsive types of self-harming clients are the most common. Whitlock and her colleagues (2008) have attempted to develop a classification system of self-harming practice categories based on the number of acts of self-harm and severity levels. Walsh (2006) has developed a classification system for self-harming clients based on three important factors: *frequency of behavior*, *methods used*, and *extent of damage caused*. With the frequency of behavior, this entails determining if this behavior is episodic or repetitive. There are two types of methods used: (a) immediate and direct bodily harm and (b) indirectly over time trying to harm one's body. Walsh also assesses the extent of harm caused per episode, common/low lethality versus major/high lethality. Determining these key factors can help inform clinical decision-making in terms presenting to the client a recommended treatment level of care or combination of treatment modalities that might best meet his or her needs.

More recently, I have developed a classification system of self-harming practices with matching treatment level of care recommendations, based on clinical practice evidenced-based experience and wisdom of specialists, findings from researchers studying self-harming clients, and the existing research findings on what seems to work clinically (see Table 1-1). I have identified five categories of self-harming clients based on the frequency of daily acts and level of severity of their engagement in this behavior: *experimenter/follower*, *episodic*, *regular/moderate*, *heavy*, and *severe*. I will describe the frequency of self-harming episodes and the key characteristics of clients in each self-harming practice category below.

Experimenter/Follower
- Infrequent solo and/or recreational self-harming with friends
- Superficial scratching, cutting, or burning
- Follows lead of peers for engaging in this behavior
- No habituation
- Precontemplators
- Females and males

Episodic
- May self-harm for a few days, a week, or longer and abstain for weeks or months
- May cut, burn, and engage in self-battery
- May engage in binge drinking and/or substance abuse
- Self-harming may occur during high stress periods or following a critical life event
- No habituation
- Precontemplators
- Mostly males

Regular/Moderate
- Random pattern of occurrence (daily to every other day), 1–3 acts of self-harming
- Cuts, burns, or uses other methods of self-harm on a regular to moderate basis

- May see concurrent bulimia, substance abuse, or sexually risky behavior
- May have past treatment history and be caring a *DSM-IV* diagnosis
- Habituation is developing
- Precontemplators
- Mostly females

Heavy
- 4–5 self-harming acts per day
- Uses multiple methods of self-harm
- May see concurrent bulimia or other eating-distressed issues, substance abuse, or sexually risky behavior
- Often have past treatment history and *DSM-IV* diagnosis
- May have emotional, physical, or sexual abuse background
- Habituation, strong compulsion to self-harm, loss of control, and physical tolerance have developed
- Experiencing psychological, physical, social, school/occupational consequences
- Precontemplators or contemplators
- Mostly females

Severe
- 6 or more self-harming acts per day
- Uses multiple forms of self-harm and has done extensive and deep tissue damage
- May see concurrent bulimia or other eating-distressed issues and substance abuse
- Have past treatment history and a *DSM IV* diagnosis
- May have emotional, physical, or sexual abuse background
- May have had a past suicide attempt
- Habituation, strong compulsion to self-harm, loss of control, and physical tolerance have developed
- Experiencing serious psychological, physical, social, school/occupational consequences
- Precontemplators or contemplators
- Mostly females

Once the client's category of self-harming practice has been accurately assessed, treatment guidelines and the matching level of care are presented to the client and his/her partner or family as possible avenues for intervention. It is important to remember that the self-harming practice category boundaries are not rigid and it is not uncommon to see some combination of characteristics from two of the self-harming practice categories with certain clients. Furthermore, with some self-harming clients we will see a progression or increase in their self-harming

Table 1-1 CLASSIFICATION OF SELF-HARMING PRACTICES AND MATCHING TREATMENT RECOMMENDATIONS

Self-Harming Practices	Experimenter/ Follower	Episodic	Regular/Moderate	Heavy	Severe
Frequency of self-harming episodes	Infrequent solo and/or recreationally self-harming with friends	May self-harm for a few days or for a week and abstain for weeks or months	Random pattern of occurrence to 1–3 acts per day	4–5 acts per day	6 or more acts per day
Key characteristics of self-harming client	• Superficial scratching, cutting, or burning • Follows lead of peers for engaging in this behavior • No habituation • Precontemplator • Male and females	• May cut, burn, and engage in self-battery for a few days, a week, or a few weeks • May see binge drinking and/or substance abuse • Self-harming may occur during high stress periods or following a critical life event • No habituation • Precontemplator • Mostly males	• Cuts, burns, or uses other methods of self-harm on regular to moderate basis • May see concurrent bulimia, substance abuse, or sexually risky behavior • May have past treatment history • Habituation developing • Precontemplator • Mostly females	• Cuts, burns, and uses multiple methods of self-harm • May see concurrent bulimia, other eating-distressed issues, substance abuse, or sexually risky behavior • Most have past treatment history and DSM IV diagnosis • May have emotional, physical, or sexual abuse background. • Habituation, strong compulsion to self-harm, loss of control • Physical tolerance has developed • Experiencing psychological, physical, social, school/ occupational consequences • Precontemplator/ contemplator • Mostly females	• Uses multiple forms of self-harm and has done extensive and deep tissue damage • May see concurrent bulimia, other eating-distressed issues, and substance abuse • Has past treatment history and DSM IV diagnosis • May have emotional, physical, or sexual abuse background. • May have past suicide attempt • Habituation, strong compulsion to self-harm, loss of control • Physical tolerance has developed • Experiencing psychological, physical, social, school/ occupational consequences • Precontemplator/ contemplator • Mostly females
Matching treatment recommendations	• Collaborative strengths-based brief therapy for individual young adult • Family therapy for adolescent if access to parents or key caretakers	• Collaborative strengths-based brief therapy for individual young adult • Couples therapy if involved in serious relationship • Family therapy for adolescent if access to parents or key caretakers	• Collaborative strengths-based brief therapy for individual young adult • Couples therapy if involved in serious relationship. • Family therapy for adolescent if access to parents or key caretakers • If not enough treatment intensity, pursue Pathways to Possibilities program	• Collaborative strengths-based brief therapy for individual, couple, or family • If not enough treatment intensity, pursue Pathways to Possibilities Program • Follow-up therapy to consolidate gains	• Collaborative strengths-based brief therapy for individual, couple, or family • Psychiatric evaluation to assess need for medication or, if suicidal risk potential is high, arrange an inpatient admission • Pathways to Possibilities Program for aftercare support if needed • Follow-up therapy to consolidate gains

behavior and in other equivalent self-destructive behaviors over time. With other clients, they may stick with one self-harming method and practice and not progress any further into more serious self-harming behavior, or abruptly decide to stop after experiencing a serious consequence as a result of this behavior, or they may begin to feel that it no longer benefits them.

Treatment planning is collaborative and the client and his/her couple partner or family have the ultimate say in what their treatment goals are going to be and with the selection of what level of care, treatment modalities, and therapeutic experiments offered in a given therapy session will best meet their needs. It is critical that we do not try and privilege our treatment recommendations, but instead, honor our clients' preferences and expectations. Research indicates that clients are better at deciding what will work best for them and predicting treatment outcomes than therapists (Norcross, 2008). Treatment matching is not a new concept but it historically has shown great clinical results with substance-abusing clients (Kissen, Platz, & Su, 1971; Miller & Carroll, 2006; Miller & Rollnick, 2002; Parker, Winstead, & Willi, 1979; Prochaska, Norcross, & DiClemente, 1994). Empowering clients to be the lead authors of their treatment plans, giving them the freedom of choice with determining the goals for treatment, and selecting from a menu of treatment modalities and therapeutic experiments offered in their sessions can help reduce client defensiveness, and psychological reactance. It fosters a cooperative therapeutic relationship and increases the likelihood of treatment retention.

The Challenges with Help-Seeking and Engaging Self-Harming Individuals

For those self-harming college students who have had negative treatment experiences in the past, they reported the following: the strong treatment focus on their deficits triggered feelings of shame, guilt, and unwarranted vulnerability; the early and exclusive use of medications was not helpful; the therapists threatened to psychiatrically hospitalize them; there was a lack of trust and respect in their relationships with their therapists; and their past therapists had imposed their own agendas on them, such as exploring for or pushing them to share their past trauma stories (Whitlock, 2008; Selekman & Shulem, 2007). Whitlock (2008) and Whitlock, Eckenrode, & Silverman (2006) found in their study with self-harming college students that they rarely actively seek mental health or medical care. Only 28% of the subjects in their research sample had disclosed self-harming behavior to a mental health provider in the past. Even after making the effort to show up individually or being brought to a mental health or medical provider, many self-harming individuals drop out of treatment. Some of the major complaints of self-harming clients for not returning to treatment are: "The therapist looked scared by my cut and burn marks and scars," "asking me too many questions," and "telling me how to live my life," "She (the therapist) lectured at me 'You really should stop this it's dangerous!'. . .Yeah. . . like don't tell me how to live my life" (Selekman & Shulem, 2007). In the last example above, the therapist prematurely used advice-giving and pushed for change with the client while the client was still in the *precontemplative stage* of readiness to change (Prochaska, et al., 1994). As Prochaska et al. have pointed out, only 20% of the clients seen in mental health and health care settings are in the *action stage* of readiness for change. Many self-harming clients would be considered *precontemplators*, that is, they do not think they have a problem even though others are concerned about them and they may have experienced some serious consequences and difficulties in their life because of this behavior. However, it is important not to assume that every self-harming client is a precontemplator. I have treated self-harming young adults and adolescents who have entered treatment in the *contemplation, preparation, action,* and *maintenance* stages of readiness for change. The stage the clients are assessed to presently reside in will determine what set of therapeutic strategies and tools the therapist should employ to match where they are at (1994) and help them advance to the next stage of readiness to change. Prochaska et al. contended that if we can empower the clients to move at least one stage further in their readiness for change process, the likelihood of a positive treatment outcome is increased.

Similar to clients experiencing difficulties with bulimia, self-harming is a hidden practice that their partners or family members may not know is occurring until a concerned friend, family member, or professional at their school or job finds paraphernalia (razor blades or other sharp objects) being used, are alerted about the behavior, or catches them in the act. Since this is a hidden practice and, for many, a coping strategy that works so well for them, they will not let others know about it for fear that they may try to get them to stop this behavior. The same mind-set operates with substance-dependent individuals who adopt the distorted perception that others pose a threat, even close friends, partners, and family members. It becomes a real double bind for the moderate to severe self-harming individual, the longing to tell others about their behavior and be socially connected and the shame and fear if his or her hidden practice is discovered.

Research and clinical practice evidenced-based experience indicates that self-harming individuals are more likely to tell a close friend if anyone about his or her self-harming behavior (Hawton & Rodham, 2006; Selekman, 2004, 2006a; Selekman & Shulem, 2007; Whitlock, Eells, et al., 2007; Whitlock, 2008; Whitlock et al., 2008). However, due to friendship loyalty, lack of knowledge about this behavior or appropriate community resources or experience with self-harming individuals, friends may not take him or her to the university student mental health clinic or tell a teacher, social worker, school nurse, or counselor about his or her friend's behavior. Furthermore, even after self-inflicting deep and serious tissue damage, self-harming individuals rarely seek medical treatment (Selekman, 2005, 2006b; Selekman & Shulem, 2007; Whitlock, Eells, et al., 2007).

Lack of Clinical Experience, Knowledge Base, and Skills

In consulting for and training mental health, health care, and school professionals worldwide, it is clear that these professionals were not only intimidated by young adults and adolescents who self-harm but felt that they lacked the clinical experience, knowledge base, and skills to do effective treatment with these individuals and their partners or families. Whitlock, Eells, et al. (2007) found in their survey with 290 directors of student mental health centers across the country the following: Only 28.3% believed they and their staffs had the knowledge and clinical skills to do effective treatment with self-harming students; 74.8% believed that they and their staffs needed more knowledge and training in order to work with this treatment population; 54% reported that self-harming clients were much more difficult than other clients with different presenting problems; and 40.2% worried about self-harming clients being a suicide risk.

CHAPTER TWO

Invitation for Possibilities: Honoring Clients' Stories and Establishing Successful Partnerships for Change

Assessing the *Spaces in Between*

For many individuals who self-harm, their behavior is cyclical rather than linear (Selekman, 2006b; Selekman & Shulem, 2007; Whitlock, Muelenkamp, & Eckenrode, 2008). Their self-harming practices may be used for periods of time to cope with specific stressors, stopped, and then resumed. With the episodic category of self-harming clients, they may go for weeks or months without a single episode. One of the most important parts of the assessment process is to explore with the client in great detail what is happening during the *spaces in between,* when they are abstaining from self-harming behavior. This begins with eliciting all of the details about their self-generated pretreatment changes. We need to find out what useful self-talk and creative coping and problem-solving strategies the client employs to avoid not caving in to self-harming and other self-destructive behaviors, even when experiencing negative and strong emotions, frustration, and high levels of stress. It also is helpful to find out from our clients in initial consultation sessions if they have experienced any positive and surprising events that happened to them or epiphanies prior to our first face-to-face contacts with them. This could take the form of reading a book or magazine article and gaining some new insight about their problem situations or trying out some new technique from a self-help book that really worked. Hubble et al. (1999) referred to this *client extra-therapeutic factor* as a *random event.* We need to know what specific and meaningful activities they engage in to fill up free time, which I refer to as *structure-building.* We need to assess what toxic people, places, objects, music, or Web sites they steer clear of. Finally, we need to find out who their cheerleaders or most avid supporters are in their social networks, including parents, siblings, relatives, close friends, and adult inspirational others who help them maintain abstinence and what specifically they say or do that helps the most (Selekman, 2005, 2006a, 2006b,; Selekman & Shulem, 2007). All of these valuable solution-building client actions by self and others serve as helpful building blocks for solution construction. By punctuating, amplifying, and consolidating these solution-building patterns of thinking, feeling, and behavior, we are inviting the client to compliment himself or herself on his or her resourcefulness. Research indicates that 40% of what counts for treatment success has to do with the therapist's expertise in capitalizing on the clients' expertise, their theories of change, expectations, self-generated pretreatment changes, and utilizing their strengths and resources in their presenting problem areas (Hubble et al., 1999).

Pretreatment Experiments for Telephone Intake Callers and Walk-Ins

Since change is already happening with our clients well before they contact us to set up an appointment or walk in to our practice settings for help, it can be of great benefit to both the clients and their therapists to further accelerate the change process by having them perform pretreatment experiments before their initial appointments. This will elicit all of the details from them about what is already working to prevent their situations from getting much worse and helping to resolve their difficulties and concerns even a little bit. The following pretreatment experiment is designed to increase clients' self-awareness levels of what works during the spaces in between they are not pushed around by their difficulties and seems to be preventing their situations from getting much worse. The caller seeking help is offered the following pretreatment experiment on the telephone:

> "We have been so impressed over the years by how resourceful, creative, and resilient our clients are at the beginning to change and prevent their situations from getting much worse well before we see them for the first time. In order for me to learn more about your resourcefulness, creativity, and resiliencies, I would like you to do a little experiment for me before we meet. I would like you to notice what is happening in your life/relationship with your (son/daughter/partner) that you would like to continue to have happen and write those things down. I also would like you to notice what specifically you are doing during those times when your (son/daughter/partner) is being (cooperative/respectful/responsible) that might be contributing to these positive behaviors happening and preventing your situation from getting much worse. Please write those things down and bring your list into our first appointment."

For walk-ins, this experiment can be modified and used prior to being seen by the intake worker or therapist. While waiting to be seen, the client and his or her couple partner, family members, or concerned friend(s) are given a form that has written on the top of the page a modified version of the telephone intake pretreatment change experiment description. They can be given pens and asked to think about and write down what they think has improved even a little bit with the self-harming person's situation and couple/family relationships and preventing things from getting much worse.

Talmon (1990) was the first brief therapist to demonstrate the therapeutic advantages of using pretreatment experiments to further accentuate clients' self-healing capacities and build off of their self-generated pretreatment changes before their first therapy sessions. Thus, the first and possibly last therapy session was used to amplify and consolidate clients' gains. Selekman and Shulem (2007), Selekman (2005), McKeel (1999), Allgood, Parham, Salts, and Smith (1995), and Weiner-Davis, de Shazer, and Gingerich (1987) have found in their research that not only are client self-generated pretreatment changes quite common, but also, when therapists amplify, consolidate, and build on their clients' pretreatment improvements, they are less likely to drop out of treatment, they are more likely to achieve their goals, and their changes tend to persist long after treatment is completed.

In two past clinics and in my current private practice setting, my colleagues and I found that when offering this experiment to parent callers, it not only greatly reduced client lengths of stay in treatment but, in some cases, by simply having parents refocus their attention on what was going *right* with their son or daughter and what specifically they were doing to promote and maintain these positive behaviors, neutralized the idea that there was a serious enough problem that warranted immediate attention and they decided to hold off on pursuing counseling and canceled their appointments. Those families that did keep their appointments often came to their initial family sessions armed with lists of four or more positive behaviors to report that had occurred between the time of the initial telephone call to our clinic and their first appointments. After the therapists in the projects amplified and consolidated their clients' pretreatment positive gains, lengths of stay in treatment were 1–5 sessions. If therapy went beyond single sessions, clients were given increasingly longer time intervals between sessions as a vote of confidence in their resourcefulness and creativity and their therapists' belief in their abilities to make further progress on their own. At both clinics, the majority of these clients were followed up with at 6 and 12 months and they had reported continuing to utilize their self-generated pretreatment changes to maintain their goals and had made further progress with their individual, couple, and family life situations.

Multiplicity: Identifying and Utilizing Multiple Client Inner Resources

Clients not only bring to us their key strengths and resources, self-generated pretreatment changes, and past successes; they also possess a wide range of empowering voices from their pasts and certain role behavior experiences, or they adopt certain personas or personalities they employed in specific situations when stuck, faced with adversity, or trying to help others, and may continue to employ with their families and friends. We are all multivoiced and multistoried. Carter (2008) and Gergen and Gergen (2007) contend that these client inner resources can be tapped to help empower him or her to have the courage to stand up to and try to conquer their presenting difficulties. The therapist can inquire with the clients about a time they have called upon an inspiring and important person's voice from their past (a grandparent/parent/older sibling/adult inspirational other) to get them fired up to resolve a stressful situation or conflict in a relationship or abstain from self-harming, getting stoned, bingeing and purging, and so forth. In a similar fashion, the therapist can inquire with the clients if they have ever in the past adopted any particular role behaviors or taken on different personas or personalities when faced with adversity or a difficult situation that helped them to successfully cope or resolve the difficulty. Carter has identified an inner family of major and minor personalities that we carry around in our heads. Some of the minor personalities she has identified are: *the guardian, the pleaser, the fighter, the wise friend, the driver, the organizer, the success, the clown, the artist,* and *the dreamer.* Once the therapist gains access to this valuable information about the clients' alter personas or personalities, role behaviors, and abilities to access particular inspiring and supportive voices in their heads, all of these inner resources can be utilized in their presenting problem areas, to empower them to get through tough times in their lives and to achieve their goals. Some examples of questions we can ask our clients to elicit these helpful inner voices and alter personas or personalities to generate solutions are as follows:

- "Can you think of a time in the past where you called upon hearing your volleyball coach's inner voice and inspiring words to help you through a tough situation you were faced with in your life?"
- "Liz, can you think of a time in the past where you called upon your dreamer persona to help give you hope and get you more fired up to pursue your goals?"
- "What role behaviors and actions did you employ in your family that benefited other family members that may be beneficial in improving your relationship with Paul?"
- "Which two of your other personas or personalities should we call upon that empowered you in the past to kick the bulimia habit that you think can help you to conquer this cutting habit?"
- "What creative ideas do you think the wise friend part of you has that we can tap to help you to stand up to cutting and bulimia when they are both trying to double-team you?"

Carmen, a 20-year-old college student and art major, was grappling with long-standing difficulties with cutting and bulimia. She had been in an eating disorder inpatient program for her bulimia and had seen several therapists before me. Prior to our first appointment, Carmen had gone two weeks without bingeing and purging and had only cut herself two times. When inquiring with her about all of the details regarding how she was able to maintain such great self-control, Carmen had attributed it mostly to calling upon her *dreamer persona,* which she had used successfully in the past to give her the hope, the drive, and determination to conquer her habits, which had been haunting her since her early adolescent years. Apparently, using mental gymnastics whenever she would start to experience negative self-defeating thoughts and feelings, she shifted her thinking to visualizing herself using her dreamer persona working for a reputable advertisement firm creating beautiful computer graphic designs and logos for companies her company had contracted with. By transporting herself into this future reality of career success with the help of her *dreamer persona,* Carmen found a valuable tool that she could use to continue to help her conquer her cutting and bulimia habits. In addition to Carmen's use of the *dreamer persona,* she found staying away from certain toxic people and places and filling up her free time with meaningful and constructive activities also helped her not cave in to cutting or bingeing and purging. Since Carmen had generated her own unique and effective problem-solving strategies, I encouraged her to do more of what was working, including using her valuable *dreamer persona.*

Key Client Resiliency Protective Factors

Another important client expertise area to inquire about is their natural resiliency protective factors and how they have used them in the past and present to cope with or overcome adverse life situations. Some clients are very creative problem solvers, seek out adults outside the home that they can get emotional support and advice from (adult inspirational others), use their strong social skills to seek out friends or adults for support rather than isolate themselves, immerse themselves in *flow state* activities when stressed out (creative writing, playing an instrument, art, dancing, etc.), rely on their good sense of humor to cope with a tough situation, persevere when the going gets rough for them, and maintain an optimistic mind-set (Anthony & Cohler, 1987; Csikszentmihalyi, 1990, 1997; Selekman, 1997; 2006b). Any past successes clients have had at using their resiliency protective factors to cope with or overcome adverse life situations can be used to cope with or master their current difficulties. When working with the parents and relatives of self-harming clients in a family therapy context, it is also beneficial to invite them to share their resiliency stories, which can offer the identified clients valuable wisdom and creative ideas about how to better cope with and/or overcome adverse current life stressors or events. The case below illustrates how a client's use of his resiliency protective factors was tapped to help him overcome a painful loss situation.

Stephen, a 19-year-old college student, had just broken up with his girlfriend of three years. They had gone to the same high school and agreed to try to maintain their relationship long distance while they attended separate colleges. In the past, there were even discussions about getting married in the future. One day his girlfriend, Melissa, had called him to say that she had met someone else and wanted to end their relationship. Needless to say, this proved to be a traumatic event for Stephen and he slipped back into burning himself on his arms with cigarettes daily for a week. Apparently, Stephen used to do this to himself when he was 14 but had stopped for 5 years. Stephen initiated this behavior after one of his closest friends moved with his family across the country. When I asked him how he overcame this painful loss, Stephen reported immersing himself in perfecting his guitar-playing skills and writing music. One day, after looking at his multiple burn scars on his left arm he had said to himself, "This is really stupid!" Instead, he channeled all of his emotional pain about losing his friend into writing some powerful ballads, increasing his guitar lessons, and getting a band together. While describing how he had overcome this adverse life event, I could tell that Stephen was really proud of himself. By inviting him to talk about his perseverance and courage to move forward, it was triggering positive emotion for him. Without even having to suggest to Stephen that he should tap this past successful use of his resiliency protective factors, he had come to the realization that his love for music could help him navigate his breakup with Melissa.

Identifying and Utilizing Clients' Key Intelligence Areas as Avenues for Expression, Learning, and Solution Construction

For the past three decades, the brilliant Harvard University psychologist Howard Gardner has been researching and implementing his multiple intelligence educational approach throughout the world (Gardner, 1993, 1999, 2004). Gardner believes that schools should individualize each child's curriculum around his or her key intelligence areas. He has identified 10 intelligence areas: *linguistic* (likes to write poetry and/or creative stories, read, possibly serve as a public speaker), *logical-mathematical* (strong analytical and mathematical skills, likes science, computers), *musical* (may sing, plays instrument(s), may write own music), *bodily-kinesthetic* (expresses self best through movement, may dance, likes drama and theater, or play sports), *visual-spatial* (expresses self best through art, photography, strong visualization skills, inventive), *interpersonal* (strong social skills, natural leadership abilities, likes group projects, prevention work, and public speaking), *intrapersonal* (good at connecting thoughts and feelings, introspective), *natural* (loves animals, appreciates and likes being out in nature, camping), *existential* (searching for the meaning of life and events that occur, is curious and reflective, interested in philosophy), and *spiritual* (may or may not be very religious, believes in the importance of having faith and hope). Not only are these intelligence areas used by individuals as an avenue for personal expression and how they learn best but in the world of counseling, they can be tapped for co-designing with clients therapeutic experiments that are built around their strengths. The case example below illustrates how to use a client's key intelligence strength area to empower her to conquer her presenting difficulties.

Tracy, a 20-year-old singles star on her university tennis team, was brought for counseling by her friend and fellow teammate, Cara, for cutting herself and on and off difficulties with bulimia. While establishing rapport with Tracy, I inquired with her if she had a baseline game or a serve and volley game. Tracy liked playing a baseline game. Next, she was asked what her best shots were. According to Tracy, she loved moving her opponents around and "getting them up to net" so that she could either "hit a passing shot down the line" or use her "top-spin lob over their backhand side." Cara interjected that "Tracy's top-spin lob has so much spin on it that it is virtually un-returnable." I observed that by having Tracy talk about her tremendous tennis skills, it was triggering positive emotion in her. Clearly, Tracy's number one intelligence area was bodily-kinesthetic. When asked about what was the most difficult for thing for Tracy to stomach in her life presently, she said, "The pressure to keep winning." Cara felt that Tracy was "too hard on herself." Although the cutting occurred on an infrequent basis, it was another way for Tracy to release the buildup of emotional pressure and uncomfortable thoughts that were trying to counter her "confident thoughts about winning." In addition to teaching Tracy mindfulness meditations to help center herself and quiet her mind, I taught her my *visualizing a movie of success* tool when pushed around by her emotional pressure and self-defeating thoughts. In the session, I had Tracy close her eyes and visualize a blank movie screen in her mind. Using all of her senses, including color and motion, she was to project onto the screen her best all-time tennis match. With her eyes closed and smiling, Tracy transported herself back to a match last year where she had beaten another top-ranked college star. She described hitting some "wicked passing shots," getting a good percentage of her "first serves in," and hitting her "top-spin lobs perfectly." I strongly recommended that whenever Tracy was being pushed around by her emotional pressure to keep winning or thoughts that were trying to counter her confident thoughts about winning, she was to go to a quiet place and access this movie of success. Tracy also had the option of using mindfulness meditation. Both of these tools proved to be instrumental in helping Tracy not resort to cutting and bingeing and purging. Furthermore, she had a good friend in Cara to turn to for support as well.

Assessing Clients' Top Signature Strengths

The positive psychology movement, which was spearheaded by the cutting-edge psychologists Don Clifton, Martin Seligman, Christopher Peterson, and Mihaly Csikszentmihalyi, grew out of these revolutionary researchers asking two important questions about the field of psychology (Seligman, 2002, 2003):

- "Why has the psychology field for decades focused most of its attention on searching for what is wrong with people in trying to identify their deficits, weaknesses, and psychopathologies?"
- "Why are we not studying what is *right* with people and individuals who are flourishing in the world and learning from them what their secrets are about how to achieve meaningful and fulfilling lives filled with joy and happiness?"

It is this latter question that these positive psychology pioneers and their colleagues continue to study. They are developing highly practical and clinically useful questionnaires and interventions to empower people to have more fulfilling lives filled with meaningful achievements and an overall sense of happiness and well-being. After conducting a rigorous and scholarly investigation of Eastern and Western philosophies and religions, and studying some of the greatest thinkers of all time, Peterson and Seligman (2004) identified six categories of virtues and 24 character strengths that are distributed across the virtue categories they call the *Values-in-Action Classification of Character Strengths and Virtues*. The six virtue categories are: *wisdom and knowledge, courage, humanity, justice, temperance,* and *transcendence*. The 24 character strengths are: *creativity, curiosity, open-mindedness, love of learning, perspective, bravery, persistence, integrity, vitality, love, kindness, social intelligence, citizenship, fairness, leadership, forgiveness and mercy, humility, prudence, self-regulation, appreciation of beauty and excellence, gratitude, hope, humor,* and *spirituality*. Peterson (Peterson, 2006; Peterson & Seligman, 2004) developed the *Values-in-Action Inventory of Strengths*, also called the *VIA Inventory of Strengths* questionnaire, which is designed for adults and identifies an individual's top five signature strengths. If requested, it will identify in the order of character strength potency the remaining 19 character strengths for the test taker. The self-report questionnaire takes approximately 40 minutes to complete. Peterson (2006) has found that the VIA measures are reliable and show validity in terms of accuracy in measuring an individual's top five character strengths.

For older children (10 and above), Peterson's colleague Nansook Park has created a shorter version of the VIA called the *VIA Inventory of Strengths for Youth*. The questionnaire invites children and adolescents to reflect on each of the 24 character strengths, rating each one (1 = not like me at all, 5 = very much like me) (Peterson, 2006). Both the VIA Inventory of Strengths for Youth and the VIA Inventory of Strengths for Adults can be taken online at www.viastrengths.org.

I often use both VIA inventories with individual adults, couples, families, adolescents, and older children to have them identify their five top signature strengths and collaborate with them on how they can be used more and utilized in contexts where the client is experiencing difficulties and they have not experimented with them in those contexts, such as in particular relationships or at school, and using them in novel ways to increase life satisfaction through involvement in altruistic acts and more engagement in old and new meaningful activities (Peterson, 2006;

Peterson & Seligman, 2004; Seligman, 2003). The following case example illustrates how to utilize a client's top signature strengths to improve his relationship with his girlfriend and make individual gains as well.

Walt, an 18-year-old college student, had an episodic type of self-battery self-harming practice that tended to occur when he would feel "really out of control with things going on in my life." His self-battery took the forms of smashing his fists into walls and engaging in some very risky skateboarding tricks that would result in fractured bones, deep bruises, gashes, and scrapes. He also would sometimes try to prevent the healing process by picking off his scabs and sometimes would get infections from doing this. Although Walt could see this pattern and even viewed it as a form of self-punishment, the infrequency of these episodes (every other month to several months down the road) did not alarm him enough to view this as a problem. Sally, his new girlfriend, was very concerned about Walt's self-harming tendencies and was responsible for getting him to me for a consultation. Walt indicated in the session that as much as he hated going to see counselors (he had seen three other therapists when he was in high school for self-battery), he did not want to lose his relationship with Sally and would do anything for her. Apparently, for months Sally had been trying to get Walt to see a counselor for the "ways he was brutalizing his body" and had threatened to break up with him if he did not get help. To help gain a better understanding of both Walt's and Sally's five top signature strengths, I had them go online and take the VIA Inventory for Strengths. They brought their test results to our next session. Both partners reported liking the questionnaire and found it quite interesting. Walt's five top signature strengths were: *bravery, persistence, zest, leadership,* and *teamwork.* Sally's five top signature strengths were: *kindness, love, authenticity, perspective,* and *zest.* We discussed how aware each partner was of their top signature strengths, how they had been using them in their separate lives, and how often they are used in their relationship to make it even stronger. Sally recognized all of her signature strengths and felt that she utilized them regularly with friends, Walt, and her family. However, she felt there was room to develop her *zest* character strength more. Walt was able to recognize all of his signature strengths and, upon discussion, could see that *teamwork* was weak in his relationship with Sally. I explored with Walt how he could tap his *leadership* and *teamwork* signature strengths to improve his relationship with Sally. It turned out that Walt was a rugged outdoorsman who had done some mountain climbing and mountain biking. He had a student membership at the local health club and at was a highly skilled wall-climber. Sally had never done these activities before but had been on some wonderful canoe trips in the past with her family and friends. I had suggested as an experiment that Walt take a leadership role and, with patient teamwork, teach Sally how to wall-climb. He thought this was a "sweet" idea and something he would enjoy doing. In addition, to help improve their relationship communications, I recommended that Walt experiment with using his *bravery* top signature strength in a novel way by taking more risks with Sally by letting her know what was happening in his life that was making him "feel so out of control," rather than "brutalizing his body" with punching his "fists into walls" and daredevil maneuvers on his skateboard. Through the help of the VIA and having the couple partners experiment with their top signature strengths in novel ways, they were better able to improve their relationship and disrupt the long-standing episodic self-harming pattern that had been getting the best of Walt on and off since high school. I also had encouraged Walt to continue to use his weight lifting, jogging, and involvement in intramural sports as healthy coping strategies, as Walt had successfully employed these in the past during the long stretches of time between his self-battery episodes.

I have offered the VIA Inventories as a pretreatment experiment to highly motivated and/or parents, young adults, and adolescents who appear in the telephone intake conversation to be in the *contemplative*, *preparation*, *action*, or *maintenance* stages of readiness for change (Prochaska et al., 1994) I do this to help increase their levels of awareness and for me to learn more about their top five signature strengths and how they can be utilized in clients' identified problem areas and in other areas of their lives. We also may learn about some creative ways they are already using their top signature strengths to better cope with or try to resolve their presenting difficulties. In addition, we also can learn about how they have met with success in the past using their signature strengths to resolve other difficulties. Most clients find their online VIA inventory-taking experiences to be both insightful and worthwhile.

New Views on Self-Harming Behavior

Historically, self-harming behavior has been viewed as occurring mostly with individuals who are diagnosed with borderline personality and posttraumatic stress disorders. To this day, many psychiatrists and other mental health professionals worldwide believe that self-harming individuals are on the road to suicidal behavior. However, recent research and clinical practice evidenced-based experience indicates that the majority of these individuals do not have an underlying personality disorder, nor do they want to die (Michel & Nock, 2008; Selekman, 2005, 2006b; Whitlock, Muelenkamp, & Eckenrode, 2008; Whitlock, 2008). Self-harming individuals not only want to live but have found that this behavior effectively helps them to cope with emotional distress and other major stressors in their lives. One area specialists in this field are in agreement about is that this behavior for some self-harming individuals follows a similar path that substance abusers do when they become physically dependent on substances. Similar to substance abusers, self-harming behavior is habit-forming, loss of control can occur, physical tolerance for bodily pain and distress develops, and individuals hooked on this behavior continue to engage in it despite serious psychological, physical, social, educational and/or occupational consequences (Miller, 2005; Selekman, 2006b; Selekman & Shulem, 2007; Whitlock, Muelenkamp, & Eckenrode, 2008; Whitlock, 2008). Another substance abuse parallel with self-harming individuals is a *maturing* and/or *bottoming out* of this behavior phenomenon. There were many Vietnam War veterans who. as young adults. gave up their heroin addictions after returning home (Robbin, 1993; Selekman & Todd, 1991). I have worked with several young adults and adolescents who had experienced serious enough psychological, physical, and social consequences because of their self-harming practices at earlier ages that they decided on their own to give up their habits. These individuals often reported that their self-harming episodes tended to cluster around stressful life events or during high-conflict periods with couple partners, parents, and peers. Once they found some inner peace, were able to get through these stressful life events, and achieved conflict resolution or abandoned toxic relationships, they were better able to quit their self-harming practices and discover more adaptive coping strategies.

Self-Harming Difficulties as Gifts and Resources

Most therapists who are faced with new or old clients who report self-harming difficulties try prematurely to get their clients to stop this behavior, by lecturing them about the dangers of this behavior, presenting them with replacement behaviors, or getting anxious and assessing with them if they are suicidal and possibly establishing a no-self-harming-or-suicide-attempt- contract with them. All of these attempted solutions are typically tried well before therapeutic alliances have been established and without coming to know the intimate relationships the clients have had with the self-harming behavior, eliciting the unique meanings of this behavior for their clients, and *how* it has been helpful to them (the positive effects) in trying to cope with the *what* (specific thoughts, feelings, bodily sensations, and life stressors) that has been oppressing them. For many self-harming clients, their cutting, burning, or whatever method they use to cope with emotional distress has been like a gift or resource for them. We need to honor and respect this and explore with them the specific ways it has been helpful to them and the disadvantages or consequences of abstaining from this habitual behavior. We need to try to crawl into their skin and live in it while we are genuinely and deeply listening to their self-harming and other meaningful personal stories. Since many self-harming clients have felt invalidated and not listened to or respected by their parents, other key caretakers, or adults, and by some of their former therapists, we have to give them plenty of room to tell their stories and avoid at all costs being narrative editors. As the late, brilliant family therapy pioneer Harry Goolishian put it best, "Knowledge is always on the way" (Goolishian & Anderson, 1988, personal communication). If anything, we need to adopt an irreverent therapeutic stance and employ reflective curiosity to learn more about our clients' ever-evolving self-harming stories. Lucinda's story below illustrates how she benefited from using a razor blade on herself and how it comforted her like a good friend would when she experienced emotional distress.

> Lucinda, a 20-year-old college student, described cutting as being "like a friend" to her. Whenever her friends would let her down, her parents would not respond to her in a supportive way, and she was feeling depressed, cutting would help soothe her. When asked about what would be the disadvantages of stopping the cutting, Lucinda responded with, "I wouldn't know how to calm myself down. I can always count on the razor blade to comfort me."

Once we come to know all of the benefits of our clients' self-harming behavior and establish solid therapeutic alliances with them, this can point us in the direction of specific therapeutic tools and strategies that can produce similar pleasurable and positive effects which we can offer them. Similar to substance-abusing clients, self-harming clients tend to be less psychologically reactive and more cooperative when they are given the freedom to choose from a menu of therapeutic strategies and tools.

Self-Harming Difficulties as Habits and Being Transformational

Self-harming behavior, like any compulsive behavior, is habit forming. Like any habitual behaviors we develop over time, these patterns of behavior are made to be broken. I like to refer to bingeing and purging, substance abuse, sexually risky behavior, and any other compulsive behaviors getting the best of the client as habits. These habits may occur more frequently and be more of a dominant force in our clients' lives around stressful life transition points, such as adolescence, leaving home to move out or go to college, family losses, and breakups. Self-harming habits are transformational and are like turning points or temporary chapters in an individual's life story. They are like the waves coming ashore and receding back into the lake or ocean. We need to have our clients experience the transformational nature of their self-harming habits. Once clients begin to embrace their self-harming difficulties as turning points or temporary chapters in their lives, they will not feel so stuck or dominated by them and other stressors they are grappling with, and will discover that liberation is only a matter of *when*. This is similar to the Buddhist position of impermanence and change being a continuous process. Happiness is part of our natural state, only obscured by attachments to certain mood states, viewing upsetting situations with tunnel vision, and clinging to unrealistic desires and expectations that veil our radiant, innate nature and limit our potential. According to the Hevajra Tantra, "We are all Buddhas by nature; it is only adventitious obscurations that veil that fact" (Surya Das, 2007, p. 22). Surya Das contends that the happiness we seek is already within us. This is the Buddha's secret. Thus, problems and difficulties are fluid and in a constant state of evolutionary flux. Negative and painful feelings and irrational thoughts are like the clouds in the sky, they are in constant motion. It also is important to impress upon our self-harming clients that the better they get at facing their difficulties and life challenges head-on, the stronger and more emotionally resilient they will become.

Therapeutic Alliance-Building: Creating a Climate Ripe for Change

Since a very small percentage of self-harming individuals actively seek counseling or medical care and may be classified as precontemplators in their stage of readiness to change—that is, they do not believe they have a problem—it is critical that, as therapists, we strive to create an inviting and safe therapeutic climate that honors and embraces their strengths and resourcefulness, which will greatly reduce the likelihood of high psychological reactance and defensiveness and help co-create a context ripe for change. We can create a therapeutic climate ripe for change and jump-start the alliance-building process by first coming to know the clients, their couple partners and families by their self-generated pretreatment changes, key resiliency protective factors, key multiple intelligences, top signature strengths, alter personas and supportive inner voices they call upon, talents, key flow state activities or life passions, and past successes. With couples and families or when young adult self-harming clients are accompanied to their initial counseling sessions by a close and concerned friend, I will ask the following complimentary questions to inject positive emotion into the office room and co-create a therapeutic context ripe for change:

- "If someone stopped you on the street and asked you (concerned partner/parents), 'What are two of Kelly's (the self-harming partner/adolescent) top strengths?' What would you tell that person?"
- "Kelly, if your best friend asked you, 'What are two things that you really appreciate about your (couple partner/mother/father/each of your parents)?' What would you tell him or her?"
- "Bill, if someone stopped you on the street and asked you, 'What are two of Steve's (self-harming person) top strengths and two things that you really appreciate about him?' What would you tell that person?"
- "Steve, what special qualities about Bill and the strength of your friendship helped pave the way for you to come here today?"

Once couple partners, parents, and the self-harming clients begin to identify key strengths and qualities they appreciate about one another, the therapist can invite participants to give both recent and past examples of these strengths and qualities in action. This will provide the therapist with valuable information about past client, parental, and couple partner problem-solving successes and potential building blocks for co-constructing solutions for the presenting problems. Some examples of these follow-up questions are as follows:

- "Jan (Kelly's partner/mother), can you think of some recent or past examples where Kelly really shined with her leadership abilities?"

- "Kelly, can you think of a time recently where Jan (Kelly's partner/mother) was really supportive?"
- "Bill, describe for me a time in the past with Steve where you came to know his courageous side that really surprised you?"
- "How specifically did he show you his courage?"

If the self-harming client comes to the initial session alone, you can ask similar types of questions as the first set of questions using empty chairs. For example, the client can be asked:

- "If your (couple partner/mother/best friend) were sitting in that chair over there, and I asked him or her, 'What are two of Jill's top strengths?' what do you think he or she would say?"
- "If your (next best friend/father) were sitting in that other chair, and I asked her or him, 'What are two things that you really appreciate about Jill as a person?' what do you think she or he would say?"

In clinical situations, where we know up front that there is a tremendous amount of conflict and invalidation occurring in the couple or family relationships, which we may witness in our office lobbies, I may not ask these types of questions until there has been some progress made with conflict resolution and with the couple or family interactions. However, more often than not, couple partners, family members, and concerned friends find it difficult not to come up with at least one positive thing to say about the self-harming client and each other.

Client Expectations and Theories of Change

Many of the self-harming young adults and adolescents and their partners and families I have worked with have experienced multiple treatment failures. It behooves us as therapists to take the time to find out from our clients what their treatment expectations are of us and what former therapists and treatment program staff had overlooked or missed with their situations. This important client information will steer us away from replicating unproductive attempted solutions by past therapists and involved helping professionals from larger systems. Conversely, it is important to inquire with self-harming clients and their partners and families what specific therapeutic strategies and tools and treatment modalities former therapists and treatment program staff had tried that seemed to work and may be worthwhile reinstating to help them to resolve their current difficulties. Furthermore, we need to know the clients' *theories of change* and treatment preferences (Hubble et al., 1999; Norcross, 2008). This consists of eliciting from the self-harming individual, his or her partner, and parents what specifically needs to be addressed or resolved in their therapeutic work with the therapist so that they will be satisfied and have an ideal treatment outcome. In addition, clients and their partners or families may know of certain types of treatment modalities or therapeutic tools and strategies that may benefit them in resolving their presenting difficulties that new therapists need to consider incorporating into their treatment regimens out of respect for the clients' wishes and belief that these interventions can work for them. The following questions can provide this important information:

- "You have seen a lot of therapists before me. What did they miss or overlook with your situation that is important for me to know?"
- "What kinds of things did former therapists and treatment program staff say or do with you and your partner/family that was a real drag for you or you think made your situation worse, so I don't make the same mistakes?"
- "I know it was hard for you to make it here and that counseling has been a real drag for you in the past. Tell me, on your way over here did you think about all of the various ways I could possibly upset you or screw up your situation?"
- "In looking back at your past treatment experiences, can you think of any specific things that former therapists or treatment program staff tried with you that seemed to help, even a little bit, that might be worthwhile testing out with your current difficulty?"
- "Sometimes when we have been in counseling before a few times, we may have learned specific strategies that seemed to work and when a big crisis occurred or life started to take a negative turn, we stop doing what had been working for us. Can you think of anything you had learned from any of your former therapists or the treatment program staff you had worked with that you found very helpful that we might want to start experimenting with now?"
- "Is there anything that is happening at school with any of your daughter's teachers or her dean that you would like me to address that is stressing her and you out right now?"
- "Is there anything you really want the teachers to better understand about your daughter that you think is important for them to know?"
- "Was there anything your last therapist failed to do or accomplish with your son's probation officer or help dealing with the juvenile justice system that you would like me to attend to?"
- "If you were to work with the most perfect counselor, what specifically would he or she do that you would find most helpful?"
- "Before you came here today, did you have a strong preference for a particular type of therapist (race, ethnicity, or gender)?
- "Which would you prefer to try first, individual, family, or group counseling?"
- "What are your best hopes that you will get out of our session today?"
- "What are your best hopes that you will get out of our work together overall?"

- "How will you know that you are really satisfied with the work we have done together?"
- "What specifically will have to change with your situation that will tell you that this time around you really succeeded in counseling?"

Client Importance, Confidence, And Hope About Changing

Motivational interviewing strategies and techniques are very effective with self-harming young adults and adolescents. This nonthreatening counseling approach embraces clients where they are at and rolls with their resistance rather than directly confronting them about the necessity of changing their problematic behaviors and taking responsibility for their actions (Arkowitz, et al., 2007; Miller & Rollnick, 2002; Rollnick, et al., 1999; Rollnick, Mason, & Butler, 2008). To help relieve any concerns that clients who have had extensive treatment histories, chronic difficulties, and are hooked on their self-harming, substance-abusing or bulimic habits might have about the therapist putting a lot of pressure on them to begin changing their behaviors in their very first counseling sessions, I will frequently share with these clients the following:

> Earlier in the session you had shared with me that you had been in a couple of different programs and saw a number of therapists before me. I just want you to know that in no way am I going to try to tell you how to lead your life or change you. That is completely up to you to decide. All I ask is if, and only if, you decide to change any aspect of your behavior or situation, that you let me know when you are ready to do that and I am prepared to help you in the best way possible. How does that sound?

In response to this supportive declaration on the therapist's behalf, often the clients look visibly much more relaxed, psychological reactance lowers, and they will respond more freely to questions.

Since many self-harming clients are in the precontemplative stage of readiness for change, they may not see initially the *importance* of changing their self-harming behavior because they have not experienced any serious consequences due to their behavior and it has worked so well for them as a coping strategy. Some self-harming clients may be so demoralized by their self-harming behavior and past treatment failures that they have little or no *confidence* that they can ever conquer this habitual behavior. As therapists, we need to take our self-harming clients where they are at, respect their desires about their lack of necessity for changing, and carefully assess their confidence levels and the specific obstacles that may be preventing them from being more confident and hopeful about changing their situations. The following categories of questions can help us to assess where the client is at with his or her importance, confidence, and readiness for change levels.

Importance (Why?)

- "What would be worthwhile about not cutting anymore?"
- "What difference would it make in your life if you stopped cutting?"
- "How else would it benefit you?"
- "What would be the disadvantages of not cutting anymore?"
- "How will you know that you really want to stop cutting?"

Confidence (How? & What?)

- "On a scale from 1 to 10, with 10 being you really want to quit cutting today, where would you rate yourself?"
- "How confident are you that over the next week you will take a step higher on that scale, up to a 4?"
- "How specifically will you get that to happen?"
- "What will you do to cope with your friends cutting around you while you are striving to get up to that 4?"
- "How will you know that you are really succeeding over the next week?"

Readiness (When?)

- "What will have to happen that will tell you that the time is now to quit cutting for good?"
- "How else will you know that you are really ready to quit now?"

Similar to assessing our self-harming clients' importance, confidence, and readiness for change levels, we need to assess their hope levels for being able to resolve their self-harming and other presenting difficulties they are concerned about in their lives. There are two critical dimensions to hope: *agency thinking* and *pathway thinking* (McDermott & Snyder, 1999; Synder, Michael, & Cheavens, 1999). Agency thinking has to do with how clients muster up the drive and determination to achieve tasks or goals they set for themselves. This can include useful self-talk and surrounding themselves with cheerleading close friends, certain family and extended family members, and adult inspirational others that are good at firing them up to complete tasks and pursue their goals. Pathway thinking has to do with clients' abilities to determine what specific steps they need to take to successfully complete tasks and achieve their goals. Some clients we work with are weaker in agency thinking in that they have not found self-talk effective and they lack a strong support system that can get behind them to ignite their motivation and determination to complete tasks and pursue their goals. Other clients may be strong in the agency-thinking department but have difficulty with problem-solving and determining the best courses of action when trying to manage tasks and pursue their goals. Scaling questions (de Shazer, 1988, 1991; de Shazer et al., 2007; Selekman, 2005, 2006b) can be useful to assess clients' agency and pathway-thinking abilities and overall hope levels, by asking them the following:

- "On a scale from 1 to 10; with 10 being you that are totally hopeful that you can kick your cutting habit and 1 meaning no hope at all, where would you have rated your hopefulness 4 weeks ago?"
- "A 1."
- "Where would you have rated it 2 weeks ago?"
- "A 4!"
- "What steps did you take to get up to that 4?"
- "What did you tell yourself to get that to happen?"
- "Have you ever used that same helpful self-talk tape to help you to achieve other goals you set for yourself in the past?"
- "Did any of your family members or close friends help fire you up to get up to that 4?"
- "Where would you rate your situation now on that hope scale?"
- "A 6! Wow! Are you aware of how you got that to happen?"
- "What specifically are you going to do to over the next week to get one step higher on that scale, up to a lucky 7?"

Through the use of the hope scaling questions we can establish an initial treatment goal with the client. Some self-harming clients are highly pessimistic, depressed, and demoralized by their inability to conquer their difficulties. These clients typically respond very well to *subzero scaling questions* (Selekman, 2005, 2006b). Some examples of subzero scaling questions are as follows:

- "On a scale of –10 to –1, with –10 meaning your situation is totally hopeless and irresolvable and –1 that you have an inkling of hope that your situation can change just a little bit, where would you have rated your situation 4 weeks ago?"
- "A –10."
- "How about two weeks ago?"
- "A –8. Are you aware of what you did to get up to that –8?"
- "What else did you, family, or friends do that helped you not slip back down to rock bottom again?"
- "Where would you rate your situation today?"
- "A –5. Are you aware of what steps you took to get up to a –5?"
- "Let's say you and I get back together in one week's time and you come in here and tell me you took some steps up to a –4, What will you tell me you did?"

In a similar fashion, the therapist can use subzero scaling questions to establish an initial treatment goal with even the most pessimistic of clients. This category of questions also is quite useful with suicidal, highly psychologically reactant, and professional clients who have had extensive treatment histories and outsmarted and defeated many therapists while on the treatment circuit.

Clients' Stages of Readiness to Change

The stages of readiness for change model developed by Prochaska et al. (1994) can be quite useful for helping us determine what specific therapeutic strategies and tools to employ with our self-harming clients. Although many self-harming clients enter treatment in the *precontemplative* stage, there are some who have already advanced to the *contemplative, preparation, action*, and *maintenance* stages of readiness to change. When working with couple partners and families, it is important to remember that the clients' couple partners and fellow family members can individually be at different stages of readiness for change than the identified clients. Therefore, we have to carefully match therapeutically what we offer to do with clients, their couple partners, and family members with their unique stages of readiness for change. As mentioned earlier, only 20% of the clients who enter treatment are in the action stage of readiness for change. However, many therapists and treatment program staff handle most of their clients as if they are already in the action stage, armed with personal goals and ready to do some hard work. When their clients fail to comply with their recommendations and do not complete therapeutic assignments between sessions, the clients are confronted about being "noncompliant," "in denial," or "resistant." It is important to remember that all clients want relief from their oppressive difficulties, especially getting people off their backs. We just have to be careful not to become resistant therapists!

When working with precontemplating self-harming clients, the use of the *two-step tango* engagement strategy can be effective (Selekman, 2005). The first step of the tango is to empathize with the clients' dilemma: they are possibly demoralized by the intractable nature of their self-harming behavior and the fact that treatment has not worked in the past, they have been dragged in to see you by their partner, parents, or concerned friends, and are experiencing strong pressure from their high school dean or some other social control agent who can enforce response and action. Next, you want to let them know that ultimately they set the agenda and determine what is talked about and that there is no hurry or need to pursue change immediately. The second step of the tango is to begin to raise the clients' consciousness level by planting seeds in their minds about the benefits of changing. This is done in a very relaxed and nonchalant manner. The therapist needs to alternate back and forth between restraining the clients from changing, and planting helpful and surprising reasons for changing their behavior. The following case example illustrates the two-step tango engagement strategy with a 16-year-old female adolescent who was not even a window-shopper for family counseling.

> Gail was referred to me for family therapy by her high school dean for cutting in several places on her arms. I had discovered from Gail's mother that she had been in counseling three times before for cutting and bulimia. Gail was very clear with me when we began the session, "I don't need counsel-

ing, I hate it, and I'm not going to talk to you!" I empathized with Gail about counseling being a real drag for her and being forced to do it by her dean. The first seed I planted in her mind was the fact that typically kids like her might have had to meet with the district psychiatrist or be referred to an emergency room to be evaluated for suicide risk and possibly psychiatrically hospitalized. Gail had a surprised look on her face and inquired with me if this was really common for other kids like her to have to "see a shrink" and possibly end up in "a nut house." I then shared with her how lucky she was and really smart to come to the session to show the dean that she was responsible and was sensitive to his concerns about her. At this point in the session, Gail looked worried and wondered whether if she kept seeing me for a little while, the dean would get off her back and she would not have to "deal with shrinks." I reassured Gail that I would agree to closely collaborate with the dean, get him off her back, and help keep the shrinks out of the picture if she would agree to commit to working together. Once Gail agreed to contract for some sessions, she began to open up about what had precipitated the most recent cutting episode and other stressors in her life.

Self-harming clients, along with their intimate partners or involved family members, may be in the *contemplative* stage of readiness for change. On some level they recognize that their habits and attempted solutions to resolve their difficulties may be problematic. However, they continue to persist using unproductive coping and problem-solving strategies that are further perpetuating their difficulties. They are stuck and ambivalent about what to do. One effective therapeutic tool to help contemplators begin to see the advantages of discontinuing engaging in unproductive coping and problem-solving strategies is *the decisional balancing scale* (see Figure 2-1); (Prochaska, et al., 1994; Velasquez, Maurer, Crouch, & DiClemente, 2001). The original decisional balancing scale had two column headings entitled *pros* and *cons*. I have changed these headings to *advantages* and *disadvantages*. On the lines below in each column, the contemplative client is to rate on a scale from 1 to 4 each item they write down in the columns. The ratings are as follows: 1 = slightly important, 2 = moderately important, 3 = very important, and 4 = extremely important. The contemplative client's ratings are beneficial to the therapist in helping guide their future therapeutic decision-making in terms of what specific barriers to change need to be removed and choosing the most appropriate strategies and techniques for accomplishing that. I have found the decisional balancing scale also to be helpful to use with clients in the early stages of *preparation*. Clients may still feel stuck or not very hopeful about being able to remove specific barriers to change or achieving whatever goals they make for themselves.

According to Prochaska et al. (1994), each time we help our clients to advance to the next stage of readiness for change we are increasing the likelihood for their treatment success. Although more the exception than the rule, some clients may have to go through a few rounds of some or all of the stages before their changes

Fig. 2-1 THE DECISIONAL BALANCING SCALE	
INSTRUCTIONS: Rate each advantage and disadvantage on a scale from 1 to 4. **1** = Slightly important, **2** = Moderately important, **3** = Very important, and **4** = Extremely important.	
Advantages	Disadvantages

really stick and they are totally confident they will not return to their self-harming or other problematic behaviors. The following guidelines will help therapists determine at what stage of readiness for change their self-harming clients are in.

Precontemplators
- Not even window-shoppers for counseling
- They don't think they have a problem
- Brought in or sent for counseling under duress, i.e., mandated clients
- May feel demoralized by their chronic difficulties and multiple treatment failures
- May have grown up in a family where no one ever modeled the benefits of changing anything
- Does not identify a treatment goal for himself/herself
- Rarely will participate in the implementation of proposed change strategies for his/her couple or family relationships

Contemplators
- On some level, recognizes there is a problem
- May feel stuck or ambivalent about abandoning certain attempted solutions or habitual patterns of behavior
- Continue to persist in certain actions that are further exacerbating
- Agency and pathway thinking may be at a low level
- May respond well to the use of the decisional balancing scale

Preparation

- Getting closer to taking action
- May be ready to begin clarifying his/her best hopes or initial goal
- May report obstacles to taking that first step in the direction of change
- The obstacles might take the form of ambivalence, fear, anxiety, or lack of confidence
- May respond well to the use of the decisional balancing scale

Action

- Confident and ready to pursue his/her initial treatment goal
- Agency and pathway thinking is at a high level
- Ready to test out proposed therapeutic experiments

Maintenance

- Feels good about having taken action toward achieving his/her goal
- May experience a gradual or sudden increase in anxiety and fea about slipping back into old problematic patterns of behavior and unproductive habits
- Very receptive to learning solution-enhancing and goal-maintenance strategies and tools to stay on track and prevent slips from occurring
- May also be receptive to participating in support or self-help groups

Termination

- Totally confident about not slipping back into former problematic patterns of behavior and unproductive habits
- Make excellent mentors, sponsors, inspirational others, and guest consultants

Important Treatment Considerations

- When seeing couples or families, you need to carefully assess at what stage of readiness for change each partner or family member is
- With any given couple or family, the couple partner and each family member might be in a different stage of readiness for change
- When designing, selecting, and offering therapeutic experiments to couple partners and family members, we need to accurately match what we offer with the unique stages they are in
- If you are not sure what stage the client, partner, or a family member is in, always err on the side of cautiousness and assume he or she is in the previous stage
- The stages are fluid and some clients can move quite quickly through the different stages in a given session
- It may take some clients a few cycles through some or all of the stages before they become permanent residents in the termination stage

Use of Letters to Engage Clients Who Are No-Shows or Prematurely Drop Out After Their Initial Consultation Sessions

Research indicates that many self-harming clients will not voluntarily seek treatment even when they have lost control of their behavior and have experienced serious psychological, physical, social, educational and/or occupational consequences (Whitlock, Eckenrode, et al., 2006; Whitlock, 2008). In some cases, even after being brought to the initial consultation session by concerned couple partners, parents, or friends, self-harming clients may drop out of treatment. I have found it to be most advantageous and worth the effort to send letters to both no-shows and clients who drop out after having their initial consultation sessions. Going the extra mile and showing these self-harming clients how much you care about them can be the catalyst to getting them to back into treatment again. For some self-harming clients who have had negative past treatment experiences or felt they could not count on their parents or other significant adults to help them, receiving a positive and caring letter from their new therapist can give them hope and makes the new counseling experience feel inviting. Clients can begin to entertain some of the possible benefits of changing their situations. When successful at helping self-harming clients to pursue or get back into treatment, personalized outreach letters can jump-start the therapeutic-alliance building process.

The letter below was sent to Rita, a 20-year-old college student and self-harming client who had temporarily dropped out of treatment after the initial consultation session and reentered treatment with me after receiving my personalized outreach letter. Like many clients who were sent personalized outreach letters, Rita thanked me for my letter and shared that she had been skeptical of counseling since it had not made a difference with her situation in the past. In Rita's case, however, my letter helped her to overcome her ambivalence about giving counseling another try. Rita had a moderate to heavy self-harming practice with concurrent difficulties with bulimia and was originally referred to me by a university physician at the student health clinic who, upon examining her, had discovered many cutting scars on her arms and legs and was concerned about her. Rita had gone to the clinic for flu-like symptoms. When she was 15 years old, Rita spent 2 weeks in an eating disorders inpatient treatment program. She had seen numerous therapists before me and had felt "misunderstood" and "not helped by them."

Dear Rita,

I am writing you this letter to let you know how much I enjoyed meeting you and how impressed I was with your courage and persistence in not giving in seeking help for your situation. My colleagues and I receive a lot of telephone calls from adults who may present with similar concerns, as when you first came in to see me, and schedule appointments but never show up for their appointments. However, you are different. You showed up! I would really like to get to know you better and help you out in the best way possible whenever you are ready to take that step. Since you made it quite clear to me that counseling has been a real drag for you in the past, I really want you to be in the driver's seat in deciding what is most pressing or stressful in your life that you would like help changing and guide me on what to avoid doing with you that other therapists did that made you feel "misunderstood" and "not helped by them," so I don't make the same mistakes. Please feel free to call me when you wish to schedule a new appointment. Next week, I currently have the following dates and time slots available for appointments. My office telephone number is _____. I look forward to our having a fresh start and learning more about your strengths, expectations of me, and helping you make your best hopes for yourself a reality.

Warm regards,
Matthew Selekman, MSW, LCSW

The same day that Rita received my letter, she contacted me to schedule an appointment. Once back in treatment, Rita was in a better place to begin addressing her self-harming and bulimia difficulties. One big motivator for change upon her reentry into counseling that had occurred right after she had dropped out of treatment was Rita's being "rejected" by a handsome male student she had been fixed up with by a close friend who was "turned off" by her "scars" on her "arms" and "legs" when they had gotten intimate with each other. In addition to helping Rita reduce the frequency of her cutting episodes, I regularly solicited feedback from her about the quality of our collaborative partnership and her satisfaction with the treatment process in order to further strengthen my therapeutic alliance with her.

With no-show self-harming clients, a modified version of the letter above can be constructed and sent out to them. If the client had been the caller, it is important to note in the letter that *it took a lot of courage to call* your practice setting and that *many people who are experiencing similar situations as them have not been able to take that big step*. Once this client makes contact with the therapist, offering to do the initial consultation session in his or her home is another nonthreatening and effective way to engage no-show and/or precontemplative clients.

Sometimes it takes a few letters to engage no-show clients and reengage premature dropout clients. For me, it has been well worth the effort to take the time to send these clients letters and show that I care and am committed to them.

The Ecological Assessment Framework: Viewing Self-Harming Difficulties with Multiple Lenses

After establishing rapport with self-harming clients, their couple partners or concerned friends, and/or families, we need to secure a clear description from the clients of the various contexts in which their behavior is embedded and who comprises the *solution-determined system*. The solution-determined system includes concerned representatives from the client's immediate family, intimate partners, close friends, adult inspirational others, other key members from their social network, the therapist, and involved larger-systems helping professionals. Once we enter a conversation about a new client who is self-harming, we become part of the solution-determined system. Ideally, if the self-harming client and his or her partner and/or family are willing to have the involved members of the solution-determined system attend the initial consultation session, it can provide the therapist with a wealth of important information about the results of the pretreatment experiment, if administered, varying problem views of the participants, treatment expectations, their best hopes and goals, theories of change, and the participants' various attempted solutions past and present. The self-harming client is empowered to share his or her concerns about what has not helped, what has worked, and how the representatives at the meeting can help him or her in the best way possible now.

Together, with the client having the lead voice, we can co-construct the *blueprint for change plan*. The blueprint for change plan consists of the following: the client and his or her couple partner and/or family taking the lead in determining treatment goals, past successful strategies to tap for achieving those initial goals, choosing from a menu of different treatment modalities and adjunct services, and selecting from a menu of session therapeutic experiments offerings to try out over the next week that are in line with those goals. Clients are free to participate in multiple treatment modalities and receive adjunct therapy components such as extra time learning mindfulness meditation or additional art therapy. Furthermore, the client and his or her partner and family can share with the members of the solution-determined system what they need most from them at the present time. By working this way, not only can therapists greatly reduce client lengths of stay in treatment but the teamwork, which cuts across all the various contexts in which the self-harming behavior is embedded in, can result in the co-generation of creative and effective solutions for resolving the presenting difficulties. This helps combat both the client's and therapist's feelings of isolation in trying to resolve the challenging and sometimes intractable self-harming behavior, particularly with self-harming clients who would fall into the heavy and severe self-harming practice categories. Although it might seem like an arduous task to mobilize all of the members of the client's solution-determined system for the initial consultation session, the earlier in the treatment process this can be initiated, the better. Even if it proves impossible to recruit all of the members of the client's solution-determined system, just having a few of these key resource people participating in sessions can be beneficial with the treatment planning and change process. Sometimes I will get written permission from the client, his or her couple partner, or parents to include former self-harming clients who are leading healthy and productive lives, or I may bring in an experienced adult inspirational others to join the team effort if it can further aid with providing extra support and helping the change process.

If the client and his or her couple partner and/or family feel uncomfortable having other members of the solution-determined system, including involved helping professionals from larger systems, participate in the initial consultation session, this needs to be respected and reintroduced at a later date when he or she, the partner and/or family feel that trust has developed with the therapist. However, it is most advantageous that the therapist get permission to begin collaborating with actively involved helping professionals from larger systems and key members from the client's social network as early in treatment as possible to learn about their attempted solutions, concerns, and expectations of the therapist.

In addition to learning more about the client's individual level of functioning, the therapist needs to gather from clients information regarding the nature of and concerns with the couple and/or family relationships, peer relationships, other key social network relationships, his or her school and/or occupational functioning, and the involvement of helping professionals from larger systems. By securing a comprehensive multilens viewing of the client in his or her social ecology, we can identify with the client, his or her partner, family, and members of the solution-determined team, which systems levels to target for interventions first.

The Ecological Assessment Framework

Young Adult/Adolescent

- Assess key signature strengths, flow state activities, multiple intelligences, resourceful alter personas, and supportive inner voices
- Assess for self-generated pretreatment changes and past successes
- Determine key resiliency protective factors for coping with past and present life stressors and losses
- Define major concerns, treatment expectations, best hopes, and main goal now
- A theory of change
- Determine stage of readiness of change, importance, and confidence levels
- Have client give detailed assessment of all past attempted solutions, including both positive and negative past treatment experiences
- Determine connectedness vs. disconnectedness to intimate other, parents, siblings, and extended family members
- Assess mood management skills and difficulties with self-regulation
- Assess for eating-distressed difficulties and body-image concerns
- Assess if there are any significant physical health conditions and past or present medication use
- Take a drinking and drug history
- Assess key triggers for self-harm and other self-destructive and externalizing behaviors
- Assess if there has ever been a past suicide attempt and any family history of suicide attempts and/or completions
- Assess benefits and disadvantages of internet usage

Couple/Family Level

- Assess key signature strengths, flow state activities, and learning styles of the intimate partner and/or the parents
- Assess pretreatment changes and key solution-building interactions in the relationship
- Identify those patterns of interaction and beliefs that contribute to the maintenance of the presenting problem
- Assess partner's and/or parents' theories of change
- Assess partner's/parent's attempted solutions, including past partner's and parents' successes
- Assess the quality of the couple relationship and the parents' marital or postdivorce relationship
- Assess stages of readiness for change of the partner and/or each family member
- Assess if the couple partner or parents have experienced any difficulties with alcohol or substance abuse
- Assess couple partner or parental concerns with Internet usage

Peer Level

- Assess who the most concerned and caring friends are
- Assess social competence skills or difficulties
- Assess peer acceptance or rejection issues
- Assess intimate partner and/or parental concerns about peer choices
- Assess peer concerns about the client

Key Members from Social Network

- Determine with the client which key members from his/her social network to recruit for future counseling sessions
- Assess details about key members' past successes at providing support and helping him or her resolve their difficulties in the past
- Assess with the client and his or her partner or parents the benefits of involving former self-harming clients and experienced adult inspirational others for added support

School/Occupational Level

- Assess school academic and/or occupational performance
- Assess if there are any learning or work-related difficulties
- Assess client concerns about particular school personnel, fellow employees, or boss

Larger Systems Level

- Identify with the client, his or her partner, and the family, what key larger systems professionals are involved with their situation

- Explore with the participating helping professionals their stories of involvement, most pressing concerns, expectations, and best hopes for the client, the couple relationship, and/or the family, and the therapist
- Determine with the client if there is any need for therapist collaboration and advocacy in school/college and/or work settings

When gathering information with clients, their couple partners, and/or families' about these other assessment areas, it is important that we give clients the benefit of the doubt that there are always spaces in between when self-harming and other problems are not occurring and partners and family members are getting along. It also is helpful to adopt the mind-set that reality is negotiable and there are many ways to look at and think about any of the client, couple, or family areas where they are experiencing difficulties.

Drinking And Drug History

Self-harming clients who abuse substances are at much greater risk for accidentally killing themselves than nonusers. Although most self-harming clients are like amateur surgeons carefully cutting around major blood vessels, when they become intoxicated their judgment and coordination become impaired and they run the risk of severing a major vein or artery. Therefore, it behooves us to take a detailed drug and alcohol history and gain a clear understanding of the client's substance and alcohol usage, including all categories of substances abused, pattern of use of each substance, changes in the amount used or initiating the use of new substances, triggering critical life events, and family history of alcoholism and substance abuse. For some of our self-harming clients with strong alcoholism in family backgrounds, they can be set up genetically for developing alcohol dependency in adolescence if they are born with a built-in chemical tolerance system in their livers; they can metabolize alcohol faster than the average person. I have worked with some adolescents as young as 12 years old who had become alcohol dependent after heavily abusing alcohol for a year and had come from families plagued with intergenerational alcoholism problems.

The *drinking and drug history form* assessment tool (see Figure 2.2) consists of three columns: age, pattern of use, and life events. When using this assessment tool, it is helpful to administer it alone with the client and closely collaborate with him or her on the content material. I like to begin with alcohol and whether or not alcoholism runs in the family. In the age column, we begin with age 0 to assess if alcoholism runs in his or her immediate or extended family. Next, we can find out how old the client was when he or she first tasted alcohol and in what context it was tried. Most clients report around 7 or 8 years old and not liking the taste of it initially. However, some clients with strong family backgrounds of alcoholism remember liking it. When asked at what age he or she started using alcohol more often, the client might report drinking whiskey at 12 or 13 years old and vodka or other hard liquors with friends after school or on weekends and have a good toler-

Fig. 2-2 DRINKING AND DRUG HISTORY		
Age	Pattern of Use	Life Events

ance for it, possibly outdrinking their friends. This would be one indicator that this young adolescent has a built-in chemical tolerance system and is at very high risk for becoming alcohol dependent. When asked about what was going on in his or her life at the time, we might learn about a painful loss, such as the death of a close grandparent or a parental separation or divorce. One common pattern with moderate to severe alcohol and substance-abusing clients are backgrounds riddled with losses that have not been mourned and resolved. Often, we will see an increase in harder liquor and substances or increases in the use of the client's drug of choice following these painful losses. There might also be the loss of a romantic relationship (which can be psychologically devastating for adolescents), loss of a close friend, loss of physical functioning due to an accident or illness, getting kicked out of school, or an abrupt family move. Once the pattern of alcohol use has been followed and corresponding critical life events are red-flagged and discussed up to the present, I will, in a similar fashion, inquire with the client about the patterns and methods of use and abuse of sedative-hypnotics, antianxiety agents like Xanex and Valium, marijuana, stimulants like cocaine or crack, methamphetamine, methcathinome ("cat'), diet pills, attention deficit disorder medications (Adderall, Ritalin, etc.), designer drugs (Fentanyl, ecstasy, Ketamine, OxyContin), opiates or pain pills (heroin, opium, Percocet, Vicodin, demerol, etc.), over-the-counter cold remedies like Coricidin, hallucinogens (LSD, magic mushrooms, etc.), and inhalants. With self-harming clients who present with eating-distressed issues, it is important to assess whether or not they are using OxyContin or methamphetamine for weight control. In addition, some self-harming clients who regularly attend rave parties may be regularly using club drugs like ecstasy (MDA) and combining them with alcohol and marijuana, which can put a tremendous strain on their hearts when lengthy periods of dancing are added to the mix. Some of these young adults and adolescents may end up in emergency rooms of hospitals because of this potentially lethal combination of activities.

The strength of the drinking and drug history assessment tool is that all of the information is coming from the client and helps them make important connections between the increase in their abuse of alcohol and other substances and critical life events, particularly losses. Once they can make this important connection they can begin to see how they employ equivalent behaviors like self-harm, bingeing and purging, and sexually risky behaviors to try to cope with emotional distress related to losses and other difficulties in their lives, which are creating serious health, relationship, school/occupational, and, in some cases, legal consequences for them.

If the self-harming client is involved in an intimate couple relationship and the partner is not participating in sessions, the therapist should find out what effect the partner's use or abuse of alcohol and other substances is having on their relationship and his or her own efforts to cut back on the use of or abstaining from alcohol and substance usage. However, if the partner is participating in the couples therapy sessions, the therapist can directly obtain his or her drinking and drug history, either with the client or alone if he or she would feel more comfortable with this arrangement.

Dimeff, Baer, Kivlahan, and Marlatt (1999) have developed both the *Brief Alcohol and Screening Intervention* (BASICS) and an *Alcohol Skills Training Program* (ASTP), which are empirically validated harm-reduction interventions for regular to heavy alcohol-binge-drinking undergraduate college students. Their harm-reduction approaches incorporate the best elements of motivation-enhancement interviewing and the stages of change models (Miller & Rollnick, 2002; Prochaska et al., 1994). For better assessing alcohol-abuse difficulties with college students, Dimeff et al. (1999) also recommended administering the following questionnaires: *Comprehensive Effects of Alcohol, Daily Drinking Questionnaire, Frequency-Quantity Questionnaire, Drinking Norms Rating Form*, and the *Alcohol Perceived Risks Assessment*.

Assessing Eating-Distressed Behavior and Body-Image Issues

Difficulties young adult women and female adolescents may be having with eating, weight control, and body-image issues are very sensitive subjects and need to be approached in a delicate and respectful manner. As mentioned earlier, research indicates that close to 50% of self-harming young adult women and adolescent females have concurrent difficulties with bulimia (Favazza & Selekman, 2003). Although some self-harming young women and adolescent females have difficulties with obesity and anorexia, the frequency of these concurrent types of eating problems are quite low among the larger young adult and adolescent female self-harming populations (Favazza & Selekman, 2003; Whitlock, Muelenkamp, & Eckenrode, 2008). Both bulimia and self-harming behavior can be viewed as equivalents in that they are efforts for young adult women and adolescent females to take back control when they are feeling like they have lost control in coping with certain life stressors and relationship difficulties.

Any discussion about eating-distressed issues needs to take into consideration the oppression of women in a patriarchal society that embellishes thinness. Women are often judged by how good they look and comply with dominate males' wishes. Many women are socialized to "be pretty," "polite," and not to assert themselves. As therapists, we need to take a political stance and be like social activists in empowering young women to challenge and break free from these oppressive patriarchal assumptions and societal expectations about how to look and conduct themselves in the world. The work of narrative therapy pioneers Michael White and David Epston adopts such a political stance (Maisel, et al., 2004; White, 1988, 2007). When assessing eating-distressed difficulties, therapists can ask the following externalizing questions:

- "Many women and teenage girls find themselves being pushed around a lot by traditional assumptions and expectations about having to have the 'perfect body shape' and 'be pretty.' These assumptions and expectations have been oppressing women for generations. What percentage of the time daily out of 100% of the time do you find yourself thinking about how you look and your weight?"
- "What percentage of the time would you say you are in charge of these traditional assumptions and expectations versus their being in charge of you?"
- "What are you going to do over the next week to be 70% in charge?"
- "When these traditional assumptions and expectations are trying to brainwash you into thinking that you are not thin enough or pretty enough, what do these assumptions and expectations coach you to do to comply with their wishes?"
- "Have there been any times lately where you stood up to these traditional assumptions and expectations and rebelled against their wishes?"
- "What do you tell yourself or do instead of caving in to starving yourself, bingeing and purging, taking laxatives or diet pills, or cutting yourself?"
- "Which would you prefer to have, a self-embracing or a self-erasing lifestyle?

In some cases, bulimic behavior may be a metaphor for family or other intimate relationship difficulties. Clients can be asked the following metaphorical questions:

- "Has there been anything that happened recently or in the past in your family or other important relationships outside the home that has been difficult for you to stomach or digest?"
- "What specifically does your father say or do that is difficult for you to digest?"

- "How about your relationship with your boyfriend or any of your close friends? Have they said or done anything lately that has been difficult to stomach or digest?"

These questions are quite useful for learning about what specific relationship difficulties the client is experiencing conflict and having a hard time coping with. It helps the client look at her bulimia as being embedded in multiple social contexts rather than viewing it as occurring due to her intrapsychic conflicts or deficits. We may learn about destructive invalidating interactions or, in a smaller percentage of cases, past or present forms of abuse occurring. The questions also are helpful for deciding whom to engage for future sessions and what relationships need to be targeted for intervention. The following case example illustrates how useful the metaphorical questions can be for zeroing in on a self-harming client's most conflicted family relationship that may need therapeutic attention early in treatment.

Juanita, 17 years old, had been plagued with bulimic and episodic cutting difficulties for five years. Her parents had been separated for a year and she had not seen her father for a long time. Her mother gave up her career to stay at home and try to help her daughter to stop these behaviors. Juanita used to be an excellent student and was was quite popular with her peers. However, she had missed many days of school and her grades had greatly declined. When she would not attend school, her peers and teachers would call her home to offer support. Juanita had seen seven therapists and three different psychiatrists over the past five years. Based on what I had observed in my initial consultation meeting with the family, school personnel, and currently involved mental health team of professionals, there appeared to be a long-standing rigidified pattern of interaction occurring: the more super-responsible the mother, the helping professionals, and her peers were in trying to save Juanita and get her to stop her self-destructive behaviors, the more super-irresponsible she was by not using all of the many coping strategies and tools to help herself that the professionals had taught her and the more she would not go to school. Early in the session I asked Juanita, "Has there been anything that happened recently or in the past in your family or in other important relationships outside the home that has been difficult for you to stomach or digest?" Immediately, she responded with "my relationship with my father." Juanita went on to say that she worried about "his drinking" and did not like when he would "swear at" her and her mother. Prior to the marital separation, Juanita and her father used to spend a lot of time playing board games together and she missed him a lot. The mother, on the other hand, was quite angry with the father and limited Juanita's contact with him. Much to my surprise, not only was the father not invited to the consultation session but he was completely excluded from participating in Juanita's family therapy sessions. Apparently, Juanita had said on many occasions in the past to her mother and the mental health team that she wanted to have some sessions with him as well. It was decided at the end of the consultation meeting that separate father-daughter sessions would be offered to Juanita so she could reconnect with him. When asked, "What would be the disadvantages of giving up your vomiting?" Juanita responded with, "For my mom to take care of me. Not just my mother but everyone to pay attention to me!" So we learned that both the bulimia and her episodic cutting had provided secondary gains for Juanita, in that they both, in a very dramatic way, demanded the attention of others. In concluding the consultation session, I recommended to the mother, school, and mental health professionals that Juanita get involved again in theater, which she had enjoyed as a child, and a catch-up plan with her course work be negotiated with her teachers so she could get back on track at school. Juanita, her mother, and the helping professionals were all in agreement with the plan. Finally, the mother also decided that she would start working and having a social life outside the home again.

Key Assessment Questions to Ask Self-Harming Clients

In helping to determine the nature and severity of the client's self-harming practice and involvement in equivalent behaviors like substance abuse, bulimia, and sexually risky behaviors, I will ask the key assessment questions below. These questions are helpful to elicit: the unique meaning of the self-harming behavior; how it benefits the client; the affects of this behavior on relationships with his or her family, intimate partner, and friends; his or her engagement in equivalent self-destructive behaviors; past physical or sexual abuse, and suicide attempts by the client and his or her family/extended family members (Juzwin, 2004; Selekman, 2006b). The key assessment questions are as follows:

- "Where did you learn how to cut, burn, or use other forms of self-harming yourself?"
- "How long have you been self-harming?"
- "Where on your body do you typically cut, burn, or harm yourself in some other way?"
- "On a given day, how often do you self-harm?"
- "What does your self-harming mean to you?"
- "In what ways does it help you?"
- "What would be some other disadvantages for you of giving it up?"
- "Do you ever experience any particular thoughts, feelings, or bodily sensations that trigger you to self-harm?"
- "What are other triggers for you?"
- "What effect does your self-harming have on your relationships with your parents and siblings?"
- "Do you self-harm alone or with your friends?"
- "Have you ever lost any friendships or intimate relationships because of

your cutting, burning, or other forms of self-harming?"

- "Do you ever engage in risky unprotected sexual behavior to try to find comfort or to hurt yourself?"
- "How often in a given week or month would you do this?"
- "If you could put a voice to your cutting, burning, or most meaningful scars, what would they say about you as a person and your life situation?"
- "Do you ever abuse drugs or alcohol to escape from your problems, numb away negative thoughts and feelings, or to just harm yourself?"
- "How often in a given week or month would you do this?"
- "Do you ever take laxatives, diet pills, or starve yourself for weight
- "How often in a given week or month would you do this?"
- "Do you ever purge or overexercise for weight control?"
- "How often in a given week or month would you do this?"
- "Has anyone ever hurt you emotionally or physically in the past and it was traumatic for you?"
- "Have you or any members of your family/extended family ever tried to take their lives in the past? Did anyone commit suicide?" (If yes, find out how long ago and methods used by the client and/or family/extended family members.)
- "When you resist the temptation to self-harm, what do you tell yourself or do that works?"
- "What specifically do your parents, older siblings, best friends, or adult inspirational others do or say to you that helps you to not cave in to harming yourself?"

Client-Attempted Solutions

In addition to inquiring with clients about their past negative and positive treatment experiences, it is important to find out everything they have tried to do to cope with and resolve difficulties in their lives, including refraining from self-harming or engaging in equivalent self-destructive behaviors. One helpful way to learn how clients may be mismanaging difficulties in their lives is to ask them to describe for you recent stressful situations that were triggering negative emotions in them and how they attempted to cope with or resolve the difficulties. Often clients' attempted solution patterns are redundant and become rigidified. These patterns play a key role in maintaining the presenting problems. By having a clear picture of the client's circular problem-maintaining patterns, the therapist will have several locus points in which to disrupt these patterns and promote change.

Mood Management Skills and Self-Regulation Difficulties

Many self-harming clients experience difficulties managing their moods, particularly negative emotions. However, it is important to first explore with our clients if there have been any times recently or in the past where they constructively responded to their negative emotions and did not succumb to self-harming or engaging in other self-destructive behaviors. By eliciting this valuable information, we can learn about specific coping or problem-solving strategies that we should encourage clients to use when they are being pushed around by their negative moods and thoughts.

We need to find out what main mood states our clients experience that are most likely to trigger a self-harming episode. As mentioned earlier, many self-harming clients report having difficulties coping with frustration and their depressed, anxious, and angry thoughts and feelings. They also have grave difficulty with self-soothing, frustration tolerance, and delaying gratification. Some clients report feeling overwhelmed by powerful waves of emotionality and experience what psychologist Daniel Goleman refers to as an *emotional hijacking* situation (Goleman, 2003). This is why the use of mindfulness meditation and other Buddhist self-healing practices (see Chapter 3) are so useful to self-harming clients in that it helps them to center themselves and learn how to quiet the wild emotional stallions in their heads. Once clients learn how to embrace their emotions and negative thoughts and neutralize their potency, they become less reactive to them. In the next chapter, I will also present highly effective *disputation skills* for empowering our clients to challenge their irrational self-defeating thoughts, which often drive their self-harming and other equivalent self-destructive behaviors (Seligman, 2002, 2003).

Couple Partner, Parental, and/or Involved Social Network Members' Attempted Solutions

It is critical to gather detailed information about the attempted solutions of all of the couple partners parents, and involved members from the client's social network (Watzlawick et al., 1974). First, I like to find out about any past problem-solving strategies that seemed to work or helped a little bit with the self-harming client. Sometimes with some further modification or adjustments, a particularly effective past problem-solving strategy may be helpful to try again. There may be past parental problem-solving strategies that worked at resolving another difficulty that the client used to have or his or her sibling had that may be worthwhile testing out with the present self-harming problem. In some cases, older siblings may have had difficulties with self-harming as teenagers and the parents came up with some effective strategies for resolving their difficulties; these strategies might be worthwhile trying with the client. Finally, there may be certain off-the-wall ideas parents had come up with in response to their son or daughter's self-harming or other self-destructive behaviors that they held back from trying out because they thought it would not work. As long as it is not punitive or abusive in any way, I may encourage the parents to give their unusual ideas a test run. In some cases, their creative problem-solving strategy may not only be quite effective but will be a better solution strategy than anything a therapist could possibly come up with.

In initial couple and family sessions, I invite the couple partner, parents, and involved members from the client's social network to describe a recent self-harming or equivalent self-destructive episode that occurred with the client and how they attempted to manage it. I have found it quite helpful and newsworthy to have the clients map out this circular problem-maintaining pattern on a legal pad or flip chart. This helps the concerned others see that despite their best efforts to express their concerns and be helpful to the clients, they are inadvertently perpetuating the self-harming and/or equivalent self-destructive behaviors they want to see stopped. Some of the most common ways couple partners, parents, and involved members from clients' social networks respond are: becoming highly emotionally reactive, lecturing about the dangers and health consequences of the client's actions, pleading with the client to stop hurting himself or herself, trying to over-protect the client and micromanage him or her, threatening to take the client to a psychiatric hospital or shipping him or her off to a boarding school or residential treatment center, yelling at the client, viewing the client's behavior as manipulative and punishing the client with a lengthy consequence, putting down or blaming the client for the high level of stress in their couple or family relationships, or emotionally disengaging from the client.

Assessing and Tapping Key Resource People from Self-Harming Clients' Social Networks

Many moderate to severe self-harming clients report feeling "alone" and socially disconnected. Part of this social isolation is due to the fact that self-harming is a hidden practice. The family, extended family members, and concerned friends may pose a threat to them in trying to get them to stop engaging in this "coping" behavior. In addition, many long-standing self-harming clients experience shame and worry that if family members and friends discover what they are doing, they will be repulsed by this behavior or be upset with them for engaging in this behavior. Once habituation and a high tolerance for physical pain occurs, the self-harming practice can become much more important than spending time with family members and friends in helping them to cope with emotional distress and other major life stressors.

To help combat self-harming clients' social isolation, I have found it to be invaluable to assess with clients who the key members from their social networks are whom they have been able to count on for support in both the past and present. This can include recruiting concerned friends, close older siblings, close relatives, and other adult inspirational others like favorite teachers and coaches they trust and really like, clergy, and adult friends of the family they feel close to. As mentioned earlier, these individuals are key members of the client's solution-determined system. We can secure this important information about who the key resource people are by asking self-harming clients the following two questions:

- "When you are really stressed out and having a tough time, which one or two of your friends whom you have really been able to count on in the past to help you out do you turn to for support?"

- "Are there any adults outside your home/on campus other than your close friends whom you feel close to that you have been able to turn to for support and advice when you have really needed it?"

The answers to these questions will provide valuable information regarding whom you can recruit for future counseling sessions once the client sees the value in tapping the tremendous support and collective wisdom these key resource people can provide, as long as the client is willing to give written consent to do this. I have created the *significant other consent form* (see figure 2.3) which can be given to the client to sign, the client's parents if a minor, close friends, close friends' parents, and adult inspirational others to secure written consent to contact these key resource people to participate in future counseling sessions. The rules of client confidentiality are clearly explained to these key resource people.

There are four treatment benefits to involving the client's key resource people in counseling sessions:

1. The client is reconnected to concerned family and friends, who can provide a strong sense of community and support for him or her.
2. Key research people can provide a diversity of fresh and creative ideas for the client, his or her partner and/or family, and the therapist to help promote change.
3. Key social network resource people can aid in the relapse prevention process by challenging poor decision-making made by the client and celebrating and reinforcing positive gains he or she is making by abstaining from self-harming and other self-destructive behaviors to stay on track.
4. Key research people can be included in solution-determined collaborative meetings with involved helping professionals from larger systems to share their insights and actively participate in the solution-construction process.

Assessing the Need to Bring in Former Self-Harming Clients and Experienced Adult Inspirational Others

Some self-harming young adult and adolescent clients we work with lack solid support systems and have highly conflicted and/or toxic relationships with their parents or key caretakers. In addition, they may be associating with a very negative group of friends who reinforce their self-harming and other self-destructive behaviors. When faced with this type of clinical dilemma, it may be beneficial to offer to the client the idea of bringing in alumni who used to have difficulties with self-harm and other self-destructive behaviors, such as substance abuse, bulimia, and engaging in sexually risky behaviors, and are now abstinent from these behaviors and leading productive lives. Not only can this provide clients with a big boost of hope that they can conquer their self-harming and other self-destructive difficulties, but the alumni can provide them with much needed positive support, encouragement, helpful relapse prevention strategies that have worked for them, and

---

Fig. 2-3 SIGNIFICANT OTHER CONSENT FORM

I/We _____ give my/our therapist _____ permission to include in my/our counseling sessions the following two friends/adult inspirational others: _____ for the purpose of providing additional support in my/our treatment. I will explain to my friends, their parents, and adult inspirational others that confidential information will be shared in our counseling sessions and that it is not to be disclosed outside of our meetings. I will obtain signatures from my friends, their parents, and any adult significant others I wish to include in my/our counseling sessions.

Signature Of Client   Date

Signature Of Parent/Guardian   Date

Signature Of Friend's Parent   Date

Signature Of Friend   Date

Signature Of Friend's Parent   Date

Signature Of Friend   Date

Signature Of Adult Inspirational Other   Date

Signature Of Adult Inspirational Other   Date

Witness   Date

Notice to client/significant others: I/We understand that this consent shall expire in 1 year from the date of our signature(s) or until the calendar date _____. I/We understand that I/we may revoke this consent at any time during my/our treatment. I/We also agree not to hold my/our therapist responsible for any violation of my/our confidentiality by participating friends or adult inspirational others. I/We (friend's parents) agree not to hold the therapist responsible for any possible negative effects of having my/our teen participating in his/her friend's counseling sessions.

---

assistance with doing better in school, securing employment, or resolving difficulties in the workplace. Depending on the clients' unique needs, the alumni often agree to be available to clients for as long as they need them for support or until they get solidly on track and establish some new, healthy peer relationships.

In clinical situations where the young adult or adolescent's relationships with parents or key caretakers are highly conflicted or there is an extreme emotional disconnection with them, it can be helpful to introduce to the client an experienced adult inspirational other who was successfully utilized to help other clients faced with similar situations. This allows clients to have a positive and meaningful relationship with a caring adult who can provide support, advice, and valuable wisdom when they need it. Once a positive relationship is established with the adult inspirational other, it can help the client to become emotionally stronger and less reactive to negative interactions with their toxic parents or key caretakers and better able to cope with life stressors.

Assessing the Benefits and Consequences of Internet Usage

For many clients, virtual self-harm communities and social network sites have been a gift in helping them feel less socially isolated. On MySpace and Xanga self-harming clients can seek and share self-harming experiences and information with others like them. On YouTube, hundreds, if not thousands, of self-harming videos are posted. Some of these sites are monitored for potentially triggering content, such as sharing self-harming techniques, while others regularly post graphic stories, poems, and art that can serve as powerful stimuli for a self-harming episode. There are some sites that show video footage of self-harming individuals using multiple methods for brutalizing their bodies.

Since there are very few if any specialized support groups offered for young adult and adolescent self-harming clients in their communities, there are a growing number of online support groups tightly monitored by mental health and health care professionals to help fill this gap. Information on how to access these online support groups can be found by visiting the following Web sites: SIARI, WebMD, and LifeSigns.

As part of the assessment process, it is critical that therapists assess with their self-harming clients, their couple partners, and/or parents how they use the Internet and determine with them how it benefits them and how it might contribute to the maintenance of their difficulties. Many therapists working with self-harming clients overlook this important assessment area. Whitlock, Lader, and Contrario (2007) and I recommend that therapists ask the following types of questions to secure this important information:

- "How often do you visit the Internet to get and share information?"
- "Have you ever visited a Web site to find out about or talk about self-harming behavior?"
- "What are other favorite sites you like to visit?"
- "What do you like to do most when you visit these Web sites?"
- "Do you like to post messages or videos or do you like to see what is new on these Web sites?"
- "Have you ever made friends over the Internet?"
- "How close do you consider your Internet friends?"

- "What do you like most about having friends that you only communicate with online?"
- "Do you ever take the advice from your friends online?"
- "Can you share with me some examples of the advice you were given by your online friends that you put to use?"
- "How comfortable do you feel hearing stories, reading poetry, or seeing pictures or videos of self-harm?"
- "Have you shared your own story on any of your favorite Web sites and how did you feel about doing this?"
- "Does what you learn or do on the Internet affect what you do when you are offline?
- "On a scale from 1 to 10, with 10 feeling totally comfortable with each one of your favorite Web sites and 1 extremely uncomfortable, how would you rate each one?"
- "Has there ever been a time or times in the past where, after visiting a particular Web site or participating in an online self-harming support group, it triggered you to self-harm?"
- "What was it about the Web site or what was said or discussed in the online support group, that triggered you to self-harm?"
- Ask a couple partner or parents: "Do you think that the Web sites or any of the online self-harming support groups that _____ has been visiting and participating in are a trigger for him/her to self-harm?"
- Ask a couple partner or parents: "How specifically do you think _____ seeking information on certain Web sites and participating in online self-harming support groups is benefiting him/her?"
- Ask a couple partner or parents: "What effect do the lengthy periods of time _____ spends visiting Web sites and participating in online self-harming support groups have on your relationship with him/her?"
- "Is _____'s excessive Internet usage creating more closeness or distance in your relationship with him/her?"
- Ask parents: "Are there any specific and outlawed Web sites that your son/daughter keeps visiting that you are concerned about?"
- Ask parents: "Do you have firm guidelines regarding your son/daughter's Internet usage?"
- Ask parents: "Are the two of you consistent and a unified team with setting limits and enforcing your consequences when your son/daughter visits forbidden Web sites?"

The answers to the above questions can be extremely helpful for collaboratively determining with clients, their couple partners, and/or parents if their Internet activity is benefiting them or serving to hinder their conquering their self-harming habits. It is important to find out if their online friends are truly providing support or are teaching them new methods of self-harming. Similarly, it is important to determine if there is a pattern occurring with the client with particular people or certain Web sites triggering self-harming episodes. As therapists, we need to ask ourselves if we also might be inadvertently reinforcing the client's unproductive conflict-avoidant coping style and poor social skills by not challenging their excessive use of the Internet. Some self-harming clients use the Internet as an escape to avoid facing family, couple, and peer conflicts. Spending endless hours having online chats, hearing and reading self-harming thematic stories and poetry, looking at pictures and watching self-harming- related videos on Web sites does not expose the self-harming client to a world of wellness and helpful places to learn adaptive coping strategies and relationship effectiveness skills. Finally, for young adults and adolescents who have recently conquered their self-harming habits, visiting a self-harming focused Web site or listening to self-harming stories in an online self-harming support group could derail them and lead to a slip or prolonged relapsing situation.

Identifying Clients' Positive and Negative Triggers

One of the most important assessment areas we need to address with the client, his or her partner, and/or the parents are both positive and negative triggers that can help prevent and precipitate self-harming episodes. It is helpful to begin this inquiry by asking the client, his or her partner, and the parents specific positive actions they have taken in both the past and the present to prevent self-harming episodes from occurring. During the spaces in between, when clients are not self-harming or engaging in other self-destructive behaviors, we need to find out what their useful self-talk tapes are, which key resiliency protective factors they utilize, and what their most helpful self-generated coping or problem-solving strategies are. We need to find out what specific flow-state activities the clients have immersed themselves in when experiencing emotional distress or other environmental stressors. Next, we can explore with the client what specifically his or her couple partner, parents, and key members from his or her social network do that help him or her not to cave in to self-harming and to stay on track. I use the *my positive trigger log* (see figure 2.4) to help clients keep track daily, for over a week, what they, their couple partner, parents and siblings, close friends, and other key members from their social networks do that triggers positive emotion and prevents them from caving in to a self-harming episode (Selekman, 2006b). Many self-harming clients have indicated that this valuable relapse prevention tool has helped them to stay on track. Similar to how self-harming episodes are cyclical, getting skilled at practicing helping oneself individually and tapping the expertise of healthy and supportive others to avoid not caving in to the urge to self-harm also is cyclical and will perpetuate positive patterns of healthier thinking, feeling, and actions for our clients in the future.

It is critical that we also conduct a detailed assessment of all of the clients' negative triggers. For self-harming clients, triggers can take the following forms: certain unpleasant mood states; oppressive recurring irrational and self-defeating

Fig. 2-4 MY POSITIVE TRIGGER LOG					
Date	What I did	My parents/ siblings	Friends	Other involved helpers	How specifically helpful

thoughts; certain bodily sensations like severe cramping during menstrual cycles; use of alcohol or other substances; gorging oneself with food; sharp objects, a lighter, matches, or other objects used for burning oneself; certain songs; physically associating with or communicating online with certain toxic people and self-harming friends; visiting certain self-harming-focused Web sites or participating in online self-harming support groups that are not tightly monitored by professionals or responsible hosts; reading poetry or stories or looking at videos involving graphic self-harming and other self-destructive behavior footage; and certain locations where self-harming behavior had occurred in the past or visits to these locations. By having the couple partner, the client's parents, and key members from his or her social network present when reviewing the client's positive and negative triggers and with the relapse prevention planning process, we can minimize the likelihood of future slips occurring and the teamwork in multiple contexts will help the client to stay on track and eventually conquer his or her self-harming problem.

Assessing the Nature of the Client's Peer Relationships and Social Skills

As mentioned earlier, moderate to severe category self-harming clients often report feeling alone. In some cases, these clients used to be socially active and had close friends with whom they regularly got together. However, as they became increasingly more out of control with their self-harming and equivalent self-destructive behaviors, this may have contributed to losing their close friendships, social ridicule, or peer harassment, both in face-to-face interactions and on online social interaction Web sites, leading to social isolation. If there are some long-standing friends who have been there for the client unconditionally, it is these friends who may be worthwhile recruiting for future counseling sessions to aid with providing added between-session support for the client, co-constructing solutions, and aiding with relapse prevention (Selekman, 1995, 2004, 2005, 2006b).

Some self-harming clients have poor social skills and experience grave difficulty with fitting in with and being accepted by their peers. It could be that the client has difficulty asserting himself/herself or taking risks, tends to clown around or act obnoxious with others too much, handles frustration or disappointment in inappropriate ways, has poor self-grooming skills, and either lacks or is weak in the ability to observe the effects of his/her actions on others. I have developed a therapeutic experiment called *observing oneself high up in a bubble*, which is specifically designed to help self-harming clients or any clients who are experiencing social skill difficulties—identify both what works for them in social interactions and how they get themselves into trouble with their peers (Selekman, 2006b; see Chapter 3). The following case example illustrates how this therapeutic experiment helped a 14-year-old self-harming adolescent who was alienating her peers due to her provocative behavior and was being scapegoated by them at her junior high school.

Julie, an eighth grader, was referred to me by her school social worker for cutting, disrupting some of her classes by showing her fresh wounds or scars to her friends, and being disrespectful toward the teachers in these classes. Julie also had a tendency to be mean to some of her peers. As the school year progressed, Julie was finding that not only were terrible rumors circulating around the school that she was "the psycho queen," but her peers, including former friends, were rejecting her as well. To further add to her being socially ostracized, on her MySpace page peers were posting mean-spirited entries and distorted pictures of her. Julie's goal in counseling was to rekindle her former friendships and stop being rejected by her peers. I offered Julie the observing-oneself-high-up-in-a-bubble experiment to provide helpful information about what she needed to do that helped her get along with former friends, and also keep track of what the friendly alter part of herself high above in a bubble observed her doing that made her peers dislike her. I gave her a small pocket notebook to record her daily interactions and the insights she gained from her observations. After one week of doing the experiment, Julie quickly learned about how showing her fresh cut wounds or scars was turning off former friends and peers rather than being viewed by them as a cool thing to do. Furthermore, she had discovered that treating her peers in mean ways was only leading to her peers "dissing" her and giving her the cold shoulder. On the bright side, Julie learned that by refraining from showing her fresh cut wounds and scars to her former friends and treating fellow peers nicely, they would talk to her and want to hang out with her. By the second week of doing this experiment and practicing doing more of what was working for her in trying to reconnect with former friends, building new relationships, and treating her peers with more respect and dignity, Julie discovered that peers in general were responding to her in more positive ways and the rumor mill appeared to be stopping. Julie was very pleased with her social success, was feeling better about herself, and was now in a better place to address her cutting difficulty and the disadvantages of continuing this behavior.

Another way we can help self-harming clients improve their social skills is through role-playing social scenarios where they experience difficulties and problem-solve together about optional ways of responding to others. In addition, having clients put themselves in the shoes of others (role-taking) and experience how they may think and feel about them in terms of their style of interacting and what they are talking about, can be most beneficial for clients in helping them gain insight into how they affect others in both positive and negative ways.

Many self-harming clients can benefit from learning relationship effectiveness skills. This can include assertiveness, communications, problem-solving, conflict-resolution, and resisting skills. Prior to teaching skills in these areas, it is helpful first if the clients can recall times where they had successfully used these skills. During this inquiry, we may learn about certain solution-building patterns and ways of thinking in interpersonal situations that we want to encourage the client to increase or experiment with in weaker relationship skill areas.

Finally, we need to explore with couple partners and parents of the self-harming clients any concerns they may have about who the latter associate with. In some cases, couple partners and parents have shared their concerns and tried repeatedly to get the clients to stay away from certain toxic and negative people and the unhealthy contexts in which they associate with them. This issue can be explored and addressed more directly in couple or family therapy sessions. The following case example illustrates how making poor choices with toxic intimate partners can have dire consequences for the client.

> Jeremy, an 18-year-old living at home with his mother, had a long history of cutting four or more times a day, substance abusing and associating with drug-using friends, doing poorly in school, and violating his mother's rules. He had been psychiatrically hospitalized twice for cutting and overdosing on pills and alcohol, was in residential treatment twice, and saw seven therapists before seeing me. Jeremy also had a long history of being rejected by girls. Much to Jeremy's surprise, he was introduced to Marne by a friend who seemed to really like him. Little did Jeremy know that Marne had a history of not committing in relationships, flirted a lot, and was known to use males and females alike for her own needs and then drop them as intimates and friends, respectively. Both Jeremy's mother and I had cautioned him about not getting too attached to Marne. Jeremy claimed that he "loved Marne" and that she was being "straight up" with him. It appeared that Jeremy put up an invisible force field regarding really listening to his mother's and my concerns. One week later, Jeremy was at a party with Marne and "caught her making out" with a friend of his. Emotionally devastated by what

he had seen, Jeremy came home, grabbed a butcher knife, and began to cut deeply into his arm, severing a tendon. Clearly, he had crossed the line from cutting for relief from emotional distress to wanting to end all feeling. Once Jeremy's mother saw what he had done, she quickly wrapped a towel around his forearm to stop the bleeding and called 911. She saved his life. After being stabilized in the intensive care unit of a medical hospital, his current psychiatrist had him admitted into an adult inpatient psychiatric program. It took this life-threatening experience for Jeremy to learn to be more cautious and careful in the future with choosing his intimate partners. Although he made a commitment to stop cutting and abusing substances after getting out of the hospital, Jeremy was experiencing terrible withdrawal symptoms: mood swings, cravings, and sleeping difficulties. I worked with Jeremy and his mother in coming up with a highly structured relapse prevention plan and having them practice together several distress management tools and strategies, such as mindfulness meditation and visualizing movies of success. As part of the relapse prevention plan, Jeremy agreed to stay away from his former "crew" of drug-using friends and certain places that would lead to him "getting stoned." I also was able to get Jeremey to identify certain early warning signs to look for in new relationships with women that would be red flags for avoiding further involvement with them. Jeremy also landed his first job, which he had felt great about and provided additional structure for him during his leisure time.

Jeremy's case situation illustrates how we need to tightly monitor heavy to severe self-harming young adult and adolescent clients who are more at risk for suicide attempts, particularly if they have already made previous attempts or come from families where other members or extended family members have made attempts or completions, have multiple risk factors for suicide potential, such as: serious romantic relationship breakups, have heavy substance abuse, have a long history of self-harm, lack a strong and healthy support system, and are failing in school or unable to sustain or secure employment. The more stressors self-harming clients are struggling to cope with, the more at risk they may be for a suicide attempt (Joiner, 2005; Miller et al., 2007).

Assessing School and/or Occupational Functioning

As part of the assessment process, we need to find out both what is going well and what is not for self-harming clients in school or college and/or in their work settings. In addition to finding out about their academic or job performance strength areas, we want to know if they are experiencing any learning difficulties. These can take the form of difficulties staying focused and concentrating, visual and auditory memory, and processing and speed. If they report that any of these areas may be presenting a problem for them, it may be beneficial to see if educational testing could be arranged to pinpoint the key learning issues so as to put in place an effective remedial plan for strengthening the identified problem areas. I have worked with a number of self-harming adolescents who were doing poorly academically and not responding well to their parents' repeated requests to complete their chores or cooperate with regard to parental limits, and it turned out through educational testing that they all had auditory memory difficulties. Test results like these can be of great benefit for parents and teachers alike, to help them better understand their adolescents' and students' processing difficulties and be more flexible, patient, compassionate, and concrete with their requests. Both young adults and adolescents can be taught specific tools and strategies for learning how to work with and make improvements in these problem areas.

We also might discover that the self-harming young adult and adolescent could benefit from some advocacy with school or college personnel by putting in place special educational remedial services and accommodations that will help him or her be more successful in school. Some self-harming adolescents labeled as having "attitude problems" are acting up because they are not retaining or understanding the classroom material and feel totally lost. Teachers might not be aware of this problem and therefore are viewing these students as being "troublemakers." I have found it to be quite advantageous to regularly collaborate with teachers and other concerned school personnel of the self-harming adolescent clients. By meeting with all of the adolescent's teachers, we can learn about what is and is not working in their classes. In some cases, certain teachers are having very few problems with the adolescent and can offer their fellow teacher peers' valuable insights about what specifically they do in their classes that works in terms of promoting pro-social behavior, cooperation, and homework completion. When collaborating with school personnel, I always adopt a one-down nonthreatening position and use curiosity to find out what teachers' concerns are, details about how they are getting stuck in the management of the students in and out of their classes, and what the best hopes and expectations are for the school personnel's work with their students and their families. After establishing rapport and treating teachers with the highest level of respect, I have found that productive teamwork can be established and change strategies are more likely to be successfully implemented in the teachers' classrooms.

Determining which Key Helping Allies from Larger Systems to Collaborate with

Self-harming clients, their couple partners, and their families need to be invited to decide which involved helping professionals from larger systems the therapist needs to collaborate with. I believe that these involved helpers can be allies who offer the solution-determined treatment system valuable expertise and experience that can be tapped in the solution construction process. In addition to learning from the helpers about the referral process, their stories of involvement, concerns, expectations, and best hopes for the clients, I like to find out from them about their past successes working with similar clients and what their *commitments* are (Kegan & Lahey, 2001; Selekman, 2005, 2006b). By commitments, I mean the various beliefs and problem views that drive the helpers' actions or attempted solutions. Similar to parents, I believe that involved helping professionals are trying to manage the clients' situations in the best way they know how based on their past experiences working with similar clients and using the strengths and resources they possess. However, unlike the parents, the helpers may be limited by the mandates of their roles in relationship to their clients and the work contexts they represent, which may have a constraining effect on what they are to look and listen for and what they can and cannot do. Ideally, if the clients are willing to have the involved helpers attend the initial consultation session, we can learn valuable information regarding the helpers' commitments up front and the client, his or her couple partner, and/or family members can reflect on how the helpers are viewing their problem situations, concerns, and best hopes for them. Furthermore, the clients can let the helpers know what has been helpful or not helpful from their previous meetings and how they can help them out in the best possible way now. As therapists, we want to maximize opportunities for the helpers to be active participants in the solution construction process and observe and hear clients' problem situations improving and being communicated about in new ways. This will lead them and the organizations they represent to be less concerned about the clients and disengage from the solution-determined treatment system.

The Blueprint for Change Plan

The *blueprint for change plan* is co-constructed with the client, his or her couple partner, and/or family in the initial collaborative strengths-based brief therapy consultation session (see Figure 2.5). The clients take the lead in determining the following: their goals for treatment, which of their self-generated pretreatment change solution-building patterns they need to increase, strengths and key intelligences, resiliency protective factors, alter personas/helpful inner voices, past successes, and key flow-state activities they need to call upon to achieve their goals; identifying which helping professionals and members from their social networks to recruit for future sessions to aid in the change effort; and selecting from a menu of treatment modality options, and initial consultation session therapeutic experiments in line with their treatment goals. Session by session the blueprint for change plan will be reviewed with the clients and, collaboratively with the therapist, they will make any necessary changes to improve upon it in terms of including additional family and social network members, new larger systems helper participants, modification of the treatment goals, adding or dropping certain treatment modalities or adjunct services selected in the initial consultation session, and discontinuing unproductive therapeutic experiments and trying new ones. There are six parts to the blueprint for change plan: *My/Our Identified Key Pretreatment Changes, Target Behaviors and/or Relationship Changes Desired Now, My/Our Identified and Key Strengths Tapped for Goal Attainment, Identification of Solution-Determined System Membership and Whom to Include in Future Sessions, Treatment Modality Selection Menu,* and *Therapeutic Experiment Selection*

Fig. 2-5. THE BLUEPRINT FOR CHANGE PLAN

My/our identified key pretreatment changes

1.
2.
3.
4.
5.

Target behaviors and/or relationship changes desired now

1. Parent's goals
   a.
   b.
   c.

2. Couple's goals
   a.
   b.
   c.

3. Young adult/teen's goals
   a.
   b.
   c.

My/our identified and key strengths tapped for goal attainment

1.
2.
3.
4.
5.
6.

Identification of solution-determined system membership and whom to include in future sessions

1.
2.
3.
4.
5.
6.

Treatment modality and selection menu

_____ Individual therapy   _____ Solution-Oriented Parenting Group

_____ Couples therapy   _____ Stress-Busters Leadership Group

_____ Family therapy   _____ Collaboration and advocacy with larger systems
                                           professionals

Therapeutic experiment menu

_____ Therapeutic experiment #1

_____ Therapeutic experiment #2

_____ Therapeutic experiment #3

Parents

Name _____ Date _____

Name _____ Date _____

Young adult/teen

Name _____ Date _____

Therapist

Name _____ Date _____

Menu. After filling out the blueprint for change plan, all participants sign their names on the bottom of the last page of the form, which makes it our official co-constructed contract. I will review each of the sections of the blueprint for change plan and the types of questions that can be asked to secure the necessary information to complete each section. Some of the questions will have been asked earlier in the initial consultation session, particularly questions that inquired about the clients' pretreatment changes, strengths, and treatment goals. However, it is helpful when filling in the blueprint for change plan with clients to further elaborate on their earlier responses and have them take the lead in determining which of their pretreatment change solution-building patterns of behavior and thinking, key strengths, and productive past coping strategies to tap to help them achieve their goals.

My/Our Identified Pretreatment Changes

This important client information will be provided when the clients discuss the results of the pretreatment experiment given to them when they had made the initial telephone call or walked into your clinic or agency. In some cases, clients will have not completed or forgot to do the pretreatment experiment or will identify later in the initial consultation session their newsworthy pretreatment changes. Therapists need to determine with the clients the specific solution-building patterns of interaction and newly generated or re-instated past successful strategies they need to increase that can help them to achieve their individual and relationship goals. Clients can be asked the following types of questions:

- "What do you need to tell yourself more often that will help you to continue to not cave in to cutting?"
- "Do you think if you continue to hang out more with Mary and Lisa (positive peers and not self-harming), you will be less likely to have a slip?"
- "Which people and places to do you need to continue to stay away from that will help keep you on track and going strong?"

- "In what ways will it benefit you when Mom and Dad continue to 'stop nagging' you about doing your homework?"
- "Jane, what specifically would you like Terry to keep doing that will give you the confidence to kick your cutting and bulimia habits?"
- "Terry, what specifically would you like Jane to keep doing that will help the two of you get along better?"

When asking pretreatment change questions, the content of the questions needs to be derived from what specifically the clients, their couple partners, or parents indicate are positive pretreatment behaviors, thoughts, and ways of feeling they need to increase.

Target Behaviors and Relationship Changes Desired Now

In this section of the blueprint plan for change, we invite the client to be as specific (who, when, where) and clear as possible about what (how) behaviors and relationship changes they desire now. The therapist's job is to ensure that well-formulated treatment goals are established. We need to negotiate solvable behavioral goals with our clients. Otherwise, vague or ill-formed goals will lead to vague and unfocused therapy. It is important for clients to be aware that goals are the start of something new, not the end of something. There are four categories of questions that are useful to ask clients to establish well-formulated treatment goals: *presuppositional*, *best hopes*, *miracle question sequence*, and *scaling questions* (de Shazer, 1988, 1991; de Shazer et al., 2007, George, Iveson, & Ratner, 1999; Selekman, 1997, 2005, 2006b). Some examples of these goal-setting questions are as follows:

Presuppositional Questions
- "Let's say you left our meeting today feeling like it had accomplished everything you were hoping for. In reflecting back on how your situation was before you came in here today and how things are really different now, what changed that you are most pleased about?"
- "Let's say this were our last session together and you left here feeling completely satisfied today. What specifically is better with your situation now?"
- "How specifically are things now better in your relationship with your mother/partner?"
- "Are you aware of how you got that to happen?"
- "What else is better in your relationship?"
- "What effect are those changes having on you?"
- "So when these changes continue to happen in your relationship with your mother/partner, will this be a sign that you are ready to stop counseling?"
- "What will be the final step you need to take that will tell you that you are really done with counseling?"

- "Let's say I had you gaze into my trusty crystal ball two weeks down the road when you have quit cutting yourself, what do you see yourself doing instead that is making you feel good and more in control of your life?"
- "Let's say I am also gazing into the crystal ball, what people am I seeing you hang out with and what are you doing with them that is helping you stay quit?"
- "Let's say we were to run into each other at your favorite shopping mall one year from today after we successfully completed counseling together, and you were eager to share with me about your many changes individually and in your most important relationships. What will be the first change you will be excited to tell me about?"
- "How is that change making a difference in your life?"
- "If you were to walk me back step by step, sharing with me along the way what your thinking and actions were that paved the way to making this change happen, what will you tell me you told yourself and did?"
- "Let's say I had, sitting over there, an imaginary time machine and the three of you hopped in there for a speed-of-light journey into a new galaxy. What you are not aware of is that when humans enter this new galaxy, all of their past problems, concerns, and worries are erased. When you come back from the future, what specifically is better with your situation?"
- "How are your new changes making a difference for you individually and in your relationships?"
- "What else is better with your family situation?"
- "How else will you know that you are really succeeding as a family?"

Best Hopes Questions
- "What are your best hopes that you would get out of our meeting today?"
- "Which one of your best hopes would need to be realized today to make this a really useful session?"
- "What will your everyday lives be like once these best hopes are realized?"
- "What are you already doing or have done in the past that may in some way contribute to these best hopes being realized?"
- "How will you know when another small step toward achieving your best hopes has been made?"

Miracle Question Sequence
- "Suppose while you are sound asleep tonight a miracle happens and all your problems are solved. When you wake up tomorrow, what specifically will you notice that is better with your situation?"
- "Are you aware of how you got that to happen?"
- "What else will you be most surprised about that changed in your relationship with your father?"

- "How will that make a difference for you?"
- "What else is better with your situation?"
- "If your brother were sitting in this empty chair, what would he notice that is better in your relationship with your mother?"
- "I'm curious. Are any pieces of the miracle happening a little bit now?"
- "Are you aware of how you got that to happen?"
- "What will you have to continue to do to get that to happen more often?"

Scaling Questions

- "So, on a scale from 0 to 10, where 0 means when you decided to seek help and 10 means the day after the miracle, where would you say you are at today?"
- "At a 4?!"
- "I'm curious, what is it that tells you you are not at a 2 or a 1?"
- "What are you going to do over the next week to get one step higher, up to a 5?"
- "What will you tell yourself to get fired up to achieve your goal?"
- "When and where will you achieve the 5?"
- "Who will you be with when you achieve your goal?"
- "What will be other signs that will tell you that you are at a 6 or higher?"
- "Let's say we get together in one week's time and you come in here and tell me you made it up to a 6, What will you tell me you did?"
- (Ask a highly pessimistic client): "On a scale from –10 to –1, with –10 meaning that your situation is totally hopeless and –1 that you have an inkling of hope that your situation can change a tiny bit, where would you have rated your situation one month ago?"
- "A –9."
- "How about 2 weeks ago?"
- "A –6."
- "Are you aware of what you told yourself or did to get from a –9 to a –6?"
- "What else did you do that seemed to help a little bit?"
- "What else are you telling yourself to not give up?"
- "Let's say we get together in 1 week's time and you come in here and tell me that you took some steps up to a –5. What will you tell me you did?"

As readers can clearly see, the above questions can help guide clients in identifying the specific changes they desire. In addition to clarifying what the clients wish to work on changing first and how they envision themselves doing this, we need to also explore with them if their selected goals are small enough, doable, and if they anticipate any possible obstacles or bumps on the road to achieving their initial goals. I call this category of questions *covering-the-back-door questions.*

Covering the Back-Door Questions

- "Do you anticipate any obstacles getting in the way of your achieving your goals over the next week?"
- "What steps do you or others need to take to remove those barriers to achieving further success in your target goal area?"
- "Let's say that over the next week you run into some unexpected and challenging bumps in the road to achieving your goal. What will you tell yourself or do to stay fired up, not give up, and continue to pursue your goal?"
- "How have those strategies you used in the past helped you to achieve other goals when the going has gotten rough for you?"
- "Do you think the goal you wish to pursue over the next week is small enough and doable or do you think we need to make it smaller or modify it in some other way to further increase the likelihood of your success at reaching it?"
- "What specifically do you need from your partner/parents to ensure that you will achieve your goal?"

Not only does covering the back-door questions help optimize the clients' success, it also encourages them to be more mindful and realistic about the journey to attaining one's goals, that it is not smooth sailing, and to anticipate that but not to give up. The covering-the-back-door questions also help clients gain an aerial, wide-angle view, looking down at their goal-attainment process to see what adjustments they need to make in thinking and in action while on their journeys to maximize success. Finally, I like to use covering-the-back-door questions for goal-maintenance and relapse-prevention purposes (see Chapter 3).

If key members of the clients' solution-determined system, such as concerned members from their social networks or involved helping professionals from larger systems, are attending the initial consultation session, the clients can be invited to share with them what their desired best hopes and goals are, so they can help clients in the best way possible. This can take the form of added support and advocacy in those larger systems the clients are involved with, to ensure that clients' special needs are getting met. If the members from their social networks and larger systems helpers feel that they can achieve the clients' goals, these goals can be written down on the blueprint-for-change plan as well.

My/Our Identified and Key Strengths Tapped for Goal Attainment

In this section of the blueprint-for-change plan, the clients are invited to share their expertise about which specific self-generated pretreatment changes, key intelligence area talents, resiliency protective factor actions, alter persona/helpful inner voices, meaningful flow-state activities, and past successful strategies to tap in empowering them to achieve their goals. If in the telephone intake conversation, the client, his or her partner, or parents present themselves as highly motivated and eager to get to work on further improving their situations, in addition to giving them the pretreatment change experiment, I will have the family members go online and complete the Values-in-Action Inventory of Strengths, and bring their questionnaire results into the initial consultation session. Prior to the consultation session, they can be asked to think about how they can use their top five signature strengths to help them to solve their difficulties. With these clients, I will ask them what ideas they came up with already for using their top five signature strengths to make improvements in the original areas of their lives that they were concerned about prior to their first consultation sessions. The following questions are useful for eliciting clients' expertise:

- "What specifically do you need to increase doing that can further improve your situation?"
- "When faced with other difficult or challenging situations in the past, what have you done to successfully cope with or resolve those difficulties?"
- "What sparkling moment from your past stands out in your mind as a great example of your resourcefulness, courage, and resilience?"
- "Which of those courageous steps that you took and helpful thoughts can you use to achieve your goal over the next week?"
- "Which of your strengths, talents, and helpful personas or inner voices should you call upon to help ensure achieving your goal over the next week?"
- "How specifically can you use your artistic and creative writing talents over the next week to not cave in to cutting yourself?"
- "What past successful parenting strategy can you reinstate over the next week that will pave the way for more cooperation with your daughter?"
- "In what ways will you use your top signature strength, curiosity, to help you to avoid getting into arguments with your partner?"
- "Which one of your adult inspirational others' voices do you need to access and hear that will get you even more fired up to achieve your goal?"

Our clients' strengths and resources are our allies and should be accessed and utilized as much as possible in all of their problem areas throughout the course of treatment. Using a strong strengths-based emphasis with our clients fosters cooperative therapeutic relationships, and triggers positive emotions in our clients, which can greatly enhance their creative problem-solving abilities and increase their investment in the collaborative change effort (Fredrickson, 2002, 2003; Selekman, 2005, 2006b).

Identification of Solution-Determined System Membership and Whom to Include in Future Sessions

We may learn about who the key members are of the solution-determined system during the telephone intake conversation and can request at that point if the caller could invite these individuals to attend the initial consultation session if the clients feel comfortable with this request. If we don't secure this information at intake, we can find out who these members of the solution-determined systems are in the initial consultation session. Ultimately, it is left up to the clients to determine what larger systems professionals and key members from their social networks they wish to have attending their counseling sessions. When clients voice their concerns about having these individuals attending their sessions, I will share some of the advantages of having them actively involved in the change effort, such as sharing their creative ideas and expertise, providing further support and advocacy for the clients in social contexts outside the home where they are experiencing difficulties, and maximizing for opportunities for the involved helping professionals from larger systems to notice and hear that changes are occurring with their situations. The last good reason for involving the helping professionals is particularly true for representatives from powerful legal systems that can enforce response and action, like the child protective agancies and juvenile and adult justice systems. Once they are less alarmed or concerned about their clients' problem situations, they will help support the change process and disengage from the solution-determined system.

In addition to determining solution-determined system membership with the clients, it also is important to invite clients to tell you whom to include in future counseling sessions. I typically begin the counseling process working with those family members or the couple partners and/or concerned friends who are present for the initial consultation session. I will then expand the system and have the clients' decide whom else to include in future sessions if change is not happening by the second session. In some cases, the true customer for change in the client's social ecology may be an older sibling, a close friend, a grandparent and/or other relative, or the referral source from a larger system. I ask clients the following types of scaling and solution-building questions to help find out whom to include in future counseling sessions:

- "On a scale from 1 to 10, with 10 being most concerned about you and 1 hardly at all concerned about you, what numbers would you give absent family members?"
- "What about your closest relatives?"
- "How about your partner?"
- "What numbers would you give to your closest friends?"
- "It may be difficult to get all these concerned people in your life to the next session. Out of all of the people that you mentioned, which two or three of them could be the most helpful to us in improving your situation?"
- "Have you called upon any of these caring and concerned people in the past to help you get through other tough situations?"
- "What did he/she/they say or do that you found most helpful in those situations?"

- "In what ways can we use his/her/their words of wisdom or effective past problem-solving actions to help you with your current difficulties?"

The last two questions above may offer therapists creative and constructive building blocks for co-generating solution strategies for the clients' current difficulties. Once we determine whom to include in future sessions, this will lead to a discussion with the clients about what treatment modalities and adjunctive services they wish to choose first and include in our blueprint-for-change plan.

Treatment Modality and Adjunct Services Selection Menu

This portion of the blueprint for change plan co-construction process involves the clients selecting from a menu of treatment modality and adjunct services offered in the practice setting. Ideally, if the therapist has enough time and the staff, a wide range of groups and adjunct services can be offered to the clients in the initial consultation session. With group treatment, it is critical that there are minimally 8 clients and ideally a male-female co-therapy team for gender balance. Certain types of groups may not be available to new clients initially until there are more participants to fill them. When the client numbers increase and the timing is good to fill groups, I will offer to self-harming adolescents the opportunity to participate in a *Stress-Busters' Leadership Group* (Selekman, 2006a; see chapter 6) and for their parents concurrent participation in the *Solution-Oriented Parenting Group* (Selekman, 200b; see Chapter 6). The clients also can select collaborative strengths-based individual, couple, or family therapy as their primary treatment modalities. In the way of adjunctive services offered, clients also may choose to have extra involvement in mindfulness meditation training, art therapy, expressive writing therapy, and yoga activities. It also is helpful to explore with the clients if they wish for their therapists to do any collaboration and advocacy with any of the involved helping professionals from larger systems who were not present in their initial consultation sessions. All of these treatment modalities, adjunctive services, and group therapies are offered in my *Pathways to Possibilities Program*, which is a nine-week strengths-based intensive outpatient program (see Chapter 7).

After the clients select which treatment modalities and adjunct services they wish to participate in, I share my reflections and recommendations with the clients. I am careful not to privilege my concerns and recommendations above the clients' desires for themselves. Together, we need to maintain a dialogue with our clients if certain treatment modalities and adjunct services they may not have selected as first choices may be a better fit for them. As part of this dialogue, we can discuss the advantages and disadvantages of their pursuing certain treatment modalities and adjunct services initially. Once consensus is reached, the treatment modalities and adjunct services will be written on the blueprint-for-change plan.

Therapeutic Experiment Selection Menu

Once we have a clear understanding of what our clients' pretreatment changes, key strengths and resources, theories of change, stages of readiness for change, treatment preferences and expectations, and treatment goals are, we can take a short break in the consultation session to think about appropriate therapeutic experiment options to offer to the clients. As part of this break, I write a *therapeutic reflection*, which consists of compliments for each client participant, underscoring their strengths and resources, positive relabeling of negative behaviors, any questions I would like them to think about during the week, and two or three experiments for them to choose from in line with their treatment goals. After the clients make their selections, these are written on the blueprint for change plan and all participants sign their names on the last page of the plan form.

CHAPTER THREE

Collaborative Strengths-Based Brief Family Therapy with Self-Harming Young Adults and Adolescents

The Collaborative Strengths-Based Brief Family Therapy Approach: An Overview

The collaborative strengths-based brief family therapy model has been evolving since 1985. What is unique about this brief family therapy model is that it integrates the best elements of change-based and meaning-based postmodern systemic therapy approaches with client-directed outcome-informed therapy, positive psychology, Buddhist mindfulness meditation practices and teachings, Navajo Indian healing practices and teachings, cognitive therapy, and art and expressive writing therapy methods (Andersen, 1991; Anderson, 1997; Anderson & Gehart, 2007; Arkowitz et al., 2007; Arviso-Alvord, 2008; Arviso-Alvord & Cohen-Van Pelt, 2000; Boscolo et al., 1987; Csikszentmihalyi, 1990, 1997; Csikszentmihalyi & Csikszentmihalyi, 2006; de Shazer, 1988, 1991; de Shazer et al., 2007; Diener & Biswas-Diener, 2008; Duncan et al., 1997; Duncan & Miller, 2000; Emmons, 2007; Epston, 1998, 2000; Fisch & Schlanger, 1999; Fisch et al., 1982; Fredrickson, 2002, 2003; Freeman et al., 1997; Friedman, 1995; Goolishian & Anderson, 1988; Haley, 1980; Hanh, 1991, 1997, 1998, 2001, 2002, 2007; Hoffman, 1988, 2002; Hubble et al., 1999; Jim, 2008; Keyes & Haidt, 2003; Lyubomirsky, 2007; Maisel et al., 2004; Malchiodi, 2003, 2008; Miller & Rollnick, 2002; Nardone & Salvini, 2007; Nardone & Watzlawick, 2005; Papp, 1983; Pennebaker, 2004; Peterson, 2006; Peterson & Seligman, 2004; Selekman, 1997; 2004, 2005, 2006a, 2006b, 2008a, 2008b; Seligman, 2002, 2003; Surya Das, 2007; Synder & Lopez, 2007; Watzlawick et al., 1974; M. White, 2007; K. White, 2008). This treatment approach is sensitive to gender power imbalance, cultural issues, the spiritual dimension of clients' lives, wider societal factors, and social injustice issues that often play a part in the development and continuance of human difficulties. The collaborative strengths-based therapist views the therapeutic encounter as being a political enterprise, particularly with women and clients of color who are marginalized and disempowered in our society. As therapists we need to take a stand and actively advocate for our clients being discriminated against and experiencing institutional racism in their schools and interactions with representatives from larger systems. The ecological, flexible, and integrative nature of the collaborative strengths-based brief family therapy approach provides therapists with a kaleidoscopic viewing of their clients' difficulties and offers multiple therapeutic pathways to pursue in order to collaboratively empower them to achieve the kind of changes they desire. Clients take the lead in determining their treatment goals, whom to include in their sessions, setting session agendas, how to structure sessions, choosing which therapeutic experiments they would like to try between sessions, and the frequency of visits. In partnership with the clients, the therapist actively collaborates both in and out of sessions with involved and concerned members of the clients' social networks and helping professionals from larger systems. Thus, this ecological family therapy approach targets interventions at the individual, family, peer group, social network, larger systems, and community levels.

Another important feature of the collaborative strengths-based brief family therapy approach is the therapist's session-by-session assessment of the quality of the therapeutic relationship and their experience of and satisfaction with the change process (Hubble et al., 1999; Norcross, 2008). Therapists can ask their clients the following questions to secure this critical information:

- "What was our meeting like for you today?"
- "What did you like the most about the meeting?"
- "What ideas did you find the most helpful that you can see yourselves putting to use over the next week?"
- "How specifically do you think those ideas or strategies will be of help and make a difference in your situation?"
- "Is there anything we did not talk about or address that you think we really need to discuss the next time we get together?"
- "Were any of you surprised that I did not ask you about certain aspects of your situation that other therapists may have asked you about in the past?"
- "Was there anything I said or did in our meeting that upset any of you that you would like me not to talk about or do again?"

By taking care of the therapeutic relationship, making the necessary adjustments to better accommodate the needs of our clients, and ensuring they are satisfied with the change process, clients are less likely to drop out of treatment, will be more invested in achieving their goals, and will have better treatment outcomes.

Finally, the collaborative strengths-based brief therapist gives himself or herself permission to take positive risks with clients by being transparent and sharing his or her thoughts and feelings, trusting his or her gut with in-session risk-taking, using storytelling, feeling comfortable using humor and sharing his other crazy and absurd ideas, and being provocative when it seems to make sense. Another critical role of the therapist is to help facilitate connection-building by strengthening parent–young adult/adolescent relationships. Thus, the creative and flexible use of self can be another catalyst for change.

Theoretical Assumptions

The following eight theoretical assumptions are highly pragmatic and offer therapists working with self-harming clients and/or their couple partners and their families a new lens for viewing their difficulties. Each of the guiding assumptions offers a wellness perspective on young adult and adolescent self-harming problems, family difficulties, and for conducting collaborative strength-based brief therapy. These core assumptions guide the therapist's thinking and actions.

Assumption #1:
All self-harming clients and/or their couple partners and families have the strengths and resources to change; they are the experts.

Throughout my professional career, I have worked with many self-harming young adults and adolescents and their couple partners and families and all of these clients possessed the necessary strengths and resources to change, even clients who had long histories of self-harming and/or equivalent self-destructive behaviors and extensive past treatment histories. By inquiring with clients about their self-generated pretreatment changes, key strengths and talents, resiliency protective factors, alter personas and helpful supportive inner voices, and past successes, this valuable information will furnish us with a gold mine that we can tap and utilize in all of the problem areas they are seeking help with. Even clients who have been traumatized in their past, offer us valuable wisdom about their resiliencies and coping and problem-solving strategies for overcoming adversity that can be used to resolve their current difficulties.

With parents, I like to inquire what their parents had done with them that helped them to cope with or resolve difficulties when they were adolescents or young adults. These past solution-building intergenerational patterns can also be used in the current presenting problem areas (Selekman, 2006b). Furthermore, the clients' parents may have come up with some effective problem-solving strategies to resolve a similar difficulty with an older sibling of the client's that might be worthwhile trying out with the client.

Assumption #2:
When young adults and adolescents have strong and secure attachments with their parents, they are least likely to self-harm and engage in equivalent self-destructive behaviors.

Two common family dynamics observed in the families of self-harming young adults and adolescents, and central themes heard in their self-harming stories, are emotional disconnection and repeated invalidation by their parents. For whatever reason, the parents are not emotionally attuned to them when they are experiencing emotional distress and in need of soothing and loving support. Over time, these young adults or adolescents come to the realization that they cannot count on their parents for emotional support, and thus take matters into their own hands by engaging in self-harming and/or equivalent self-destructive behaviors to soothe themselves.

Attachment research has indicated that when parents have established strong and secure attachment bonds with their children, they have a cohesive sense of self and identity, they self-regulate their emotions well, they have positive feelings about their bodies, they tend to be self-confident and take pride and joy in their personal accomplishments, they are resilient, and they have trust in and feel comfortable reaching out to others when they need support (Bowlby, 1988, 1979; Ainsworth, 1978). It is never too late to further strengthen the attachment bonds between parents and their children.

As therapists, one central role we need to play in our family therapy work with self-harming young adults and adolescents is to serve as catalysts for connection building. The more we can help strengthen the emotional connections between parents and their self-harming children, the less likely they will be to resort to self-harming and other self-destructive behaviors. Strong parent-young adult/adolescent emotional connections promote resilience and emotional insulation to help them better cope with negative emotions and stressors.

Assumption #3:
Self-harming, equivalent self-destructive behaviors, and other difficulties are more likely to occur when young people's lives lack a strong sense of purpose and are unbalanced.
The Navajo Indians have an important teaching and value called *Hozho* or "Walking in Beauty" (Arviso-Alvord, 2008; Arviso-Alvord & Cohen-Van Pelt, 2000; Jim, 2008; White, 2008). When people are "Walking in Beauty," they are leading a harmonious and balanced life strongly connected to their cultural identity and values, regularly exercising, maintaining a healthy diet, engaged in meaningful activities, firmly rooted in their relationships with parents, siblings, grandparents, other extended family members, their clan, friends, and in their relationship to animals, nature, the environment, and to the Creator. This is a continuous and circular process that the individual needs to honor, respect, and keep in balance. We are all interconnected to each of these important dimensions of our lives. Our lives become much more meaningful and fulfilling and we tend to be physically and mentally stronger when we keep all of these dimensions of *hozho* in balance. Similar to the Buddhist ultimate state of being of *enlightenment*, the ultimate hozho state of being is one of *contentment* (Arviso-Alvord, 2008). If a combination of these important dimensions of *hozho* are in a state of unbalance

and we lack a sense of purpose in life, we become emotionally and physically vulnerable to developing both psychological and physical difficulties. Many self-harming clients' lives are in a state of imbalance on multiple dimensions of *hozho*. I have worked with numerous self-harming clients who lack a sense of meaning and direction in their lives, are not taking care of themselves physically and spiritually, and are very disconnected from their parents, elders, and their cultural identities and values. It is critical as therapists that we carefully assess the above dimensions of *hozho* with our clients and help them to achieve more balanced and harmonious lives.

Assumption #4:
All self-harming clients want relief from oppressive difficulties.
Although self-harming clients may be brought for treatment by concerned family members, their couple partners, and/or friends and initially do not voice a desire to stop their self-destructive behaviors, this does not mean that they are resistant or that they do not want help to better cope with or resolve the difficulties going on in their lives. It is the therapist's job to listen carefully and observe for clues about how the self-harming clients want to cooperate. We need to carefully match what we say or try with clients in our sessions with their unique stages of readiness for change, theories of change, and key strengths. In some cases, the oppressive difficulties the clients want help with are getting a parent, their couple partner, concerned friends, the referring person, or other larger systems professionals off their back. They may want more freedom and less oveprotective micromanagement from their couple partner or parents.

Some of our self-harming clients are oppressed by dominant stories that have been written about them. These stories may have been coauthored by their concerned parents or key members from their social networks, such as their peers and mental health professionals ("she is manipulative and trying to get even with us," "she is an emo queen," "she is a cutter," "he is a borderline"). Once published on the Internet, in a client case file, circulated as school gossip, or locked in as a central family belief, it is difficult for the self-harming client to have a new script and to escape into a different reality or more preferred story. White (2007) suggests that as therapists we need to listen carefully for traces of *subordinate story lines* in the dominant problem-saturated stories of our clients, which can serve as entry points to underscore their resourcefulness, values, hopes, and dreams for themselves. It is these alternative story lines that can be expanded upon with clients and harnessed for co-authoring more preferred stories.

Cooperating with self-harming clients' initial goals for themselves and reducing the oppressive stressors in their lives will help pave the way for clients to feel better and cope better and be less likely to resort to self-harming and equivalent self-destructive behaviors as their coping strategies. Furthermore, this therapeutic activity will also help prevent premature dropout situations.

Assumption #5:
Change is inevitable and there are always spaces in between self-harming episodes.

Change is a continuous process and self-harming behavior is no exception. No young adult or adolescent is always self-harming, even clients with heavy to severe category self-harming practices. As mentioned earlier, self-harming behavior, like any habitual behavior, is cyclical and is never occurring nonstop. Again, like good Sherlock Holmes and Miss Marple detectives, we need to inquire about what is happening during the spaces in between one self-harming episode or act and the next. We can ask self-harming clients what they tell themselves and do instead of caving in to self-harming acts or engaging in equivalent self-destructive behaviors. It also is helpful to find out what their couple partners, parents, concerned friends, adult inspirational others, and other key members from their social networks say or do that helps them refrain from self-harming or engaging in equivalent self-destructive behaviors. It is these helpful effective coping and problem-solving strategies that we need to increase, which will further reduce the clients' need to resort to self-harming and other self-destructive behaviors.

Assumption #6:
Self-harming clients and/or their couple partners and families take the lead in determining their treatment goals.

Self-harming clients and/or their couple partners and families need to be invited to take the lead in determining their treatment goals. We need to go with whatever self-harming clients wish to change first with their life situations, even if it has nothing to do with the self-harming behavior, or any equivalent self-destructive behaviors they are currently engaging in. However, our job is to make sure that we negotiate solvable, small, and realistic goals with our clients to maximize for their success. It is important to educate self-harming clients and/or their partners and families that goals are the beginning of something new, not the end of something, and to try and enjoy the journey, no matter how challenging it may be. I have found that once we empower our self-harming clients to achieve small changes in their target goal areas, these can ripple into larger changes in other important areas in their lives. Their self-confidence, hope, and expectancy levels will further increase once they meet with success in their goal areas.

Assumption #7:
Problems are unsuccessful attempts to resolve difficulties.

For many of our clients, their self-harming and concurrent equivalent self-destructive behaviors are attempted solutions to help them to cope with emotional distress and other stressors in their lives. Even after falling into the depths of their moderate to severe self-harming practices, they cling to the promise and belief that their beloved coping strategies will help them to get by and feel better in spite of the serious psychological, physical, social, and school and/or occupational consequences they may begin to experience or have been experiencing already. Self-harming clients are not alone in getting locked into rigid ways of thinking and responding to emotional distress by mismanaging life difficulties. Their couple partners and parents also get stuck doing *more of the same* in how they think about and respond to the self-harming clients' habitual behavior and other concurrent self-destructive behaviors or difficulties. I have found it helpful to map out on a flip chart or legal pad how self-harming clients and/or their couple partners and parents try to manage their presenting problems when they occur. I secure this information by asking the clients, couple partners, or parents to describe a motion picture of how they responded to a recent self-harming episode or some other problematic behavior of the clients and to track the whole subsequent circular and recursive chain of behaviors that followed. By doing this, all parties involved can see how, in their best or most loving efforts, they are perpetuating the very difficulties they wish to resolve. Nardone and Watzlawick (2005), Nardone and Salvini (2007), Watzlawick et al. (1974), and Fisch et al. (1982) have written extensively about how it is our clients' attempted solutions that are the problem.

Nardone and Salvini (2007) have found through the use of *strategic dialogue*, which is a mutual search and inquiry with clients using specific strategic questions regarding their attempted solutions for trying to resolve intractable symptoms and difficulties, often epiphanies occur spontaneously in which clients come up with their own unique solutions. They discover how, in their best efforts to resolve or better cope with their difficulties, they have perpetuated them. So by coming to know their problems through their attempted solutions, clients can begin to see how they have imprisoned themselves, and now have gained the wisdom and freedom to pursue new actions that make important differences in their lives.

Assumption #8:
There are many ways to view a client's self-harming behavior and/or equivalent behavior, none more correct than others.
Each self-harming client's story is unique and we need to honor and respect this fact. As therapists, we need to be careful not to privilege our explanations why we think our self-harming clients engage in this behavior and how it benefits them. Unfortunately, there is a tendency in the mental health field to make the diagnostic leap that anybody who engages in self-harming behavior must have a borderline personality disorder, was physically and sexually abused and has posttraumatic stress disorder, or is suicidal. Using meta-analysis quantitative and qualitative research methods with clients seeking help for a variety of presenting problems and randomly assigned to different treatment approaches, Wampold (2001) found that diagnosis was irrelevant in terms of treatment outcome. After interviews were conducted with thousands of clients and hundreds of therapists involved in his research, what was reported as most significant for the clients were the therapists' skills and abilities to establish strong therapeutic alliances and collaborative bonds with them, not knowing their diagnoses or the type treatment

approach they had received. We need to take the time to come to understand our clients' self-harming stories, how they have found this particular behavior and equivalent self-destructive behaviors to be of great benefit to them, and the disadvantages of abandoning them. For our self-harming clients, the map is the territory (Hoffman, 1988). Therefore, when offering alternative constructions of their problem explanations and situations they need to come close to fitting or be acceptable to the clients' views (Andersen, 1991). The same is true when offering replacement distress management tools and strategies to self-harming clients. Just because certain replacement distress management tools and strategies work for 1 of the therapist's past 10 self-harming clients does not mean that they will work with his or her new self-harming clients. It is important to remember that research indicates our self-harming clients' theories of change and treatment preferences and expectations should dictate what therapeutic strategies or treatment modalities can best benefit them (Hubble et al., 1999; Norcross, 2008).

The Session Format

When starting up with new clients it is important at the beginning of the session for the therapists to let them know about the session format. I first let the clients know that there will be two parts to the session. They are told that the first part of the session will consist of them telling their stories, sharing their treatment preferences expectations, and concerns, and providing important background information about their situations, including learning more about their strengths and resources and the results of their pretreatment change experiment that was given to them during the telephone intake conversation. Next, I share with the clients that the second part of the session is devoted to talking about *solutions* and *change* and, more specifically, where they want to be *when* they have a *successful* treatment outcome. I then let new families know that I like to spend the early part of the session with the whole family group in order to gather important family background information, time alone with the parents, and then give the young adult or adolescent his or her individual session time as well. Following my individual session time with the young adult or adolescent, I let the family know that I like to take an intersession break to reflect on my observations and what they had said earlier in the session about their situation. I then construct the *editorial reflection*, which consists of underscoring family members' pretreatment changes, resourcefulness, and resilience, positively relabeling negative behaviors, asking questions about the family drama that I am still curious about or questions I would like family members to ponder over the next week, and two or three therapeutic experiments that are in line with their goals. Finally, the session concludes with my going over the blueprint plan for change form with them, filling it out together, and inquiring with family members about what their perceptions and feelings were about the quality of our developing therapeutic relationship and their session experiences.

I have observed over the years that when I share with clients how the second part of the session will focus mostly on *solutions and change*, it grabs their attention. They usually smile, move forward in their chairs, and are visibly enthusiastic about what is to come. In fact, I will sometimes take a mini-break midway into the hour after completing the first part of the session, step out of the office room, and then come back into the room and begin the second part of the session talking about solutions and change. I also have gotten similar reactions from clients by switching office rooms with the clients conducting the first part of the session in a colleague's office and then moving everyone into my office to talk about solutions and change. By doing this, we are creating firm boundaries between *how things are and were* (problems and concerns) and *what will be* (solutions and change) happening in your office. This can greatly increase the clients' expectancy levels that change *will* happen and it is only a matter of *when*.

Subsystem Work: Engaging Parents and Self-Harming Young Adults and Adolescents

The early part of the session is devoted to coming to know the clients by their strengths, talents, and expertise. Problems, concerns, client expectations, and important family background information are discussed. I will attempt to establish mutual treatment goals with the parents and the young adult or adolescent. However, which is often the case, the young adult or adolescent will not agree with or see eye to eye with behaviors their parents want them to change. The parents' goals may be too unrealistic or they may want to see multiple behaviors changed all at once. Often, this results in the young adult or adolescent getting defensive or argumentative and his or her so-called attitude problem flaring up that the parents had been complaining about earlier in the session. In these situations, this is where establishing separate treatment goals and working with subsystems can be helpful.

Parental Subsystem Work

When meeting alone with the parents, therapists have an opportunity to strengthen their alliances with them, find out more about their past parenting successes and untested ideas that they had held back from trying, thinking they would not work, and negotiate a smaller and more realistic treatment goal for their sons or daughters or for themselves. Parents also can be offered one or two therapeutic experiments to try out over the next week. To find out from the parents what specific behaviors they engage in that may be backfiring or adding more fuel to the fire in their conflicted relationships with their son or daughter, I ask the following questions:

- "If your son/daughter were sitting in that empty chair over there and I asked him/her, 'What is the number one thing that your parents do that really pushes your buttons and gets you the most upset,' what would you tell me they do?"
- "Okay, so it is your yelling behavior that he/she would say gets him/her

the most upset. If I were to ask him/her to rate that behavior on a scale from 1 to 10, with 10 being yelling hardly at all and 1 yelling all of the time, where would he/she have rated it a month ago?"

- "At 1. How about 2 weeks ago?"
- "At a 4. Are you aware of how you got from 1 to a 4?"
- "What specifically do you think your son/daughter would say is helping you reduce your yelling?"
- "Where would he/she rate your yelling today?"
- "At a 5. What specifically would he/she say you're doing that got you one step higher on that scale?"
- "Let's say you decided as a goal to want to further reduce your yelling. What are you going to do over the next week to get one step higher, up to a 6?"

Some parents are so upset with or emotionally disconnected from their sons or daughters that they may not be willing in the first session to begin working on specific behaviors they are engaging in that may be contributing to the maintenance of their sons' or daughters' self-harming or other difficulties. Since these parents may be in the contemplator stage of readiness for change, they will not include themselves as part of the solution construction process. However, they may be receptive to playing detective for the therapist by carefully observing daily for any pattern changes or exceptions in their son or daughter's problematic behaviors. The parents are instructed to notice what is happening during those encouraging times when the problematic behavior is absent or only happening a little bit. If the parents are receptive to doing this, they also can be asked to pay close attention to what *they* are doing during those encouraging times that may be contributing to them happening. Often, parents make important discoveries in the dual observing roles that can lead to a dramatic shift in how they view and interact with their sons or daughters.

With so-called *boomerang kids*, that is, self-harming young adults who have struggled to make it in the world on their own after futile attempts to move out of the family home or flunked out of school or were asked to leave their colleges because of serious mental health, substance-abuse, or legal issues, parents need to have firm guidelines and expectations for their returning young adult kids if they are going to live at home (Haley, 1980). Some important guidelines and expectations parents need to establish with their young adult sons and daughters are as follows: getting a job and keeping it, paying some rent, helping out around the household, treating the parents and younger siblings with respect, staying out of legal trouble, not abusing substances, not exhibiting violent behavior. As clear and important as these guidelines and expectations are for young adults that are living at home or who just returned home, some parents have grave difficulties enforcing their rules either because they are guilt-ridden or they have a long history of being inconsistent with their kids. It is the therapist's job to help these parents be a strong unified team, prepare themselves for extreme challenges from their young adults, and stick to enforcing their rules and serious consequences if they continue to violate their rules. The toughest aspect of the consequence-enforcement process is the point where the parents will no longer tolerate the violation of their rules and have to ask their young adult sons or daughters to leave their house. Out of fairness to their adult kids, they should be given a warning that this will happen by a certain date without any negotiations unless they make a commitment to turn the situation around and follow all of the parents' rules. With some young adult situations, the parents' threat, presentation of a date for them to leave if things do not change, and elimination of their previous revolving-door rescuing pattern are enough for them to get in gear and start taking responsibility.

Once their young adults do return home, it is equally important to have the parents play detective and keep track of their sons' and daughters' responsible steps and efforts to get better prepared to succeed in the world the next time they move out or return to college. Taking steps like actively seeking employment, taking a class or two at a local community college, refraining from using substances or self-harming, helping around the house, treating the parents with respect, and having conversations with one or both parents about future career aspirations should be acknowledged and celebrated by the parents. Their return home may be a second chance for some of these young adults to resolve past conflicts with their parents and establish the kind of future relationships they desire to have with them.

Subsystem Work with the Young Adult or Adolescent

During this individual session time with the young adults or adolescents, we can strengthen our alliance with them, find out more about their treatment preferences and expectations of us, try to negotiate the parents' goal or establish a separate treatment goal, explore with them if there is anything they did not talk about in the company of the parents that they think you should know about, specific parental behaviors they would like you to change with the parents that make them the most upset, and your offering to serve as an intergenerational arbitrator in negotiating with the parents any privileges they want. Depending on the clients' stage of readiness for change and their establishing an initial treatment goal will determine if I will offer them one or two therapeutic experiment options. For many young adults and older adolescents, they may be in the precontemplative stage of readiness for change or less invested in changing their behavior and relationship with their parents or the family situation and are more focused on launching out of the family nest to move out and work or go away to college. With these clinical situations, it may be more therapeutically beneficial to support the client's developmental strivings for more autonomy, building self-confidence regarding his or her future plans, and provide him or her with more individual session time or see him or her individually and the parents separately but maintaining a systemic treatment focus and address their relationship conflicts indirectly. If the parents are willing and/or desire to work on their relationship, they can be seen separately to help them renegotiate their marital relationship as their son or daughter begins the leaving-home process (Carter & McGoldrick, 1989). Conjoint family therapy sessions can be conducted to manage any adjustment issues the family may be experiencing during this major family life-cycle change, which can be as tumultuous as the earlier adolescence stage may have been for them.

Interviewing for Possibilities: Co-Creating Compelling Future Realities with Our Clients

We can use therapeutic questions to tap clients' expertise and establish well-formulated treatment goals with vague, withholding, pessimistic, and demoralized clients. Many of the self-harming clients, their couple partners, and their families have experienced unproductive inpatient and/or outpatient treatment in the past, which both has had a demoralizing effect on them and has further exacerbated their difficulties. This can contribute to their having a very low level of trust and faith in a new therapist's or treatment program's ability to help them. With these clients, the use of *goal-setting clarification*, *coping sequence*, and *pessimistic sequence questions* can assist therapists in establishing well-formulated treatment goals and foster cooperative relationships with them.

Some of our self-harming clients who have had extensive treatment histories will have long stories to share about their past negative treatment experiences and chronic difficulties. In some cases, the client or another family member may be harboring a secret or have been holding back from sharing a concern or habits they are struggling with, like self-harming, bulimia, substance abuse, or sexually risky behaviors that, out of fear and safety concerns, they have held back from disclosing to their families. Therefore, we have to be careful not to be narrative editors and give them plenty of room to share their long problem-saturated stories. The use of *conversational* and *reversal questions* can open up space for family members to take risks and talk about the *not-yet-said* (Anderson, 1997; Goolishian & Anderson, 1988; Selekman 2005, 2006b). Once these clients have had the space to be historians about their past treatment experiences, serve as helpful advisors to the therapist, and possibly share the unspeakable (a family secret), a specific focus for the future direction of treatment that the clients would like to pursue often will evolve out of this meaningful therapeutic conversation. At this point, the clients may be in a better place to articulate their treatment goals. I will present each of these categories of questions below.

Goal-Setting Clarification Questions
- "Over the next week, when your son takes some steps to show you that he has a 'better attitude,' what specifically will you see him do?"
- "What difference will that make for the two of you in your relationship with him when he shows you he has a 'better attitude'?"
- "How will you respond differently to him?"

- "What else will he do that will tell you he has a 'better attitude'?"
- "How specifically over the next week will your daughter show you that her self-esteem level is increasing?"
- "What else will you need to see your daughter do that will tell you that her self-esteem level is continuing to improve?"
- Ask the client who says, "I don't know": "Let's say you took more time to reflect on my question about what specifically you would like to change today. What do you think the first thing that might pop into your head might be?"
- "If you did know, what would be high up on your list?"
- Therapist asks a sibling of client or his/her couple partner: "If _____ did know, what do you think he/she would say?"
- "Why do you think he/she would say that?"
- "What kind of difference do you think it would make in his/her life when that changes?"
- Ask when a withholding client disagrees with his/her sibling or couple-partner: "So you don't agree with your sister/brother's/couple partner's thinking about what you really want to change?"
- "What specifically do you want to change first, instead of what your sister/brother/partner had said for you?"
- Ask the parents who want three behaviors changed at once: "Okay, you have said that there are three things you want your daughter to change immediately: swearing at you, which we will call scale A; not doing her homework, which we will call scale B; and respecting your curfew time, which we will call scale C. Earlier you presently rated her at a 5 with the swearing, a 3 with not doing her homework, and a 4 with respecting your curfew time. What affect would a change on scale C over the next week have on scales A and B?"
- "So you think she would be less tired the next day, not swear as much, and get her homework done if she comes home at a reasonable time and respects your curfew. How many nights over the next week of respecting your curfew would be a small sign of progress for her?"
- "So if she could come home on time 3 out of 7 days, you would be really happy. Let's say she achieves your goal for her. Would that earn her a 5 on scale C?"

Coping Sequence Questions
- "It sounds like at times things are getting really out of hand with your arguing. Tell me how do you prevent things from getting much worse?"
- "In what ways is that helpful?"
- "What else are you doing to prevent things from getting much worse?"
- "The situation sounds really challenging at times. How are you managing to cope with this to the degree that you are?"
- "What does your mother do that seems to help a little bit?"
- "In what ways does that help to diffuse the argument?"

- "Can you think of anything else the two of you have been doing to prevent things from getting much worse?"
- "Out of the two creative strategies ("making a time-out hand signal" and "physically separating from each other" for a period of time) you and your mother came up with to prevent things from really escalating and getting much worse with the arguing, which one of these strategies do you think could help make a little bit more of a difference in helping the two of you argue less?"
- "On a scale from 1 to 10, with 10 being the two of you "physically separating from each other" for a period time when an argument arises most of the time and 1 just digging in more, defending your position, and not trying to separate, where would you have rated yourselves 4 weeks ago?"
- "At a 1. How about 2 weeks ago?"
- "At a 2. Are you aware of how you got yourselves one step higher on that scale?"
- "What else did you do to get up to that 2?"
- "Where would you rate yourselves on that scale today?"
- "At a 4. How do you account for your getting two steps higher up on that scale?"
- "Let's say we get together in 1 week's time and you come in here and tell me that you took one step higher on that scale, up to a 5. What specifically will you tell me you did?"

Pessimistic Sequence Questions

- "Some parents in your situation would have thrown in the towel with counseling a long time ago. What keeps you trying and hanging on by a thread with your son?"
- "What would be the tiniest change you would need to see happen with Harvey over the next week that would give you an inkling of hope that your situation can improve a little bit?"
- "On a scale from –10 to –1, with –10 being that your situation is totally hopeless and irresolvable and –1 that you have a glimmer of hope that eventually we will be able to make a little bit of headway with Harvey's burning himself, where would you have rated your situation 1 month ago?"
- "At a –10. How about 2 weeks ago?"
- "A –9. Are you aware of what you did to prevent the situation from staying rock bottom at a –10?"
- "Where would you have rated your situation a week ago?"
- "A –7. What specifically did you or Harvey do that got all of you two steps higher on that scale?"
- "Let's say we get together in 1 week's time and somehow all of you are able to take your situation one step higher, up to a –6. What will you tell me you did to pull off this big feat?"
- Ask a highly pessimistic self-harming young adult living at home: "Sylvia,

some young women in your situation might have wanted to check out of life by now. What are you telling yourself to move forward with your life and not give up?"

- "How do those words of wisdom from your water polo coach give you a little more hope with your situation?"
- "How about with your parents? Can you think of anything they have said or tried with you in the past that seemed to help a little bit?"
- Ask parents who are highly pessimistic: "Some parents in your situation would have tried to put their daughter in a boarding school, residential treatment center, or, better yet, up for adoption. What has stopped you from pursuing those options?"
- Ask emotionally disconnected and/or laissez-faire parents: "Let's say this Friday night at midnight a police officer rings your doorbell and tells you that your son is no longer with us. What effect would that have on your marital relationship?"
- "What would you miss the most not having him around anymore?"
- "How else would it be difficult for you to go on with your lives not having him around?"
- "Who will attend his funeral?"
- "What will the eulogies be?"

Conversational Questions

- "You have seen a lot of therapists before me. What did they miss with your situation that is important for me to know?"
- "What specifically will have to be addressed or happen in our work together that would send you off feeling completely satisfied with what we did together?"
- "What kinds of things did your former therapists and treatment program staff do that were upsetting to any of you and you think contributed to making your situation much worse?"
- "What have we not talked about that, if resolved, could make a big difference in your relationship with your father?"
- "What questions do you think I have avoided asking you about your situation that you think are significant?"
- "If you pretended to be my family therapy supervisor observing us working together, what unhelpful views about any of you or ideas about your situation do you think might be in my head that are blocking me from being truly present, deeply listening, and helping you in the best way possible?"
- "I am working with another family just like you and I am totally stuck. Do you have any advice for me about how I could best help that family out?"
- "If you were to work with the most perfect family therapist, how would he or she converse with you and try to accomplish with you that would tell you that this therapist is really competent and will without any doubts help your family change?"

- "Marjorie, what would it mean to you and how would it make a difference in your relationship with your parents if you could trust them with secrets?"
- "I'm curious, Melinda. Was there anything you told yourself before you came in here today that you were not going to talk about in our meeting today?"
- "What is the courageous conversation you have not had with your parents that, when you eventually decide to have it, could really move your relationship forward with them in a more positive direction?"
- "If there was one thing that hasn't yet been said in order to reach a deeper level of understanding about your (cutting/situation), what would that be?"
- "What question, if answered, could make the most difference to the future of your relationship with your parents/your couple partner/individual situation?"
- Asking the client who appears to be the family savior: "Who do you worry the most about, your mother or your father or both of them?"
- Asking the client: "What's missing in your relationship with your father/ mother that, if it were present, would make a big difference?"
- "So if your father would "devote more quality time doing things" that you would "like to do with him," that would make a big difference for you?"
- "Okay, to help your father out with this important change you desire in your relationship with him, what would be one step he could take over the next week that would indicate to you that he has really taken your request to heart?"
- Ask the father: "Do you think your son's goal is doable or do we have to modify it in some way?"
- Ask the client: "How else will you be able to tell that this time around is really different with your father and he is truly delivering?"
- Ask parents who appear to be conflict avoidant or detouring their conflicts through their self-harming son or daughter: "Do the two of you argue enough?"

Reversal Questions
- "What advice do you have for your parents so they can argue less?"
- "What advice do you have for your parents about what kind of consequences another teenager just like you would respond best to?"
- "Do you have any recommendations for your father about what he could do differently when his anger is trying to get the best of him?"
- "If you have a slip, what are two things you want your parents to do that could help you to quickly get back on track?"
- Ask Evan the client: "If your parents decided to spearhead a major family mood climate change at home, what specifically would you recommend they do as leaders that could benefit everyone in the family?"
- "What specifically would they have to work on changing first as family leaders conducting this broad-scale family mood change mission?"
- "Their nagging. On a scale from 1 to 10, with 10 being only nagging once

in a while and 1 nagging all of the time, where would you rate your parents today on that scale?"

- "At a 2. In your mind, what specifically will you need to see them do over the next week to get up to a 3?"
- Ask the parents: "As the leaders of this important family mission, is your son's goal for you over the next week too big or do you think you can pull it off?"
- "Out of respect for you as the family leaders, what specifically do you need to see Evan do that can help pave the way for you to achieve his goal for you?"

Some of our self-harming clients and their families will describe their self-harming behavior or presenting difficulties as being oppressive and intractable, and seemingly having a life all of their own. With these clients, I have found it most advantageous to externalize the self-harming behavior or main presenting problem they voice the most concern about. What is most important when externalizing clients' presenting problems is that their language in describing them and their beliefs about them are used in co-constructing the problems into objectified entities that have been trying to get the best of individual family members, their family relationships, peer relationships, other key social network relationships, and relationships with involved helping professionals from larger systems (Selekman, 2005; White, 2007; White & Epston, 1990). *Percentage questions* can be used instead of scaling questions once the clients' presenting problems have been externalized (Selekman, 2005; White, 1986). This category of questions helps the clients, their families, involved members from their social networks, and larger systems have a quantitative measurement of what percentage of the time they are standing up to or in charge of the problem versus the problem's getting the best of them at the beginning, at second and subsequent sessions, and by the conclusion of treatment. Below are some examples of externalizing and percentage questions.

Externalizing Questions
- "If 'cutting' were to pack its bags and leave your life for good tomorrow,what would you miss the most not having it in your life anymore?"
- "If there were any special qualities or aspects of 'cutting' that you would wish to keep, what would those special qualities or aspects be?"
- "Nancy, who is in charge of your skin, 'cutting' or you?"
- "Nancy, have there been any times lately where you stood up to 'cutting' and reclaimed your skin?"
- "In what ways have your scars left a bad taste in your mouth about 'cutting' being more a foe than a friend?"
- "Nancy, have there been any times lately where you outtricked 'cutting' and did not cave in to its wishes to claim your arms as battlefields?"

- "In what ways does 'cutting' divide the two of you (the parents) in determining how best to respond to Nancy after a slip?"
- "How long has bulimia been pushing all of you around?"

Percentage Questions
- "Nancy, what percentage of the time are you and your parents in charge of 'cutting' versus 'cutting's' being in charge of you?"
- "So 'cutting' is 50% of the time in charge. What steps will you need to take as a family team over the next week to regain more control over 'cutting' and be 60% of the time in charge of it?"
- "How else will you be able to tell as a family team that you are in charge 60% of the time?"

Practical Guidelines for Empowering Parents to Prevent and Constructively Manage Inevitable Self-Harming Slips

Most recently, there has been a proliferation of practice-oriented and self-help books written by self-harming treatment specialists, that offer those parents—who have young adults and adolescents struggling with self-harming and other equivalent self-destructive behaviors—parenting guidelines to help strengthen their relationships, improve their communications, and constructively respond when their kids experience self-harming episodes (Hollander, 2008; Levine, 2006; McVey-Noble, et al., 2006; Plante, 2007; Selekman, 2006b; Walsh, 2006). While some of these books do provide some "hands-on" strategies and tools for parents to use that can empower them to help their sons and daughters resolve their self-harming difficulties, the majority of them are not systemic or strengths-based in their theoretical orientations and do not offer a wide enough range of therapeutic interventions that can produce major changes in parents' outmoded beliefs about their kids' behaviors and change entrenched problem-maintaining family interactions.

Often when parents do discover that their sons and daughters are engaging in self-harming and other equivalent self-destructive behaviors, they respond to them in extreme ways: they are highly anxious and worried, they yell at and lecture at them, they threaten to put them in an inpatient or residential treatment program, or send them off to a boarding school, they punish them with extreme consequences, or they emotionally disconnect from them. Similar to therapists who are inexperienced in treating self-harming clients, parents are often intimidated, shocked, and perplexed by this behavior and are at a loss for what to do.

I will provide practical guidelines that we can teach parents regarding how to create home environments and stronger relationship bonds with their sons and daughters that can greatly reduce the likelihood of self-harming or equivalent self-destructive behaviors from occurring. I will then present guidelines for how parents can constructively manage inevitable future slips that their sons and daughters may have and how to quickly and confidently get them back on track.

Prevention Strategies

1. Parents need to create positive and upbeat home environments that are inviting and nurturing, and their kids need to know that they are available for emotional connection and support when needed by them. We need to encourage parents to strive for the daily goal of giving their kids four to five compliments and/or show positive gestures toward them and limit their complaints to one a day if even necessary. The 5 to 1 ratio of compliments to one complaint per day has been shown in couples' research as one of the major factors that keeps couples together and (Gottman & Gottman, 2006). This important research finding applies to parent-adolescent relations as well. Self-harming adolescents have reported that they tended to be much more cooperative with and act out less when their parents expressed their love and appreciation toward them and were empathically attuned to them during the times they were experiencing emotional distress and needed comforting from them. (Selekman & Shulem, 2007).

2. When their self-harming young adults or adolescents accomplish something that they are pleased with and/or display responsible behaviors, the parents need to respond with praise and take pride and joy in their kids' accomplishments and celebrate their important gains. They also can let their kids know how pleased they are with them by leaving notes or cards in their bedrooms or in other heavily frequented locations in the house. This is known as *active constructive responding* and contributes to parents and their kids having more positive and stronger relationships. *Passive constructive responding* would consist of parents giving their sons or daughters hugs, kisses, or high fives to acknowledge their accomplishments (Gable, Reis, Impett, and Asher, 2004). Gable et al. found these two forms of constructive responding present in highly satisfied and flourishing couple relationships. Having parents make a more concerted effort to positively and constructively respond to their kids' accomplishments can set in motion purposeful positive relationship patterns that can strengthen and sustain their connections with them over time.

3. Parents need to set limits and consistently enforce their consequences when their kids violate their rules and get into trouble. However, rather than using the same old standard fare of taking privileges away and lengthy grounding periods, parents should experiment with *positive consequences* (Selekman, 2005). Positive consequences take the form of doing good deeds in the community and other kinds of altruistic acts that are time-limited and serve as the kids' consequences. For some self-harming young adults and adolescents, their positive consequence experiences can boost their self-esteem levels and be both character-building and life-changing.

4. Parents need to model the responsible use of nicotine, alcohol, prescription medications, and food. They need to show their kids that there are healthy

ways to manage work stress and emotional distress, such as exercising, meditating, yoga, engaging in meaningful flow-state activities, and hobbies.

5. Parents need to learn what their kids' triggers are for self-harming and engaging in equivalent self-destructive behaviors. They also need to learn the same distress management tools and strategies that are being taught to their kids and practice using them at home with them. By doing this with parents, we can create a solid bridge from our offices to the clients' homes. Parents can monitor their kids practicing using their coping strategies and tools at home. For example, if parents observe that their daughter appears to be experiencing emotional distress after receiving an upsetting e-mail from a friend, they can ask her, "Which tool do you think can be most helpful to you right now, the sound meditation or visualizing movies of success?"

6. Once parents know *where, when, what,* and *with whom* self-harming episodes are most likely to occur, they can intervene early with support, soothing, distraction, and whatever other strategy that staves off a budding self-harming slip.

7. Parents need to closely monitor and limit their kids' computer usage and the Web sites they are visiting. Immediate consequences should be provided when their kids visit forbidden Web sites that glorify and encourage self-harming and other self-destructive behaviors.

8. Parents need to be educated on how self-harming behavior differs from suicidal behavior. They need to know that most self-harming young adults and adolescents use this behavior as a coping strategy for managing emotional distress and to quickly soothe themselves.

9. Parents need to know that self-harming behavior is complex, can be caused by many factors, and is habit-forming. Therefore, parents need to be patient, supportive, and try to gain a better understanding of how this particular coping strategy has been benefiting their sons or daughters.

10. Parents need to avoid playing detectives with their kids and asking them daily, a few times a day, "Do you feel like hurting yourself?" Also, they should avoid asking their son or daughter daily if they could check his or her body for fresh scratches, cuts, or burn marks.

11. Parents of self-harming adolescents should avoid overscheduling them in too many extracurricular activities, avoid putting too much pressure on them regarding academic achievement, and avoid imposing on them unrealistic performance expectations in concerts, theater, and athletic events.

12. Parents should reward their kids with praise and special privileges for staying on track, for not having any slips, and for exhibiting better choice-making and responsible behavior in all areas of their life. A short-term reward could consist of the young adult or adolescent being taken to his or her favorite restaurant. It is important to educate parents that slips are normal and inevitable, and go with the territory of change.

13. Parents need to make a commitment to *spending quality time together* as a family and engaging in fun and meaningful activities that the young adult or adolescent would like to do with one or both of them. Research indicates that this is an important characteristic of strong families (DeFrain & Stinnett, 1992; Stinnett & O'Donnell, 1996). The more parents and their kids can accrue positive experiences together, the more their relationship bonds will strengthen, which will provide emotional insulation for their kids to better cope with emotional distress and life stressors.

14. Parents should regularly solicit feedback from their kids on how well they are doing in the parenting department and welcome any advice or suggestions they may have for improving their relationships with them. This shows their kids how much they love and care about them and their willingness to go to great lengths to make the relationships better.

15. Parents need to be educated about Buddhist healing practices such as nonattachment (not clinging to negative thoughts and feelings and unrealistic expectations for themselves and their kids) and using mindfulness meditation to quiet their minds. By practicing using loving-kindness and compassion with themselves and their kids, they will prevent parental burnout and will be better able to be more present with their kids. This will help strengthen their relationships.

Constructive Parental Management Strategies

1. Following a self-harming episode, parents should avoid, at all costs, responding with anger, lectures, disgust, hysteria, further overwhelming them with their anxiety, threatening their kids with institutionalizing them, or emotionally disconnecting from or giving up on them. Instead, they should be supportive of them and try to comfort or soothe them with calming voices and/or by hugging them. They should try to gain a better understanding from their son or daughter about what had triggered his or her slip. Parents need to make direct eye contact and listen carefully to their son or daughter's story. They need to validate his or her thoughts and feelings before offering any advice.

2. Parents can ask their kids the following questions to gain a better understanding of why they are self-harming and/or engaging in equivalent self-destructive behaviors and what specifically they can do as parents differently to reduce the likelihood of future slips or prevent prolonged relapsing situations:

- "How can we best provide support or comfort to you right now?"
- "Now that we know that you are cutting yourself, what does it mean to you?"
- "In what ways has it been helpful to you?"
- "How long have you been cutting?"
- "How often do you cut?"

- "Where on your body do you cut?"
- "Have you tried to stop?"
- "What happened when you tried to stop?"
- "Is there something going on in your life right now that is really stressing you out that you would like some help with?"
- "In what ways have we contributed to your cutting yourself?"
- "What specifically should we avoid saying or doing with you?"
- "What would you like us to change first that you would really appreciate that would make you happier?"
- "How will that make a difference in our relationships with you?"
- "Is there anything missing in my relationship with you that, if it were present, would make a big difference in helping us get along better?"

3. If the parents have asked many of the above questions and are still feeling at a loss for what to do, they can always draw from both their own and their parents' past successful parenting strategies. The parents can first brainstorm and identify what they have done in the past to resolve other difficulties with their self-harming adolescent as well as with his or her older siblings that may have had similar difficulties at the same age, that can serve as a road map for future success with the current self-harming difficulty. They also can access what their parents had done with them as adolescents to help them better cope or resolve their difficulties in adolescence. Parental storytelling about their tough teen struggles is another effective way to strengthen their relationship bonds with their kids.

4. If the parents are willing to take a hard look at their own blocks or constraints from their families of origin, we can explore with them what assumptions and patterns of interaction from their relationships with their parents may be contributing to difficulties in their current relationships with their self-harming young adult or adolescent. We may learn that the same invalidating interactions, patterns of emotional disconnection when there is conflict, and problems with providing empathy have a life all their own and they are trying to wreak havoc in their current relationships with their sons or daughters. These patterns can be externalized as one possible therapeutic option to pursue in these case situations.

5. With highly entrenched and chronic self-harming situations where the parents have been disempowered by their young adult or adolescent sons or daughters due to constant threats of hurting themselves or trying to take their lives, the therapist coaches the parents to use Gandhian nonviolent passive resistant tactics to take back control (Omer, 2004). This includes staging a sit-in in their young adults' or adolescents' bedroom in front of their door, refusing to budge until they come up with some solutions for their challenging behaviors. They are to sit as long as it takes for their sons or daughters to present some useful ideas for improving their behavior.

The parents also can put together a written document that states that they will no longer tolerate their sons' or daughters' behaviors (listing all the behaviors that must change) and they are taking the family in a new direction. They make a commitment to stop yelling, getting into power struggles with him or her, nagging, or making threats. The parents also let their sons' or daughters' know that they will no longer support the conspiracy of silence regarding not letting extended family members and close friends of the family know what has been going on in their household. When parents can commit to changing their ways and enforce their new contract with their son or daughter, dramatic changes can occur. It is important to coach parents to both strike when the iron is cold (the son or daughter is in a relaxed state or has not escalated) and reach out with positive gestures of affection and praise when their son or daughter is treating them with respect and taking responsibility.

Another important area to cover with parents of self-harming adolescents is for them to establish relationships with their friends' parents. There is no expectation that they become best friends. By having a network of parents working together as a team and letting one another know if they just heard or learned about something to be alarmed about involving their kids, such as the empty house where the kids are planning to have their unsupervised Friday night party is important information to share with fellow parents to prevent crises and police involvement. Adolescent clients have shared with me that it is much more anxiety-provoking for them when the parent squad "busts" their party than when the local police department does. Once parents know where the house or rave party is that their kids had no permission to attend, I have had some parents visit these parties, look for some of their sons' or daughters' friends and inquire if they have seen them. Although this would not be considered "cool" by their sons or daughters, the parents are letting their kids know that they care and mean business with enforcing their rules.

Distress Management Tools and Strategies
The Chilling Out Room
The *chilling out room* was developed for three purposes: a) to provide clients with a quiet, sacred space in which to decompress when experiencing emotional distress and feeling tempted to self-harm or engage in equivalent self-destructive behaviors; b) to provide a multisensory experience that triggers positive emotion and teaches self-harming clients healthy and effective ways to get relief from emotional distress; and c) to help disrupt long-standing habitual patterns of thinking and action that have maintained the self-harming and equivalent self-destructive behaviors of the clients. Although I have implemented the chilling-out room concept with individual young adults, it tends to be much more effective with couples and families.

The first step for implementing this multisensory change strategy is for the self-harming young adults or adolescents and their parents to select a room in their house or apartment that will serve as the designated chilling-out room. When clients lack adequate space to devote a whole room for implementing this change strategy, I have had these couples and families select a corner in a larger room to serve as the designated *chilling-out corner* or *zone*. Some families like putting up an artistic-looking sign that the adolescent has created to make the room more official. The room or corner of a larger room needs to have a window in it or by the corner.

The second step is for the young adults or adolescents and their parents to pick out some colorful and fragrant flowers that will be right by the window. This will provide the self-harming young adults or adolescents with the opportunity to utilize their *visual* and *olfactory* senses.

Next, the self-harming young adults and adolescents take the lead in creating a library of interesting and colorful art books that intrigue them (they can take out books from the local public library). As part of this library, they can include photo albums with photos of fun social outings with friends or their couple partners and family. This is another opportunity to access their visual sensory channel.

They are to create a music library in which the self-harming young adult or adolescent takes the lead with music selections. I have them select music they find relaxing, but the tunes cannot be ones that have led to triggering negative emotions, self-harming episodes, or engaging in other self-destructive behaviors in the past. Once I have developed an alliance with the self-harming young adults or adolescents and they see the value in this change strategy, I turn the clients on to some relaxing, contemplative, centering music that plays on multiple senses, such as the music of Native American flute player Carlos Nakai, jazz musician Lonnie Liston Smith's *Astral Traveling,* and Miles Davis's *Circles.* If the clients find these tunes helpful and are interested in hearing some additional music of mine, I will bring in some new musical offerings for them to hear and select from.

Many self-harming young adult and adolescent clients enjoy art. There needs to be a wide range of art supplies made available to the clients, such as an easel for painting, pastels, colored pencils and crayons, and fresh clay. The use of fresh clay plays on our *tactile* sensory channel and is a great way to take the clients' mind off of unpleasant thoughts and feelings and demands their visual attention. Most people like to run their hands through fresh clay because it feels nice and it is a relaxing activity.

The only ground rules for using the chilling-out room or corner are that the clients are to stay in the room or corner using the resources available to them until they are totally centered or emotionally balanced and ready to interact with their couple partners, family members, or friends. The second ground rule is that couple partners or other family members are not allowed to disturb or enter the room or corner area when it is being used by the clients. This is the clients' sanctuary and safe sacred space to decompress for as long as they need it.

I have had such great success with the chilling-out room concept that the clients' couple partners and parents have used it as a way to stave off arguments and power struggles and to center themselves when stressed out. Some parents have used it with other siblings as well.

Mindfulness Meditations and Experiments

Mindfulness meditation is one of the most effective coping and centering distress management tools that we can teach self-harming young adults and adolescents. Being mindful is embracing everything that happens in the miraculous moment, including unpleasant thoughts and feelings that enter our mind while we are trying to focus on a specific bodily sensation or object in our environment. Research indicates that people who maintain a daily mindfulness practice can lower their blood pressure and heart and breathing rates; can decrease sympathetic activity in their automatic nervous systems; can enhance their right brain functioning; can strengthen their immune system; can improve their muscle relaxation abilities; can improve their concentration and problem-solving abilities; and can lower stress and causes relaxation by containing, moderating, and regulating cortisol flow. There is an increase in the number of influenza antibodies found in regular meditators' bodies compared to bodies of nonmeditators, and it cools down a revved-up amygdale (Bennett-Goleman, 2001; Davidson, 2003; Kabat-Zinn, 1990, 1995; Rosenkrantz, Jackson, Dalton, Dolski, Ryff, Singer, et al., 2003). Studies with Buddhist monks who have been meditating for decades show heightened brain activity in their left prefrontal cortexes, which is where positive emotions reside. In their right prefrontal cortexes, researchers found that the monks had lowered activity, which has been linked to anxiety and negative emotions (Post & Neimark, 2007). Psychologically, these monks experience a stable sense of serenity and contentment, which is caused by enlightenment. There is a mind-brain that is active, attentive, and very well-focused (Lutz, Greischar, Rawlings, Ricard, & Davidson, 2004). Finally, in the depths of their meditative states, Buddhist monks report experiencing a sense of timelessness (Goleman, 2003). A similar experience happens for individuals immersed in their flow-state activities where they lose track of time while they are engaged in a meaningful activity working with a sense of effortlessness that is deeply pleasurable (Czikszentmihalyi, 1990). I use the following mindfulness meditations and experiments with my self-harming clients: the *sound meditation*, the *food meditation*, the *candle meditation, cloud shape watching*, and *wave watching*.

The Sound Mediation

This meditation helps clients relax and get centered through listening to sounds occurring around them. After getting comfortable in a chair or on a couch in a quiet place in their homes, they are to close their eyes and carefully tune in to all sounds they hear around them. They are to simply label the different sounds they hear around them in their mind without getting too attached to any one sound. I like to have clients do this for 10–12 minutes. Ideally, if the clients can practice using this meditation and others described here at least twice a day for a few weeks, they will develop competency in both entering and staying in a deep meditative state. Many of the self-harming and other clients I have had experiment with this meditation in my office have fallen asleep after doing it because they were so relaxed.

For other clients having trouble doing the sound meditation, it may be beneficial to bring in some music that plays on all of one's senses, like Lonnie Liston Smith's *Astral Traveling* tune. (A great rendition of this tune is on Pharoah Sanders's CD *Thembie*.) I have clients silently try to not only identify different instruments they hear but visualize the images of animals in their minds that are produced by the sounds they hear. After doing this with *Astral Traveling* or other music, clients often find it easier to do the sound meditation.

The Food Meditation

The food meditation taps all of one's senses. What is critical when having clients practice using this meditation is to do each step very slowly and devote 2–3 minutes to each step. The food product used can be either a raisin or a piece of popcorn. Since most people like popcorn, it may be a better bet unless you have a raisin-loving client. The steps for doing this meditation are as follows:

1. Clients get comfortable in an office chair or couch.
2. Therapists place a piece of popcorn in the clients' left palm.
3. Clients are to carefully study the shape, coloring, and shadow around the piece of popcorn.
4. Accessing their olfactory sensory channel, I have the clients carefully smell the piece of popcorn and try to identify what they smell silently to themselves.
5. Next, the clients are to slowly pick up the piece of popcorn with their right hand and place it in their mouth without biting down on it yet. I have found it useful in heightening the sensory experience to have the clients close their eyes at this point. The clients are to roll the piece of popcorn around in their mouth.
6. The next step is for the clients to bite down into and chew the piece of popcorn slowly and finely, without swallowing it.
7. Finally, the clients are to describe silently to themselves whatever sensations they experience as the chewed-up piece of popcorn travels down their esophagus and enters their stomach.

While doing this meditation, clients are literally transported to popcorn land! They are totally immersed in the popcorn experience and have taken a vacation from their problems for 12 solid minutes.

The Candle Meditation

Clients begin this meditation by finding a quiet room and getting comfortable in a chair or couch. On a table, clients are to place a tall lit candle and for 10–12 minutes stare into the flame. While doing this, clients are to note the colors within the flame, anything else they see within the flame, and its ever changing shape.

Cloud Shape Watching

Most people during a given day look up at the sky at clouds and are often surprised to see recognizable objects such as animals and human head shapes. Cloud shape watching can be fun and can feel like being an explorer chartering unknown territory, looking for the familiar. This mindfulness experiment can help liberate our clients from the inner emotional turmoil they experience when triggered by negative life events. When they begin to experience emotional distress, clients are instructed to go outside when it's light out and carefully look up at the sky for any recognizable objects in the cloud formations. Like a fun game, each time they practice using this distress management strategy they are to write down their observations, and try to top the number of recognizable objects they had discovered while studying the clouds on previous cloud-watching missions.

Wave Watching

Another effective mindfulness experiment is to have clients get out of their head when beginning to experience emotional distress by going to a local lake or ocean beach, stand by the edge of the water, and carefully watch waves coming ashore and returning back to their source. I like to share with clients that life's difficulties or problems are like waves: They can be big, rough, and powerful at times, but they are in a constant state of flux and always return to their source. Therefore, difficulties or problems are not fixed or permanent but are transformative. In general, most clients who regularly practice using this mindfulness experiment report seeing this connection and feeling less victimized by their unpleasant thoughts and feelings and their self-harming and other difficulties. They also find the combination of watching and listening to waves coming ashore or striking the rocks or reef healing and relaxing.

With all of the above mindfulness meditations and experiments, some self-harming clients may have a hard time entering and sustaining their meditative states because of intruding thoughts. I recommend that the client first label whatever thoughts enter his or her mind, such as "There goes a worrying thought," and view this thought as an invited guest into his or her home. Invited guests are greeted with warmth and treated with respect and can stay as long as they wish. Another good analogy is to share with the client that the intruding thoughts are like the clouds in the sky that are always in perpetual motion; eventually, they will clear out, revealing their beautiful blue sky self. By offering these positive ways of viewing their negative intruding thoughts, clients can embrace them and not be troubled by them; they can return their main focus and concentration to whatever object they are carefully observing.

Urge Surfing

Closely related to wave-watching is *urge surfing*, which has shown great clinical results with substance abusers (Bowen, Witkiewitz, Dillworth, & Marlatt, 2007; Marlatt, Bowen, Chawla, & Witkiewitz, 2008; Marlatt & Kristeller, 1999). I have found the use of urge surfing to be quite applicable for goal maintenance and the prevention of slips with self-harming clients. In urge surfing, self-harming clients capture in their minds the image of them riding through big waves on their surfboards, maintaining their balance and boards. This serves as a metaphor for constructively managing urges and cravings to self-harm or engage in equivalent self-destructive behaviors. Clients are first taught to label whatever bodily sensations, thoughts, or feelings they experience and to enter their minds and cultivate a nonattached and curious stance in relationship to these potential triggers or urges to self-harm or engage in equivalent self-destructive behaviors. Clients learn to accept and embrace these bodily sensations, thoughts, and feelings that naturally occur during the maintenance stage of readiness for change (Prochaska et al., 1994). They learn that there is no need to try to suppress or avoid them. Once clients get skilled at maintaining their surfboards even when faced with big and powerful waves, they are less likely to wipe out and have slips or prolonged relapse.

Key Buddhist Principles and Healing Practices

Practicing Nonattachment

All human beings at some time or another fall into the mental trap of becoming too attached to negative thoughts and feelings and fixed beliefs about what and who upsets us, what we do not have and must have to feel more complete, more fulfilled, and successful, and what and who we want to have more control over. The more attached we become to the above thoughts, feelings, and beliefs, the more frustrated, depressed, anxious, and out of control we become. This is a ripe and vulnerable mental state for self-harming, bingeing and purging, substance abuse, or engaging in sexually risky behaviors for quick emotional relief or self-punishment.

One way to help our self-harming clients cultivate nonattachment or detachment from their negative thoughts, feelings, and fixed beliefs is to have them visualize themselves gradually gaining distance from what they desire or are upset about (Lowenstein, 2005). Therapists can have clients find a comfortable chair or couch to sit on and a quiet place in their home. Next, clients are instructed to think about something they desire or are upset about, accessing its image in their mind. Have them carefully examine the thoughts and feelings connected to this attachment. Clients are asked to visualize in their mind, seeing themselves standing next to the image of what they desire or are upset about. After doing this, they are to capture the same image in their mind again, but standing farther away from what they desire or are upset about. This step can be repeated again, with clients now visualizing themselves standing at a much farther distance from the image of what they desire or are upset about. Clients need to practice this visualization daily, particularly when they find themselves ruminating about frustrating or negative things that happen to them or desiring something that they don't have control over. Once clients are skilled at using this exercise to become nonattached, they will feel more liberated and gain wisdom about what they can and cannot control and how not to self-impose their own emotional misery.

The Four Noble Truths

While on his spiritual journey to enlightenment, Buddha one day sat under a pipal tree and came up with his *Four Noble Truths* based on the insights and wisdom he had gained and experiences he had in the world. The *First Noble Truth* is about suffering, unhappiness, grief, discomfort, and despair. These forms of suffering occur when we desire something or someone and cannot obtain it. The *Second Noble Truth* was Buddha's attempt to diagnose the cause of human suffering. He believed that suffering was caused by our quest for pleasure and avoidance of pain and discomfort, craving to be reborn, existence and nonexistence, and certain things we don't have. With the *Third Noble Truth*, Buddha proclaimed that the way to free ourselves from suffering was through "indifference to desire and freedom from desire" (Lowenstein, 2005, p. 35). The cure for suffering was by following the *Middle Way* or the *Eightfold Path*. Through the Buddha's further in-depth study and reflection on the Middle Way evolved the *Fourth Noble Truth*: the Eightfold Path. For the Buddha, he found the Middle Way on his spiritual journey by reflecting on the benefits of living a life between his former existence of living a life of wealth and royalty and the personal challenges of gaining inner wisdom and strength, trying to survive in a world filled with poverty, starving people, and social injustice. In his Eightfold Path, the Buddha argued that in all of our thoughts and actions we should strive to become balanced, harmonious, skillful, or "just right" (Lowenstein, 2005). The Buddha's Eightfold Path guidelines are as follows:

1. *Right view or understanding:* This brings us closer to the Buddha's teachings.
2. *Right thought or intention:* It is our duty to bend our will and understanding of the Buddha's teachings.
3. *Right speech:* This encourages us to speak to others without falsehood and malice
4. *Right action:* We should be honest and nonviolent with others.
5. *Right livelihood:* We should pursue a life free from greed, hurtful behavior, and exploitation.
6. *Right effort:* We should use our energies in a balanced and skillful way.
7. *Right awareness:* We should develop an alertness both to our inner processes and to outward events.

8. *Right concentration:* This reminds us that our meditation should always be focused (Lowenstein, 2005, p. 37).

For the Buddha, practicing all of the Eightfold Path guidelines daily can provide life-enhancing wisdom. It offers guidance on how to change our negative and rigid thoughts and feelings and fixed beliefs so we can lead lives of happiness and freedom. Linehan (1993a) was one of the first psychotherapy pioneers to incorporate Buddhist principles and healing methods in a clinical treatment model. The Middle Way and other Wise Mind Buddhist methods and principles comprise one of the core skill areas Linehan teaches her clients (Miller et al., 2007).

The Four Immeasurable Minds

According to Hanh (1997, 1998), there are *Four Immeasurable Minds*. They are: *metta* (love), *karuna* (compassion), *mudita* (joy), and *upekkha* (equanimity). All four of these mind states are interconnected and work together. For Buddhists, providing joy and happiness to others is an important value. Reaching out with loving-kindness and compassion to those in emotional distress, even people we find challenging or people we would consider our enemies, is a highly cherished Buddhist value. Equanimity means maintaining one's emotional balance or center when faced with or experiencing stressful life events or difficult people. We embrace the fact that with stressful life events and difficult people we are bound to experience unpleasant bodily sensations, thoughts, and feelings that are all naturally occurring, are part of what is happening in the moment, and with patience and acceptance will pass, and we will be just fine.

Hanh (1998) recommends practicing the *metta meditation*. This consists of first practicing getting skilled at learning how to love oneself, mastering effective ways to bring joy and happiness into one's life, and being compassionate with oneself. Once skill develops on this level, we can practice bringing more love, kindness, joy, and compassion to our relationships with intimate partners, family members, and extended family members. After further increasing our skills, we can practice using loving-kindness and compassion with our friends and acquaintances. The final challenge and the true test of solid skill development is to begin experimenting with bringing love, joy, happiness, and compassion into our relationships with difficult people or our enemies. It is my strong belief that we would have a much less violent world if more people practiced mindfulness meditation and used loving-kindness and compassion with one another.

Turning Arrows into Flowers

At some point or another, our self-harming clients may experience their bosses, colleagues, teachers, parents, peers, or friends saying or doing something that is hurtful or even aggressive toward them and putting them on the defensive and wanting to retaliate in some way. Many self-harming clients have grave difficulty managing their anger and frustration and they take it out on themselves through self-inflicted violence, or they externalize it. I have worked with some male self-harming clients who both fracture bones in their hands by punching their fists into walls and doors and lash out at others when angry and frustrated. Since these kinds of responses may end up being costly in terms of serious consequences at work or school, fuel more social ridicule, and cause loss of jobs and friends, they need to find a way to respond constructively. The Buddha's closely related experience right before his enlightenment offers us a wise and valuable solution for responding to these challenging life situations. He had been attacked by Mara, the Tempter, and the Evil One. Mara and his army of demons shot thousands of arrows at the Buddha, but as the arrows neared him, instead of trying to retaliate, he turned them in his mind into flowers and they fell harmlessly by his feet. According to Hanh, "We can all practice so that we can receive the violent words and actions aimed at us and, like the Buddha, transform them into flowers. The power of understanding and compassion gives us the ability to do this. We can all make flowers out of arrows (2003, p. 13). The Buddha's story of how best to respond to angry, aggressive, and threatening people can be valuable wisdom for our clients.

Visualization Experiments

Most young adult and adolescent self-harming clients have no difficulties with visualization and guided imagery. Many of these clients are talented writers and artists and possess the natural abilities to tap their imaginary powers and inventiveness to access metaphorical objects, seeing themselves in action in different settings, and other images requested to visualize while doing these experiments. Similar to the mindfulness meditations and experiments, visualization experiments can help our clients disrupt negative thoughts and feelings and focus their attention on images that can trigger positive emotion for them. Two visualization experiments are presented here that our clients can use when experiencing emotional distress: *embracing the dragon to release the princess/prince* and *visualizing movies of success*.

Embracing the Dragon to Release the Princess/Prince

This visualization and guided imagery experiment can be quite effective with self-harming adolescents. Throughout their childhoods, in stories, cartoons, TV shows, and in movies, adolescents were exposed to dragons, princesses, and princes. Most children really enjoy fairy tales and stories that involve these powerful and wise characters.

I begin this visualization experiment by having the adolescents close their eyes. They are then to visualize an image of a big and powerful fire-breathing dragon. While seeing in their minds the dragon, I share with clients that "cutting" (whatever clients call their self-harming behavior) has been like a dragon for them in that it is strong and powerful and has helped them like a good friend. It has given them both the courage to not give up and a high level of tolerance for pain. With a few breaths of fire, the dragon can temporarily and quickly get rid of their inner pain and bad feelings or thoughts. I share with clients, "As you have discovered, it really works!"

However, we discover in life that even the best of our friends at one time or another may let us down and not deliver for us or do something that may get us into trouble or alienate others. Our relationships with dragons leaves us with scars and burn marks, may lead to our losing close friends who are replaced with toxic ones, may get us into trouble at school. We may learn some other unhelpful habits like regularly getting stoned, convincing ourselves to throw up or starve ourselves to lose weight, may get us to a shrink, medicated, and the worst-case scenario, possibly hospitalized!

On the upside of our relationship with dragons, which is a positive thing about them, is that they can transform into caring, sensitive, and wise princesses and princes (I have the clients access an image of a princess or prince, depending on their gender). By nurturing, respecting, and thanking the dragon for all of the good things it has done for you (I have the clients see themselves in their mind thanking and hugging the dragon), it will transform into a princess or a prince who will empower you in many positive ways (I have the clients visualizing the dragon disappearing and themselves transforming or turning into a princess or a prince). It will lead you to find more positive and healthy ways of getting emotional relief and pleasure, choosing better friends to hang out with, helping you not to get into trouble in school or with your parents, and taking back control of your skin and your life. You will find yourself being more self-confident, having more self-respect, and being accepted by more positive peers.

With self-harming adolescents who love to read fairy tale–like and fantasy books and write creative stories, they can identify with this visualization and guided imagery experiment and begin to see how initially self-harming was like a strong friend who soothed them and helped them to get through some tough situations in their lives. However, they also begin to see that the costs of maintaining their friendships with self-harming outweigh the benefits. Self-harming clients are invited to pay homage to all the positive aspects that this behavior has provided for them. By so doing, the adolescents can feel okay about letting go of self-harming by showing respect for it. They are liberated and free to create a new story where they become the kinds of princesses or princes they would like to be.

Visualizing Movies of Success

Visualizing movies of success is a highly effective distress management tool for disrupting client habitual patterns of thinking and action that fuel and maintain self-harming, eating-distressed, substance-abusing, and sexually risky behaviors. This tool is easy to learn and implement in any context. The self-harming young adult or adolescent is to get comfortable in a chair or couch in a quiet place in their home. The steps for doing this visualization are as follows:

1. The clients close their eyes and see the image of a blank movie screen in their mind.
2. Next, the clients are to access a movie of some past sparkling moment in their life where they had accomplished something that they were very proud of. The clients are to use all of their senses, including color and motion to capture the fine details of their movie.
3. If the clients are having a hard time identifying a past sparkling moment of personal achievement, they can access some past special place they had visited with family or friends and a magical or most special image from this experience.
4. The clients should practice viewing this movie in their mind for 12 minutes.
5. The clients are instructed to practice accessing this movie and turning it off at least 1–2 times per day over the next week.
6. When experiencing any stressful life event (arguing with parents, peer conflicts, etc.) or experiencing any emotional distress during the next week, they should practice using this tool instead of caving in to cutting, bingeing and purging, getting stoned, or practicing unsafe, unprotected sex to get emotional relief or to self-punish.

Theresa, a 17-year-old, was referred by her family physician for difficulties with cutting and gouging deeply into her skin with sharp objects, bulimia, and depression. She had been in a 2-week eating disorder program and seen numerous therapists since she was 12, when these behavioral difficulties had first begun. This coincided with the sudden death of her biological father from a heart attack. Theresa was very close to her father. One way to think about her bulimia was it must be difficult to stomach or digest the loss of her father. By the time I had seen Theresa, she had moved into the action stage of readiness for change. She was tired of looking at her scarred-up and disfigured body and the numerous infections she had gotten by not using sterile sharp objects for cutting and gouging herself. On her own, she was regaining more control over her bulimia problem. I introduced Theresa to the visualizing-movies-of-success coping strategy. Theresa used to be an accomplished violinist and had her all-time best performance when she was 15 in an old church. She was playing three of the six "Concerti Grossi," classical pieces by one of her favorite composers, Corelli. With her eyes closed and using all of her senses, Theresa was to project onto the blank movie screen in her mind a movie of her giving this outstanding performance. I asked her to listen carefully in her mind to the first piece she had played, which was "Concerto #12 in F Major," access how she was dressed, seeing faces in the crowd and the beautiful interior of the church, literally transporting herself back to that magical moment. With her eyes closed, Theresa was smiling and it was quite obvious that this whole experience was triggering positive emotions for her. Theresa enjoyed this experience in my office so much that she decided to start taking violin lessons again to further perfect her skills. I had her practice 1–2 times a day, accessing this movie of success and using it whenever she experienced emotional distress or any stressful life events that would both serve as triggers for self-harming or bingeing and purging. Theresa also found the sound meditation to be of great benefit to her. Family therapy helped facilitate strengthening her emotional connection with her stepfather, who was a professional violinist and on the road quite a lot.

Notice What You Will Do to Overcome the Temptation or Urge to . . .

There are always spaces in between self-harming and engaging in other equivalent self-destructive behaviors. The *notice what you will do to overcome the temptation or urge to . . .* distress management strategy can be of great benefit to clients with habit problems like self-harming, bulimia, and substance abuse (de Shazer, 1985; Selekman, 2005). On a daily basis for 1 week's time, clients are to carefully notice what they tell themselves or do to avoid caving in to self-harming, bingeing and purging, or binge-drinking or abusing drugs. This distress management strategy helps increase the clients' awareness about what works, that is, their key solution-building patterns of thinking and acting that they need to increase to help reduce and eventually eliminate the self-harming and equivalent self-destructive behaviors that had been oppressing them with serious physical, psychological, social, and school/occupational consequences.

Body-Scanning

Body-scanning is a powerful way to help self-harming clients relax, center themselves, and regain personal control when experiencing emotional distress. I like to have the clients find a quiet room in their home and lie down on a bed, couch, or on the floor. The clients are to first locate inside their body a location where they are experiencing some physical discomfort. After doing this, the clients are to locate a place on their arm or leg where they feel totally relaxed. Next, they are to return to the location in their body where there was some physical discomfort. The client can then locate another place on their arm, leg, or inside their body where they feel totally relaxed. The clients then return to the original location of physical discomfort. What eventually happens for the clients after alternating back and forth from relaxed locations on the body to the location where they were experiencing physical discomfort is that this pain or tension goes away. After regular practicing using this effective distress management tool, the clients discover that they have regained personal control and are more centered.

Disputation Skills

According to Seligman (2002, 2003), among the most important life skills that young people should be taught are *disputation skills*. Having an open and flexible mind and not adopting a tunnel-vision mindset when negative life events occur can help us not fall prey to depression and anxiety difficulties. Four disputation tools that I have found to be quite useful to self-harming clients are: *searching for evidence, searching for alternative explanations, implications,* and *usefulness*. Once skilled at using these disputation skills, clients can maintain an optimistic mind-set in frustrating and adverse life situations, which will enhance their resilience and self-confidence, and empower them to master future challenging situations.

With self-harming adolescents, I like to simultaneously teach their parents disputation skills so that they can help their kids become more proficient in using these tools when experiencing emotional distress or reacting negatively to upsetting family interactions or disappointing situations that occur with them or with their peers. Parents are encouraged to practice using these tools both at work and in the parenting department. I encourage parents to share with their kids how they both used their disputation skills successfully and unsuccessfully at work in responding to frustrating situations and difficulties with their bosses or colleagues. In the parenting department, I encourage them, when upset with their kids, not to cling to one explanation for or adopting a tunnel-vision way of responding to their son or daughter's self-harming or other negative behaviors. Research indicates that when parents adopt an optimistic explanatory style in response to their kids' disappointing life events or negative behaviors, it empowers them to quickly bounce back with confidence, not give up, and better cope with the stressors that are fueling their negative behaviors (Dweck, 2006; Selekman, 1997; Seligman, Reivich, Jaycox, & Gillham, 1995).

Playing a Super Sleuth Detective Searching for Evidence

Most self-harming young adults and adolescents like detective stories and murder mysteries. I like to begin introducing the *searching for evidence* disputation skill by asking clients who their favorite detective or murder mystery writers are. I like to know what specifically they like about the lead detectives in their favorite authors' books. Next, I will ask them who their favorite TV and movie detectives are and why they like them. This discussion helps clients get in the spirit of experimenting with this disputation skill.

Searching for evidence involves having clients pretend to be their favorite detectives and carefully looking for hard evidence or solid clues to support their explanations for why frustrating and disappointing events occurred in their lives. As an experiment, the clients can be asked to keep track on a daily basis how they view negative life events that occur and then search for evidence to support their most potent explanation (Seligman, 2003). Often clients come back after their daily investigations empty-handed, with no hard evidence to support their narrow and rigid explanations for why these events occurred.

Using the Mind as a Kaleidoscope: Searching for Alternative Explanations

Closely related to the disputation skill searching for evidence is *searching for alter-*

native explanations (Seligman, 2003). In introducing this disputation skill to clients, I find out with them what their experiences have been like using a kaleidoscope. I discuss with them that what is so special with kaleidoscopes is their ability to provide the viewer with not only multiple images of an object but colorful and beautiful designs as well. Next, I share with clients important constructivist assumptions that are similar to the kaleidoscope viewing experience (the viewer constructs reality; we can never adopt a God's eye view to look at ourselves in relationship to others; there are many possible explanations for every event that occurs in the world (Hoffman, 1988)).

Over 1 week's time, the clients are instructed to think of and write down daily the second, third, and fourth possible reasons why negative events occur in their lives. Clients who get good at using this disputation skill find themselves being less emotionally reactive and less likely to cave in to self-harming behaviors or engaging in equivalent self-destructive behaviors when frustrating and disappointing life events do occur. Over time, clients find that their thinking, when faced with negative life events, becomes much more flexible and open to all possibilities.

The Implications and Usefulness of Ruminating About Negative Life Events and Clinging to Narrow and Rigid Views

Some self-harming clients cling to all of their negative thoughts and feelings following a disappointing or frustrating negative life event long after it occurred. This can fuel *catastrophic thinking*, that is, they think for the worst about all of the people involved in the negative life event, themselves, and what is to come in the future for them (Seligman, 2003; Seligman et al., 1995). What the clients don't initially understand is that the more they ruminate about what somebody had done to them or why situations ended up being negative experiences for them, the more depressed, anxious, and miserable they make themselves feel.

I invite clients to take a hard look at the *implications* and the *usefulness* of not letting go of their negative thoughts and feelings and narrow ways of viewing frustrating and other negative life events. I ask clients the following types of questions:

- "Does dwelling on _____ make you feel happier or does it bring you down?"
- "How do you know that because Phil let you down yesterday, he will continue to do so in the future?"
- "How can you be absolutely certain that this way of thinking about Phil and your relationship with him is true?"
- "Do you think worrying about having another slip will help you stay on track or set the stage for your having another one?"
- "Does it help you to believe that you can control Mandy, or does this thought lead to you feeling more out of control?"

Questions like these help clients begin to see how their rigid, negative, and catastrophic thinking gets them into trouble emotionally with themselves and with others in their lives. Similar to other disputation skills discussed, both implications and usefulness help clients be much more open-minded and flexible with their thinking.

Flow-State Activities

All self-harming clients have engaged in certain leisure-time activities that were both meaningful and pleasurable to them and where they would lose track of time. These *flow*-state activities could be writing poetry and creative stories, doing artwork, writing and playing music, cooking, building things, or dancing (Csikszentmihalyi, 1990, 1997). Clients can be encouraged to pursue these activities when experiencing emotional distress or following some stressful negative life event.

Research indicates that our brains are hardwired to derive a deep sense of satisfaction and pleasure when physical effort produces something tangible, visible, and meaningful. This emotional pay-off is called an *effort-driven reward*. We also experience an increased perception of control over our environment, more positive emotions, and enhanced resilience against depression and other mental disorders (Lambert, 2006)—all good reasons to have our self-harming clients identify and increase their involvement in their choice flow state activities.

For those self-harming clients who have stopped engaging in these flow-state activities, I will explore with them which ones they found to be most meaningful and the most pleasurable that they could see themselves reinstating. Immersing oneself in flow-state activities can be a great coping strategy for disrupting negative thoughts and feelings that were triggered by a frustrating or stressful life event. By filling up self-harming clients' leisure time with as many flow-state activities as possible, we can reduce the likelihood for them to cave in to hurting themselves when they begin to dwell on negative thoughts and feelings, and it can help increase their life-satisfaction levels by immersing themselves in these meaningful and pleasurable pastimes.

My Positive Boost Kit

Another useful distress management strategy is to have clients carry a pouch or over-the-shoulder small bag in which they can carry a variety of small possessions that trigger positive emotion for them when experiencing emotional distress or trying to stave off a slip after being triggered. In the *positive boost kit* they can carry the following items that trigger positive emotion for them: a key chain or other memento from a special trip, a good-luck charm, photos of close friends and special places they have visited, special cards or small and thoughtful gifts from friends, and so forth. A lot of self-harming adolescents have found the positive boost kit very helpful for relapse prevention purposes.

Journaling

Pennebaker (1998; 2004), Campbell and Pennebaker (2003), Lepore and Smyth (2002), Pennebaker and Graybeal, 2001, Klein & Boals (2001), Crow (2000), Lepore

(1997), and Pennebaker and Susman (1988) have written about the psychological, behavioral, social, and health benefits of having clients journal about their traumatic events and major conflicts with family members and friends rather than talk about these emotionally charged life events in therapy. Some of the positive psychological effects of having clients journal about traumatic past events, major conflicts with family or friends, or current stressors are: feeling happier and less negative and having a reduction in depressive and anxiety symptoms (Lepore, 1997; Pennebaker, 2004). On a behavioral level, journaling about traumatic events, conflicts with family and friends, or current stressors improves working memory. College students given this journaling task tended to get higher grades than students who were not journaling (Klein & Boals, 2001). Pennebaker and Graybeal (2001) found that journaling can enhance individuals' social competence. Journal writers in their study were more talkative, laughed more easily and often, had improved listening skills, and their close friendships were reported to be stronger. In terms of the physiological health benefits of journaling, Lepore and Smyth (2002) found that expressive writing strengthened individuals' immune systems. Crow (2000) found in his study that expressive writing reduced participants' blood pressure. Pennebaker and Susman found that college freshmen who were given the expressive writing task to journal about past traumatic events and major conflicts with family members and friends had 43% less doctors' visits in a year than students who wrote about superficial and nonemotional events.

Pennebaker (2004) recommended that when journaling or doing any type of expressive writing, writers should follow guidelines:

1. *Acknowledge your emotions openly:* The writers need to be able to label both the negative and positive feelings connected to a past traumatic event or major conflicts with family members or friends.
2. *Construct a coherent story:* Try to create a meaningful story of what happened to them and how it is affecting them now
3. *Switch perspectives:* Try to view the traumatic event or major conflict with family members or friends through the family members' or friends' eyes.
4. *Find your voice:* The writers need to express themselves openly and honestly. They need to find a voice that reflects who they think they are.
5. *Writing method:* The writers need to select the writing method that feels most comfortable to them (Pennebaker, 2004, pp. 12–13).

Humor Journal

One way to help our self-harming clients get pleasure and receive a dose of endorphins in a positive way is through the use of humor. Clients can be instructed to purchase an inexpensive journal or scrapbook that they will use as their *humor journal*. On a daily basis, they are to write in or cut out and place in their humor journals any funny jokes or stories they read in newspapers, popular books, or favorite magazines, or heard from friends, family members, teachers, TV shows, or movies. This also includes cutting out funny cartoons or pictures from newspapers and their favorite magazines and placing them in their journals as well. When experiencing emotional distress, the client can look through their humor journals to get a good laugh and trigger positive emotion. The humor journals also can be placed in the book library section in their chilling-out room as another great reading option to look at as a way to get a good laugh and emotionally decompress.

Gratitude Log

Self-harming clients can greatly benefit from keeping a *gratitude log*. By recording daily what we feel blessed about in our lives, our health, family, good friends, positive school or work experiences, mastering a new skill, accomplishing a difficult task, overcoming an adverse life situation or illness, or doing good deeds, we will be better able to cope with negative and frustrating life events. Research indicates that having and showing gratitude increases our optimism and happiness levels, decreases negative emotions and increases positive emotion, helps us be more empathic with and socially connected to others, can calm our nervous systems, and improves sleep quality, particularly when writing in the log right before going to bed (Emmons, 2007; Emmons & McCullough, 2004). The ability to notice, appreciate, and savor life is strongly associated with life satisfaction (Peterson & Seligman, 2004). Finally, Watkins, Scheer, Ovnicek, & Kolts (2006) found that gratitude can serve as an important resiliency protective factor, aid in mood repair, and reduce posttraumatic stress disorder symptoms with trauma survivors.

The client can be instructed to purchase an inexpensive journal book and write in the middle of the top of the first page MY GRATITUDE LOG. Underneath this heading, they are to write two headings over two columns: *Date* and *What I'm Grateful For* (see Figure 3.1).

Self-harming clients can use their gratitude log in three ways. When in the throes of experiencing emotional distress, the clients can review their gratitude log to trigger positive emotion. Second, to help combat difficulties with sleeping, the clients can make it a nightly habit before they go to bed to add a new entry to their gratitude log and also review past entries. The gratitude log also can be added to the book library in the designated chilling-out room as another good reading option for triggering positive emotion.

My Epiphany Journal

We all have moments in our lives where some quote, work of art, scene from a play or movie, musical piece, personal life experience, or experiences that have happened to others who we are close to or are inspired by trigger in us epiphanies. These epiphanies might take the form of a new way of looking at a present life difficulty or situation, insights into past life events, a sudden vision of new possibilities for us in our futures, chance events that have symbolic meaning, or valuable wisdom gained from certain life experiences.

Fig. 3-1 MY GRATITUDE LOG	
Date	What I'm grateful for

The *My Epiphany Journal* is a way for clients to keep track of and write about meaningful epiphanies that they experience, which can be regularly referred to for wisdom and new ideas on how to view and negotiate life's challenges that they might encounter (see Figure 3.2). The journal format has a "date" column, an "epiphany" column, "sparked by" column, and "wisdom gained and applied to" column.

I recommend to clients that they regularly consult their epiphany journals for valuable wisdom and helpful ideas they can apply to current difficulties in their lives. For many clients, simply reviewing their epiphany journals can trigger positive emotions and elevate their hope and optimism levels about their futures. Finally, the client's My Epiphany Journal can be added to the book library in their designated chilling-out room.

Date	My Epiphany	Sparked By	Wisdom Gained	Applied to

Fig. 3.2 MY EPIPHANY JOURNAL

Get Out of Your Head and Reach Out to Others

Another powerful way to help self-harming clients get relief from emotional distress is to encourage them to get out of their heads (focusing on their negative thoughts and feelings) and do something nice for family members, a couple partner, close friends, a neighbor, destitute others, or an organization in the community. This can include doing volunteer work. Gandhi believed that happiness depended on what we could give, not on what we can get. Seligman (2002, 2003) contended that an important dimension to one's leading a meaningful life involves giving to others. Unfortunately, thanks to high technology and other material trappings, many young people today are only thinking about "Me, Myself, and I" and not about how they can make a difference in their schools, communities, and in the lives of others. Post and Neimark (2007) have found that adolescents who do volunteer work and regularly engage in altruistic acts in their communities are least likely to engage in self-destructive and other risky behaviors, have reduced depressive symptoms and suicide risk, do not have low self-esteem, have an increased sense of feeling more in control, have higher grades in school, and continue service work in their futures. In general, engaging in altruistic behavior reduces risk of illness, increases longevity, and enhances social competence. The bottom line is that when we reach out and help others, we help ourselves in the process and make our lives more meaningful.

When discussing this distress management strategy with self-harming clients, I take into consideration their key strengths, skills, and interest areas. Ultimately, the clients need to choose the type of volunteer work or altruistic act they would like to do. Once they decide what they would enjoy and get some personal fulfillment from doing it, I will assist them in finding volunteer activities in their communities or brainstorm what specific good deed they would like to do and for whom or what organization.

Contact Close Friends or Your Adult Inspirational Other

A final distress management strategy that self-harming clients can pursue is contacting close friends or his or her adult inspirational other for support and advice. We need to drive home the message to our self-harming clients that there is never the need for them to be alone with their difficulties or personal crises when they occur. As mentioned earlier, it is helpful for the therapists to know which friends and adult inspirational others clients have turned to for support and advice in the past and who and how specifically were they most helpful to them. The most consistently helpful friends and adult inspirational others should be at the top of their contact lists when needing support and advice. I have found it quite helpful to involve these key members from the clients' social networks in counseling sessions.

Major Therapeutic Experiments and Family Connection-Building Rituals

In this section of the chapter, several therapeutic experiments that draw from the clients' strengths and imagination powers and can help facilitate family connection-building are presented. I will describe each one, and the types of clinical situations where they can be most helpful. I'll offer guidelines about specific learning styles and intelligence strength and skill areas of self-harming clients and their families that would be required to get the most benefits from the therapeutic experiment offered. Case examples will be provided.

Imaginary Time Machine

The imaginary time machine (Selekman, 2005, 2006a) is one of the most versatile family therapy experiments that can be used at any stage of treatment. Most young adults, adolescents, and family members find this playful experiment to be fun to do and a great way to tap their creative problem-solving abilities and inventiveness to generate their own unique solutions. Often the young adults and adolescents demonstrate to their parents their competencies and strong desire to have more positive relationships with them while doing this experiment. As a family group they gain insight into their past successes in their relationships, and the experiment invites them to be co-architects of the kind of future relationships, they would like to have with one another. There are six different ways I use the imaginary time machine: *bringing back the best from the past to facilitate connection-building*; *resolving past conflicts and traumatic events*; *experiencing future selves to establish new parent-adolescent relationships in the now*; *the family adventure trip*; *saying "Hello" to say "Good-Bye" to lost parents, siblings, or close relatives*; and *taking the imaginary time machine anywhere in time*.

Bringing Back the Best from the Past to Facilitate Connection-Building

One powerful way to strengthen self-harming clients' relationships with more emotionally disconnected parents they are longing to get closer to is to instruct the clients to hop into the imaginary time machine and take it back to a place in time in the past where they felt close to or a closer connection with their more emotionally distant parents. Before time-traveling, the clients need to be instructed to apply all of his or her senses to the experience, including color and motion. The other participating parent is instructed to be in the listening and observing position. The client can be asked the following questions:

- "Where is he or she planning to take the time machine to?"
- "How old are you at this time?"
- "What does the location look like?"
- "What are you doing with your father/mother?"
- "What are you talking about?"
- "What are you enjoying the most about this special experience with your father/mother?"
- "What else is special about this experience?"
- "If you were to bring back any aspects of this special experience with your father/mother and want to have them happening today, what specifically would you want to put in to place or have him or her do?"
- "How would those changes make a difference in your relationship now with him/her?

Once the clients have returned from time-traveling, we can facilitate dialogue between them and the disengaged parent to see how they can begin to reinstate some, if not all, of the best elements from the clients' time-traveling experience in their relationship now. If there are certain obstacles reported that may get in the way of implementing the kind of changes the clients would like to have happen in the relationship, we can brainstorm with them as to how we can remove those barriers to building in more closeness in the relationship. The other parent in the listening and observing position can offer their ideas about how the barriers can be removed and any other suggestions for implementing the kind of changes the clients desire with their disengaged parent.

Resolving Past Conflicts and Traumatic Events

Having clients go back in time also can offer them a second chance to resolve conflicts with, or say parting words and good-byes to, a parent, grandparent, or sibling they did not have an opportunity to see before their deaths or to distant non-custodial parents or past romantic significant relationship partners who have cut off all communications with them. By having clients travel back into their pasts, they enter alternative histories that differ from their recorded histories. They can act freely, without the constraint of consistency with their previous histories. The imaginary time machine empowers them to achieve mastery and to inject positive emotion into their past realities where they may have experienced painful losses or other traumatic events. For some self-harming clients, the past traumatic events have had lingering negative effects and have continued to haunt them to the present day. In these situations, self-harming behavior may be used to help them to cope with unpleasant memories and feelings connected to the traumatic events.

I will only have self-harming clients go back in time and revisit a past traumatic event if this is their goal, they have reduced the frequency of their self-harming episodes and other equivalent self-destructive behaviors, and they appear to be more emotionally solid and confident that they can handle this challenging task. While doing this experiment, clients are free to let me know while trying this experiment if they wish to stop because it feels too uncomfortable to confront the traumatic event.

To help illustrate the preparation and the types of questions I ask clients before having them embark on their challenging journeys back in time, Tanya, 17 years old, was asked the following questions to help prepare her for her strong desire to change the quality of her relationship with her father, Boris:

- "What if you could change the past?"
- "What past painful or traumatic event involving you and your father and possibly other family members do you want to change?"
- "If you were to hop into my imaginary time machine and go back to that time, what specifically will you change about that situation?"
- "What difference will those changes have on you individually and in your relationship with your father?"
- "What else will you change about this event so that it is less toxic, you will feel more in control, and you will be free to establish a better relationship with your father?"
- "Now that you are done making those changes and you have rejoined me in the session, was there anything new that you learned from this experience that you will put to immediate use in your relationship with your father?"

- "Are you convinced that your father will be a better listener and want to do those fun activities with you now?"
- "What if it blows up and he struggles to be able to do those things that you desire from him. What are your plan B and plan C?"

As part of the preparation process, it is important for the therapists and clients to have well-thought-out backup plans if their best hopes for changes in the relationship do not happen or the whole situation spirals in a negative direction either while doing the experiment or after having the time-traveling experience.

Tanya was originally brought for counseling by her mother, Tara, for cutting, depression, poor grades in school, and running around with a lot of "Goth kids" of whom her mother did not approve. Tara felt that Tanya had a lot of "unfinished business with her alcoholic father" (Boris). According to Tara, before Boris's alcoholism problem got out of control, he was a loving father and husband. When intoxicated, Boris became violent and verbally threatening toward family members. One time at the age of 13, Boris had slapped Tanya in the face after she swore at him for hitting Tara. Since this incident, Tanya has felt very ambivalent about her relationship with her father. Although Tanya has been very pleased with her father's 3 years of sobriety and regular attendance at Alcoholics' Anonymous meetings, his trying to be a better father, and trying to treat her mother with more respect, she disclosed that she still harbored a lot of anger and sadness about how he was in the past. To try to cope with these overwhelming feelings and before she would have a visitation with him, she would cut herself as a way to self-soothe and combat these unpleasant feelings. I offered her the opportunity to take my imaginary time machine back in time and say what she would have really wanted to say to her father and accomplish whatever else she would have wanted to do so that her past relationship with her father would no longer "haunt" her today. Tanya took the time machine back to age 13 when she had been slapped by her father. The first thing she would have done differently was preventing herself from being hit, not swear at her father, and get herself, her younger brother Steven, and her mother out of the house until her father had sobered up. Typically, on Sundays her father would remain sober for the bulk of the day. While back in time, Tanya would have approached her father on that first Sunday to tell him how much she loved him and missed all of the past times they would "bike ride and hang out at the mall" together. She also would share with him how his "drinking worried" her and that she and other family members may get "seriously hurt" and how "scary" that is for her to live with. After returning from revisiting this traumatic event with her father and her former relationship with him, Tanya courageously agreed to have a family meeting with her father and me to say directly to him what she had said to him when she had traveled back in time. Boris had recently contacted me to see if we could do some family meetings with Tanya, so the timing was perfect to do a father-daughter session. Tanya wanted to see if her father would want to reinstate their "going bike riding and hanging out at the mall" again. I asked Tanya to think about other hopes and goals she had for their relationship. To help cover the back door for Tanya, I asked her if she had any concerns about her father's ability to really listen to and validate her. Tanya did not think this would be a problem. However, she had planned not to let her guard totally down in our meeting with her father. Tanya left our session very confident and hopeful that her relationship with her dad would get stronger.

The family session with Boris and Tanya went extremely well. Boris listened intently to Tanya's concerns and feelings about the devastating effects his alcoholism had on the family, and how it has continued to haunt her to this very day and contributed to the distance in their relationship. Boris was totally open to reinstating the "long bike rides and hanging out at the mall" to bring back some of the good from the past. He also included reinstating "going out for ice cream," which Tanya forgot to mention as a favorite pastime of both her and her father. The biggest and most unexpected surprise was Boris's doing a great job of educating Tanya about the disease of alcoholism and how his father was a "violent drunk," "treated him in a mean way at times," and eventually died from alcoholism before she was born. Apparently Boris had never shared this information with Tanya about his father. Tanya's thinking about her father had changed in the session after learning about the victimizing effects alcoholism had had on her father, her family, and her paternal grandfather. Through the use of externalization questions (White, 2007), Tanya began to see the real villain in her family story as being alcoholism and not her father. Over time, as Tanya's relationship with her father grew stronger, her depression lifted, she stopped cutting, and she broke ties with her "Goth crew" of friends. As can be seen from Tanya's situation, when clients can go back in time and say what they have to say to a parent, sibling, relative, former romantic partner, or a friend who had hurt them, they have an opportunity to do things differently by having more personal control and being equipped with a well-thought-out action plan, and this can help them achieve mastery and neutralize the emotional impact of a traumatic event, which can liberate them from the shackles of their painful pasts.

Experiencing Future Selves to Establish New Parent-Young Adult/Adolescent Relationships in the Now

A third way the imaginary time machine can be used is in case situations where the self-harming young adults or adolescents are being defined by the parents and past mental health professionals as being "losers," "kids who don't want to grow up," "stoners," "borderlines," or "bipolar." These young people can either be adolescents who are engaging in self-destructive behaviors, doing poorly in school, and have had possible legal involvement, or young adults labeled "boomerang kids," in that they have attempted to leave home a few times, do poorly away at college, are struggling emotionally to cope away from home, engage in self-destructive behaviors, may have brushes with the law, and, in general, fail in the world. The parents of these young adults and adolescents are often burned out, highly pessimistic, demoralized, resentful, and reaching the ends of their ropes with their kids. For these parents, straightforward types of therapeutic interventions, psychiatric hospitalizations, residential placements, kicking these kids out of the house, or having a revolving door back into their homes, usually leads to further exacerbating their kids' difficulties.

What is wonderful about the future is that it is a gold mine for many possibilities, even with the most entrenched and demoralized families. When we can open up space for family members to envision future realities of positive and more satisfying relationships and family members' successes, this can dramatically alter fixed family beliefs, disrupt long-standing emotionally invalidating family interactions, trigger positive emotion, and boost family members' optimism and hope levels about what is to come. Albert Einstein described it best when he said, "Imagination is everything. It is the preview of life's coming attractions." Having self-harming young adults or adolescents take the imaginary time machine into the distant future, where they have become successful adults and are getting all of the details about how this will greatly improve family relationships and produce other important changes, is a very exciting prospect for all family members involved who have been on a perpetual emotional roller-coaster ride with the clients. The following case example of 20-year-old Stuart and his family illustrates how the imaginary time machine paved the way for rekindling hope for his frustrated and demoralized parents that their son could have a positive future.

> Stuart had been referred to me by his primary care physician for his 5-year episodic pattern of self-harming behavior, which included "punching and burning himself when frustrated and angry." When away at college his freshman year, he was arrested twice by university police for being drunk and disorderly and had ended up in the university hospital after drinking too much at a party. He had flunked out of his first year of college and had to return home. During his adolescent years, he had been psychiatrically hospitalized one time for burning himself, spent 1 year in a residential treatment center, and had seen seven therapists before coming to see me with his parents. In addition to the parents' concerns about Stuart's self-harming behavior and binge-drinking, they wanted him to get a job and maintain it as long as he was living at home. On the upside of things, Stuart's key intelligence strength area was *logical-mathematical,* which was reflected by his precol-

lege 'A' grades in math, chemistry, and computer sciences. He had been a champion chess player in high school and created his own computer games. His future goal for himself was to "make a lot of money working for a major computer gaming software company" in their research and design department. Although he rarely talked about his future aspirations with his parents, the dominant story coauthored by his parents and former therapists who had given up on him was that he would "never amount to anything," that he was "a borderline," and he was "a resistant patient." The parents constantly compared Stuart to his highly successful sister who had gone to a top Ivy League school and had landed an upper-level-management position working for a major corporation on the East Coast. In our second family session, I introduced the idea of Stuart hopping into my imaginary time machine and taking it into the future where he was now 30 years old, had a great job working for a major computer software company, had his own apartment, and was quite satisfied with his life. Stuart smiled while filling in the details of this future context of success for him. I then asked him to imagine having Sunday night dinner at his parents' house as the new, highly successful Stuart and how they will be talking to him and treating him differently. Stuart said his mother would "hug and kiss me and tell me how proud she was of me." He claimed his father would ask him to "go to a Sox baseball game" with him and he would inquire with him about "the different projects I was working on at my job." In response to this future scenario of success, the parents were smiling and "pleased to hear" that Stuart "really wants to succeed" and "make something out of his life." After introducing the idea that if we pretended the future was now, Stuart was asked what his first step is going to be to make this career goal happen for him. Stuart reparted that he will enroll at a local community college that had special courses in computer gaming, graphic art design, and animation. When asked what his parents could do help support him, Stuart was quick to say, "Stop comparing me to Mary" (his sister) and "Stop telling me I won't amount to anything." The parents were unaware that these hurtful words had fueled his self-harming and binge-drinking difficulties. I taught Stuart mindfulness meditation and disputation skills to help him better manage his negative thoughts and moods, not self-harm, and stop abusing alcohol.

Family therapy sessions were continued to help resolve past and present family conflicts and further improve the family communications. Stuart continued working toward getting a college degree and was able to sell one of his computer games to a software company, which was interested in talking with him about future job possibilities once he completed his college education. This exciting incentive helped give Stuart the drive and determination to turn his life around. We had individual sessions to help him stay on track and consolidate his gains.

Stuart eventually came to the conclusion that self-harming and binge-drinking were not going to be part of his new life path and he quit both of these self-destructive behaviors.

The Family Adventure Trip

What if frustrated and stuck parents discovered that their self-harming son or daughter had great leadership abilities and possessed other strengths that they never knew about? Can family relationships change in a context of adventure and surprise? The answer to these questions lies in the power of the family adventure trip use of the imaginary time machine. Similar to the families like Stuart's who have been through the mill with having their self-harming kids in different treatment programs and to many therapists, life becomes doom and gloom and any semblance of family members playing and having fun together totally disappears. The whole parental focus is on the self-harming client's negative behaviors and what crisis is going to happen next.

To help inject some adventure, surprise, and playfulness into these families' lives, I have my self-harming young adult or adolescent clients hop into the time machine with their families and take them anywhere in time and in the world on an adventure trip where they will be the fearless leaders. I ask the clients the following questions when setting up the family adventure trip context:

- "Where in time and in the world would you really like to go on a family adventure trip?"
- "As the fearless leader, what other strengths will your parents and brother come to know that you have on this adventure trip?"
- "In what ways will you show your leadership skills in action?"
- "How will you help your mother be less anxious on that African safari?"
- "How will you help your father chill out when you are in that shark cage in the Great Barrier Reef?"
- "Do you think your bravery and courage will be enough to inspire your younger brother to keep trying to reach the summit of Mount Everest?"

Mary Jane, 16 years old, had a long history of cutting, bulimia, and engaging in sexually risky behaviors. She was psychiatrically hospitalized three times for her cutting and bulimia. Mary Jane had seen five therapists before me. Her parents were feeling stuck and at a loss for how to help their "out-of-control" daughter. After a difficult 2 years, they had decided to emotionally withdraw from Mary Jane to try to cope. Little did they know that emotional disconnection was the complete opposite of what Mary Jane had desired from them. The parents described a doom-and-gloom atmosphere in their home for the past two years. Mary Jane's key intelligence strength areas were *bodily-kinesthetic*, *interpersonal*, and *visual-spatial*. She was a talented swimmer and dancer. Mary Jane was quite popular and considered one of the "cool kids," which the parents learned from the school social worker who had referred her to me for family therapy. To help inject some adventure, surprise, and playfulness into our family sessions, which had started off being too serious and negative, I introduced the idea of having Mary Jane be her parents' fearless leader and take them anywhere in time and in the world in the imaginary time machine on a family adventure trip. Mary Jane decided to take her parents to the English Channel in the summer of 2009 to cheer her on when she becomes "the first female adolescent in history to swim from England to France." Although her parents were strong swimmers, Mary Jane would want them just to swim the first mile or so with her to provide encouragement and support. I asked the parents what strengths they will come to know about Mary Jane while cheering her on. The father said that she is "courageous and gutsy." The mother added that she can be "goal-driven and persevere when faced with a big challenge." When asked why she had selected swimming the English Channel, Mary Jane shared that she had "thought about doing this one day" and that she "missed those days in the past" when her "parents cheered" her on at her swim meets and "saw the good" in her. The parents were very impressed with Mary Jane's ambitious goal for herself and it gave them hope that she could change. I asked if the parents had noticed any times lately where she displayed her "courageous and gutsy" or "goal-driven and persevering" strengths in action. Both parents were able to identify for the first time examples of Mary Jane showing these strengths with completing some tough school assignments and with a recent modern dance performance. The parents were encouraged to change the family atmosphere and carefully observe for those times when Mary Jane showed them her key strengths in action and any displays of better choice-making. They were to practice being her cheerleading squad when those sparkling moments would occur.

By redirecting the parents' attention on what Mary Jane was doing right and having them be her cheerleaders, this served to inject more positive emotion into their relationships with her, and in turn, helped her feel more appreciated and loved by her parents. In reflecting back on how her situation used to be prior to having family therapy with me, Mary Jane openly admitted to me that the cutting, bulimia, and "sleeping around" were attempted solutions to comfort herself and "find love outside the home" after her parents had decided to emotionally disconnect from her.

One of the bonuses of this use of the imaginary time machine is that self-harming clients have so much fun imagining their family adventure trips and being in a leadership role that they wish to spearhead such a trip for their families. Although parents may not be able to afford expensive trips to Europe, Africa, the Amazon River, or the Great Barrier Reef off the northeast coast of Australia, to name a few adventure spots, they are often asked by their parents to research more affordable alternative family adventure trips like hiking up or climbing up small to medium-sized mountains, white-water rafting, canoe trips, or long-distance cycling trips.

Since Mary Jane's family used to go camping and canoeing when she was younger, she got her parents to agree to go on a canoe trip with her in Colorado. The parents were most impressed with Mary Jane's leadership skills in planning out all of the details of where they were going to canoe, mapping out their adventurous journey on the river, and finding a nice lodge for them.

Saying "Hello" in Order to Say "Good-Bye" to Lost Parents, Siblings, or Close Relatives

With some of the self-harming clients we will work with, their self-harming and equivalent self-destructive behaviors may have really gotten out of control following the sudden and traumatic loss of a parent, sibling, or close relative. Since many self-harming clients have difficulties with managing their moods and self-soothing, the loss of a family member or extended family member may be emotionally devastating for them. For example, Lewinsohn, Rohde, and Seeley (1996) found that adolescents who had made multiple suicide attempts were under the age of 12 when they had a parent that died. Often self-harming clients never had an opportunity to say good-bye to the family member or relative who died. This situation is even more psychologically complicated for the self-harming clients who have unresolved conflicts with the departed family members or relatives or if they had been abused by these people in some way, and were never able to confront and resolve these issues with the departed perpetrators.

In case situations, where the self-harming clients are grappling with unresolved mourning issues, conflicts, or unfinished business with departed family members or relatives, the imaginary time machine can give them a second chance to go back in time and say whatever they need to these family members or relatives while they are still alive, so they can begin grieving and make peace with their pasts. Most important, this use of the imaginary time machine can be the catalyst for facilitating the mourning process. After time-traveling, clients frequently cry and begin talking about the family members or relatives they lost, sharing personal material that they had never opened up about before with their families. Having parents bring in family photo albums that include pictures of the departed person also can be helpful with the family mourning process.

I also use this imaginary time machine strategy to help young adult and adolescent self-harming clients finish business with former romantic partners and close friends who suddenly broke up with them or closed the door on their relationships with them without any explanation. The clients in these situations never had an opportunity to find out the "why" of the relationship terminations and to express or confront them. Similar to using the imaginary time machine to resolve past conflicts and traumatic events, it can help liberate them from the negative effects of being rejected by past romantic partners and former friends who continue to haunt them today. They can go back into the past with personal control, say what they have to say to people who hurt them, and finally close the door on these relationships.

Taking the Imaginary Time Machine Anywhere in Time

A final way to use the imaginary time machine is to give the young adult or adolescent self-harming clients the freedom to take the imaginary time machine anywhere in time. Some clients take the time machine into the year 3000 and discover alien beings on another planet who taught them interesting and valuable scientific ideas that could greatly benefit us Earthlings. Other clients have gone back in history and hooked up with historical figures that they are having conversations with about their important work, which might spark some helpful ideas that they could try to implement in their families or at school or college. I will instruct both the future alien beings and historic figures to hop into the time machine with the clients and join us in the session as guest consultants. I will ask clients the following questions:

- "What new inventions or new ways of handling parent-teen conflicts would the Zagnot (alien being) introduce to your family that you think would help?"
- "How do you think that invention can improve your relationship with your parents?"
- "What advice would Gandhi have for you and your mother so you can argue less?"
- "So if one of you were to stage a sit-in, the other would stop arguing because you lost your verbal sparring partner. Would we then have peace?"
- "What would Lebron James (Cleveland Cavaliers NBA star) suggest you try doing differently with your mother so you can score more buckets with her?"
- "If Aristotle were sitting behind you in your algebra class, what would he whisper in your ear that you should do?"
- "Let's say Martha Graham asked if she could create a new choreography of your life. What would be the main themes of the dance performance?"
- "What will the stage props and set design look like?"
- "How will you and the dancers be dressed?"
- "What dance moves would be used?"
- "What would be the music?"

Invisible Family Inventions

The *invisible family inventions* therapeutic experiment is particularly effective with self-harming adolescents who are strong in the *visual-spatial* and *logical-mathematical* intelligence strength areas (Selekman, 2005, 2006b). Adolescents strong in these skill areas tend to have very creative, inventive, and curious minds. In setting up this playful and fun therapeutic experiment, adolescents are asked the following questions:

- "If you were to invent a machine or a gadget that would benefit other teens

and families just like you and your family, how would it work?"
- "What would it look like?"
- "What special features would it have?"
- "How, specifically, would it benefit you?"
- "How about your parents?"
- "How about your sister?"
- "How will having and using this machine regularly with your parents improve your relationship with them?"
- "How else can this machine benefit your family?"

Barry, 14 years old, was referred to me by his school social worker because of the burn marks on his arms and suspicions that he was abusing drugs and dealing drugs on school grounds. Prior to seeing me, Barry had been to four other therapists for burning himself and alcohol and marijuana abuse. His parents were quite angry with Barry because his grades were poor, he continued to drink and abuse marijuana, and he violated their rules. According to the parents, they were constantly yelling at and arguing with Barry. Barry was angry at his parents for always being on his "case about everything" and "being compared to his dorko" 12-year-old brother, Peter, who got "straight A's" and attended the same junior high as he did. In our first family session, it was quite obvious that Peter was the favorite son of the parents, by the way they interacted with him and boasted about his academic accomplishments. One thought that popped into my head was that his burning behavior was a metaphor for his feeling burned by his parents' undying positive praise and attention given to Peter. When asked about what he liked about burning himself, he claimed it was the "numbing feeling" he would experience and how it would take his "mind off of" his parents yelling at him. Barry's top strengths were designing Web sites for friends and relatives and graphic art design. He also was a talented cartoonist. When instructed to come up with an invisible family invention that would benefit him and his family, Barry came up with a very interesting machine called "The Anti-Arguing Machine." His machine would have the ability to detect two situations in the arguing cycle to intervene, when one family member seemed to be "picking a fight or button-pushing" and when both parties were rapidly escalating with "swearing and saying mean things" to each other. When the machine would detect these two things happening, it would send off "invisible waves" that would "physically repel" the argument instigator away from the family member he or she was picking on or disrupt the escalation process between two family members by "repelling them apart" and "keeping them apart" until they both "cooled down." The highly creative and humorous machine feature of Barry's invention was that it would produce a "cartoon of caricature drawings" of family members picking fights or having a heated argument with one another so that they could see how "absurd the whole situation is." Not only did Barry's parents find his invention intriguing and very creative, but they also agreed that the "arguing problem had gotten absurd and out of hand." I explored with them the idea of trying to build an Anti-Arguing Machine together and pick a location in the house where most of the family arguments tended to occur. I also recommended that when argument slips did happen, maybe they could be shortened in duration and Barry could create a humorous cartoon, making caricature drawings of the family members involved, so that they could get a good laugh together, make peace, and get back on track. The parents and Barry left the session more hopeful and eager to try out this idea.

In most cases, the adolescents and families who really enjoy doing this experiment spontaneously decide on their own to go home and try to build these machines or gadgets. The great news was that Barry and his family did follow through and to the best of their ability they created an Anti-Arguing Machine that they used as a reminder for catching themselves picking fights with one another and stopping arguments that were getting out of hand. In fact, they placed the Anti-Arguing Machine in their family room where they tended to have most of their arguments. The Anti-Arguing Machine concept seemed to work so well that Barry did not feel the need to make his cartoon drawings because the arguments were so short-lived and of such low-grade intensity that there was no need to make them. As Barry felt more appreciated by his parents and they began to notice and celebrate his strengths and accomplishments, he stopped burning himself and he discontinued his substance abuse as well.

The Famous Guest Consultants Experiment

This family therapeutic experiment can help strengthen families' problem-solving skills and invites them to play together to generate their own unique solutions. The therapist sets the context by asking family members what would happen if they were to put themselves in the minds of their most favorite famous people to harness creative ideas and wisdom from them. What potential solutions would grow out of their mind-expanding experiences for resolving their presenting difficulties? The famous people can be the following: artists, authors, historic figures, philosophers, musicians, politicians, sports stars, TV and movie actresses, actors, popular talk-show hosts and hostesses, celebrity chefs, and well-known and popular book and cartoon characters. Family members are to come up with two or three famous people apiece who they will pretend to put themselves in their minds. After this step is accomplished, family members are to put their heads together and speculate about how each of their famous people may view their problems and how they would go about solving them based on what they know about what they are famous for and their knowledge and skills. Family members often come up with some very creative ideas for improving their situations. Some examples are as follows: One father felt that he was being "too loose and laissez-faire" with setting limits on his daughter, so he thought about the architect Frank Lloyd Wright and beginning to lay down some "Prairie Style" structure for her (more rules and consequences); a 17-year-old self-harming adolescent who was a talented artist was influenced and inspired by the Surrealist art of Salvador Dalí, and thought about his famous painting *The Persistence of Memory*, which features bent and stretched clocks. He felt his "parents were way to rigid with their rules" and "too controlling" with him and needed to "be more flexible and trusting of" him by experimenting with giving him a "later curfew time;" or a mother who highly regarded and put herself in the mind of "the first female Supreme Court Justice Sandra Day O'Connor" who made it clear that the high court's role in our society was to "interpret the law, not to legislate." This mother felt that she was constantly pulled into the middle of breaking up verbal disputes between her self-harming daughter and her husband and was tired of both parties "pulling on" her arms "to legislate for each of their positions, which Sandra Day O'Connor would refuse to do." The mother in this family case situation decided to step out of the middle and stop being the buffer between her husband and her daughter, which forced the two of them to learn how to resolve their conflicts on their own.

One new twist to this therapeutic experiment that I have had success with is having each family member not only think like their chosen famous guest consultants but pretend to act like one or two of them in relationship to other family members. Family members have a lot of fun pretending to be their famous guest consultants and generating creative solutions to their presenting difficulties living in their skin. It also becomes like a game of charades for family members trying to figure out who is acting like whom.

This therapeutic experiment can be used in both individual and group therapy settings. It also is a great creative problem-solving activity to use in peer supervision with colleagues struggling with stuck cases.

Young Adults/Adolescents Mentoring Their Parents

One way to facilitate family connection-building or strengthen weak young adult/adolescent–parent bonds is to place a young adult or adolescent in charge of mentoring 1 or both parents for one week's time. For whatever reason, one or both parents have emotionally disengaged from their young adult or adolescent son or daughter. Sometimes this occurs when parents are frustrated with them or view their son or daughter's intractable self-harming behavior as "manipulative" or a "trump card" they pull as way to control or disempower them. Other parents may be emotionally spent due to severe marital problems, job stress, loss of employment, serious health, mental health, or substance abuse problems, and so forth that have contributed to their emotional disconnection from their self-harming son or daughter. As research indicates, self-harming adolescents in particular want to "grow into" their relationships with their parents, unless the parents are extremely emotionally toxic or unless the threat of some sort of abuse is feared (Selekman & Shulem, 2007).

If the young adult or adolescent self-harming clients voice a strong desire to get closer to one of their emotionally disengaged parents, placing them in charge for 1 week's time as the parents' mentors or teachers can empower them to shine in the hearts and minds of their parents. The young adults or adolescent clients need to take their top skill area and make a commitment to teaching the emotionally disengaged parent in one week's time a beginner's level of competence in their top skill area. The parent and son or daughter make a weekly schedule of training sessions that will be protected and sacred time together. There will be no cell phones, gadgets, or interruptions by the other parent or the siblings during the daily 30 minutes or longer training sessions if they wish to add more time. The other training session rules are that the parents can only be students and not authority figures, they must be respectful listeners, and they must attend all of the scheduled training sessions, unless there are dire emergencies that come up that were beyond their control. If this happens, the parents must make up their missed training sessions. I have had young adult and adolescent self-harming clients teach their parents how to do different types of artwork, cooking, building items out of wood, sewing, playing an instrument, and so forth. Often parents are amazed with how patient, sensitive, and competent their sons and daughters are in their teacher roles. They discover sides to them that either were unnoticed because the main focus had been on their self-harming or other behavioral difficulties, which overshadowed their competencies, or they never knew that their kids possessed such marvelous skills.

Jenna, 16 years old, was referred by a school psychologist for her cutting and depression. She had recently been psychiatrically hospitalized for what school officials thought was suicidal behavior. Jenna had cut herself deeply at school after she had discovered that friends were spreading terrible rumors about her. According to Jenna, she had been cutting on and off for the past three years and the recent cutting episode was to get emotional relief from being hurt by her peers, "not to die." However, wanting to err on the side of cautiousness, school administration strongly recommended to her parents that Jenna be hospitalized. Knowing that Jenna's top intelligence area strength was *visual-spatial,* using art in our work together seemed to be the best way to help Jenna express herself. In addition to building on her strengths and teaching her visualizing movies of success, disputation skills, urge surfing, and mindfulness meditation, she wanted to work on strengthening her relationship with her emotionally disengaged father. Her father was depressed because he had been laid off from a great paying job and was helping out in his family's business, which was a thankless job. Her father agreed that he and his daughter had drifted apart and he was willing to try to change the situation. After I introduced the idea of putting Jenna in charge of being his mentor for 1 week, they both agreed to try it out. Jenna was a talented sculptor and agreed to teach her father how to make recognizable sculptures of animals and people. They came up with a schedule of training sessions for the next week.

In our next session, the father and Jenna came back much more animated and closer as a father and daughter. The father raved about Jenna's "great teaching abilities." Apparently, they had "many laughs together" as the father would "grossly mess up" and struggle mastering the sculpting skill. They both agreed that they needed to find other fun things just the two of them could do together.

Observing-Oneself-Up-High-in-a-Bubble

When working with self-harming young adult and adolescent clients who have difficulties with establishing and maintaining relationships or poorly developed observing ego capacities, the *observing-oneself-high-up-in-a-bubble* experiment can be of great benefit to them (Selekman, 2006b). The self-harming clients are asked for 1 week's time to pretend that a friendly part of them will be carefully watching them high up in a bubble above them with all of their social encounters. This friendly part of them in the bubble will keep track of what they say or do that seems to help them to establish rapport with new acquaintances and sets in motion the building of new relationships. The friendly part of them also will keep track of what they do that triggers ridicule or rejection from others or seems to turn other people off. The clients are given a small pocket notebook to carry around with them to write down what insights they gained from the friendly part of their social encounters that occur each day of the week. This experiment also can be employed in self-harming clients' interactions with family members to gain valuable insight on the affects of their behaviors on them. Often, self-harming clients report that this experiment has helped them to establish and maintain new peer relationships, repair and reestablish old relationships with peers, and step outside and watch themselves better in social encounters and in family interactions. It helps them shift gears with their behavior when necessary to improve the quality of the interactions with friends and family members.

My Favorite Author Re-writes My Story

When working with self-harming clients who are strong in the *linguistic* intelligence area, this expressive writing experiment can tap their reading and writing skills and imagination powers. The young adults or adolescents are first to think about who their most favorite author is. Based on what the clients know about the types of books their favorite authors' like to write, their unique writing style, what it is about the characters in their favorite authors books that have really resonated with them, they are to write the opening pages (5 to 10) of a new book that their favorite authors are writing about them. What is so powerful about this therapeutic experiment is that it helps clients liberate them from their former dominant problem-saturated stories and can open up space for them to pioneer new directions in their lives. Simply by writing about themselves in different roles and people in the new story, it may spark new ways of being in relationship to others or in the world in the here and now. Some clients have found this therapeutic experiment to be so beneficial that they write well beyond the 5–10-page limitation and continue to make new discoveries about themselves and the unlimited possibilities for the kinds of people they can become. Therapists can ask clients the following questions to help guide them with this creative writing experiment:

- "Knowing your favorite author's books and writing style, what new character would he/she create for you?"
- "What special qualities, talents, or interests would your new character have?"
- "Would you be the lead character?"
- "What would the other characters in your new story about you be like?"
- "Would you have a new family or would you keep some of your current family members in your life but change how they are as people?"
- After completing the writing experiment ask the client: "Are there any aspects of your new character or elements/themes from your new story about you that you plan to implement in your current life?"

My Extraordinary Newspaper Headline

This expressive writing experiment also can be used with self-harming clients who are strong in the *linguistic* intelligence area. The clients are to imagine picking up the *Chicago Tribune* newspaper or whatever their major newspaper is in their city or town and reading a big printed headline on the very front pages of their newspapers about something they had accomplished that was big enough to make the news. The clients are given 1 week to write the headline, a few paragraphs describing the accomplishment, and include excerpts from the interview with the reporter who wrote the article. For depressed and traumatized clients who feel like prisoners in their pasts, this expressive writing experiment can provide a strong dosage of positive emotion and raise both their hope and optimism levels about the kinds of future accomplishments and possibilities they would like to make happen for them.

You at Your Best Story

Peterson (2006) has found that this expressive writing experiment can boost client happiness and counter debilitating negative emotions. Research indicates that this expressive writing experiment shows great results with depressed and anxious clients and can help these clients sleep better. The clients are instructed to write a short story (two to four pages) about some sparkling moment from their past where they had accomplished something that they were very proud of. It could be a stellar athletic, drama, or musical performance or helping someone in need, such as a fellow student being harassed or bullied, a homeless person, an elderly person, or doing something kind for a neighbor. The clients are free to choose what they write about. After writing the story, the clients are to bring it in to the next session and read it to their therapist. Every night before the clients go to bed, they are to read the story, which ends the day on a positive note and can help them sleep better.

I have added another component to this expressive writing experiment. After completing the story, the clients are to underline with blue ink their *agency thinking*, that is, how they got fired up or which friends or family members got behind them to make this accomplishment happen. With red ink, the clients are to underline their *pathway thinking*, that is, the steps that they took to achieve their accomplishment or goal (McDermott & Snyder, 1999). The added bonus of eliciting this important information from the clients is that we can extract the best of what worked in the past to use in the clients' present goal area. This can include useful self-talk, which faithful cheerleaders (close friends and family members) they can count on to support their efforts to achieve their goals, and certain behavioral actions that succeeded in the past and can be tapped in the goal-attainment process.

Three Good Things

Many self-harming clients adopt a tunnel-vision way of viewing negative life events that happen to them. They also tend to have catastrophic thinking and what is going wrong in their lives. To help broaden their perspectives and adopt a wide-angle-lens viewing of them in the world, I will prescribe to them *the three good things* therapeutic experiment (Peterson, 2006). On a daily basis, self-harming clients are to keep track of three good things that happen over a 2-week period. At the end of each day, the clients are to write down in a journal or logbook all of the details about each good thing that happened to them, by responding to the following questions:

- "What was the good thing?"
- "Was this a new good thing, or has it happened to you in the past, but not in a while?"
- "Who was involved with the good thing happening?"
- "How did you personally contribute to the good thing happening?"
- "When the good thing happened, how did it make you feel?"
- "How has this good thing made a difference in how you view yourself and your situation?"
- "Has this good thing made a difference in your life?"
- "What will you need to do or who will you need to involve to make this good thing happen again?"

Refocusing clients' attention on what is going *right* in their lives and increasing their awareness that they are active participants in making these good things happen can decrease depressive and anxiety symptoms, trigger positive emotion, and elevate their expectancy, hope, and optimism levels about having brighter futures ahead (Peterson, 2006). Furthermore, by having these clients do this experiment over 2 weeks, they will begin to see patterns of their own behavior that tend to promote good things happening to and for them. They learn who their social cheerleaders are in their lives, people who both inspire and motivate them, which toxic people or contexts to steer clear from, and what specifically they are already doing individually that works, that is, their special competencies and useful self-talk.

Planning Out Your Perfect Day

Similar to the three-good-things therapeutic experiment, the *planning out your perfect day* experiment can rapidly decrease depressive and anxiety symptoms and increase both positive emotion and happiness levels (Peterson, 2006). The clients are instructed to plan out their perfect day. The clients can ask themselves the following questions:

- "What specifically could I make happen tomorrow that would make me feel great?"
- "Who do I need to associate with during the day that will put me in a great mood?"
- "What else can I accomplish tomorrow that by the end of the day and looking back, I will say to myself, 'I am really proud of you'?"

The clearer the clients' plans are with the details or steps they will take to create a perfect day for themselves, the more likely it is to happen. At the end of each day, not only are clients to record in a journal or logbook all of the details about what made it a perfect day for them, but they are to rate on a scale from 10 to 1, with 10 being the *best day of my life* and 1 being *it was the worst day of my life*. Peterson (2006) has constructed the following rating scale for this therapeutic experiment:

Rating Scale for the "Plan Out Your Perfect Day" Experiment

10 = Best day of my life
9 = Outstanding day
8 = Excellent day
7 = Very good day
6 = It was a good day
5 = It was an average day
4 = It was a subpar day
3 = It was a bad day
2 = It was a terrible day
1 = It was the worst day of my life (pp. 43–44)

As readers can clearly see, it is very difficult for our clients to have bad days when they are rating and carefully planning out their perfect days. Similar to the three-good-things experiment, clients will begin to see important patterns of behavior, ways of thinking and feeling, and socially who they need to increase their involvement with that can produce 6-and-above rated days. Conversely, they can identify certain maladaptive coping strategies, ways of thinking and feeling, and toxic peers and adults who can bring them down to 4-and-below rated days. On a cautionary note, it is important to make our clients aware of the fact that sometimes in our best efforts to make good days happen for ourselves, unexpected things happen to us individually, socially, and in our families that can derail us. These experiences should be viewed as temporary and as opportunities to help us exercise our resiliency and human ability to bounce back and get back on track. This soft prediction of potential dips or temporary derailments that clients may experience while trying to make their perfect days happen will help keep them on their toes, not perceive these unexpected experiences as their fault, and keep in the back of their minds options for constructively managing these challenges.

Using Your Top Signature Strengths in Novel Ways

Once self-harming clients have taken online the Values in-Action-Inventory of Strengths questionnaire, they can begin to experiment with using their top signature strengths in novel ways. This therapeutic experiment, when conducted over 2 weeks' time, decreases depressive symptoms and boosts both positive mood and happiness levels for clients (Peterson, 2006). The experiment also affords clients the opportunity to use their top signature strengths to accomplish the following: expand their knowledge in new and specific interest areas, establish new flow-state activities to immerse themselves in, and use them creatively to resolve difficulties they have been struggling with or to benefit others. In some cases, clients have already met with success using their signature strengths in certain areas of their lives but never thought to experiment with deploying them in contexts where they are still experiencing difficulties. I provide below some specific examples about how clients can use their top signature strengths in novel ways:

Humor
- Make at least one person laugh or smile daily for 1 week.
- Try to be more playful with your parents and siblings for one week.

Curiosity
- Go to the local art museum and discover an artist who paints and draws like you and do further reading on that artist.
- For your upcoming family trip, play explorer and read up on the history of some of the historic sights you will visit so that you can educate your family on what you had learned about the sights before the trip.

Leadership

- Go out of your way to make a new student at your school feel welcomed by you.
- For your science class study group, find some additional library or online resources that you can read and share with your fellow group members to help the five of you put together a solid and interesting science project.

Social Intelligence

- Use your social skills to help a new student who is being harassed by peers learn how to best manage this challenging situation.
- Help a friend who just broke up with his or her boyfriend or girlfriend get back on track with his or her life.

Persistence

- Use the same drive and determination you regularly demonstrate with achieving in school and in sports to resolve your recent conflict with your mother.
- Over the next week at your dance practices, take great pleasure in mastering the steps of the new dance you will learn for your upcoming musical.

Forgiveness

- Think of a good friend who let you down who you have stopped talking to and offer him or her forgiveness.
- Request a meeting with your father, who you have not talked to for a month after your last big argument, and offer him forgiveness.

The Gratitude Letter and Visit

When working with self-harming clients who are strong in the *linguistic* and *intrapersonal* intelligence areas, have been traumatized, are moderately depressed, or feel like prisoners in their pasts, the *gratitude letter and visit* can effectively trigger long-lasting positive emotion for them and greatly reduce depressive symptoms (Selekman, 2005; Seligman, 2002, 2003). The clients are instructed to write letters of gratitude to past mentors or adult inspirational others who had provided them with valuable support, advice, meaningful words of wisdom, and possibly taught them certain skills that have benefited them in positive ways. After the clients write drafts of the letter, these can be brought in to the next session and they can read them and get editorial support and prepare for the visit portion of this therapeutic experiment. When the clients are ready to read the final versions of the letters to their past mentor or adult inspirational others, they are to call them to arrange a date, and read it to them. I have found that more often than not clients find their gratitude visits to be both emotionally uplifting for them as well as for the past mentors or adult inspirational others. In fact, clients have reported experiencing hugs and tears during these gratitude visits. The added bonus for the therapist is that we have learned about a valuable resource person that the clients may agree to have participate in future counseling sessions, in order to build in more support and to tap their wisdom and expertise with the solution construction process.

The Compliment Box

For families in which there is a great deal of negativity, blaming, and low family morale, the compliment box therapeutic experiment can help improve family communications and inject high levels of positive emotion into their family relationships. The families are instructed to get an old shoe box and cut a slit in the top. On a daily basis, family members are to write down on slips of paper things that they appreciate about one another and sign their names on the slips. They can write about what special qualities they like about one another, both recent and past meaningful things they had done that were greatly appreciated and not forgotten, and things that they noticed that other family members had done that they were impressed by or thought was great. Each evening after dinner, the family members are to set aside a minimum of 30 minutes to take turns blindly reaching into the shoe box and reading each other's compliments. I like to have family members bring in to the next family session their most meaningful and special slips to share with me. My only house rule with the compliment box is that every family member gets a compliment, even young children in the family.

Imaginary Feelings X-Ray Machine

Some self-harming clients have grave difficulty identifying their thoughts and feelings and expressing themselves through verbal means. To further complicate matters for these clients, they tend to have more psychosomatic complaints, such as headaches and stomachaches. Other self-harming clients are strong in the *intrapersonal* and *linguistic* intelligence areas and have no difficulty expressing themselves verbally and in writing (journaling). The imaginary feelings X-ray machine experiment can work quite effectively with both of these types of clients (Selekman, 2005, 2006a, 2006b).

In order to do this art therapeutic experiment, there needs to be adequate floor space in one's office. You will need a roll of paper that is comparable to meat-wrapping paper. The paper has to be thick enough that it will not tear or wrinkle easily. Next, the self-harming adolescents are to lie down on the long rolled-out sheet of paper, choose a color crayon, and have a family member draw the outline of their body with the chosen crayon. I have the clients pretend that they have a special X-ray machine that can show us pictures of what their feelings look like inside (Figure 3.3). The clients are to draw what feelings they think they have inside and where in their bodies they think these feelings reside the most. They are to draw scenes from their life depicting these different feelings. For the first time clients may reveal to their fellow family members their emotional turmoil and certain unpleasant feelings connected to past and present painful life events or conflicts. This can elicit family members' empathy and support and open up the lines for communications. Meaningful family dialogue can occur about the identified painful life events and unresolved conflicts, which may be maintaining the clients' emotional distress and self-harming behavior.

Polly, 15 years old, who had just started cutting on her arms and lower neck, was taken to the emergency room by her parents, where she was admitted to an adolescent psychiatric unit for three days. Polly was angry with her parents for institutionalizing her. She hated going for counseling and refused to open up in the company of her parents. Apparently, she had seen three other therapists in the past for bulimia and greatly disliked counseling. She also was angry at her parents for not giving her enough freedom and keeping her from seeing a boy she liked, whom her parents did not approve of because he was a known drug user. To help forge a therapeutic alliance with Polly, I decided to meet alone with her and tap her artistic abilities and use art therapy methods with her. I invited her to make an imaginary feelings X-ray. While lying down on a long sheet of paper, I traced the outline of her body. When I turned the machine on she was to draw pictures of what she thought her feelings looked like, preferably scenes from her life that best captured how they looked. She drew chaotic lines over her stomach, which represented everything she could not stomach or digest going on in her life, such as family and peer conflicts. Flames were burning over her heart, which represented her anger toward both her parents and peers she was upset with. She drew jagged lines in her head region, representing the sharp and painful depressed feelings, and a dark circular object in which the depression was housed. Finally, she drew different colored cut marks on her arms and neck region (see Figure 3.3). Polly courageously agreed to show her parents her powerful feelings X-ray. According to the parents, this was the first time that Polly had opened up to them in a long time about the stressors that were going on in her life and the painful feelings connected to them. Polly was able to more calmly discuss her issues with her parents and was willing to listen to their concerns. Although the parents would not budge on the new boyfriend issue, they did agree to give her more freedom and the opportunity to take responsibility with this new privilege.

My Family Story Mural

Both young adult and adolescent self-harming clients who are strong in the *visual-spatial* intelligence area greatly enjoy doing this art therapeutic experiment (Selekman, 2005, 2006b). On a long sheet of paper, clients are instructed to create a mural of their family story. The sky's the limit in terms of how they want to depict family members in shape, form, facial expressions, postures, arrangement of family members in terms of closeness and distance, how they are dressed, and background design (see Figure 3.4). I have found it useful to have clients do a family story mural drawing in first sessions, midway through the treatment process, and when ending treatment as another measurement of individual and family changes.

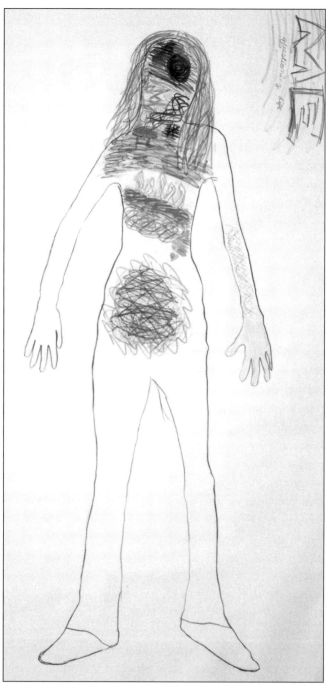

Fig. 3.3

Often, family members' position placements change as improvement occurs, as emotional connections are strengthened, and as conflicts are resolved in family relationships. Similar to the imaginary feelings X-ray machine drawing, the family story murals can be quite revealing about the family dynamics and politics and open the door for families to directly address their conflicts.

Connie, 16 years old, had been referred to me for cutting, depression, and for family conflict. Connie was attending an alternative school for students with behavioral difficulties because of her "cutting problem." She had cut herself a few times at her regular high school and the school administration felt that because of her emotional problems and cutting, she should do better in the alternative school. After being psychiatrically hospitalized, it was very difficult to get Connie to open up with her parents in the same room. Since one of her natural gifts was art and her key intelligence strength area was visual-spatial, I decided to use art therapy experiments with her as a nonthreatening way to open up about stressors in her life and the family conflicts. Connie was bitter about the school administration and her parents agreeing to hospitalize her after a serious cutting episode at school and she was enraged with her friends for spreading bad rumors about her being "a whore." Following her discharge from the hospital, she was on official "lockdown" at home and not allowed out with friends for weeks. Even while on lockdown, her mother would go through her bedroom looking for sharp objects and asking her a few times a day if she had cut herself. While meeting alone with Connie in a family therapy session, I asked her to create a family story mural (see Figure 3.4). Connie created one of the most shocking and powerful family story murals I had seen in a long time. She drew herself as this tiny and gray dead-looking person detached from the family. Her depictions of the parents in the drawing were very accurate in terms of facial expressions and body postures. When asked why she drew herself the way she did, Connie shared that she felt like she had no voice in the fami-

Fig. 3.4

ly, and when she would speak, "no one would ever listen." She went on to say that she could be "a dead corpse and no one would notice." To err on the side of cautiousness, I asked Connie if she had thoughts about or was thinking about taking her life and she said, "No! I don't have the guts to do it." Connie courageously agreed to show her parents her drawing and they were completely shocked by it. They had no idea that Connie felt so small and insignificant. Her mother asked her what they as parents would "need to do to help you be full size, more alive-looking, and standing closer to the family." Connie responded, "You need to listen to me! I want my freedom back!" Both parents agreed to test the waters with Connie and allow her to start going out again. Thanks to the use of the family story mural Connie was not only able to get her freedom back, but it demanded that her parents listen to and respect her needs as a full-size family member.

Drawing Out Oppressive Thoughts, Mood States, and Habits

When working with young adult or adolescent self-harming clients that are strong in the *visual-spatial* intelligence area who report being regularly oppressed by certain thoughts, mood states, or habits, we can externalize these difficulties by having them draw out with crayons, pastels, colored pencils, or markers on construction paper what these oppressive thoughts, mood states, or habits look like to them. Sometimes clients will do a series of drawings that capture a particular mood state or the many sides of a habit. If the clients are musically inclined, you can have them come up with a song title for their drawing. If the clients are feeling ambitious, they can write the lyrics for the song as well.

Katarina, 17 years old, had been cutting herself daily, multiple times a day and more deeply for the past year. She also has had problems with bulimia, depression, and, more recently, having fleeting thoughts of wanting to take her life. At the age of 15, she had overdosed on her antidepressants and drank some vodka with the pills. Katarina had three past psychiatric admissions and numerous outpatient treatment experiences. Her parents were extremely overprotective, particularly her mother. According to Katarina, her mother would drive around and follow her when she walked over to a friend's house in the neighborhood. She also would get called by her mother on her cell phone numerous times once at the friend's house. There were many times in the past where the parents would not allow her to go out on weekend nights. Knowing that Katarina was a highly talented artist, I had asked her draw for me what "depression" looked like to her. Next, I asked her to think of a song title for each of her drawings. Katarina's first drawing captured her sad and tragic-looking facial expression, with messy unbrushed hair, and she had heavy chains wrapped around her body (see Figure 3.5). The chains had a twofold meaning for her: "the depression weighted me down" and "I feel like a prisoner in my family." Her song title for the first

Figs. 3.5, 3.6

drawing was "Tangled Up in Blue." Katarina's second drawing resembled the famous Norwegian artist Edvard Munch's *The Scream*, in that she depicted herself with hands holding her head screaming as if she were going crazy (see Figure 3.6). Her song title for the drawing was "Temporary Insanity." I suspected that there was a family secret that the mother might be harboring that was contributing to her extreme pattern of overprotective parenting behavior. In our third family session, I asked Katarina's mother, "Is there something you told yourself before you came in here for the first session, maybe something unpleasant to talk about, that you were not going to talk about in our meetings together?" After a brief period of silence in the room, the mother tearfully shared that over the past year she had been thinking a lot about her departed sister Sonia, who had been gang-raped and killed at the age of 17. According to the mother, her sister Sonia was a "hell-raiser" and totally disregarded their parents' rules, did drugs, and slept around. The mother vowed that if she ever had a daughter, she would really "clamp down to prevent another disaster from happening." Although Katarina knew that her mother had a sister and she would have had an aunt, she thought her aunt had died from pneumonia. This was the story that Katarina's mother had been telling her since she was a child. At this point, the whole focus in family therapy switched from Katarina's difficulties to this being an unresolved family mourning situation. Future family sessions became rich in storytelling about Sonia and looking at family albums and mourning her loss with the added involvement of the maternal grandmother in our sessions. Katarina was making good use of art, music, mindfulness meditation, urge surfing, and visualization tools to conquer her self-harming, bulimia, and depression difficulties. The best news of all was that Katarina was given much more freedom once the family secret was revealed, the mother began the mourning process, and her catastrophic thinking was stabilized.

Soul Collages

I use soul collages with individual self-harming clients who are strong in the *visual-spatial* intelligence area. The *soul collage* art experiment offers the young adult or adolescent self-harming clients the opportunity to depict to the best of their ability what they think their soul would look like if we could see inside their mind. The first step of this art experiment is to have the clients look into a mirror and draw the shape of their head on a sheet of white tag board. Next, the clients cut out of magazines and newspapers pictures and words that reflect the contents of their soul. They are free to draw on and in the open space areas around the cut out pictures with colored markers, pencils, and crayons. The therapist can ask the following questions to help guide the collage-making process:

- "What does your soul look like?"
- "What objects or images would we see in your soul?"
- "If we saw certain flashing words or messages emanating out of your soul like flashing neon signs, what would they be?"
- "How does your soul shape the person you are?"
- "If you had an opportunity to change your soul, what changes would you make?"

Often, self-harming clients make important discoveries about themselves by doing this art experiment. With some self-harming clients, this art experiment can jumpstart the self-healing process and help purify their souls.

Surrealist Art Solutions: Making the Unreal Real

Many self-harming young adults and adolescents are strong in the *visual-spatial* intelligence area and like to express themselves through art. One expressive art experiment that taps their imaginative powers is the *Surrealist art solutions experiment*. I like to begin this experiment by showing some pictures of some of the most famous paintings by Salvador Dali and René Magritte to my clients to get their creative juices flowing, and to provide them with visual examples of what I would like their art works to resemble. I share with them some background information about the Surrealists and what inspired and guided these artists' thinking and art, such as: symbols and themes from fairy tales, symbols and images from their dreams and forbidden fantasies, the random, the illogical and absurd, humor, and time distortion, as well as themes of wandering without a destination, and the suspension of the laws of nature (Whitfield, 1992; Neret, 1994). In addition, I share with my clients that our dreams are a theater of the "not-yet-said" for us, that is, there are no inhibitions, our forbidden fantasies are expressed, are wishes come true, we can resolve conflicts and difficulties any way we wish, there is a sense of timelessness, our imagination runs wild, and we can live with uncertainty.

To begin the Surrealist art solutions experiment, I have clients identify a current individual, family, or peer relationship difficulty. Next, I ask them if they have had any recent or past dreams or fantasies or absurd or off-the-wall thoughts about these difficulties that have not been expressed. Using paint, crayons, or colored pencils and a large sheet of white construction paper, they are to produce a surrealist art work that captures this difficulty visually. If in their dreams or fantasies they have generated potential solutions—no matter how absurd, taboo, or off-the-wall they may be—they are to incorporate this into their paintings or drawings. Some clients may want a week to reflect on this experiment and keep track of and write down the themes from their dreams related to their difficulties. I will request that they try and complete their artwork over the week and bring it to the next session.

Once the client completes the Surrealist art solutions experiment, I will ask him or her the following questions:

- "What was your inspiration for your painting or drawing?"
- "What are the main themes of your painting or drawing?"
- "What do the symbols or objects in your painting or drawing mean to you?"
- "In looking at and reflecting on your art work, did it spark in your mind any new views about or potential solutions for the difficulty you selected to paint or draw about?"
- "If Dali and Magritte joined us in our session and were looking at your painting or drawing, what do you think they would be most intrigued by in your art product?"
- "Knowing what you know about Dali and Magritte's art work, why do you suppose they were so struck by _____ in your painting or drawing?"
- "What interpretations or useful ideas would they come up with for you based on seeing your art product and learning more about the inner workings of your mind that you think will help you to resolve your difficulty?"

Not only do self-harming clients enjoy doing this fun expressive art experiment, but it also sparks some creative and potential steps toward resolving their difficulties.

Nadia, a 15-year-old struggling with episodic bouts of cutting, weight gain, and family conflicts, had difficulty opening up in our family therapy sessions.

Knowing that one of her natural gifts was art, I decided to see her alone for a session and offer her the *Surrealist art solutions experiment.* Nadia produced an interesting art product. She drew herself as a purple elephant in a bowl of fruit to depict that everything in her life is supposed to be "peachy." When asked what she meant by the word "peachy," Nadia shared with me that she did not want her parents to worry about her and she wanted to "put up a good front" or the illusion to them and her peers that everything was fine with her. Apparently, her father had won the purple elephant at a carnival and had given it to Nadia as "a gift to hug" when ever she was upset about something. However, whenever she needed needed a real hug or emotional validation from her father, she rarely received it. Instead, he would only focus on her poor grades, weight gain, and negative behaviors. The last interesting aspect of Nadia's art product was a shower head that was "spraying and drowning" her with a "lot of water pressure," which represented the many problems in her life, such as: "fitting in with peers, academic performance, weight issues and societal views about this, and family problems." After completing her interesting drawing, Nadia courageously showed it to and discussed it with her mother. The mother and I had learned from Nadia that the symbols and themes in her drawing were part of a reoccurring dream she had been having. Nadia's mother had no idea how overwhelmed Nadia was feeling about the multiple stressors in her life that were plaguing her. She offered to provide Nadia with more support with each of these stressors and to help her to better cope with her "difficult father." The father was reluctant to participate in family therapy, despite several attempts by me to try and engage him.

A Cautionary Note About Responding to Self-Harming Clients' Artwork

Once clients complete their art products, therapists need to avoid at all costs making any interpretations or privileging their thoughts about the meaning of the symbols and objects in their drawings or collages. Instead, therapists need to use curiosity and ask open-ended questions of the clients to learn about the meaning of the symbols and objects in their drawings or collages. Before asking the clients questions, the therapist should invite family members to be the first to ask questions and reflect on their drawing or collage. The more questions asked and different ideas exchanged, the more new meanings can be generated from the clients' artwork.

The Secret Surprise

The *secret surprise* experiment (O'Hanlon & Weiner-Davis, 1989; Selekman, 2005) is particularly useful with clinical situations where there have been some client self-generated pretreatment changes and the parents have observed times where their self-harming sons or daughters are coping better and making good choices. In setting up this playful experiment, I meet alone with the self-harming clients and have them come up with two secret surprises (one for each parent) that they can pull over the next week. The surprises have to be actions that the parents will notice and really appreciate. The clients are not allowed to tell the parents what the surprises are; they will have to figure them out. After reconvening the parents for the editorial portion of the session, the therapist is to share with the parents that over the next week there will be some positive surprises their sons or daughters will be making happen and they will not tell them what they are; the parents will have to play Sherlock Holmes and Miss Marple and try to figure them out. In the next session, the family is to compare notes to see if the parents should become private detectives. This upbeat and fun therapeutic experiment often triggers positive emotion for all family members and helps strengthen their relationships.

I have used the secret surprise with couples; however; I have each partner simultaneously pulling the surprises and both partners have to figure out each other's surprises. In school settings, in an effort to improve teacher-student relationships, I have had the students (my clients) pull the positive surprises in class (not clowning around, not disrupting the class, and other surprises like turning in overdue assignments, talking to the teachers in a respectful way) and the teachers are to try to figure out what their surprises were. This therapeutic experiment can alter the teachers' negative mind-sets about the clients "always having an attitude problem" in their class.

Do Something Different

This therapeutic experiment is particularly useful with parents who are stuck doing more of the same with their young adult or adolescent self-harming sons or daughters, such as: "My way or the highway!"; the more super-responsible they are, the more super-irresponsible the sons or daughters are; incessant nagging and yelling, lectures, threats, kicking the young adults out of the house and taking them back no matter what; rescuing them from having to accept consequences for their negative behaviors; and trying to buy quiet through gift-giving. For these parents, it has become like a broken record; they are way too predictable. As a powerful way to help them to get unstuck, I will introduce the *do something different* experiment (de Shazer, 1988, 1991; Selekman, 2005; 2006b). I share with the parents the following:

> "In your best and most loving efforts the two of you have tried to change your son or daughter's upsetting behaviors However, your responses have become so familar and predictable that rather than getting the kind of results you are looking for, you are inadvertently further exacerbating these behaviors. So as an experiment over the next week, whenever your son or daughter pushes your buttons or you are tempted to try to rescue him or her or be too super-responsible for your son or daughter, I want you to experiment with doing something different than your typical responses. Your responses can be off the wall, humorous, surprising, as

long as they are totally different from anything your son or daughter has ever experienced from the two of you before."

Parents often have a lot of fun with this playful therapeutic experiment. They have done strange or outdated dances, started singing out of the blue, acted and dressed in bizarre ways, and performed well enough to earn Academy Awards. Parents also find that their reflective skills are enhanced by this experiment. Rather than being highly reactive to their self-harming sons' or daughters' upsetting behaviors, they can step back, size up the situation, and think about their options in the way of the best parental responses for the given situation. Parents are empowered, feel more in control, and begin to enjoy their roles more.

Similar to the secret surprise experiment, I will use this change strategy to improve teacher-student relationships. I will have the teachers experiment with doing things differently in relationship to the students (the clients). The self-harming clients can be instructed to use this experiment when they have voiced a desire to change a relationship with one of their parents or a sibling. They become the agents of change for their family. I also use this experiment in my *Stress-Busters' Leadership Group* (see Chapter 6).

> Sally Ann, 12 years old, would threaten to cut herself if her maternal grandmother would not give her what she wanted when she wanted it. She also was engaging in sexually risky behavior and contracted the HPV virus and other sexually transmitted diseases. Both of Sally Ann's parents had longstanding substance abuse, mental health, and legal issues. The maternal grandmother had been granted custody of Sally Ann because of her parents' past abuse allegations. When living with her parents there were no limits or structure provided for Sally Ann. The grandmother had tried everything from being nurturing and flexible to lecturing, yelling, trying to reason with her, and grounding her, but none of these attempted solutions seemed to curtail Sally Ann's provocative and cutting behaviors. The grandmother was at her wit's end and ready to try anything. I gave the grandmother the do-something-different experiment to try out. In our next family session, the grandmother reported that she had come up with some very off-the-wall responses and other new actions that truly confused Sally Ann and led to a dramatic shift in her behaviors. The grandmother bought some "goth-looking clothes, black torn fishnet stockings, black lipstick, and put on heavy black eye shadow makeup." When Sally Ann came home from school and saw her, "she freaked out!" While in shock, the grandmother asked Sally Ann to teach her some of "the dances she liked to do." Next, she asked Sally Ann if she would take her out "clubbing." The most provocative and off-the-wall tactic the grandmother tried was when Sally Ann would threaten to cut herself, she would invite her into the kitchen and "lay out a variety of knives on the kitchen counter and demonstrate the way each one cut into vegetables."

Again, Sally Ann was very confused by her grandmother's new response to her threats and had asked her a few times if she was okay. In fact, three times she got Sally Ann to cut and chop up vegetables so they could make stir-fry dishes together. According to the grandmother, "Sally Ann loved my stir-fries." Not only did the grandmother gain Sally Ann's respect and trust, but she discovered that she was "pretty cool" as well. The grandmother felt much "more in the driver's seat" in better managing Sally Ann's behaviors and Sally Ann was able to eliminate the cutting problem.

Pretend The Miracle Happened

In clinical situations where neither the parents nor their self-harming sons or daughters can identify any self-generated pretreatment changes or past successes at resolving difficulties, the *pretend the miracle happened* experiment can be useful (de Shazer, 1991; Selekman, 2005). I have done this with both clients and their parents. While meeting alone with the self-harming clients, I get them fired up to do this experiment by asking them to "imagine really blowing" their "parents' minds" over the next week. The clients are instructed to pick a few days over the next week to pretend to engage in the most important miracle behaviors the parents want to see them engage in that they had identified earlier in the session during the miracle inquiry. While pretending, the clients are to notice how they respond to them. Often clients are delighted with how effective this experiment can be at changing the way their parents interact with them. Sometimes I will reverse this experiment and have the parents pretend to engage in their sons' or daughters' miracle behaviors they would like to see from them and notice how they respond to them while they are pretending. I have parents do this experiment in my *Solution-Oriented Parenting Group* (see Chapter 6).

Looking Back/Looking Forward

The *looking back/looking forward* therapeutic experiment (Connors, Donovan, & DiClemente, 2001) is particularly useful for helping self-harming clients see how life may have been quite different when they were rarely or not self-harming at all in the past and some of the major costs of engaging in this behavior for them now. The clients can be asked to respond to the following questions:

- "Do you remember a time in the past where everything was going well for you?"
- "What has changed?"
- "What was your life like before you started 'cutting' and 'getting stoned'?"
- "What were you like back then?"
- "What was the difference between the you of 5 years ago (first started 'cutting' and 'getting stoned on drugs') and the you of today?"
- "In what ways have 'cutting' and 'getting stoned' stopped you from moving forward with your life?"

Next, the clients are to try to imagine a changed future once they reduce or eliminate their "cutting" or "getting stoned." The following questions can be asked:

- "What are your hopes for the future?"
- "Ideally, how would you like things to turn out for you?"
- "If you are feeling frustrated now in your life, how would you like things to be different?"
- "What are the options or choices for you now?"
- "What will be the best results you could ever imagine when you make a change?"

These new future images of themselves may be quite appealing to them and pave the way for reducing or possibly stopping their cutting and drug use.

My Documentary About Me

When working with self-harming young adults and adolescents who are strong in the *visual-spatial*, *bodily-kinesthetic*, and *intra-personal* intelligence areas who like photography and seeing films, they will be great candidates for making *my documentary about me*. In planning out how they are going to begin making their documentaries, clients need to first decide which most important life events they wish to include in their movies. They can show photos, conduct interviews with key people from their family stories, and visit and film significant past places they used to live or visited that were most meaningful to them. In addition, they need to think about important life themes, the musical score for their films, and any special sets or props they would like to make and include in their documentaries. Once they have completed their documentary, the clients are to bring in a DVD or videotape version of their documentary, which can be $1\frac{1}{2}$ to 2 hours in length for a screening and interview with their therapist and their family. Family members can be free to ask them any questions about the clients' documentary and share anything new that they learned about them from seeing the film. The therapist also needs to hear from the clients what they learned about themselves or their family story from this rewarding and meaningful experience. This therapeutic experiment is particularly important for clients who are trying to make sense of their personal stories. Hauser, Allen, and Golden (2006) found in their research with at-risk psychiatrically hospitalized adolescents that *narrative coherence* can serve as an important resiliency protective factor.

Choreographing a New Life

With self-harming clients who are strong in the *bodily-kinesthetic* intelligence area and are passionate about dancing, they will enjoy doing the *choreographing a new life* therapeutic experiment. The clients are instructed to choreograph two dance pieces, one that reflects their current situation and a second dance that captures them liberated and free from their past difficulties. They can choose if the first dance will be about self-harming, some equivalent self-destructive behavior, or some other difficulty in their life. The second dance will reflect their freedom from self-harming or some other difficulties in their life and how life has changed for them. Once the clients have created both dances, they can either be filmed and shown in the next therapy session or performed live in front of family, relatives, and/or friends.

Before the clients begin creating their dance pieces, therapists can ask the following questions to help guide the process:

- "In best capturing your current situation, what themes or story lines would you want reflected in your first dance piece?"
- "What style of dance would you use, jazz, hip-hop, ballet, or some other type of modern dance?"
- "What type of costume would you wear?"
- "What type of music will you play?"
- "Would you create a special type of set and have props?"
- "Would you involve a friend or do this solo?"
- "What will be the main themes or story lines in your second dance about your changed life?"
- "How will your dance style, music, and costume be different?"
- "What changes would you make with the set and props?"

After viewing the film of the client's dance pieces or watching a live performance, family members, relatives, and invited friends are free to reflect on the experience and ask questions. The therapist can explore with the clients if they learned anything new about themselves from being choreographer of their own life. Furthermore, the therapist can find out what new dance steps the clients plan to begin using in current areas of their life where they may still be experiencing difficulties.

Working with Disconnected Families

Disconnected families can be extremely challenging to work with. In addition to the self-harming adolescent's difficulties, the parents may have severe marital problems, and mental health and/or substance abuse difficulties. The other siblings may have emotional or behavioral difficulties as well. Because everyone else in the family is struggling with their own individual and relationship difficulties, the emotional connections are weak and changing one part of the family system often does not promote change in the other parts of the system, particularly with the self-harming adolescent. Many therapists make the mistake of working with the whole family group, thinking that this will eventually lead to the self-harming adolescents changing. When this is attempted, it often leads to the therapist feeling stuck, frustrated, or overwhelmed because it is a Herculean task to change the self-harming adolescents in a family therapy context in which all other family members' difficulties will overshadow their unique needs and the lack of support will only serve to maintain their self-harming behavior.

With disconnected families I have found it to be most advantageous to work with subsystems and individuals separately and establish separate treatment goals and therapeutic work projects. Thus, the change process will occur from multiple pathways simultaneously. Once improvement occurs with individual family members and in family relationships, conjoint family therapy sessions can be reinstated. The therapist can directly facilitate connection-building with the self-harming adolescents and their parents once their marital, mental health or substance abuse difficulties are resolved and they are more emotionally available to their sons or daughters.

In case situations where the parents' severe marital or postdivorce conflicts are extreme, one or both parents have serious mental health or substance abuse problems, and family interactions are highly destructive when all family members are in the same room together, I will use a *one-person collaborative strengths-based brief family therapy* approach with the self-harming adolescents. The self-harming adolescents can choose which family relationship they wish to change and they will serve as the agent for change. We will map out on a flip chart or legal pad a problem-maintaining pattern of interaction they wish to change in the designated family relationship. Role-plays and role-taking (the adolescents put themselves in the shoes of other family members to try to experience how they experience the clients) are used to behaviorally rehearse implementing change strategies and scenarios. The therapists can offer the clients a variety of therapeutic experiments for them to test out with the designated family member or relationship they wish to change. As Szapocznik and colleagues have demonstrated through their treatment outcome research over the past 20 years, it is possible to change an entire family system with one family member (Szapocznik, Hervis, & Schwartz, 2003; Szapocznik & Kurtines, 1989; Szapocznik & Williams, 2000).

Staying the Course or Shifting Gears: Guidelines for Second and Subsequent Family Sessions

In second and subsequent family sessions, we need to first elicit detailed feedback from family members on the steps they have taken toward goal attainment in their target goal areas. The therapist can ask: "So what's better since I saw you last?" or "So, what further progress have you made?" If the family reports a wealth of changes, the therapist needs to amplify and consolidate all of their gains, check in on the scaled target goal areas to assess where they rate themselves now with goal attainment and any further changes they had made that had not been mentioned earlier in the session, and encourage them to both increase their identified solution-maintaining patterns and continue to use whatever therapeutic experiments seemed to be most helpful to them. It is critical to cover the back door with the family and see if there are any concerns that they wish to share or anything else that needs to be resolved that had not been discussed earlier in the session. Asking questions like: "Is there anything that any of you are concerned about that if left unaddressed, could come back to haunt us later?" or "What would you have to do to go backward at this point?" or "Let's say you have a slip over the next week. What steps could each of you take to prevent a major backslide from happening?" The family also can be offered a mini-vacation from counseling as a vote of confidence to them for their great work. They can choose between 2 or 3 weeks. I refer to this category of clients as the *better* group.

The *mixed opinion* family will come in reporting some progress but will be eager to talk about the big argument or the slip they had on Thursday. In a respectful way, the therapist first needs to acknowledge the family's concerns about the big argument or slip and encourage them to share with the therapist what was going well on the other days of the week. Making this therapeutic move helps neutralize the idea that these events were catastrophic and decrease the strong negative emotion connected to the big argument or the slip, triggering positive emotion and raising family members' hope levels. After amplifying and consolidating the gains family members did make and checking in on their target goal area progress, we can revisit with the family if there are any leftover concerns about the big argument or slip. We also need to assess with the family if they found the offered therapeutic experiments helpful or if they would like to try something new. If the latter, the therapist needs to come up with a better-fitting experiment or two that might have a better shot of helping the family make further progress in their target goal areas. For example, if difficulties tend to occur on a random basis, the therapist needs to offer experiments that take this into account or are to be conducted on a random basis. We need to cooperate with the unique cooperative response patterns of each family member.

If the family comes back in the second or subsequent session reporting that nothing has changed with their situation, nor can they identify times or certain contexts or relationships that have improved even a little bit, the therapist can ask coping questions (de Shazer et al., 2007; Selekman, 2005, 2006b) to see if the parents or self-harming young adults or adolescents can explain what specifically they are doing to prevent their situation from getting much worse. This may produce some specific parenting or coping strategies that are preventing their situations from really escalating. These can be amplified and consolidated and the parents and the client should be encouraged to increase doing more of what works. If they continue to be pessimistic, then the therapist should use the pessimistic sequence (Berg & Miller, 1992; Selekman, 2005, 2006a) to find out what is preventing the parents from throwing in the towel with family counseling, institutionalizing their son or daughter, or kicking him or her (young adult) out of the home. Similar to the positive results that the coping questions can produce, pessimistic questions can be the catalyst for dramatic changes in family interactions and open up space for the therapist to facilitate connection-building in the parent–young adult/adolescent relationships.

Some *same* category families do not respond well to the above solution-focused therapeutic strategies. In those cases, I will *go back to basics* with clients to see what adjustments need to be made with negotiating a smaller goal, discussing whether the clients wish to negotiate a new goal, or finding out if there are some new environmental stressors that are disrupting the goal-attainment process. There may be a mismatch with the therapeutic experiments initially offered and family members' stages of readiness for change, or the true customer for change may not be present in family sessions. We can determine the true customer for change in the client system by asking the clients the following question: "On a scale from 10 to 1, with 10 being most concerned about you and 1 the least concerned about you and your situation, what numbers would you give absent family members, close relatives, close friends, adult inspirational others, or involved helping professionals from your college/school or other larger systems?" The higher the number on the scale these key resource people from the client's social network are rated will indicate the necessity for their involvement in future family sessions.

Other therapeutic pathways we can pursue with same-category families are tracking problem-maintaining family interactions that may be enabling the self-harming young adults and adolescents to continue engaging in this and other equivalent self-destructive behaviors. This circular-problem-life-support system can be mapped out on a flip chart or legal pad so family members can see how in their best efforts to try to manage the clients' presenting behaviors, they are inadvertently further exacerbating them. Pattern intervention strategies can be used, such as changing the order of involvement, add something new to the context in which the difficulties occur, change the context or times in which the difficulties occur, have the clients pretend to engage in their habitual behaviors, make it an ordeal to engage in any self-destructive behaviors, predict slips, or prescribe the do-something-different experiment (de Shazer, 1988; O'Hanlon, 1987; O'Hanlon & Weiner-Davis, 1989; Selekman, 2005, 2006b).

Another therapeutic pathway that can be pursued is to externalize the problem (White, 1995, 2007). This therapeutic strategy is particularly useful with clients who describe their presenting difficulties as being oppressive and seemingly having a life all of their own. Once the main presenting difficulty is carefully co-constructed, the therapist can use a habit control ritual (Durrant & Coles, 1991; Selekman, 1997) or other narrative therapy rituals (Epston, 1998; Freeman et al., 1997) to empower the family to break loose from the clutches of the problem and be liberated to pioneer a new direction with their lives. I like to have family members regularly work out together and have strategizing meetings to strengthen their team skills and to be as physically and mentally fit as possible in order to outtrick and eventually conquer the problem. The habit control ritual can be implemented at school, as well, if the problem is wreaking havoc there.

In some cases, the therapist has not offered the self-harming clients enough therapeutic tools and strategies for adequately managing their unpleasant negative moods and powerful self-defeating thoughts, which can continue to fuel self-harming and equivalent self-destructive behaviors. If this proves to be the case, the therapist will need to offer new therapeutic tools and strategies that might do a better job at helping the clients quiet their mind, be less reactive to their negative moods, and successfully challenge and disrupt the self-defeating thought patterns. Finally, it may be useful to revisit the family's blueprint for change plan to see if we need to make any adjustments with the target goal areas or with any other aspects of the original plan.

With families that fit into the *worse* category, we can begin with using pessimistic questions to see if this opens the door for producing a small change. If pattern intervention strategies or a narrative approach has not been tried, these two therapeutic strategies are viable options. If the family has not responded to either one of these therapeutic approaches, there may be certain constraints or blocks, family secrets, or untold family stories that are contributing to the family's presenting difficulties getting much worse. The use of conversational questions (Andersen, 1997; Anderson, 1991; Goolishian & Anderson, 1988; Selekman, 2005, 2006b) may help uncover family secrets or significant untold chapters in the family's story that had never been shared before that may be blocking the change process and keeping outmoded beliefs intact. Two other therapeutic options with worse-category families are involving a colleague or colleagues to serve as a reflecting team (Andersen, 1991; Friedman, 1995) or using a therapeutic debate team approach (Papp, 1983). With the reflecting team format, colleagues can be in the observing position in the therapy room or behind a one-way mirror and approximately 40 minutes into the hour the team will have a conversation in front of the family introducing ideas that are neither too different nor too unusual from how the family views their difficulties. The team has to be careful not to bombard the family with too many ideas. They are free to probe for the *not yet said* (Anderson, 1997; Goolishian & Anderson, 1988), which may be family secrets. After 6–7 minutes of reflecting, the family is invited to offer their reflections on what the team had to say about their situation. Good team reflections can lead to shifts in meaning and how family members view their situation, which in turn can lead to changes in their family interactions.

The therapeutic debate involves having one colleague take the side of the self-harming young adult or adolescent and one team member taking the side of the parents and conducting a debate in the company of the family about the dilemmas or constraints that are keeping them stuck as a family (Papp, 1983). Family members are free to chime in and add their thoughts or challenge the team debaters' thoughts. This can lead to lively discussions and helping the treatment system get unstuck. I have added a new member to the debate team. I like to have a colleague represent the main presenting problem's position in the family drama to gain a unique-in-the-mind-of-the-problem perspective and have its voice represented in the debate (Selekman, 2006b).

Staying Quit: Family and Individual Goal-Maintenance Strategies and Tools for Covering the Back Door

Goal-maintenance and helping self-harming clients stay on track is a family affair. It is important to educate self-harming clients and their families that slips go with the territory of change. They are reminders that we need to tighten up with the structure and they keep us honest and on our toes. After a slip I share with clients, "We could not have made headway if we did not have a slip." There are five important components to goal maintenance and reducing the likelihood of self-harming clients having slips: *structure-building*; *consolidating questions*; *using peers and key resource people in the social network as a natural relapse prevention support system*; *identify early warning signs*, and *family constructive response scenario planning*.

Structure-Building

I once worked with a middle stage alcoholic woman who said, "Keeping me busy keeps me out of trouble." It was these valuable words that became her daily mantra, which helped her to abstain from alcohol, get a job, be more emotionally present with her children, and regain her co-parenting leadership role again. By filling her free time up with as many healthy, meaningful, and pleasurable activities that she could come up with, she was able to stay quit. *Structure-building* consists of filling up one's leisure time with as many healthy, meaningful, and pleasurable activities as possible. Self-harming clients can fill their free time up by: immersing themselves more in their flow-state activities, doing hobbies, volunteering or performing other good deeds in their communities, exercising and/or playing sports, socializing with positive peers, participating in support groups, and spending as much time as possible in healthy contexts. As part of the structure-building process, I have clients record daily on their My Positive Trigger Logs useful self-talk and self-generated effective coping strategies and positive and supportive responses and contributions from their parents, siblings, friends, and involved helping professionals from larger systems that generate positive emotion and help them to stay on track and not to have slips. When self-harming clients do not have a tight structured plan in place, the likelihood of self-harming slips occurring and/or engaging in equivalent self-destructive behaviors like bulimia, substance abuse, and sexually risky behaviors is greatly increased.

Consolidating Questions

Consolidating questions are designed to help amplify and consolidate clients' gains in their presenting problem and other areas of their lives. They help underscore where clients had been before treatment, the changes they had made happen, and where they hope to be in the future when they have made even further gains for themselves. These questions also increase clients' awareness of their *news of a difference*. One way to elicit clients' news of a difference is to place them in the expert consultant role and invite them to share with you what they would recommend you do with other clients just like them. Another way to help consolidate clients' gains is to externalize their solutions. Some examples of consolidating questions are as follows:

- "So what is better, even a little bit, since the last time we met?"
- "Let's say I had you gaze into my imaginary crystal ball 2 weeks down

the road. What further changes do you see yourselves making?"

- "Is that different for you to do that?"
- "Are you aware of how you pulled that off?"
- "What changes are we seeing you make happen in your relationship with your mother?"
- "What would you have to do to go backward at this point?"
- "How are you viewing yourself differently now as opposed to the former you who was imprisoned by 'cutting'?"
- "Let's say you have a slip over the next week. What steps will each of you take to prevent a major backslide?"
- "Slips are like teachers and offer us valuable wisdom. What did you learn from that slip on Tuesday that you will put to use the next time you are faced with a similar stressful situation?"
- "Let's say 2 weeks into your 3-week vacation from counseling you experience a slip or things start to unravel in your goal areas. In looking back, what would you have wished we had addressed or resolved before you went on vacation that might have prevented that slip from occurring?"
- "Let's say we have an anniversary party 1 year from today to celebrate your staying quit from 'cutting' and 'bulimia' and your family's successes after we stopped family counseling together. What further changes will you be eager to tell me about that you made happen?"
- "What will I be the most surprised to hear about?"
- "What else will you tell me that is going great?"
- "If I were to work with another family that is struggling with the kinds of difficulties you used to have, what advice would you give me to help that family out?"
- Ask the parents: "What would you recommend that I should share with the parents that really worked for you in the parenting department with your daughter?"
- Ask the daughter: "What words of wisdom would you recommend to the daughter in the family that could help her quit 'cutting'?"
- "What should I avoid trying to do or saying to the daughter that might really turn her off or will not work?"
- "It what ways can you call upon 'talking to myself' to help you to stand up to 'cutting' if it tries to seduce you again into 'carving' yourself up when things are not going well with your friends?"
- "With the upcoming party, where you will have to see these friends, how can use 'my mantra' to not allow them to invite 'cutting' to take advantage of you in this vulnerable situation?"
- "Which one of your 'movies of success' can you play in your mind in your bedroom, a movie that is powerful enough to help you not cave in to 'cutting's' wishes to take advantage of you if an argument should erupt with your mother and you are feeling angry and frustrated?"

Using Peers and Key Members from Clients' Social Networks as a Natural Relapse Prevention Support System

Once the self-harming young adults or adolescents identify close and concerned peers and other key resource people from their social network, these individuals can be recruited for helping the clients, their partners and/or families stay on track and reduce the risks of having slips and to further consolidate their gains. The clients can be invited to share with the key members from their social networks what specifically they could do to help them maintain their goals and make further progress. It is helpful for the key members to learn from the clients not only what they have already been doing that the clients have appreciated and found most helpful, but what their negative triggers are that could possibly lead to a slip back into self-harming or equivalent self-destructive behaviors. In some cases, clients have worked out a 24-hour crisis hotline and telephone tree system with actively involved members from their social networks that they can call at anytime of the day if they feel vulnerable and are feeling like self-harming. Knowing that these key resource people are so committed to them and their continued progress is very comforting and provides a solid and healthy safety net for them.

Even if clients have not had one slip for a long period of time and appear quite confident about not going backward, it is critical for them to clearly spell out for the participating members from their social networks what specific steps they need to take to constructively help them to manage slips, should they occur. Clients also should share with the participating members from their social networks what to avoid saying or doing that can make their situations much worse. Knowing the specific details about how best to respond can help clients quickly get back on track, and prolonged relapsing situations can be prevented.

Identifying Early Warning Signs

A critical component of goal maintenance and relapse prevention and for covering the back door with clients once they make process is *identifying early warning signs* of goal-attainment areas starting to unravel, rapid increases in individual family stress levels, and budding crises. In addition to amplifying and consolidating family gains, therapists need to inquire with families in second and subsequent sessions their concerns about maintaining their progress in their target goal areas, having a slip, an increase in old or new individual or family stressors, and potential crises happening. Failing to intervene early enough, not addressing these client concerns, or things unraveling in their target goal areas can result in prolonged and disastrous relapsing situations occurring and can contribute to clients feeling like they are back to square one. Therapists can ask clients the following questions:

- "Is there anything we have not talked about up to this point, that unless we address it soon, it could lead to a major relapsing or crisis situation happening?"

- "Is there anything else going on outside of our target goal areas that any of you are concerned about that could come back later to derail your progress unless we resolve it now?"
- "Up to now you have been making tremendous progress. Is there anything we have not talked about or addressed that, unless taken care of, could present problems for you down the road?"
- "Once this issue is resolved, how will that make a difference with your situation?"
- "How can your family help you to better cope with your breakup with Peter and not slip back into 'cutting' again?"
- Ask a crisis-prone family: "Where will the next crisis happen?"
- "What time of the day?"
- "Who will be involved with it?"
- "What steps will each of you take to diffuse it?"

Family Constructive Response Scenario Planning

Another effective way to cover the back door and help clients to stay on track is to use *family constructive response scenario planning*. This consists of having clients imagine worst-case scenarios happening with their situations once they have made great strides in or have achieved their target goals. After they have identified the worst-case scenarios, the family is to generate sets of constructive, concrete steps each member can take for each of their worst-case scenarios. By fostering family teamwork and sharpening their solution-determined responses in this way, they will be better equipped to manage stressful events that were not expected to happen. If one of their worst-case scenarios should occur, they know the necessary steps to take to constructively manage it.

Case Example: Co-Constructing Change with Solution-Determined System Teamwork

Referral Process

Bonnie, a 17-year-old, was referred to me by her school social worker for her "serious cutting problems," "bulimia," "depression," and "poor grades" in school. In the morning of the referral, she had just made "four deep cuts into her left arm," which had prompted an immediate call to her mother and to me. According to the school social worker, Bonnie had been "increasing her cutting more deeply into her arms over the past month" because of "the emotional pain she feels inside" due to "three painful losses she experienced this past month." When asked about the three losses, the school social worker reported that her "boyfriend of 2 years broke up with her, her maternal grandmother died from a stroke, and the parents divorced" all in the past month. Apparently, Bonnie's boyfriend "dropped her to start dating a popular female student." Bonnie was "very close to her maternal grandmother" and "her stroke was unexpected." After the parents had separated prior to the divorce, the father only had contact with Bonnie's 14-year-old brother, Zack, and there were "no communications with her," which was a "big emotional blow for her." To further complicate the loss situation for Bonnie, she had disclosed to the school social worker that over "the past few months her mother had emotionally distanced from her" as well.

The school social worker had seen Bonnie on and off for the past 2 years for cutting, bulimia, depression, and her poor academic performance. "Bonnie's English and art teachers" also had been providing her with "support over the past school year." Her dean had met with Bonnie a few times as well. She also had infrequent visits to the school nurse's office to look at her cut marks and clean them out. Bonnie had been psychiatrically hospitalized twice in the past for "cutting, depression, and bulimia." She also had "seen three therapists in the past for individual treatment."

Telephone Intake

Linda, Bonnie's mother, contacted me immediately after returning home from taking her daughter to the hospital emergency room. Bonnie had required stitches for two of the deeper cuts on her arm. I inquired with Linda what her theory was why Bonnie was cutting and having such a tough time now. She quickly reeled off all of the losses she was dealing with in a short amount of time. Linda also pointed out how she individually had been depressed as well about the loss of her mother and the divorce situation. She openly admitted that she had not been providing enough emotional support for Bonnie lately. Linda shared with me details about Bonnie's past treatment history. She believed that the past psychiatric hospitalizations and outpatient treatment were due to concerns about her being suicidal and her eating disorder. Linda felt that all of the arguing that went on with her "ex-husband Bob and jealousy Bonnie felt because she thought that he loved our son Zack more than her" contributed to these behaviors. Apparently, Zack was a great athlete and her ex-husband was "a jock." He used to coach Zack's Little League baseball team and they played basketball a lot together.

When asked about who the concerned and key members from their social network were, Linda said that her father and sister had very close relationships with her. She also pointed out that Stella, the school social worker, her dean, the school nurse, and Bonnie's English and art teachers really cared about her as well. I asked Linda if all of these adults could attend our first family therapy session and she granted verbal consent. I also requested that she secure Bonnie's approval to do this as well.

In an effort to identify Bonnie's and the family's self-generated pretreatment changes, I asked her to conduct the experiment of carefully noticing prior to our first family session what specifically she noticed happening in her relationship with Bonnie that she would like to continue to have happen, what Bonnie was doing to help herself, as well as things she was doing to promote these positive behaviors. Furthermore, she was to keep track of other things she was doing to prevent Bonnie's situation from getting much worse. Linda was asked to write her observations down and bring her list to the first family session.

The First Family-Solution-Determined System Collaborative Meeting

Four days later, we were able to schedule the first family-solution-determined system consultation meeting in my office at a time when all of the involved school personnel and relatives could attend. Unfortunately, the school nurse could not attend because she needed to remain on school grounds. After establishing rapport with all of the participants, I began the meeting by asking Linda and Bonnie to read off their list of self-generated pretreatment change discoveries. Bonnie pointed out that her mother had been "really supportive lately" and "more understanding" with how "sad" she felt about "everything that has happened" to her. When asked if these were new behaviors with her mother, she mentioned that since her "father had moved out" of their house she has "not been emotionally there" for her. Linda openly admitted that she had been "depressed" and apologized for "not being there" for her over the past months. She made a commitment to fix this problem and provide more support. Bonnie gave her mother positive feedback that she noticed that she was really trying to remedy this situation. Linda smiled and reported a recent sparkling moment with Bonnie prior to our meeting. Cindy, one of her close friends, had "let her down after they had made plans to get together." Rather than going to her bedroom to "cut herself" or "bingeing and making herself throw up," she approached Linda to tell her how upset she was about "getting blown off." According to Linda, this was a "big change" for Bonnie. I responded with, "Wow! Are you aware of how you did that?!" Bonnie pointed out that she felt more comfortable going to her mother and thought she "would listen." The school personnel, maternal grandfather, and maternal aunt chimed in with praise for Bonnie. All of the school personnel and the relatives shared with Bonnie that she should feel free to go to them for additional support if she needed it. The school social worker and English and art teachers shared with the group that they had noticed that Bonnie already had been seeking out their support more lately as well.

Although the dean was encouraged by Bonnie and her mother's recent gains, he made it quite clear that if Bonnie continued to "cut herself on school grounds" that he would not have any recourse but to have her see "the district psychiatrist and recommend a psychiatric hospitalization due to school policy." The dean contended that he was already "bending the school policy by not enforcing the school district policy" regarding this behavior and he also was worried about a "student-cutting-contagion effect happening" as a result of "Bonnie's getting away with" this behavior. He acknowledged and was pleased that Bonnie was taking steps to help herself by seeking out the school personnel participating in the meeting for support but made it clear that there cannot be another cutting incident at school. I shared with Bonnie that she was "very lucky that she had not been hospitalized by now." I pointed out that "I have seen many teens over the years who got busted at school for cutting and ended up being psychiatrically hospitalized." Bonnie shared with the group that she was not going to cut again at school.

In thinking how it might be helpful for all members of the collaborative meeting to learn about Bonnie's self-harming story, I invited her to share with the group how the cutting has been helpful to her and what some of the triggers are that lead her to engage in this behavior. Bonnie shared with the group how emotionally devastating the loss of her maternal grandmother and her boyfriend were for her. She further added that she was deeply hurt by her father's "checking out of her life" after her parents' divorced. Bonnie pointed out to the group that her brother, Zack, "has always been Dad's favorite child." According to Bonnie, cutting helped her to "fight off sad feelings" and "stop bad thoughts" like: "I feel like my dad loves Zack more than me," "I can't count on my friends," and in the past, "I can't count on Mom." Linda shared with Bonnie both that she will now be able to count on her "for support" and that she really does believe that her "father loves" her. Bonnie also shared with the group that sometimes she gets so "mad and frustrated" with her life situation that she punishes herself by "cutting deeply" into her skin tissue. When asked if she has ever had thoughts of taking her life, Bonnie made it quite clear that she would never do that to her parents and she has never felt that way. Again, the members of the collaborative meeting shared with Bonnie that she could count on them for support when she needed it. In response to the participants' comments, I asked Bonnie to try to share with some of them what they have done so far that she has appreciated and found helpful. Bonnie shared that Stella the school social worker was "a good listener," was "very caring," and "taught me some helpful tools to not cut." When asked about what specific tools she found most helpful, Bonnie said that Stella had taught her how to "challenge my thoughts" when they were "trying to make me cut myself." Bonnie shared two examples of how this worked. She reported that both the English and art teachers were "good listeners" and "very understanding." Bonnie reported that her grandfather and aunt often were "supportive and kind" to her and that she greatly appreciated her relationships with them. Her grandfather had tried to help her better cope with the loss of her grandmother through giving her "a lot of support and sharing heartfelt stories" about her that Bonnie had never heard before.

Prior to concluding our initial family-solution-determined system collaborative meeting, Bonnie and Linda thanked everyone for coming and offering all of their support to help them through some "tough times." I also thanked all of the participants for taking the time in their busy schedules to come to the meeting and offer their support. The dean chimed in and shared with Bonnie that he would be "more than happy" to make himself "available to" her if she needed "someone else to talk to at school." I complimented Bonnie and Linda on the "steps they were already taking to keep the lines of communication open, Bonnie's taking talking risks with Linda instead of cutting risks," and I shared how pleased I was to hear about "Linda's allowing Bonnie to grow back into her relationship with her again despite her own individual struggles, which will provide her with a strong sense of security and feeling appreciated by her." The group consensus was that the next meeting should be just with Linda and Bonnie to further strengthen their relationship and for Bonnie to learn tools and strategies for not caving in to cutting herself. The following therapeutic experiments were offered to the family and meeting participants:

1. Bonnie was given the My Positive Trigger Log to fill in daily and bring to the next session.
2. Bonnie was to notice daily the various things she did to overcome the urge to cut herself or binge and purge.
3. Linda and the meeting participants were asked to keep track of further responsible steps they observed Bonnie taking to help herself and what they may be saying or doing that seems to promote these positive behaviors.

When asked about what everyone thought about the meeting, the school participants, grandfather, the aunt, and Linda felt they gained a better understanding about Bonnie's self-harming behavior and how it was directly related to family and peer stress and the recent losses she was struggling to cope with. Again, the family shared how much they appreciated everyone's coming to provide support and commitment to help out in the future.

The Second Family Session

Linda and Bonnie came to our second session in great spirits. Bonnie had gone "a whole week without cutting" herself once! She attributed it to her mother and her talking more, having "girls' nights out going out to eat and shopping," "the My Positive Trigger Log" helping her do more of what made her happy, such as "drawing, hanging out with close friends, taking her dog out for long walks in the park" near their home, and "seeking out support from" her grandfather and aunt, and the school social worker, and English and art teachers when she needed it. Bonnie even drummed up the courage to confront her father "about not being available" to her and wanting to see him. They scheduled a visit. I amplified and consolidated all of Bonnie's and Linda's gains. Linda shared with Bonnie how proud she was of how hard she was working to turn her situation around.

I met alone with Linda to praise her on her great work with Bonnie and address any concerns she may still have. I wanted to alert Linda to the inevitability of future slips that may occur, which may take the form of a big argument or Bonnie's having a cutting or binge-purge episode. I stressed to Linda the importance of not being emotionally reactive but being calm and comforting Bonnie if she should have a slip. We discussed the importance of maintaining an optimistic stance and helping her get back on track. I encouraged her to keep the lines of communication open. When asked about doing some session work on Bonnie's relationship with her father or her brother, she felt "it would be of great help for Bonnie to have a closer relationship with her dad," but it was important to assess her emotional readiness to begin having father-daughter sessions with her.

I met alone with Bonnie to further underscore her great progress and see if she would like to try a session with her father. She clearly was on the border of contemplation and preparation stages of readiness for change when it came to wanting to have a meeting with her father. I introduced to Bonnie the decisional balancing scale so that she could look at the advantages and disadvantages of meeting with her father to resolve their differences. Some of the advantages of doing this work for Bonnie were: "I would be happy about having a better relationship with him" and "Maybe we could start playing tennis alone together again." The disadvantages or fears of trying to improve her relationship with him were: "What if he does not follow through with his promises?" and "What if he continues to favor Zack over me?" I validated her feelings and concerns. I shared with Bonnie that her concerns made a lot of sense. Bonnie courageously agreed to do the meeting with her father.

I checked with Bonnie on how well she was coping with the loss of her grandfather and boyfriend. She shared that although these "losses were initially difficult to cope with," she was "better managing" her "sad feelings" about them.

I discussed the importance of structure-building and to continue to use the My Positive Trigger Log and keep track of new coping strategies she was coming up with to stay on track. As far as the bulimia issue goes, Bonnie confidently shared that she "had not had a binge-purge incident for several weeks" and felt that she had "control over it." I asked Bonnie if for her the bulimia represented her not being able to stomach or digest Zack's closer relationship with her father. Bonnie admitted that their tight relationship has been "very difficult to digest," in that when she was younger she felt she was "closer to" her father. She also connected this problem to why she was fighting daily with Zack. In addition to doing sessions with her father, I asked Bonnie if she would like to resolve her difficulties with her brother as well and she requested to do this after we did at least one session with her father. Bonnie agreed to call her father and invite him to come to our next session. Prior to ending the session, I introduced Bonnie to the visualizing movies of success and the sound meditation distress management tools to use as other helpful coping strategies for staying on track.

The Third Family Session

Bob, Bonnie's father, brought her to our family meeting. After building rapport with Bob and helping him feel warmly welcomed, I stated the purpose of the meeting and how important it was for Bonnie to have a closer relationship with him. On the top of Bonnie's agenda, she wanted to begin by sharing with her father how much she missed the days when she was younger and they would play tennis every Sunday morning and then go out for breakfast. Bob acknowledged that he missed those fun times as well. I asked Bonnie to pretend that I had an imaginary time machine sitting in the corner of the room that she could hop into and take back in time to her most memorable tennis outing with her father. I asked her how old she was at the time, what was most special about this event, how she was playing, and who was winning. She was asked to apply all of her senses to the time-traveling experience, including color and motion. Bonnie had a big smile while describing aloud how she was "on the top of my game" and "running my father ragged on the tennis court with great slice serves, drop shots, and top-spin lobs over his backhand side." Bob was smiling and said that "Bonnie could have given Venus Williams or Maria Sharapova a tough time on that day." He shared that "Bonnie is an excellent tennis player and used to be nationally ranked." This was the first time she had beaten her father in straight sets. Bob shared that he really "took a thrashing from Bonnie on that day." In watching the two of them laugh and relive this positive tennis outing, it was clear that playing tennis together had been a real joy for them in the past. Bob suggested that they play tennis together over the weekend and that he would like to reinstitute this Sunday morning tradition with Bonnie. Bonnie was delighted and "looking forward" to bringing back this fun Sunday morning tradition.

Bob apologized to Bonnie for not making himself more available to her after he moved out. He shared that he was having to do a lot of business travel and was trying to get his "life on track again." Bob also shared that he thought Bonnie was really mad at him about the divorce situation. Bonnie clarified that "the divorce was the right thing to do" because of all of their "arguing and conflicts." She shared that she was more upset about why he would cut off communications with her and "only talk with or see Zack." Bob admitted that this was wrong and said he would try to be more available to her in the future. I predicted that as they got closer, Zack would probably antagonize Bonnie more. Bob pointed out that if Zack starts annoying Bonnie more, she is to let him know and he will deal directly with his son. Bonnie found this to be reassuring.

In closing out the family session, Bob agreed to participate in all future family sessions and to continue to work on improving his relationship with Bonnie. Bob said that he found the session to be very useful and really wants to "see Bonnie happier." Bonnie was delighted with how the session turned out and hugged her father.

The Second Family-Solution-Determined System Collaborative Meeting
Present at our next family-solution-determined system collaborative meeting were Bonnie, Linda, Bob, the grandfather, the aunt, the school social worker, the dean, and both the English and art teachers. When asked about what further progress Bonnie was making, all participants acknowledged that she was doing a great job of communicating with them, there were no reports of cutting incidents at school, her grades were improving, and she appeared to be "happier." Bob reported that he had two really enjoyable tennis outings with Bonnie. Bonnie shared with the group that she was really confident that her relationship would continue to grow stronger with her father.

As predicted, Zack started antagonizing Bonnie more as she was getting closer to their father. However, she let her father know about this and he directly addressed this problem with Zack. Everyone agreed that Zack should be invited to the next regular family session. The English teacher shared that she used to have similar problems with her younger brother after her parents divorced. When asked about how she managed this situation with him, she shared with me and the group that she really wanted to have a better relationship with him and that they were "both in the same boat of wanting more individual time" with their father. Somehow her brother "could see the light" and how they needed to "support each other" with missing their father. Bonnie thought she would try out this strategy.

The next family-solution-determined system collaborative meeting was scheduled for 3 months down the road, with the understanding that if there were any concerns by any of the participants, they would communicate with one another by telephone. The group consensus was that Bonnie had made incredible progress and they were feeling less alarmed about her cutting difficulties.

The Fourth Family Session

Both parents attended the family session with Bonnie and Zack. The parents and Bonnie happily reported that there were "no cutting or binge-purge episodes" between sessions. Bob brought up the sibling-conflict issue and stated that he would "not tolerate anymore fighting between them" and that he was going to "strive to find the balance of spending equal amounts of time with them separately." Zack shared that he really missed his father and wanted to spend more time with him. Bonnie voiced the same concerns and suggested that maybe their father would be willing to try adding joint visits with both her and Zack as a compromise. Although Zack was initially not too thrilled about trying this out, he eventually agreed to try it. Both kids acknowledged that they were so impressed with how their parents were being "civil and respectful" toward each other in our session. They hoped that their parents could keep this up when it came to visitations and holiday gatherings in the future.

I decided to meet alone with Zack and Bonnie to consolidate some of the gains that they were making in our family session. In an effort to find out about their past successes spending quality time together, I asked about what they have done in the past to get along with each other. Zack said they really enjoy playing Ping-Pong together. Bonnie said that they have played X-Box and computer games together without any problems. We also discussed how they push each other's buttons. Zack had a long history of going into Bonnie's bedroom to annoy her. Bonnie did not like when Zack would put her down in front of his friends when they were hanging out at their house. I got both siblings to agree to a peace treaty and reinstating some of the fun activities they used to do together in the past.

The Final Family-Solution-Determined System Collaborative Meeting

Our last family-solution-determined system collaborative meeting was up at the school. Present at the meeting were Bob, Linda, Bonnie, the grandfather, the school social worker, the dean, the school nurse, and the English and art teachers. The aunt could not make the meeting and Zack was in class. All of the school staff reported that Bonnie had made major changes. They said that "she was happier," "there were no reports of cutting," and "her grades have greatly improved." The parents chimed in how proud they were of how well Bonnie was doing. When asked what she would have to do to go backward at this point, Bonnie shared confidently that she "no longer thinks about cutting or bingeing and purging anymore" and can only see herself "going forward." I asked the parents the same question. Both parents acknowledged that they have learned the importance of "putting your kids before anything else, no matter what your personal problems are." They both planned to continue to be more present and emotionally available to Bonnie when she needed support from them. The group mutually agreed to discontinue the family–multiple helper collaborative meetings due to Bonnie's great progress. Our last family session was scheduled for 6 weeks down the road.

The Last Family Session

Present in our last family session were Bob, Linda, Bonnie, and Zack. The parents reported that Zack and Bonnie were getting along much better. I learned that their "Ping-Pong matches were quite intense and competitive" but there was "no name-calling or fighting." Bob reported that he and Bonnie were regularly playing tennis together and protecting their special Sunday time together. The joint visit experiment with Bob and both kids worked out just fine and they planned to try it again. After amplifying and consolidating their gains, we mutually agreed to terminate treatment.

Telephone Follow-Up

I spoke with both Linda and Bonnie at 6 and 12 months and there were no reports of cutting or bingeing and purging. Bonnie shared that "my relationship with my father had never been stronger" and she had a "better relationship with Zack." In addition, she got back into playing tennis competitively and actually won a local tournament. She had a part-time job in a music store and got accepted into her first-choice college in New England. Linda shared that "Bonnie was no longer depressed" and "much more confident."

Post-Therapy Case Reflections

Bonnie's case situation nicely illustrates the power of working with the family-solution-determined system. Having key resource people from the adolescents' social network, including actively involved and concerned helping professionals from larger systems, provides the adolescent or young adult and his or her family with tremendous support, and a diversity of fresh and creative ideas for resolving their current difficulties. It can help the youth and the family stay on track once change occurs. I have found that working in concert with all of these individuals makes the therapeutic process briefer. Bonnie disclosed in treatment that she had found it to be quite comforting to know that she had strong support from both her school and her relatives.

One core issue that I addressed in family therapy sessions was the emotional disconnection process that had occurred with Bonnie and both of her parents. The combination of the loss of the maternal grandmother and parental divorce had led to Bonnie's mother's emotionally withdrawing from her due to her own issues with depression and loss. Following the divorce situation, Bonnie's father had cut off contact with her as well. This was particularly devastating for Bonnie because she used to have a very close relationship with her father prior to the divorce; without her mother emotionally available to her there was no parent around to provide emotional support. This led to Bonnie taking matters into her own hands and cutting herself as an attempt to soothe herself. To help counter the negative effects of the emotional disconnection family problem, I encouraged Bonnie to increase her involvement with her grandfather, aunt and the caring and concerned school staff that had attended our solution-determined system collaborative meetings.

After strengthening Bonnie's relationship with her mother, I began working on rebuilding her relationship with her father. In the first family therapy session with her father, I made use of my imaginary time machine and had Bonnie go back to a place in the past where she had felt very close to her father. Bonnie took the time machine back before the divorce situation to a Sunday morning when she was enjoying trouncing her father on the tennis court. This time-traveling experience triggered lots of positive emotions for both Bonnie and her father. Her father had declared in our session that he would reinstate Sunday morning tennis and breakfast with Bonnie as a way to bring them closer together. He also made a commitment to be more present in Bonnie's life.

The last part of the family therapy work was to alleviate another stressor for Bonnie, which was her conflicted relationship with her younger brother, Zack. Once I got the two siblings to reinstate past enjoyable activities they could do together and to see how they were both in the same boat with their postparental divorce wishes to see their father more, they stopped bickering and were more supportive of each another.

Case Example: One-Person Collaborative Strengths-Based Brief Family Therapy with a Young Adult

When working with self-harming college students living on campus grappling with unresolved family-of-origin issues, a one-person collaborative strengths-based brief family therapy approach can be used. The clients can choose which family relationship they wish to change in telephone interactions with this family member, during school holiday breaks, and summer break periods. They will be exposed to and will be offered a variety of therapeutic experiments that are in line with their goals, key strengths and intelligence areas, stages of readiness to change, and theories of change that can be tried out to accomplish the family relationship changes they desire. This treatment format can be combined with conjoint family therapy when the parents and/or siblings come to visit the clients on campus. Sometimes, I will set aside a block of 2–3 hours to have a marathon family session when the clients' families are in town and there are a lot of target or goal areas in need of direct intervention. The following case of Heather illustrates how it is possible for an individual family member to change family relationships and make significant family system-wide changes.

Referral Process

Heather, 20 years old, was referred to me by her university student mental health center counselor. She was cutting and burning herself 4–5 times per day, smoking marijuana, and occasionally binge-drinking, and at times starving herself after troublesome telephone conversations with her mother or after visits with her. According to Heather, her mother put a lot of pressure on her to be an 'A' student and used her as a junior therapist and confidant after arguments with Heather's father and to help her with her personal problems. Recently, Heather's father was diagnosed with a rare form of cancer, which has led to an increase in telephone calls from her mother for support. These emotionally charged telephone calls would trigger Heather to slash deeply into her skin, burn herself on her arms with a cigarette, or starve herself for a few days. At times, Heather would feel guilty about not being home to comfort her mother and help out with her father. Unfortunately, home for Heather was on the West Coast and visits were limited to school holidays and summer break periods. Heather felt very much entangled in the family web.

Heather's past treatment history consisted of multiple individual treatment experiences and one inpatient psychiatric hospitalization following a serious suicide attempt by overdosing on her mother's Xanex and barbiturates. She was 17 years old at the time. The psychiatrist who had treated her in the hospital had diagnosed her with borderline personality disorder because of her cutting and equivalent self-destructive behaviors. Over the past 2 years, her student mental health center counselor, Madeline, had tried dialectical behavioral therapy with Heather. However, she had felt that this treatment approach was not working. Madeline felt that it might be worthwhile for Heather to try a radically different treatment approach and referred her to me. She wanted me to address Heather's lack of a solid support system on campus. Apparently, Heather had shared with her that her extreme self-harming and equivalent self-destructive behaviors had cost her several friends. Heather would frequently share with her how alone she felt. She does, however, have one friend, Cassie, who has been there unconditionally for her.

The First Therapy Session

I began the first session with coming to know Heather by her key strengths. I asked, "If your best friend, Cassie, were sitting in this empty chair over here and I asked her, 'What are two of Heather's top strengths or talents?' What would Cassie say?" Heather said, "Heather is a BFF" (best friend forever) and she is "very smart." I asked Heather to give some specific examples of what she thinks Cassie would cite as BFF-like behaviors. Heather said, "I can always count on her" and "she is a very caring and sensitive person." I explored with Heather if Cassie was a charter member of her fan club! Heather laughed. I then asked her to give some examples of her being a really dependable person that others can count on. She gave examples of being "a big support to Cassie after her boyfriend had broken up with her." She also said that in class group projects her fellow students could "always count on" her to "contribute valuable information" and "put together a solid presentation."

I shifted gears and began to explore with Heather the spaces in between times when she was not self-harming and engaging in equivalent self-destructive behaviors. I discovered that spending long periods of time "hanging out with Cassie," "writing poetry," and "doing" her "homework at the university library rather than in the dorm room" helped. She found that if she "spent too much time alone" in her "dorm room" she would be "more likely to hurt herself" or "get troubling calls" from her mother. I made a mental note that these were important behaviors that needed to be increased.

Next, I began the goal-setting process with Heather. I caught her up on what her counselor, Madeline, had shared with me about her and her family politics. Heather stated that the number one relationship she wished to change was with her mother. I asked her how she would really know that she was succeeding at achieving this goal. According to Heather, "I would assert myself when my mom would call and let her know how things were going with my classes and what was going on in my life." She further added, "I will tell her that I love her and care about her but that I have a lot on my plate and can no longer be her shrink." I cautioned Heather about the second statement she wished to share with her mother and the potential costs of telling her this. Heather admitted that her mother would probably "lay a massive guilt trip on" her for saying that at this point. Heather and I mutually agreed for her to share the first statement with her mother to see how she handles that as a starting place for beginning to change their relationship.

I asked Heather to describe a blow-by-blow description of a recent conversation she had had with her mother so he had a sense of how they interact with each other. The circular interaction map of this recent conversation was drawn out on my legal pad (see Figure 3.7). Together, we analyzed the chain of events that led to her slashing and burning herself badly. I explored with Heather if along the circle there was something else she could have done differently rather than getting defensive, succumbing to guilt, and turning to self-punishment by slashing and burning herself. I felt this was a great opportunity to use disputation skills training. I asked, "Heather, does getting defensive with your mother make you feel more or less in control of yourself?" I also asked her, "When you surrender to guilt, does it make you less or more vulnerable prey to slashing and burning yourself?" Heather was beginning to see the implications and lack of usefulness of thinking and emotionally responding to these upsetting conversations with her mother was only serving to perpetuate her self-harming and equivalent self-destructive behaviors. I also pointed out that there are many ways to view other people's actions that

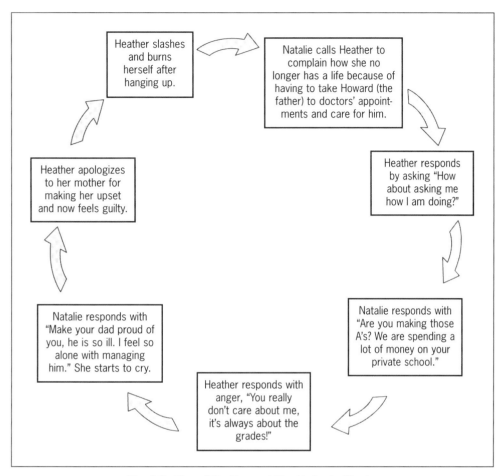

Fig. 3.7 Map of Heather and Her Mother's Circular
Problem-Maintaining Interaction

appear to be unreasonable and invalidating to us, not just that we made them upset and it is our fault. In reflecting on this destructive and invalidating pattern of interaction with her mother, Heather could see how her mother would play "the poor victim role" and she would serve as her mother's "caretaker." We did a role-play reenacting the same telephone conversation where she would play herself and I would play her mother. However, this time around, Heather would respond differently to her mother. After saying hello, she gave her mother a very warm and enthusiastic greeting and launched into sharing with her three good things that happened with her classes and something fun she did with Cassie. While playing her mother, I was caught off guard and surprised by Heather's new behaviors and did not know how to respond. Next, Heather really surprised me by how she responded to her mother's invalidating response. Rather than getting defensive and worrying about hurting her mother's feelings, she thanked her and her father for sending her to such a fine university. After this surprising response, it was very hard for her mother to respond with tears and lay a guilt trip on Heather. Once we completed the reenactment of the telephone conversation, Heather was not thinking about or feeling compelled to hurt herself.

In closing out our session, I complimented Heather on her hard work in the first session, her perseverance with not giving up with helping herself, and her creativity in generating some novel responses to test out in trying to disrupt this long-standing invalidating pattern of interaction with her mother. I also complimented her on establishing a solid friendship with Cassie and using her for added support when she needed it, writing poetry, and having good insight about how allowing herself to be alone in her dorm room in the evening could lead to self-harming and that it was better to do her homework at the university library. I encouraged Heather to bring Cassie to the next session. Heather thought this was a great idea and signed off on my significant-other consent form. She was offered the following therapeutic experiments to choose from and try:

1. To practice using her new tactics or responses in telephone and in face-to-face conversations with her mother
2. To use the My Positive Trigger Log to identify and increase using coping and problem-solving strategies that work
3. To continue to write poetry and do her homework in the university library in the evenings
4. To continue to use Cassie as a support person and bring her to the next session

Heather left our first session very satisfied and more confident about changing her relationship with her mother.

The Second Session

Heather brought Cassie with her to the session. The great news was that Heather had an opportunity to test out her new telephone tactics with her mother. According to Heather, her tactics totally changed the topic to such a degree that her "mother wanted to learn more about" her "college life" and what she was "learning new" in her "English class." This was her mother's "favorite subject in both high school and college." I gave Heather a big high-five and explored with her how she drummed up the courage to experiment with her new tactics. She stated that she was "feeling much more confident" to take the risk. To top it off, Heather did not have the desire to self-harm at all after having her conversation with her mother. She also went "6 out of 7 days without slashing or burning" herself. I asked her how she had pulled this off. Heather stated that she was "keeping very busy" and was doing more of what was working. She had a good explanation for her having a slip over the weekend. She had gone to two parties and "drank and smoked marijuana" and "came home and felt depressed about this and slashed and burned" herself. However, the self-harming episode was short-lived and not as bad as it typically was. She had called Cassie for support after the self-harming episode. I normalized the slip and encouraged Heather to share with me the wisdom she had gained from this experience that she will put to use the next time she is at a party. Heather could see how drinking and smoking marijuana made her vulnerable prey for bad judgment and self-harming. She planned to make a commitment to abstain from alcohol and marijuana usage. Cassie shared that she was "really proud of Heather" and believes this time around she was committed to changing. I asked Cassie to share what ideas she had for structure building to help minimize Heather's caving in to hurting herself. Cassie strongly recommended that Heather go with her to her "wonderful yoga class." She also recommended that they "go for long bicycle rides on the old prairie path together."

In concluding the session, I complimented Heather on her tremendous courage and for the great work she had done over the past week. I complimented Cassie for being such a loyal and great friend and contributing her helpful ideas. We discussed the importance of structure building and adding the yoga class and bicycling activities to her weekly regimen for helping her stay quit from hurting herself. As a vote of confidence to Heather, I gave her a 2-week vacation from counseling. I offered her the following therapeutic experiments to do while on vacation:

1. Plan Out Your Perfect Day and then rate each day (10 = Best Day of My Life, 1 = Worst Day of My Life)
2. You at Your Best Story
3. Continue to use My Positive Trigger Log
4. Try out the yoga class and long bike rides with Cassie

The Third Session

Two weeks later, Heather came back with Cassie, again armed with both therapeutic experiment materials to present. Her planned-out perfect days ended up "averaging 7–6.5 ratings." Her "lowest-rated day was a 5." When asked what she would have rated her lowest days before working together, Heather said, "The days would have ranged from 3 to 1." She observed that by hanging out more with Cassie and their new friend, Karen, doing yoga, biking, studying in the library in the evenings, not drinking or smoking weed, writing more poetry, regularly referring to her My Positive Trigger Log for ideas when stressed out," and reading her You at Your Best Story nightly before she went to bed all helped her steer clear from hurting herself.

For her You at Your Best Story, Heather wrote about how she had won a high school state poetry competition. This was the first time she had ever received an award for anything in her life. Heather shared how she got herself fired up to read her poem in front of 500 people. She thought about her favorite poet, Emily Dickinson and "imagined seeing her face in the back of the room carefully listening to and being impressed by" her writing abilities. To this very day, Emily Dickinson had served as a big source of inspiration for Heather. I asked her what her most favorite Dickinson poem was and she said, "I'm Nobody, Who are You?" When asked about the meaning of that poem for her, Heather responded with, "The poem lifts your spirits when you are feeling alone because it reminds us that there are other people in the world who feel alone at times. Therefore we are never really alone." Heather shared that the You at Your Best Story experiment was a big emotional uplift for her. She also found that reading it every night before she went to bed helped her to sleep better.

Finally, we talked about how much Heather was enjoying taking the yoga class and biking with Cassie. She said that both activities really "relaxed" her and that she was "getting into excellent physical shape." Heather also disclosed that her "father was responding well to a new cancer treatment." As far as Heather and her mother, she was "less emotionally reactive" to her and felt "much more in control during and after conversations with her." When asked about what might make her go backward at this point, Heather was hard-pressed to see this happen. She pointed out, however, that if she stopped keeping busy and hanging out with Cassie, she could see slips happening. I presented a worst-case scenario to test the waters with Heather and asked if she did have a slip, what would be her first couple of steps that she would take to get back on track? Heather said that she would "call Cassie or Karen" and "go to the library to do work" and "at all costs, get out of the dorm room."

After complimenting Heather and Cassie, she was encouraged to keep doing more of what was working to keep her on track. When stressed out or feeling at a loss for what to do, she was reminded to consult with her My Positive Trigger Log. As a vote of confidence, Heather was given a month-long vacation from counseling. Heather was quite confident that she would stay on track.

The Fourth Session

Prior to my scheduled session with Heather, she had called me to see if her visiting mother, Natalie, could come to our meeting with her. Heather thought this would be a great opportunity to do further work on their relationship. Natalie was unaware that Heather had been cutting, burning, starving herself at times, and abusing alcohol and marijuana. Heather was not going to say a word about the self-starving and alcohol and marijuana abuse to her mother.

Natalie was very friendly and seemed to be quite pleased with how Heather was able to maintain her 4.0 grade average. Heather shared with her mother that she was so glad that they were "getting along better" and that they were having "less emotionally stressful conversations." She courageously and gently pointed out to her mother that she could "no longer serve" as her "confidant and shrink" when she was "stressed out by Dad" or she was having her "own personal difficulties." Much to Heather's surprise, Natalie validated her daughter's feelings and said that she would "stop pulling her" into her "personal difficulties." In fact, since Heather had been telling her mother how much she was enjoying her counseling experience, Natalie shared that she was "going to see a therapist privately." Heather praised her mother for seeking out help for herself. In a very loving and sensitive way, Natalie put her arm around Heather and shared with her that she loved her dearly and that she knows that she could "always call her if she needed support" and "don't worry about stressing me out." Heather found this reassuring and was happy about the changes her mother was making. We wrapped up the session with Heather reflecting on where she was at the beginning of treatment and where she was now, including her sharing what she used to do. This was another sign of Heather's courage and willingness to take positive risks with her mother. Although Natalie was initially alarmed to hear about Heather's past self-harming and other self-destructive behaviors, she could tell that she was in a solid place presently. Natalie shared with Heather that she was very proud of her.

The Last Session

Heather came in smiling, with both Cassie and Karen. Cassie had convinced Heather and Karen to go on an out-of-state bicycle trip with her. Heather reported "not having any slips, no alcohol or marijuana use, and [being] in the best physical shape" she has ever been. Her father continued to respond well to his cancer treatment. She also was having a much less stressful and more positive relationship with her mother. I amplified and consolidated all of Heather's remarkable gains. I asked Heather, "What is your consultation fee if I needed you to come in and help me with another young woman who was going through what you used to struggle with?" She responded with, "No charge! I would be happy to help her out." We mutually agreed to terminate and I thanked Cassie and Karen for all of their support.

Telephone Follow-up Calls

I was only able to reach Heather at 6 months. At that time, she was still not self-harming, self-starving, or abusing alcohol and marijuana. Her father was functioning much better physically. Heather and her mother continued to have a much more positive relationship.

Post-Therapy Case Reflections

With Heather's long history of self-harming and engaging in equivalent self-destructive behaviors, even the most seasoned of therapists could be intimidated by her presenting difficulties. What further compounded and exacerbated Heather's difficulties was her feeling entangled in her family web, in spite of living on a college campus quite a long way from her home. For years, Heather had served as a confidant and junior therapist for her mother and had tremendous pressure placed on her to be a straight-A student. While away at college, her mother frequently called her to solicit her support in dealing with her father and personal issues. Heather's parents would not ask about how she was doing or if she needed anything from them. Whenever she would attempt to confront her mother, this would result in her laying a guilt trip on Heather, which would fuel self-harming and other self-destructive behavior episodes.

To help Heather disentangle herself from the powerful family politics and be less emotionally reactive, I had Heather describe a recent telephone conversation she had with her mother and mapped it out on paper so she could visually see the circular problem-maintaining interaction with her mother. Heather found this to be very beneficial and could see how she not only got herself invalidated but there were locus points around the circle where she could experiment with new responses and be in control. The use of disputation skills were helpful to Heather in that she could see how her way of thinking in response to her mother's invalidating interactions or guilt trips would lead her to hurting herself. Once Heather met with success at disrupting this pattern on the telephone and changing the direction of the conversation with her mother, she felt much more self-confident, more in control, and less emotionally reactive to her.

Heather was very creative and resourceful. She was a gifted writer and strong in the linguistic-intelligence area. Well before I started seeing Heather, she had come up with some very effective self-generated coping strategies, such as writing poetry, "hanging out a lot" with her close friend Cassie, and doing her homework at the university library. I encouraged her to increase these behaviors.

Since Heather's friend Cassie was her number one cheerleader, I found it quite useful to have her participate in our sessions. It has been my clinical experience that once I establish rapport with my clients' friends and actively involve them in the treatment process, the friends are committed to the change effort and will support their client friends to stay on track and be successful in the world.

Finally, the use of the positive psychology interventions Plan Out Your Perfect Day and You at Your Best Story were designed to increase Heather's happiness level and trigger positive emotion, which helped counter some lingering negative emotions she was still experiencing. With the help of the Plan Out Your Perfect Day experiment Heather learned other behaviors she needed to increase to further improve her situation. Clearly, Heather became much more balanced in mind, body, and spirit.

CHAPTER FOUR

Collaborative Strengths-Based Brief Couples Therapy with Self-Harming Young Adults

Couples and Help-Seeking Partners Presenting with Self-Harming Difficulties and Other Concerns

Couples and help-seeking partners presenting with self-harming difficulties and concerns are not radically different from most distressed couples. They tend to argue or have conflicts about power and control dynamics, closeness and distance in the relationship, extra-relationship affairs, boundary problems with their families of origin, and possible concerns with substance abuse and eating-distressed behaviors. In addition, the *leaving home* stage in general is a stressful time for young adults and their parents, which can contribute to individual partner and couple relationship difficulties (Carter & McGoldrick, 1989; Haley, 1980). Since self-harming behavior closely resembles and may progress over time like substance abuse behavioral difficulties, the help-seeking partner in the contemplation or action stage of readiness for change may be locked into a rigid rescuing or too-responsible role and pattern of interaction similar to the behavior of the partner of an alcoholic or substance abuser, which, in his or her extreme efforts to help the self-harming partner, further perpetuates his or her problematic and super-irresponsible behaviors. In some cases, the help-seeking partner may also self-harm or engage in equivalent self-destructive behaviors like substance abuse, bulimia, or sexually risky behaviors, which can greatly contribute to maintaining the self-harming partner's behavior.

I have worked with some young adult couples with self-harming and other difficulties where the *Four Horsemen of the Apocalypse* played a significant role in the rapid deterioration of their relationships. The Four Horsemen of the Apocalypse are *criticism*, *defensiveness*, *contempt*, and *stonewalling* (Gottman & Gottman, 2006,

2008). Stonewalling is one of the most frustrating for couple partners to cope with in that the partners' withdrawal from conversations and offering no physical or verbal cues on where they stand on anything in a given conversation or on important issues can be quite difficult to live with. The use of silence can be a powerful weapon to throw the partner off balance and control what is and is not talked about in the relationship.

Another unique aspect of young adult couple relationships is the fact that this might be both partner's first experience with a serious intimate relationship, so they are charting new territory. Because they are often not married, the back door is always open to exit the relationship when conflicts or problems seem insurmountable. In fact, it may not have to get to this point when one of the partners might decide to go outside the relationship to get certain needs met or abruptly end the relationship.

Engaging Couples with Self-Harming Difficulties

Often, the initial caller seeking help for their self-harming partner is the customer and in the action stage of readiness for change. As research has indicated and clinical practice evidence-based experience has shown, a very small percentage of self-harming clients seek out mental health treatment (Whitlock, 2008; Whitlock et al., 2007). Therefore, the entry person into the couple system is the concerned partner who may or may not be able to convince the self-harming partner to pursue couples therapy.

Coaching Help-Seeking Partners to Facilitate the Engagement of Their Reluctant Self-Harming Partners Entry into Couples Therapy

There are four different coaching strategies I use with help-seeking partners: *use of a pretreatment experiment to generate new ways of viewing and doing, track and modify the conversational interaction pattern regarding seeking couples therapy or treatment, the help-seeking partner presents self as the troubled partner in the relationship,* and *having the self-harming partner bring a close friend with them to the first couples therapy session.*

Use of a Pretreatment Experiment to Generate New Ways of Viewing and Doing

When help-seeking partners call me to share their concerns about their self-harming partners and would like to bring them in for treatment or couples therapy, I will request that on a daily basis the calling partner keep track of what they are doing to prevent the situation from getting much worse with the self-harming partner. I also will point out to the help-seeking partners that self-harming behavior is cyclical and there are always spaces in between or gaps of time from one self-harming episode to the next and for them to keep track of what is happening during those times that they would like to continue to have happen. Furthermore, I request that the help-seeking partners keep track of what they are doing during the non-self-harming periods of time that promotes the kinds of positive behaviors and interactions they would like to see happen more with the self-harming partner and in their relationships. Finally, the help-seeking partners are to bring in their lists to the initial consultation session. In some cases by simply refocusing the help-seekers' attention on what is both competent about and working with the self-harming partners, this can change the help seekers' viewing of their partners, which in turn can change their interactions. Sometimes, based on an increased awareness as a result of the pretreatment experiment, the help seeking partners will spontaneously decide to increase their solution-building patterns, which can lead to a reduction in the self-harming partners' problematic behaviors. In both cases, the shifts in the help-seeking partners' viewing of the self-harming partners and changing the ways they interact with the self-harming partners can make the idea of going for couple's therapy less threatening for the latter if partners agree that there is further work to be done on their relationship. I have had some couple situations where the help-seekers' changes in viewing and doing in relationship to their self-harming partners were so dramatic that the help-seeking partners ended up calling to cancel their initial appointments as a result of implementing their pretreatment change experiments.

Track and Modify the Conversational Interaction Pattern Regarding Seeking Couples Therapy or Treatment

If the pretreatment therapeutic experiment does not lead to any significant changes in the mind of the help-seeking partners, another useful coaching strategy is to invite the callers to give me a blow-by-blow description of how they try to convince their self-harming partners to go either for couple's therapy or for individual treatment. While talking on the telephone, I will create a circular interaction map on a sheet of paper to write down step by step how they approach and talk with the self-harming partner about going for counseling, their tone of voice, posture when talking, the specific words used, and how the self-harming partners respond to them each time they speak. In some cases, simply by having the help-seeking partners hear themselves describe their unproductive actions or picturing in their minds what they are doing that inadvertently is contributing to the self-harming partners' reluctance to go for treatment can open up space for possibilities. Help-seeking partners learn through this therapeutic exercise that the self-harming behavior and possible equivalent self-destructive behaviors are embedded in a redundant circular problem-maintaining pattern of interaction and they are active participants in maintaining the very behaviors they wish to see changed. I will ask the help-seeking partners the following questions to assist them in coming up with more productive ways to approach and respond to their self-harming partners:

- "When you first approach your partner about going for counseling with you, what other words can you use other than: 'You really need to get help or else . . .' or 'You are really stressing me out'?"

- "What do you think it is about your tone of voice or your body posture that may be putting her on the defensive?"
- "How do you think raising your voice or trying to mother your partner may blow up for you in getting him to go for counseling with you?"
- "What words do you think you could experiment with when approaching Alison that will make it much more inviting for her to want to go for counseling with you?"
- "What adjustment in your tone of voice and body posture could you make that could put Wanda less on the defensive?"
- "Do you think it would be less threatening for Tabitha to go for counseling if you shared with her that you really want to do it as couple rather than insisting that she get therapy for herself?"

The Help-Seeking Partner Presents Self as the Troubled Partner in the Relationship

A third coaching strategy therapists can try with help-seeking partners who are having grave difficulty bringing their reluctant self-harming partners into couple's therapy is to have them present themselves as the ones who are struggling to cope and having difficulties. I strongly encourage help-seeking partners to pretend like they are striving for Academy Award–winning performances in selling their self-harming partners on the idea that they are the troubled partners that really need their assistance with the solution-generating process and to get unstuck. It is very hard for even the most reluctant of self-harming partners to rebel against their confused, bungling, and struggling partners. Once the self-harming partners go for the bait of trying to help out their troubled partners and may have met their match with the extent of their difficulties and inabilities to resolve them alone, they may agree to go for couple's therapy to get assistance for their troubled partners.

Having the Self-Harming Partner Bring a Close Friend to the First Couples Therapy Session

Some reluctant self-harming partners may warm up to trying out a couples therapy session if they can bring their closest friend with them. The presence of close friends makes going for counseling much less threatening and anxiety-provoking and can pave the way for engaging them in treatment. Although the friend may be biased and supporting the self-harming partner's position with the couple's difficulties, he or she may be able to offer both a unique perspective on the couple's relationship dynamics and some fresh and creative problem-solving ideas that could help stabilize the self-harming behavior. After establishing good rapport with and tapping the expertise of the friend, the self-harming partner will be much more receptive to meeting alone with his or her partner and discussing couple treatment goals, depending on what stage of readiness for change he or she is in.

Doing Couples Therapy with One Partner

Doing couples therapy with one partner is a viable option when either all of the above coaching strategies fail to engage the self-harming partner for treatment or the help-seeking partner thinks it would be best for him or her to serve as the agent of change for their couple relationship and come alone to therapy. Their decision to want to conduct the treatment process this way could be for the following reasons: the self-harming partners dislike therapy and have not responded well to it in the past, they want to learn alone effective therapeutic strategies and tools to change their partners by themselves, or they are protective of the self-harming partners and do not want to increase their stress level by bringing them into counseling, out of fear that it could lead to an increase in the self-harming behavior. All is not lost if we cannot engage the self-harming partners. We can track with the help-seeking partners the circular problem-maintaining sequences of interaction in which the self-harming episodes are embedded in and offer a variety of change strategies to disrupt these patterns. Since the help-seeking partners are the customers for change in most cases, they are highly motivated to begin implementing change strategies to resolve the self-harming and other possible equivalent self-destructive behaviors.

In some cases, the help-seeking partners may be in the contemplation or preparation stages of readiness for change and the therapist can use the decisional balancing scale to help them see the advantages and disadvantages of continuing to engage in unproductive attempted solutions and opening up their minds to experimenting with new and more productive ways of responding to self-harming episodes after they advance into the preparation and action stages of readiness for change.

If change is not happening with the absent partners' self-harming and or possible equivalent self-destructive behaviors and the relationship situations are getting much worse, I will strongly recommend the need for me to intervene directly with the absent partners. This can include having the help-seeking partners bring them into the next session or, if they do not think this will work, allowing me to contact the absent partners on the telephone and offering to do a home visit if that could help with the engagement process. It is important once the self-harming partners agree to meet with the therapist either in their home or in the office that they offer to see these partners as many times individually as they saw the help-seeking partners individually to balance things out. With some couples with self-harming difficulties, you can change both the help-seeking partners' fixed beliefs about ways of interacting with the self-harming partners, and yet the latter's symptoms or difficulties remain intact. This tells me that possibly the self-harming partner may continue to be experiencing inner emotional chaos, and mood management difficulties. They may have an emotional coping style and/or lack the tools for soothing themselves. Once engaged in couples therapy, I will offer to teach the self-harming partners mindfulness meditation, disputation skills, and other useful distress management tools to empower them to better manage negative moods and self-defeating irrational thoughts.

What Works in Couples Therapy

There is no existing treatment outcome research on what works clinically with young adult couples grappling with self-harming and possible other equivalent self-destructive difficulties. Therefore, we have to rely on existing treatment outcomes and other research and clinical practice evidence-based wisdom with couples to guide therapeutic experiment design and selection. Gottman and Gottman (2006, 2008) have done the most groundbreaking research with couples. They have been able to predict with 94% accuracy which couples will succeed and stay together and those couples that will divorce and break up if not married. They have identified the following important couple strategies they need to master in order to keep their relationships flourishing:

1. Establish a rule in the relationship that for every negative statement or complaint made by one partner he or she will have to come up with five positive things to say or compliment the other partner about.
2. When there is a conflict or argument that erupts one or both partners need to attempt to repair and soothe the other partner either during the conflict or argument or right after it.
3. Reduce the likelihood of the four horsemen of the apocalypse doing further damage to the relationship by educating and increasing the couple's awareness of early warning signs or what triggers are for them.
4. It is important to educate couples about the research finding that 69% of the conflicts couples have are often never resolved (Gottman & Gottman, 2008). The therapist needs to help couples respect each partner's differences rather than trying to change them. It is important to have partners look at how their differences benefit the relationship.
5. Couples need to learn how to compromise and agree with each other rather than fight about decisions that have to be made.
6. After an argument or if one partner is not in a good place, the other partner needs to turn to him or her and try to physically comfort his or her partner.
7. Help the couple identify positive sentiment patterns of interaction that increase positive affect and seem to strengthen the emotional connection in the relationship.

Gable et al. (2004) found in their study that when partners shared with each other positive events in their lives and the other partners responded with strong interest, a lot of enthusiasm, and complimented them, it enhanced their positive affect and well-being and the interpersonal benefits were high ratings of relationship satisfaction and increased intimacy. Gable et al. also found that partners who fairly consistently responded in this active constructive and positive way to their partners' positive events were rated as being more committed to the growth and stability of their relationships than partners who tended to respond to their partners' reports of positive events in a passive or invalidating way.

Challenging Couple Treatment Dilemmas

Working with High-conflict Couples

When working with high-conflict couples, I will first attempt to work with the couple together. However, if the first session keeps digressing into intense blame-counterblame destructive couple interactions, and they cannot agree on anything, I will see each partner separately and establish separate treatment goals and therapeutic work projects. Not only does this simplify the therapist's job but it is a more productive course of action until the couple situation becomes more stable. It is critical that the therapist let the partners know the house rule that the therapist will not harbor any secrets while seeing them separately. I will let both partners know that if one or both partners divulge and entrap me in a secret, I will have no other recourse than pursuing the following two options: (a) tell the other partner or (b) terminate treatment. Once relationship progress occurs as a result of seeing the partners separately or unless one or both partners object, I will reinstate couples sessions again. Their new positive solution-building patterns of interaction will be amplified and consolidated.

If the couple is still having difficulties with fighting and arguing, I have had success using the following therapeutic experiments with these couples:

1. One or both partners can hold up a red card, like referees do in soccer matches when there is a penalty, whenever an argument is about to begin or if it begins to escalate.
2. For every blaming statement or complaint made by a partner, that partner needs to come up with five positive things to say or compliment the other partner about (Gottman & Gottman, 2006, 2008).
3. The partners can practice repairing and soothing each other during or after an argument or conflict occurs (Gottman & Gottman, 2006, 2008).
4. The blaming or arguing pattern (the couple needs to label the pattern) can be externalized and an anti-pattern-breaking ritual can be implemented to empower the couple team to conquer the oppressive pattern.
5. A structured couple fighting experiment can be implemented to teach the partners how to fight or argue fairly. They are to schedule different times each day of the week to fight or argue for 10 minutes (each partner gets 5 minutes apiece). Anything left over to argue about beyond the allotted 10 minutes they are to write down and bring to their next scheduled fighting or arguing session. In each scheduled fighting or arguing session, the partners take turns flipping a coin to determine who goes first. After a partner completes a turn, he or she says, "Thank you, dear." After the 10 minutes allotted, they can do something fun either together or separately.

All five of the above therapeutic experiments are quite effective at disrupting long-standing blame-counterblame and other destructive couple interaction patterns, help couples feel more in control, and enhance their problem-solving and conflict-resolution skills.

Working with Dual Self-Harming or Equivalent Self-Destructive Behavior Couples

The challenge of working with couples where there is self-harming and equivalent self-destructive behaviors like bulimia, substance abuse, or gambling occurring with both partners is that the partners' habit difficulties mutually reinforce each other's problematic behaviors. I will first try to elicit from couple partners important information about self-generated pretreatment changes and any past successes they have had. If there are no pretreatment changes or past successful problem-solving or coping strategies reported, I have found it useful to track one of the couple's typical circular problem-maintaining sequences of interaction when self-harming or other equivalent self-destructive behaviors occur and how each partner responds to the other. When mapped out on a flip chart or a legal pad, each partner can learn about how they inadvertently maintain the very behaviors they want changed with their partners. It is also helpful to accurately determine with the partners the stage of readiness for change at which each partner is presently and match what we do therapeutically with where they are. If it appears that the severity of each partner's self-harming practice, bulimia, substance abuse, or gambling problems overshadows each partner's unique needs, it is difficult to establish mutual treatment goals, and treatment compliance is in question, I will recommend seeing each partner separately. I will share with the partners my house rule about not harboring any secrets and how I will manage this situation if my rule is violated. Separate treatment goals and therapeutic work projects can be established. With partners presenting with substance abuse difficulties, I will take a comprehensive drinking and drug history. If there are serious physical and withdrawal concerns, I will involve a physician who specializes in addiction medicine to assess the need for medical monitoring and a detox. Once progress is made both individually and with the couple relationship, I will bring the partners back together to amplify and consolidate their gains and explore with them if they have a joint relationship goal they would like to work on. After each partner has been able to greatly reduce or achieve abstinence from their habitual behaviors, a tight structured plan needs to be put in place to help them stay on track and reduce the likelihood of slips or prolonged relapse situations.

Birchler, Fals-Stewart, and O'Farrell (2005, 2008) have developed *Behavior Couples Therapy*, which is an empirically validated treatment approach for couples presenting with alcohol and substance abuse problems. Many of the therapeutic experiments they recommend for these challenging couples are quite applicable to working with dual-self-harming or equivalent self-destructive behavior couples. They highly recommend that partners know each other's triggers and reduce exposure to toxic people and places and mutually triggering partner behaviors, such as nagging, complaining, yelling, and threats of leaving or ending the relationship, which lead to self-harming and equivalent self-destructive episodes. Each partner needs to be coached and needs to practice reinforcing only abstinent and responsible behaviors. When abstinent and responsible behaviors do occur with each partner, the other partner is to do something rewarding and enjoyable that the abstinent partner would like to do. In an effort to help partners focus more of their attention on what is working in their relationship, they have the partners do the therapeutic experiment *Catch Your Partner Doing Something Nice* (Birchler et al., 2008). This therapeutic experiment helps create a more positive emotional climate in the couple relationship. The partners are to practice their positive behaviors and do something nice and caring for each other each day as well. If the couple is rigidly entrenched in their problem-maintaining patterns, the following change strategies can be employed:

1. Pattern intervention strategies can be used, such as adding something new to the problem context, exaggerating problematic behaviors and patterns, scheduling behaviors, and making engaging in certain problematic behaviors an ordeal.
2. Having one or both partners do something surprising and different when they each engage in problematic behaviors.
3. Externalize the self-harming, bulimia, substance abuse, or gambling (whatever the clients call their habits or problematic behaviors) or client-identified patterns that are oppressive and pushing them around.
4. The therapist can wonder aloud with the couple what all of the disadvantages will be for their relationship and each of them individually if the self-harming, bulimia, substance abuse, or gambling difficulties were resolved.

Case Example: Empowering a Couple to Conquer a Long-Standing "Rejection Pattern"

I first saw Shana and her parents when she was 16 years old and heavily abusing alcohol, marijuana, and cocaine, cutting herself, failing in school, and experiencing intense conflicts with her parents over her declared lesbian sexual orientation. The mother was from Colombia and a staunch Catholic and the father was from Iran and for him, any form of homosexual behavior was not tolerated in his household or homeland. At age 17, Shana started getting involved with lesbian older adolescents and young adult women and was caught by the parents in her bed with one of her girlfriends. She was kicked out of the house for a lengthy period of time. While out on the streets and without any money, she made a serious suicide attempt. After being psychiatrically hospitalized, the parents took her back home until she finished her senior year of high school and then kicked her out again. The parents brought Shana back to see me again with the highly unrealistic goal of my talking her out of being lesbian and just be normal. Efforts on my part to help the parents be more understanding and supportive of Shana would be met with anger and refusing to budge from their position of their daughter's needing to change. Although the parents refused to continue family therapy sessions, they continued to allow Shana to see me.

Shana was able to get a job and live with a friend until she could save enough money to get out on her own. Because Shana and I had made such a strong connection in the past, she would call me once in a while to schedule an appointment or two to get support and encouragement over the next 3 years. Shana finally landed a good-paying job and was involved in the best relationship she had ever been in. She was living with her new Latina partner Maria at Maria's mother's house. Maria's parents were divorced. Apparently, Maria's mother was very accepting of her sexual orientation and had no problem having Shana live with them. The mother owned a three-flat house and allowed Maria and Shana to live in the empty first floor apartment, paying very little rent. Maria's father had emotionally cut himself off from Maria after she had come out to her parents. Apparently, he was a very devout Catholic and a traditional Latino man who viewed her behavior as "sinful." They had not spoken since Maria was 18.

After the first 8 months of living together, the honeymoon period had abruptly ended and the couple began fighting daily over "Shana's being too clingy and possessive" and "Maria's flirting and dancing with other women and drinking too much at the lesbian bars and clubs" they frequented. Shana would confront Maria and try to get her to leave with her and they would have an argument. This would result in Maria's spending the night out and Shana's coming home and cutting herself. Shana convinced Maria to go with her to see me. In order to learn from Shana and Maria what they were doing to prevent things from getting much worse with their relationship, I asked them both to carefully observe what they were doing daily to prevent their situation from really escalating and ending the relationship and to write their observations down and bring their lists to our first couples session.

The First Couples Therapy Session

After establishing rapport with Maria and having Shana catch me up on her work and other aspects of her life, I asked each partner to share what they were doing to prevent their situation from really escalating and getting much worse. Shana said that she was trying to "cut back on confronting Maria" as much and "giving her more breathing room." Maria chimed in that she "really could not tell that Shana has cut back on her smothering" behavior. She also was upset about "Shana's cutting on her arms and legs." Shana shared that she was "having a real hard time coping with her flirting right in front" of her and then "spending the night out." She said that her "emotions go haywire" and then she "cuts" herself "to calm down."

Both partners agreed that they "missed" how their relationship was in the beginning when they had "first hooked up." In an effort to learn more about what was working with their relationship when it was at its all-time best, I had the couple hop into my imaginary time machine and take it back to when they "first hooked up." The atmosphere in the room greatly changed and both partners seemed more relaxed when talking about their past positive behaviors. According to Maria, they were "having great sex and were more physical," "Shana was not smothering me," they went to the "movies a lot," "went for romantic walks along the lakefront when the sun was beginning to set," "we went shopping," and less frequently, they "enjoyed dancing together at lesbian clubs." Shana shared that they used to "hang close together at the clubs" and "Maria did not dance with anybody else." She said that she used to "love the great sex" and "romantic walks" as well. Maria pointed out that "Shana was not cutting back then." Shana countered with sharing that Maria was "not drinking as much back then either." Maria shared that they were "happier back then." When asked what specifically they were doing "back then" that made them "happier," Maria stated that there was "more playfulness and fun in the relationship back then." Shana chimed in: "Yeah, we joked around a lot and made each other laugh." With the help of the imaginary time machine, it injected positive emotion into the couple relationship and gave them a mini-vacation from their negative, problem-saturated current state of affairs. In addition, I learned a great deal from the partners about important solution-building patterns of interactions and activities they could reinstate in the here and now that could improve their relationship. However, when I explored with the partners if they could see themselves reinstating these positive behaviors in their relationship, they were both very skeptical that it would work.

Clearly, the dance clubs and bars were presently a toxic place for this couple. Maria's flirting, dancing with other women, and binge drinking triggered Shana's cutting. Shana's possessiveness and smothering would lead to Maria's hurting her by sexually acting out with a woman she would go home with from the club or bar. Shana pointed out that Maria would not drink that much out of the club or bar scene. In fact, they rarely bought beer or other alcoholic beverages when they would go grocery shopping.

At this point in the session, I began the goal-setting process. Maria wanted Shana to "stop smothering" her and "stop her cutting" because she was worried that she "might kill herself." Shana pointed out to Maria that if she wanted her to stop doing this she would have to "stop flirting, dancing with, and spending the night with other women!" She further added, "I don't know how long I can take this anymore!" Maria shouted: "I think you should move out!" Shana pointed out to me that this is what Maria said to her last partner right before she left her home for good when they were having serious problems. I decided to take a risk with the couple and introduce a new way of viewing their current problem situation. I asked the partners to label what they would call the pattern of the way they talk to each other. They both agreed on the label "rejection." I then introduced the new idea of co-constructing their problems into "the rejection pattern" that had a life all of its own and was trying to destroy their relationship. The "rejection pattern" had already driven a grand canyon of distance in their relationships with their parents over their sexual orientations and was now trying to brainwash each of them to engage in the very behaviors (the smothering, possessiveness, binge drinking, flirting, dancing with and sleeping with other women) that will lead one or both of them to end their relationship. I raised a dilemma with them and asked, "Are we going to allow the 'rejection pattern' to create havoc in your relationship or are the two of you going to join forces and be a strong team and put an end to its reign in your lives?" Both partners responded with a strong emotional reaction and indicated that they were not going to allow the "rejection pattern" to "continue to ruin" their relationship. I pointed out that "rejection patterns" are very clever and well-rooted patterns that don't give up easily. They also strike couple partners when they are least expecting it. Maria asked me, "What can we do to stop it?" I strongly recommended that they begin to "anti-rejection pattern-proof" their relationship. This would include working hard to refrain from saying and doing things to each other that would put each of them in an emotionally vulnerable state, such as steering clear from smothering, cutting, drinking, flirting, dancing and sleeping with other women, and blaming and threatening each other about ending the relationship. I pointed out that these behaviors send out invitations to the "rejection pattern" to take advantage of them individually and as couple when they are in this vulnerable state and add fuel to the fire. It was Maria's idea that they "should stay away from the clubs and bars for a while." Shana shared that this was a great idea because she will "feel less likely to cut" herself if she "did not have to worry about what Maria would do at the clubs or bars."

I returned to the goal-setting process and asked the couple: "What percentage of the time do you think you were currently in charge of the "rejection pattern" versus the "rejection pattern" was in charge of you?" The partners agreed that they were currently 50% of the time in charge of the "rejection pattern." In setting a goal for the next 2 weeks, I asked the couple, "What steps are you going to take over the next week to get up to being in charge of the 'rejection pattern' 60% of the time?" Maria reiterated that "we will stay away from clubs and bars" and she would "not drink." Shana made a commitment to "stop smothering Maria and not cut."

After a brief intersession break, I shared my editorial reflection with the couple. I complimented both partners for their resiliency and perseverance in their unique attempts to overcome adversity and try to find a healthy relationship to get their needs adequately met. I pointed out that they really do both have a lot in common and really understand the emotionally devastating effects that "rejection patterns" have on individuals and family relationships. I told them that their relationship was at a crossroads and the "rejection pattern" is currently testing each of the partners to see how committed they are to growing their relationship or allowing it to collapse. I further shared, "So as a couple team you have to make a choice. Are you going to allow the 'rejection pattern' to succeed and complete its mission at destroying your relationship, or are the two of you going to unite and conquer it for good, so that it will wish it never invaded your relationship?" Both partners were fired up to work together as a team to defeat the "rejection pattern." I shared with them that it will be a tough battle and they need to train together to be fit for a fight because "rejection patterns" do not die easily. Maria came up with the idea of them getting a couples membership at the YWCA so they could work out together. Shana thought this was a great idea as well. I offered the couple an anti-pattern-breaking ritual to work on over the next 2 weeks. They were daily to keep track of what they told themselves or did to stand up to the "rejection pattern" and not allow it to get the best of them. They were also to keep track of the times when the "rejection pattern" achieved victories with them. The partners were asked to create a chart where they could record their couple team victories in one column and in the other column record the "rejection pattern's" victories over them. I predicted that the "rejection pattern" may give them a run for their money and try to thwart their efforts to take back control of their relationship from its strong grip on them.

The Second Couples Therapy Session

Two weeks later, the couple came back, eager to share how well they were doing as a couple and individually. They brought in their chart to show what worked. They got their membership at the YWCA and were working out together daily. They reinstituted their romantic evening walks along the lakefront. There were no reports of smothering, cutting, drinking, flirting, dancing with or spending the night out with other women. In fact, the couple stayed away from dance clubs and bars. They also reported having better sex and in general having more physical contact. When asked what they would rate their strong start to take back control of their relationship from the clutches of the "rejection pattern," they rated themselves to be 70% in charge. I responded with a big "Wow!" I gave them both big high fives for their great job. I explored with them what their secret for success was. Maria shared that "we kept on telling ourselves that we have to be a team." I asked them if the "rejection pattern" had had any victories over the 2-week period. Shana shared that there was one time where Maria and she "almost got into an argument over something small but we were able to resolve it." Again, I praised the couple on their excellent teamwork.

I decided as a vote of confidence to the couple that I would give them a 4-week vacation from counseling. Prior to ending the session, I predicted that the "rejection pattern" would try to spoil their vacation when they were least expecting it and how it was important to back each other up and keep chanting their mantra: "We have to be a team." When asked about they what they were going to do over the next week to be 80% of the time in charge of the "rejection pattern," both partners planned to increase doing what was working for them.

Third Couples Therapy Session

Although the couple felt they achieved their goal of being 80% in charge of the "rejection pattern," Maria had gone out with a former girlfriend who was visiting from out of town and had a few drinks with her. This had led to Shana's anxiety level increasing and cutting herself. They also had a short-lived argument about what this ex-girlfriend meant to Maria. However, Maria reassured Shana that she and Shana "were exclusive" and she was "not interested in" her "ex-girlfriend anymore." When asked if this was different for Maria to respond this way with Shana, the latter indicated that she had found Maria's behavior to be very comforting. I asked if they could foresee anything else happening over the next break period that could open the door to the "rejection pattern" doing some serious damage to their relationship, and neither partner felt they would let this happen.

On the upside of things, Shana had landed a great-paying job at a hospital, and the couple was still working out and going for long romantic walks along the lakefront. Maria shared that their sex life was greatly improving and that they were being much more playful with each other. After complimenting both the couple and each partner individually, I asked them when they wanted to come back, in 5 weeks or 6 weeks. The couple opted for 6 weeks. When asked what they would do to get up to 90% in charge of the "rejection pattern," they planned to go to an out-of-state beach park for the weekend. Both partners felt this would be another test to see how strong their relationship was getting. In the past, whenever they would be alone for a long period of time, they would end up having arguments.

The Final Couples Therapy Session

The couple came in glowing and quite pleased with their great progress. Their weekend getaway was "wonderful without one argument!" I gave both partners high fives. There were no reports of "cutting or drinking." Things had been going so well that the couple had "talked about canceling the appointment." In an effort to further consolidate their gains, I pulled out my imaginary crystal ball and had each partner gaze into it, telling me what further changes they see themselves making 1 year from now. Maria saw them in their "own apartment with a pet dog." Like Shana, she saw them "going out of state to get married." Shana saw herself "taking some college classes and working toward an associates degree at a local community college." Both partners saw themselves "very happy" and having an even "stronger relationship." After complimenting the couple, we mutually agreed to terminate couples therapy.

Telephone Follow-Up Calls

I spoke to each partner at 6 and 12 months. Not only was their relationship even better than the last office visit, but they had gotten their own apartment, they got a beagle, which they named Waldo, and Shana was taking evening college classes. There were no reports of cutting, drinking, or extra-relationship difficulties.

Post-Therapy Case Reflections

One of the biggest challenges working with Shana and Maria for me was trying to remain neutral and balanced with both partners. Since I had a long treatment history with Shana, I had to be careful not to favor or inadvertently take her side when discussing the couple's conflict issues. In the very first couple session, I worked hard to build a therapeutic alliance with Maria so that she could trust me and not feel that I was biased and taking Shana's side when discussing their difficulties.

Although the couple did report some sparkling moments or times when they were getting along, these positive events did not fit with the dominant story, which was Shana's not being able to trust Maria because she was "binge-drinking," "flirting," and sometimes "spending the night out with other women." Maria's part of the complaint story was Shana's "smothering," trying to control her, and "cutting." These behaviors would compel her to take back control and relieve stress by flirting, binge-drinking, and sleeping with other women. When Maria would engage in these behaviors, Shana would feel more out of control and begin cutting herself. Both partners resorted to emotion-driven and self-destructive coping strategies, which only made matters worse for the couple relationship.

The major therapeutic breakthrough that united the couple as a team and propelled their relationship into a more workable place was the use of externalizing the "rejection pattern," which was a family-of-origin pattern that had been oppressing both partners for a long time. For Shana, once she had begun the "coming out" process with her highly religious and conservative parents, they kicked her out of the house and cut off all contact with her. Maria's father, a devout Catholic and "traditional Latino man," emotionally and physically cut himself off from Maria when she had attempted to "come out" to him and her mother. Both partners agreed that they were being victimized by this oppressive pattern that had hurt them in previous intimate relationships and was haunting them in their current relationship. They accepted the challenge of working closely together as a team to take back control of their relationship from the "rejection pattern" and put an end to its reign over them. Through a lot of solid teamwork, the couple successfully conquered the "rejection pattern" and established a much more satisfactory relationship.

Case Example: It Only Takes One to Tango: Couples Therapy with One Partner

The Initial Consultation Session

Bill, a 21-year-old college senior and business major, had been referred to me by his mother. I had treated her for depression 3 years ago. Bill was seeking help for how to help his girlfriend Stacy stop cutting herself. Apparently, she had refused to go to the student mental health center on their college campus and see another therapist in the community with him. Stacy also made it quite clear to Bill that "counseling does not work." According to Bill, Stacy had seen "five therapists beginning in junior high and throughout high school for cutting and bulimia." Stacy's opinion was that her "cutting and bulimia had gotten much worse as a result of going to counseling" and that her "therapists never really understood her." Rather than putting any more pressure on Stacy, Bill decided to come to me to get "some advice on how best to manage" his situation with Stacy "without rocking the boat with her." Bill shared his concerns about Stacy's cutting 3–4 times per day and sometimes quite deeply. When asked about any past successes or self-generated pretreatment changes that helped even a little bit, Bill could not offer any examples or sparkling moments of hope. I asked Bill what his theory was of why Stacy was engaging in the cutting behavior. He believed it was due to her being "a perfectionist who came from a high-achievement-oriented family." Stacy had shared with him once that the cutting helps her "to relieve stress and frustration." Bill reported that "when Stacy did not get an 'A' on a test or a paper, she would cut very deeply into her skin."

When asked to share all of his attempted solutions, Bill quickly pointed out that he has "tried everything!" He has "pleaded with her to stop, gone through her dorm room to remove all sharp objects, asked to check her arms, asked her if she felt like cutting, tried to get her to go for counseling, and confronted her about stopping." I asked Bill to describe a motion picture of how he responded to a recent cutting episode with Stacy. Bill had "suspected she had just cut herself after speaking to her on the telephone" and came to her dorm room to investigate the situation. When he "asked if she had cut herself" and "wanted to check her arms, Stacy got very angry and defensive" and asked him to leave again. Bill refused to leave until she told him the truth. Stacy finally admitted that she cut herself. Bill tried to comfort Stacy by hugging her. Stacy asked him to leave. Bill left and called later in the evening to see if she was okay and to make peace with her. Later that night, Stacy had finally opened up to him about being upset about Bill's "putting his friends and his upcoming Fortune 500 company recruitment interviews" before her. Bill let Stacy know that he needed "a little space from her" and he "needed to focus on the business interviews to hopefully land a great job after graduation."

At this point in the interview, I asked Bill the miracle question to begin the goal-setting process. Bill quickly pointed out that "Stacy would not be cutting herself anymore," they would "not bicker as much," she "would not be so hard on herself with academic achievement," and they "would enjoy each other's company more." When asked what effect all of these changes would have on him, Bill shared that he would be "less stressed out," he would not be compelled to play "detective with her anymore," and they "would have a better relationship." I asked, "If I were a fly on Stacy's dorm room wall watching the two of you and listening to your conversations with her after the miracle happened, what would I hear you talking about?" Bill responded with, "We would be making fun date plans rather than my interrogating her like a detective." I asked Bill where they would be planning to go. Bill shared that they would be "going ice skating and having dinner out." He also reported that he would "not even bring up the word 'cutting' when we would get together." I then asked Bill the following: "If Stacy were sitting in that empty chair over there, what would she be the most surprised and pleased that changed with you after the miracle happened?" Bill responded with, "She would say: 'I am glad that you finally have stopped treating me like a crime suspect being questioned.'" I asked what else Stacy would see changed in their relationship. Bill pointed out that Stacy would be "happy" that they "were spending more time together." I asked Bill, "I'm curious. Have there been any pieces of the miracle happening a little bit already lately?" Bill quickly pointed out that there had been "two days over the past week" where he was "certain there was no cutting going on." When asked how he might have contributed to that, Bill shared that on one of the days he had "not mentioned a word about cutting" and on the other day they "spent the whole day by the lakefront lying together under a tree being loving toward one another." Bill discovered that "hugging and hand-holding" seemed to "put Stacy in a good mood."

At this point in the session, I asked Bill, "Let's say you left here completely satisfied with our consultation session and everything you were hoping for happened. What will be the number one thing that you will notice first that changed with your situation?" Bill said, "I will not be playing detective with Stacy anymore." I further added, "I will stop being so preoccupied with her cutting." I asked Bill a scaling question. "On a scale from 1 to 10, with 10 being not playing detective at all and 1 being playing detective all of the time with Stacy, where would you have rated yourself a month before this consultation session?" Bill said he was "at a 1." When asked where he would have rated himself 2 weeks ago, he said, "A 4." I inquired with him about the steps he had taken to get up to a 4. Bill pointed out that there had been some days where they had "spent long periods of time together without any mention of cutting." I asked Bill, "Are you aware of how you did that?" Bill responded that it was "tiring to argue about the cutting issue" and some days he can succeed at "keeping it out of my mind." To get a baseline of where Bill would rate himself now on the scale, he said he was "at a 5." Bill contended that he thought he was at a 5 because he and Stacy were "being more loving with one another lately." I asked Bill, "What are you going to do over the next week to get one step higher up, to a 6?" Bill shared with me that he was going to try to "refrain from playing detective with Stacy" and try to "reduce the amount of time" he "thought about her cutting issue."

After a brief intersession break, I shared my editorial reflections with Bill. I complimented Bill on how caring and insightful he was and committed to improving his relationship with Stacy. I shared with him that I thought it was great that he did "not want to rock the boat with Stacy" by trying to force her to see yet another therapist and was already on to some creative and useful strategies of his own creation that were working. I offered Bill two therapeutic experiments:

1. Bill was to pick a few days over the next week to pretend to engage in both his individual miracle behaviors and Stacy's miracle behaviors for him. While pretending, he was to carefully notice how Stacy would respond.
2. Bill was asked to notice what he would do daily to overcome the urge to dwell on Stacy's cutting issue. However, if he should cave in to impulse and start thinking about her cutting issue, he was instructed to write down the thought on a piece of paper, read it, and then crumble it up and throw it away.

Bill thought both of these experiments could be helpful to try and he agreed to test them out.

The Second Session

Bill came back 1 week later with a great report. He reported that he "went a whole week without bringing up once the cutting issue with Stacy!" When asked about if he was aware of how he resisted the temptation to play detective with her, Bill shared that he would silently talk to himself and say, "Don't do it!" He also would go to the bathroom in Stacy's dorm room and look in the mirror and say to himself, "It's okay, stop worrying." There were two occasions away from Stacy where Bill had to write down on paper his worrying thoughts, read them, and throw them away. He found this strategy to be very helpful. Bill shared that he and Stacy were "getting along really well" and "she seemed much happier." I consolidated and amplified all of Bill's gains. Bill rated himself "between a 7 and an 8." I asked Bill, "An 8– or a 7 + ?" Bill went with the 8–. Next, I asked Bill what the next step would be that he will take to get up to a 9–. Bill said that he will continue to do the experiments and what was working. He planned to shoot for "a whole week of not worrying once about the cutting issue." I complimented Bill on his hard work and great progress. I pointed out that slips go with the territory of change and if they should occur, they are a sign that Bill was making headway and he should view them as valuable teachers of wisdom regarding where we need to tighten up. As a vote of confidence, I wanted to offer Bill a choice when he wanted to come back, in 2 or 3 weeks. He decided to come back in 3 weeks.

The Last Session

Three weeks later, Bill happily reported that he had "made it to a 10!" He continued to avoid "not playing detective with Stacy." He "did not have any worries about the cutting issue." In fact, Stacy approached him and said that she has "totally stopped cutting for the past 2 weeks." Instead of cutting, Stacy was "getting better at not being so hard on herself with her academic performance" and "regularly taking both aerobics and pilates classes at the university gym." Sometimes, Bill and Stacy would go to the gym together. Bill was saving the best news for last. He had "landed a six-figure position with a Fortune 500 company!" Upon graduation, he would begin his new job and planned to ask Stacy to marry him as well. After consolidating all of Bill's gains, we mutually agreed to terminate.

Telephone Follow-Up Calls

I spoke to Bill at 6 and 12 months. He reported that he loved his new job and that he had married Stacy. They purchased a condo together near the lakefront. There were no reports of cutting or any reoccurrence of Stacy's former bulimia problem in either of the two telephone conversations. I also had received a call from Bill's mother thanking me for helping her son.

Post-Therapy Case Reflections

Bill's case example nicely illustrates the importance of honoring a client's theory of change, treatment preferences, and how it is possible to change a client couple relational system through one partner. It is my contention that clients should take the lead in determining their goals, deciding who attends counseling sessions with them, determining the treatment modalities they wish to pursue, and the frequency of session visits, and setting the counseling session agendas. By being sensitive to and respectful of Bill's wishes to be seen individually, this helped establish a cooperative relationship with him. Bill was highly motivated and in the action stage of readiness for change.

In exploring Bill's unproductive attempted solutions at trying to change Stacy, it was a newsworthy experience for him. He could see how being too overprotective and playing the detective role with Stacy would only serve to fuel more conflict in their relationship and further maintain her self-harming behavior. Bill also discovered that incessantly worrying about her would result in his experiencing negative self-fulfilling prophecies and make him feel more worried, have more catastrophic thoughts, and feel more miserable. Once Bill was able to avoid the temptation to let his worries drive his actions in relationship to Stacy and abandon his unproductive habitual patterns of behavior, he helped pave the way for the kind of changes he desired with Stacy's situation, and their relationship greatly improved.

CHAPTER FIVE

Collaborative Strengths-Based Brief Therapy with Self-Harming Young Adults and Adolescents

Working Individually with Self-Harming Young Adults and Adolescents

With self-harming young adult and adolescent clients where you have limited to no contact with their parents or they would prefer individual counseling, a collaborative strengths-based brief therapy approach can be a viable treatment alternative to couples or family therapy. When working with young adults who are attending a university or college out of state, the only access the therapist may have to their parents is during their visits to the campus prior to a holiday or school year breaks. It is during these times that the therapist can capitalize on this great opportunity to do direct family work if the young adults have identified family conflict or relationship changes that are one of their treatment goals. If this is the case, the therapist can set aside a few hours to do a marathon session. Between the infrequent parental visit times, the young adults can try out therapeutic experiments designed to help improve their relationships with their parents or siblings, either on the telephone or when visiting their parents during holiday and school breaks. However, there are many young adults who may or may not be college students who want to work on relationship difficulties or on their own unique individual issues. Ultimately, the young adults take the lead in determining the focus of treatment and their goals.

For therapists working in school and residential treatment settings with self-harming adolescents, it may be difficult to schedule parents during the day for family therapy sessions because of their work schedules. The school social worker, psychologist, and counselor may not have time to provide this service during their hectic workdays. And because of geographic reasons or that the adolescents are wards of their home states, they may only have the adolescents to work with. Although it is my bias and strong belief that family therapy is the treatment of choice for self-harming and other adolescent behavioral difficulties, there are some clinical situations where I will only work alone with the adolescent. I will work individually with an adolescent when a combination of the following family dynamics are present: The parents have severe mental health and/or substance abuse problems, the parents have severe marital and postdivorce conflicts and cannot tolerate being in the same room together, the adolescent refuses to open up in the company of their parents because of their intense conflicts, safety issues are in question for the adolescents and other family members, family therapy has not worked in the past after multiple attempts, and the best thing we can do for the adolescents is to help them become more resilient, learn independent living skills, and launch out of the family nest into adulthood. If the adolescents discuss family conflicts or relationships they wish to change, a one–person collaborative strengths-based brief family therapy approach can be used and they can serve as the agent of change for their family. Therapeutic experiments can be offered that the adolescents can implement in their efforts to change their interactions with a particular family member or a family relationship. Once tested out and evaluated, the adolescents and the therapist scan determine together what works, what to discard, or which new therapeutic experiments to try.

Co-Constructing Tribal Circles of Caring Others to Support Isolated Self-Harming Young Adults and Adolescents

Some self-harming young adults and adolescents report feeling alone and isolated and not being able to count on their biological or foster parents, key caretakers, extended family members, or, in some cases, their peers. In these situations, I have found it quite effective to co-construct with clients a *tribal circle of caring others*. I used to work in a clinic in a very poor community with a lot of gang activity where the adolescents had serious self-harming and other behavioral difficulties and came from families with parents who had heroin addictions, alcoholism, and severe mental health problems. Many of these youths turned to their second family in the community, the street gang, to try to get their needs met. To help prevent these adolescents from becoming alcohol or drug dependent, taking their lives, and ending up killed on the streets or incarcerated, my colleagues and I came up with the idea of co-constructing with them tribal circles of caring others comprised of adults and healthy peers who they identified as truly caring about them and had possibly helped them in the past get through some tough times. The adolescents in our program identified the following people: responsible relatives, clergy, community leaders, former coaches, teachers, concerned and caring adult neighbors, healthy peers from former neighborhoods who had stayed in touch, or possibly non-gang-involved or non-substance-abusing peers. Not only did we find that this tribal network of caring and committed adult inspirational others and healthy peers wanted to make themselves available to these struggling youths, but they would generate highly creative solutions to help them turn their lives around. For example, a participating priest in one of our tribal circle of caring others' collaborative meetings helped get one of my drug-dealing and self-harming gang-involved clients off the street and working in his church so he could learn how to earn money legally. A concerned adult female neighbor hair stylist offered to serve as a mentor for a female self-harming and substance-abusing adolescent client of mine to help perfect her hair-styling skills and maintain her future interest in doing cosmetology work. Once the members of the tribal circle are engaged, the rules of confidentiality are explained and all participants and minors' parents are asked to sign off on the significant other consent form.

With self-harming young adult college students reporting feeling alone and isolated, I have used a similar strategy of organizing a tribal circle of caring adults, such as favorite professors who they have tightly bonded with and they trust, student mental health counselors, university clergy, local caring relatives or close adult friends of the family, or one or two friends on campus who would be willing to participate in the change effort. I will also recommend the involvement of my former college-aged self-harming alumni who are now abstinent, doing well in college, and leading more meaningful and satisfactory lives. In addition to offering support and creative solutions, the young adult clients will feel a strong sense of community and establish meaningful connections with healthy and caring people who they can count on. Having the tribal circle of caring others actively participating at the beginning and through the conclusion of treatment can offer individual clients multiple perspectives on the important changes they have made, which can further increase their awareness levels about what works and empowers them.

The other advantage of organizing a tribal circle of caring others for both self-harming young adults and adolescents is that it decentralizes therapists from being the main support people for these clients. The members of the tribal circle of caring others take over with providing the continued support and helping them to stay on track. In some cases, self-harming young adults and adolescents have established long-lasting, meaningful relationships with members of their supportive tribal community.

Case Example: Breaking Free from the Clutches of "Feeling Invisible" and "Cutting and Burning": Empowering a College Student to Take Back Control of Her Life

Referral Process

Samantha, a 19-year-old college freshman, was referred to me by her student mental health counselor Mandy for cutting and burning herself 4–5 times per day since the beginning of her first school year on campus. According to Mandy, "Samantha has made no friends" and describes herself as "feeling invisible" in her classes and on campus. Efforts to "hook her up with social activities or support groups on campus" had proven to be futile, in that "Samantha fails to follow through." Prior to coming to the university, Samantha had two past psychiatric admissions for cutting, depression, and anorexia and had seen six outpatient therapists since she was

14. The student mental health center psychiatrist diagnosed Samantha as being depressed and placed her on Zoloft. In spite of Samantha's depression, she was able to maintain a straight-A grade point average. Mandy also shared with the author that Samantha described her family as being "highly dysfunctional" and her parents "invalidating her a lot as a teenager." Out of frustration and feeling stuck, Mandy referred Samantha to me for a consultation.

The Initial Consultation Session

I spent the early part of the consultation session coming to know Samantha by her strengths. She had been an A student throughout her entire academic career and was particularly strong in math, science, and computer skills. Samantha shared with me that she always "experienced social ridicule for being so smart" and "never felt like" she "fit in with the popular kids." Since coming to the university, Samantha had felt "like an invisible person" both in and out of her classes. Samantha could not identify one pretreatment change or any time recently or in the past where she felt visible in and out of class or even back in high school. When asked about what her theory was why she was not more visible to others, Samantha described herself as being "shy" and being so "scarred up" on her "arms and legs from cutting and burning" herself that she did not want people to see this side of her and "deliberately avoided having close contact with others." Samantha went on to say that she felt like she created her "own prison" for herself in that she wanted to fit in socially and make some friends, but, on the other hand, she did not want people to discover how she was "brutalizing" her body with her self-harming practice. Samantha shared with me that the cutting and burning served two purposes: It made her "feel something" and it was "a way to punish" herself for "not being good enough." I used curiosity with Samantha and asked her, "Is that your voice talking about 'not being good enough' or someone else's voice from your past?" Samantha quickly pointed out that it was her "father's voice talking" and that her "parents are high-achievement-oriented and always put pressure on" her "to get straight A's in school." "They expected me to always study and be at the top of my high school class so I could get into the best universities." She also stated that her parents were not very affectionate with either her or her older brother who lives in Europe.

When asked what specifically she wanted to change now, Samantha shared that she wanted "help with getting out of the prison" she created for herself. I asked, "Let's say over the next week you figure out how to pick the lock of your prison cell door and begin to escape from being invisible. What will be the first step you will take with your new-found freedom?" Samantha responded with, "Take a risk in one of my classes and initiate a conversation with another student." I then asked, "What will you tell yourself or do to drum up the courage to pull off this big step over the next week?" Samantha shared that she was "not sure" but that she had "to start somewhere." I asked her, "Is there one particular student you have in mind in one of your classes who seems nice that you will talk to?" Samantha shared that there was this "friendly girl in her biology class" who she would approach. I explored with Samantha what specifically she will talk to this student about. Samantha thought it would be "best to start talking about the biology class" and then "talk about her other classes" and "how she liked being at the university." In an effort to cover the back door and emotionally fire up Samantha to take this big step, I externalized the problem and raised a dilemma with her. I asked, "In what ways do you think 'being invisible' will try to sabotage you before you approach this 'nice student'?" Samantha responded with, "Well, when the time comes to take the risk and talk to her, I won't do it." I raised the following dilemma with her: "So, is 'being invisible' a friend that protects you from being discovered (protecting her self-harming practice) or does it prevent you from growing and taking risks in your life?" Samantha agreed that caving in to "being invisible" was keeping her "in prison" and that she needed to "take this step now!" I asked Samantha, "How will you outsmart 'being invisible' when it tries to infiltrate your mind and thwart your effort to talk to the 'nice student'?" Samantha firmly and confidently responded with, "I won't let it happen!" We mutually agreed that this would be her initial treatment goal.

After taking a brief intersession break, I complimented Samantha on her courage and perseverance. I complimented her on already showing "being invisible" who is going to be in charge of her life by showing up for this consultation with a complete stranger. I went on to say, "Being invisible could have brainwashed you to not take any more risks with counseling and continue to be its prisoner." Samantha smiled and nodded her head. I offered the following therapeutic experiments for Samantha to choose from:

1. Pay close attention to what you will tell yourself and do to frustrate "being invisible" when you take your courageous step to talk to the 'nice student.'
2. In order to learn more about the times when "being invisible" and "cutting and burning" are not teaming up and doing their dirty work against you, notice what you will do to stand up to them and "take the step now" to take back control of your life.

Samantha agreed to try out both of these therapeutic experiments. We scheduled our next appointment for the following week.

The Second Session

I began the second session by inquiring with Samantha what further progress she made at standing up to "being invisible" and not allowing it to sabotage her goal. Samantha proudly reported that she "spoke to Marnie (the nice student) after the biology class and it went really well." I asked her, "What is your secret about how you pulled that off?!" Samantha responded with, "When "being invisible" was trying to undermine my efforts to take this risk, I told it, 'You are not going to get away with this'!" She went on to report that "Marnie asked" her "to get coffee with her" and she "actually went." I responded with, "Wow! I don't know if 'being invisible' will be able to cope with the risky daredevil you have become!" Samantha laughed and jokingly said, "Yeah, it better watch out because being visible feels pretty good!" I asked her, "How do you view yourself differently now versus the former you who was held captive in prison by both 'being invisible' and 'cutting and burning'?" Samantha stated that she felt more confident and liked having her freedom." Her next goal for herself was to "ask Marnie if she would like to go out for dinner." To help co-create a positive, self-fulfilling prophecy and pave the way for Samantha to achieve her new goal, I introduced my imaginary crystal ball and had her gaze into it, seeing herself having dinner with Marnie and describing all of the details about what day and time they will go out, where they are eating, how she will be dressed, the specifics about what she will be talking about with her, and how well the conversation was going. Samantha did a beautiful job describing all of the details .

I wanted to make Samantha aware of the fact that "being invisible" and "cutting and burning" will not give up easily and could strike when she is least expecting them to do their dirty work. I asked her, "How specifically will you not allow them to undermine your special dinner with Marnie?" Samantha disclosed that "cutting was trying to strip me of my confidence after talking with Marnie." Apparently, after talking with Marnie she had gone back to her dorm room and carved deeply into her left arm. Samantha shared that "it was as if cutting took over my mind and made me do this." I asked her what its brainwashing thoughts were and she said, "I will not let go of you" and "I will not share you with anyone else." I explored with Samantha how she prevented this slip from becoming a prolonged relapsing situation. She stated, "I was able to tell myself I have got to stop this!" When asked how committed Samantha was to breaking free from the clutches of "cutting" and its tag team partner, "burning," on a scale from 1 to 10, with 10 being totally committed, she said she was at "a 7." I asked her where she would have rated herself back when she was seeing Mandy (the counselor at the student mental health center). Samantha rated herself at "a 1." I explored with Samantha other steps she had taken over the past week to get up to a 7. She observed that "keeping busy with schoolwork, going for long walks, and doing yoga in her dorm room" helped her to not cave in to cutting or burning. We talked about the importance of structure-building and filling up her free time with as many healthy and constructive activities as possible. To clarify her goal for herself over the next week, Samantha reiterated that she "will go out for dinner with Marnie" and "not come back to" her "dorm room and cut or burn" herself. Again, I cautioned her about "being invisible" and "cutting and burning" reasserting their power and trying to get her back in prison and sabotaging her special plans with Marnie. I introduced the My Positive Trigger Log to help increase her awareness of her positive triggers and what works to stay on track. I also taught Samantha the sound and food meditations, urge surfing, and body scanning as methods she could use to center herself and be less reactive to "being invisible" and "cutting and burnings" efforts to take over her mind.

Following the brief intersession break, I complimented Samantha on her great work and tremendous ability to bounce back after having a slip and not throwing in the towel or allowing this to be an excuse for "being invisible" to make her surrender to it and go back to imprisoning herself. I encouraged her to continue to keep busy with her schoolwork, go for long walks, and do yoga. I offered Samantha a 2-week vacation from counseling as a vote of confidence. However, while on vacation I recommended that Samantha:

1. Practice using the sound and food meditations, urge surfacing, and body scanning coping tools and strategies
2. Keep track of her positive triggers and fill out the My Positive Trigger Log
3. Increase the frequency of her long walks and yoga.

The Third Session

Samantha came in pleased with the big steps she had taken. Not only had she gone a whole week without cutting or burning herself even once, but her dinner went great with Marnie and they had become "closer friends" as a result of it. In fact, they had gotten together five times over the 2-week interval period. When asked where she would rate herself in her commitment to conquer "cutting and burning," she gave herself a 9. I asked Samantha what her secret was to achieve a 9 performance over the past 2 weeks. Samantha reported that "going for long walks both alone and with Marnie in the forest preserve park, doing yoga, the meditations, urge surfing, body scanning, keeping busy with schoolwork all helped." She found the My Positive Trigger Log helpful for discovering other ways to trigger positive emotion and as a reminder of what to do when stressed out. Apparently, she had gotten a B grade on a history paper and she was tempted to cut herself but looked at her My Positive Trigger Log and called Marnie to go for a long walk. When Samantha came back from the nice and relaxing walk with Marnie, she "decided to do the food meditation," to further "take her mind off the paper." I made a big deal about how well she had handled this challenging situation. After complimenting her excellent week and fancy footwork with staving off a near slip, I encouraged her to keep doing more of what was working. I asked Samantha when she wanted to come back, in 3 or 4 weeks, and she decided to schedule an appointment in a month.

The Last Session

Prior to our next session, Samantha had called me to see if she could bring Marnie to the meeting. After establishing rapport with Marnie, I discovered that she used to cut herself in high school. Apparently, with Samantha's increased confidence level and more stable positive mood, she had the guts to let Marnie know about her hidden self-harming practice. Samantha was quite surprised to discover that Marnie used to have this difficulty. When asked how she had conquered her self-harming practice, Marnie pointed out that both playing volleyball and working out had given her more pleasure than the cutting did. In fact, Marnie had gotten

Samantha to join her intramural volleyball team. Not only was Samantha enjoying playing on the volleyball team, but she was making new friends as well. Also, on the upside of things, Samantha reported that she was now "at a perfect 10!" I asked her, "Are you aware of how you did this?!" Samantha shared that she had not cut or burned herself once, was "going for long walks, doing yoga, the meditations, urge surfing, body scanning," and continued to find "the My Positive Trigger Log helpful." However, what Samantha was most pleased about was that she had "Marnie in my life."

To test the solidity of Samantha's changes, I asked her what she would need to do at this point to go backward. She confidently said, "It's not going to happen!" I asked her, "What if you get a B grade on a paper or test?" Again, Samantha confidently stated, "I won't let this get to me and I know I will have other chances to pick up my grade in the class." In an effort to highlight differences and Samantha's gains, I had Marnie reflect on the former Samantha when she first had met her and how the new Samantha is today. Marnie stated that "Samantha used to be shy and quiet-spoken but is now more spontaneous and fun to hang out with." She further added that "Samantha has become friends" with some of her friends as well.

After a brief intersession break, I complimented Samantha on her tremendous progress and how fortunate she was that Marnie was in her life. Samantha felt at this point she no longer needed any further counseling. We mutually agreed to terminate.

Telephone Follow-Up

I spoke to Samantha only at 6 months because I was unable to reach her 1 year later. At this time, Samantha had "gotten an apartment with Marnie off school grounds near the university." She had become closer with Marnie's friends and continued to engage in healthy and constructive activities during her free time or when she was "stressed out." There were no reports of cutting or burning.

Post-Therapy Case Reflections

Samantha presented for counseling with me with quite an extensive treatment history and with a self-harming practice that could fall into the heavy to severe practice categories. In carefully listening to her long self-harming story, it was clear that she had been oppressed by cutting and burning and "being invisible" for a long time. When I am working with new clients who are describing their difficulties as oppressive and seemingly having a life all of their own, I will externalize the problem. After externalizing both the "being invisible" and "cutting and burning" problems, I raised dilemmas with Samantha and got her fired up to take back control of her life from the clutches of these difficulties. Samantha responded with a lot of positive emotionality in response to the externalizing questions, which helped liberate her from the jail cell that these difficulties were keeping her imprisoned in. Once out of the jail cell, Samantha was free to take risks and pursue a more preferred and healthy direction with her life.

I also made good use of presuppositional language and embedded hypnotic commands with Samantha to further empower her, such as: "Notice what you *will* do" and "take the step *now* to *take back* control of your life." In addition, the use of the imaginary crystal ball further empowered Samantha to co-create a positive self-fulfilling prophecy with her situation.

Once Samantha was on the road to change, I covered the back door by stressing the importance of structure building, consolidating her gains, using prediction ("being invisible" and "cutting and burning" may try to sabotage her gains and strike when she is least expecting it), and My Positive Trigger Log. Since Samantha was so bright and resourceful, I encouraged her to increase doing more of what was working.

Finally, I was so delighted to witness Samantha's tremendous growth socially. She not only succeeded at establishing a solid relationship with Marnie but with Marnie's friends as well.

Case Example: "I Can't Count on Mom and I Can't Count on Dad": Helping an Older Adolescent Soar on His Own

Referral Process

Sean, a 17-year-old high school senior, was referred to me by his school social worker, Mindy, for burning, cutting, and self-battery. Mindy claimed that Sean had been self-harming "every day to every few days up to 4–5 times a day." According to Mindy, "Sean had been engaging in these behaviors since age 14. All of Sean's life his 2-year-older brother Paul has bullied him and the parents were unable to stop him." At the current alternative school Sean was attending, there also are "gang-involved students that have harassed and bullied him" as well. These negative experiences and frustrating situations trigger Sean to "punch himself in the face, pour lighter fuel on his arm and set it on fire, or he will burn himself with a cigarette or cut deeply into his arm with a razor blade." After he was psychiatrically hospitalized three times by the school district psychiatrist affiliated with his former high school for his self-harming behaviors, he was placed in Mindy's alternative school. He had been diagnosed with borderline personality disorder, obsessive-compulsive disorder, and bipolar disorder. Sean had been placed on Depakote and Wellbutrin but he did not take his medication as prescribed. Since age 14, Sean had seen nine therapists. Mindy stated that "family therapy had not worked in the past because of both frequent session cancellations and the parents' resistance to attend sessions." Mindy pointed out that since Sean's parents had divorced when he was 12, his "father has completely checked out of Sean's life." His mother was "very depressed and anxious and unable to keep a job." Apparently, she had been "inconsistent with attending meetings" with Mindy and Sean's teachers. "The family was experiencing financial difficulties but the father was responsible, paying child support and helping out with his sons' basic needs."

When asked about Sean's strengths, Mindy described Sean as being "very bright, a gifted artist, and a wizard on the computer." Mindy had been seeing Sean daily, sometimes twice a day, when he would "come to school in a bad place emotional-ly" or to stave off a self-harming episode at school "after the negative peers would harass or bully him." Due to her hectic schedule and a big caseload of students, Mindy decided to refer Sean to me.

The First Therapy Session
Sean's mother dropped Sean off at my office and went to run some errands. Sean shared with me that this is how it has been since his parents' divorced. "I can't count on my mom and I can't count on my dad." Apparently, this was his mother's pattern of dropping him off at therapists' offices and then disappearing for the hour. He said his father would call him "out of the blue to arrange a visit and then call and cancel or fail to show up period!" I validated Sean's feelings about being let down by his parents and asked him to please let him know while we were work-ing together if he felt misunderstood or not supported by me.

At this point in the session, I shifted gears to come to know Sean by his strengths. He proudly shared his expertise with computers, particularly his unique and creative graphic art, logo, and Web site designs. To earn some money, he has designed Web sites and logos for his mother's friends, neighbors, and some local small businesses. I shared with Sean that I would love to see some his graphic art designs. Sean agreed to bring in some of his artwork. When asked about his future career dreams for himself, Sean pointed out that he would really like to do graph-ic art design work for a major computer company. Sean was visibly quite animat-ed and excited about his career plans.

Before initiating the goal-setting process, I wanted to make sure he did not repli-cate any of the unproductive attempted solutions that Sean's former therapists and inpatient staff had tried with him in the past. I placed Sean in the expert consult-ant role and invited him to share what former therapists and inpatient staff had said or tried with him that made him upset or had iatrogenic negative effects. Sean was quick to mention that some of his former therapists kept their distance with him, as if he "were poisonous" or "a monster" when he would talk about "hitting, burning, and carving into myself." He said, "They were scared of me." Sean further added, "They loved giving me labels like borderline personality disorder, OCD, and bipolar disorder." In fact, two of his therapists had him psychiatrically hospitalized first before agreeing to work with him. Sean "hated taking medication" because of the "terrible side effects," and he stated that "they really didn't work anyways." I asked him, "You have seen many therapists before me. Was there anything they missed or overlooked with you or your situation that is really important for me to know so I can help you out in the best way possible?" Sean was quick to say, "I'm not crazy! Try to understand me and how frustrating my life is living in a family where your parents are useless and your brother is like a loose cannon!" I validat-ed Sean's feelings, offered empathy and support, and thanked him for his expert advice about what to avoid doing with him and what could be helpful in our work together. Sean gave me some helpful feedback about how he appreciated his interest in "what was good about" him. Apparently, his former therapists' "only wanted to talk about my problems and get inside of my head."

To begin the goal-setting process, I asked Sean the following question: "Let's say we were to look at a DVD movie of you 1 month down the road when your life situation has changed. What will you see in the movie that is different with you and your situation?" Sean said, "I will stop hurting myself." I asked Sean, "What will we see you doing instead of hurting yourself in the movie, when your brother, the peers at your school, or your mother is frustrating you?" Sean pointed out, "You will see me shaking off their words, holding my head up, and walking away from them."

I then asked, "What else will we see you doing differently in the movie?" Sean shared, "I will be hanging out more with Sandy (his girlfriend), spending more time making new graphic art designs for my portfolio for future job interviews, and getting out of the house more." Sean also shared that he would be "happier" and "feeling more in control of my life." When asked what specifically we will see happening in the movie that will make him feel "happier" and "feeling more in control." Sean stated, "You will see me hanging out more with Sandy and I am doing better in school." I asked Sean what we will see him doing differently in his classes that will help him do better grade-wise. Sean shared, "You will see me sitting in the front of the classes paying attention, taking good notes, and turning in my homework." I asked him, "Are any scenes from this movie already happening in your life now?" Sean responded with, "Sandy and I have been spending a little more time together, I have made several new graphic art designs, and I have not hurt myself for the past three days." I asked, "Are you aware of how you were able to make all of those wonderful things happen?" Sean shared, "Hanging out with Sandy and spending hours making more graphic art designs makes me happy and relaxes me. When these good things are happening, I am less likely to hurt myself." I made a mental note about needing to increase Sean's involvement in these activities to reduce the frequency of self-harming episodes. I then asked Sean, "How will you know that you really succeeded in counseling?" Sean said, "I will stop hurting myself even when my brother, peers, and my parents frustrate or hurt my feelings." I asked Sean the following scaling question: "On a scale from 1 to 10, with 10 being you are no longer hurting yourself and 1 hurting yourself all of the time, where would you have rated yourself a month before coming here?" Sean said, "At a 1." When asked about 2 weeks ago, Sean said he was "at a 4." I explored with Sean how he had gotten four steps higher, up to a 4. According to Sean, "Spending more time with Sandy and trying to ignore my brother and the gangbangers at school." He currently rated himself to be "at a 6." Again, I played detective and wanted to know the specific steps that Sean had taken to get up to a 6. Sean stated, "Hanging out more with Sandy who just told me that she 'loved' me, ignoring my brother and the gangbangers, and making some new graphic art designs." I asked the following question to establish Sean's initial treatment goal: "What are you going to do over the next week to get up one step higher, to a 7?" Sean said, "Spending even more time with Sandy, keep ignoring or walking away from people who bring me down, and try and not hurt myself for the whole week. I commended Sean on his ambitious goal of going a whole week without hurting himself but shared my concerns about setting such a big goal for himself since the self-harming had been happening for such a long time and things happen that are beyond our control. Sean agreed that if he could go "4 out of 7 days" he "would be happy."

After a brief intersession break, I complimented Sean on how his situation reminded me of a sign in one of my colleague's offices that reads: "Please solve your problems before you come in here so I can help you more." Sean smiled. I complimented him on already coming up with effective ways to not cave in to hurting himself: "hanging out more with Sandy," which makes him "happier," making "more graphic art designs," "ignoring his brother and the gangbangers" when they are trying to hurt or frustrate him, and "getting out of the house more." I introduced to Sean the My Positive Trigger Log to keep track of and write down what he and others do to help him not cave in to hurting himself and triggers positive emotion for him. I offered Sean the following therapeutic experiments to try over the next week:

1. Pretend that the DVD movie is your reality right now and increase your time spent with Sandy, make more graphic art designs, ignore and walk away from your brother and the gangbangers, and get out of the house more.
2. Notice what you will do and others do daily to help you avoid the temptation to hurt yourself. Write those things down on your My Positive Trigger Log.

Shortly after I saw Sean, I called Mindy (the school social worker) to let her know that he had shown up for his session and how well it went. Mindy was delighted to hear that I had made a good connection with Sean and that he had showed up. We agreed to stay in touch and collaborate.

The Second Therapy Session

Sean came in reporting an excellent week. He went 6 out of 7 days without hurting himself! When asked about how he had pulled this off, Sean responded with, "Hanging out with Sandy more and spending more time making graphic art designs," and "ignoring and walking away from my brother and the gangbangers" when they were trying to hurt him. He found the My Positive Trigger Log to be helpful because it reminded him of what his "options were" when he would "feel frustrated or down." Apparently, the one cutting incident was "not deep" and was short-lived. It had occurred following an upsetting call from his father. He just called to "check in" with Sean, "not to get together." Sean was "angry at" his dad, and said, "I decided to not tell him but take it out on me." I provided support and understood Sean's dilemma about being angry but not wanting to alienate his father any further by getting him mad at him and wanting to keep the door open to him. I provided empathy and support. I also pointed out to Sean that at this point it might be helpful to try to use the same strategy he uses with his brother and the gang-bangers, that is, of ignoring and walking away from the upsetting telephone call, realizing that he can take back control of the situation rather than allowing it to frustrate him or bring him down. Sean agreed that this could work.

I explored with Sean how he was able to not allow the cutting incident to escalate into him burning and punching himself. Sean responded with, "I called Sandy right away and she helped me not really lose it." Other good things that happened over the week was his brother Paul was "not bullying or name-calling as much," and Sean "did well on two tests" in school. Sean rated himself "at an 8!"

I amplified and consolidated Sean's many gains over the past week and asked him if he would like to meet a friend of mine who was a computer graphic art designer to learn more about this career area. Sean thought this was "really sweet" (cool). In order to do this, I informed Sean that he would have to get written consent from his mother first. I also told Sean that if he would like to bring Sandy to a meeting, he could do that as well. Due to Sean's hard work and tremendous gains, I gave Sean a vacation from counseling as a vote of confidence. Sean elected to take a two-week vacation from counseling. While on vacation, I encouraged him to keep doing more of what was working and take steps to get up to an 8.

Prior to seeing Sean again, I called Mindy to update her on his progress. Mindy also reported that Sean appeared to be "happier" and in "brighter spirits." She was also pleased that he appeared to be "getting a better handle on his self-injuring behavior."

Third Therapy Session

Present in the next session were Sean, Sandy, and Yuri, my computer graphic designer friend. They became his tribal circle of caring others. Mindy, his school social worker, another member of this tribal circle of caring others, could not attend this meeting because of work commitments. I had secured consent from both Sean's mother and Sandy's mother to have both Yuri and Sandy participate in our meeting. Sean reported having a great vacation from counseling. He earned his 8 rating by "not hurting" himself "once over 2 weeks' time!" I played cheerleader and made a big deal about this great accomplishment. Both Sandy and Yuri also applauded Sean's big step. He shared that he and Paul (the older brother) were getting along better. Sandy gave Sean a lot of praise for turning his situation around and was very happy about "being exclusive" with him.

Yuri looked through Sean's portfolio of graphic art designs and was very impressed with his work. I had talked with Sean about seeing if he could apprentice with him. Yuri was glad to set aside some weekly time to help Sean further hone his computer graphic art design skills. Sean was thrilled about this terrific opportunity. Sandy thanked Yuri for being so kind and generous. After complimenting

Sean on his great progress and thanking Sandy and Yuri for coming and continuing to empower Sean to soar, we mutually agreed to meet in a month.

When updating Mindy about Sean's progress on the telephone, I thought it would be great for her to attend the next and possibly last session due to his tremendous progress. It also would be a wonderful opportunity to have her highlight where Sean was at the beginning of the school year and where he was at now. Finally, I wanted Mindy to meet my friend Yuri, who agreed to serve as Sean's mentor and adult inspirational other.

Final Therapy Session

Sean came to our session in great spirits. Not only had he not hurt himself once and things were fine with Sandy, but his grades had gone up considerably. He thanked me for hooking him up with Yuri and said he had learned a great deal from him already. Apparently, Yuri was working out with his boss a summer employment opportunity for Sean after he graduated. Yuri became a combination adult inspirational other and a fatherlike figure for Sean. Later in the meeting, Mindy, Sean's school social worker, joined us. I had Mindy highlight where Sean was at when he was at his worst at the beginning of the school year and where he was now. Mindy pointed out that he had been self-harming almost daily for a time at the beginning of the school year and nearly failing academically. Now, she said, "Sean is like a new person, happy, not hurting himself, not letting people get to him, and doing great academically." Mindy told him, "I am really proud of you." Sean was sporting a big smile and thanked Mindy for "all of your help." She told Sean, "You made it happen!" After consolidating all of Sean's gains and having his mother join us at the end of the session to reflect on his great progress as well, we mutually decided to terminate treatment. His mother completely supported Sean's work with Yuri with the hope that it may lead to future employment opportunities for him.

Telephone Consult with Yuri

I made myself available to Yuri if there were any concerns he had about Sean. Yuri felt that he and Sean had a great relationship and that he was getting better with his graphic art design abilities. Yuri was able to work it out to bring Sean aboard with his company over the summer to see how he handles it. His boss was very impressed with Sean's work.

Telephone Follow-Up Calls

I reached Sean and his mother at 6 and 12 months. The best news was that Sean was working at Yuri's company. Sean's mother shared with me that she was very proud of Sean. Sean had seen his father a few times and the "visits went well." He and Paul were "getting along better." Since Sean was starting to make "enough money to pay rent on a nice apartment," he and Sandy were apartment hunting so they could live together.

Post-Therapy Case Reflections

One of the major themes strongly emphasized in this case example is the importance of seeing beyond all of the alleged *DSM-IV* labels and psychopathology Sean was supposed to have, focusing more on identifying his key strengths and flow-state activities, and utilizing them to empower him to resolve his difficulties. This case example also illustrates the importance of placing clients who have had multiple treatment experiences, particularly negative ones in the expert consultant role, to ensure that therapists avoid replicating unsuccessful treatment strategies. Sean was quick to point out what had not worked and further exacerbated his difficulties. By taking the time to do this, I was able to rapidly develop a strong therapeutic alliance with Sean.

Once Sean had moved into the action stage of readiness to change, my use of the DVD movie pressuppositional questions about how his situation will look after it changed helped Sean clearly define his ideal treatment outcome picture. Sean offered very clear indicators or signposts about how he will know that change really happened. This question also helped co-create a positive self-fulfilling prophecy for him.

Another important component of the treatment process that helped contribute to Sean's success was the use of a tribal circle of caring others. To help combat his overwhelming feelings of sadness and despair about not being able to count on his parents for support and feeling alone, I co-constructed with Sean a tribal circle of caring others, which consisted of his school social worker, Mindy, his girlfriend, Sandy, and the author's friend, Yuri. The bonus with Yuri's involvement is that he served as both a mentor and an adult inspirational other for Sean. With Yuri's help, Sean was able to secure a job with Yuri's company and pursue his passion doing computer graphic art design work.

CHAPTER SIX

Collaborative Strengths-Based Group Therapy Approaches for Self-Harming Young Adults, Adolescents, and Their Parents

Rationale for Group Therapy for Self-Harming Young Adults and Adolescents

Very little has been published about the use of group therapy with young adult and adolescent self-harming clients and their parents and/or families. With the increasing popularity of Marsha Linehan's dialectical behavior therapy (DBT) approach for borderline personality disorder clients, her therapeutic model is being used in a group therapy format both in inpatient and outpatient settings. More therapists are using DBT groups for treating clients exhibiting self-harming and equivalent self-destructive behaviors in their clinical settings. Miller et al. (2007) were the first published DBT pioneers to use this approach in a concurrent parent and adolescent group therapy format. I have developed an eight-session psychoeducational skill-based secondary prevention group called *The Stress-Busters' Leadership Group* (Selekman, 2006b) for adolescents presenting with self-harming and equivalent self-destructive behaviors, which has recently been expanded to nine sessions, and I have added some new didactic material and therapeutic strategies and tools to further aid group participants in helping them conquer their difficulties (discussed in this chapter). It is a portable skill-based group that can be run in any school or treatment setting. This group can be modified and adopted for small groups for self-harming young adults on college campuses as well.

There are a number of excellent reasons why therapists or treatment programs should offer group therapy as a treatment modality option for self-harming clients and/or their parents. For self-harming clients, being able to choose from a menu of treatment modalities can reduce their psychological reactance and help foster a cooperative relationship with them at the very beginning of treatment. The group modality also helps them combat feeling alone, socially isolated, or emotional disconnected from their parents or key caretakers or peers. Self-harming young adults and adolescents may feel that it is less threatening to open up and work on their difficulties with group participants their own age than in the company of their parents or key caretakers. The group can provide them with a strong sense of community, support, and hope. Group participants will experience a sense of universality and feel understood, in that they are not alone with self-harming and other equivalent self-destructive difficulties. Group members are often at different stages of readiness for change and can learn from one another what works and what has not been helpful in coping with and trying to manage emotional distress and life stressors.

Parents with self-harming young adult and adolescent kids also feel isolated, and at a loss for both understanding this intimidating and what appears to be life-threatening behavior and how to constructively manage or respond when their kids have self-harming episodes. Furthermore, since self-harming is often a hidden practice and has benefited the self-harming young adults living at home or adolescents in coping with emotional distress and family and other life stressors, they may perceive family therapy as a threat and may be reluctant to go for counseling with them. This makes psychoeducational skill-based groups for parents a viable therapeutic option. I have heard from many parents at the beginning treatment and have received numerous e-mails from parents around the country that there is a lack of educational materials and parents' support groups for parents who have kids self-harming. For this reason, I have modified my *Solution-Oriented Parenting Group* for parents of self-harming adolescents (Selekman, 2005; discussed in this chapter).

Important Considerations When Starting New Groups

When beginning new groups for self-harming young adults, adolescents, and their parents, it is important to consider the following: offering a psychoeducational versus a traditional therapy group format, running a closed versus and open-ended group, running a heterogeneous versus homogeneous group with gender makeup, age range, and presenting problem, determining the number of group participants, and the recruitment and screening process.

Psychoeducational Versus a Traditional Therapy Group Format

It is my contention that there are many more benefits to running psychoeducational groups for self-harming clients and their parents than using a more traditional therapy group format. Since many self-harming clients struggle to cope with managing negative emotion and self-defeating thoughts, delaying gratification, interpersonal conflict, and self-soothing, a psychoeducational skill-based group can empower them to learn a plethora of strategies and tools that can help them strengthen these important self-management and interpersonal skill areas so they are less vulnerable prey to emotional distress and family and other life stressors.

My concern about having self-harming clients in a more traditional therapy group setting is that having participants sharing their self-harming stories in graphic detail (their methods such as bloodletting or inflicting significant tissue damage through cutting and burning themselves) and talking in great detail about painful and stressful life difficulties can become a powerful trigger for a self-harming episode following the group session. Newly abstinent group participants may be put at risk for a slip or a prolonged relapsing situation when listening to these graphic and emotionally charged self-harming stories. This type of therapy group format may be of benefit to self-harming clients who are in the termination stage of readiness for change, totally confident that they will not slip back into their self-harming practices and looking to work on other issues going on in their lives.

Although there is a growing proliferation of online support groups for self-harming clients, many of them are not tightly monitored or run by licensed mental health professionals, which may not make them necessarily the healthiest and most helpful group to participate in. As described above, if participants are just sharing their self-harming methods and graphic self-harming stories, this will only serve to maintain group participants' self-harming practices rather than help them to conquer their challenging habits.

Running a Closed Versus an Open-Ended Group

When I fill psychoeducational skill-based groups like my Stress-Busters' Leadership and Solution-Oriented Parenting groups, I close the groups until there are enough numbers to start new groups. It is highly disruptive to group cohesion development and the treatment process to add new participants once the group has begun. In addition, new group members would have missed important skills taught in early group sessions.

Using an open-ended group format is particularly useful for self-harming clients who are seeking additional support once they are solidly abstinent and wishing to work on other issues. They also may find that the ongoing support of a group can help them to stay on track. I have had adolescents who have participated in Stress-Busters' Leadership groups and parents who completed Solution-Oriented Parenting groups who decided to keep meeting in order to keep providing support for one another and serve as guest consultants for future groups my colleagues and I run.

Running Heterogeneous Versus Homogeneous Groups

When starting a new group for self-harming young adults, adolescents, and their parents, I like to have a female co-therapist and have gender balance with the group participants. I match the participants by age range. For the Stress-Busters' Leadership Group, I will have 12–14-year-olds, 15–18-year-olds, and 19–21-year-olds together. With Solution-Oriented Parenting groups, I will recruit and accept parent participants who have kids developmentally the same age range.

Ideally, the group participants should primarily be struggling with self-harming difficulties. However, as mentioned throughout this treatment manual, self-harming clients often symptom-switch and may have equivalent problems with bulimia, substance abuse, and engaging in sexually risky behaviors. If these other difficulties are the primary reasons for the group referral or seeking participation in the group, and the self-harming behavior is beginning to increase, I will include them in the group. If the self-harming behavior is rarely occurring and bulimia and substance abuse are much bigger issues for the group candidates, I will refer them to other groups being offered by colleagues or other programs in the community that can better meet their needs.

Determining the Size of the Group

I typically limit both of my parenting groups to a maximum of eight group participants. I have found that if the group size gets too big, it becomes more difficult to manage and group cohesion becomes more difficult to achieve. With Solution-Oriented Parenting groups, I combine single, married, and even divorced parents if they can be civil and respectful toward each other in the group. For single parents, they feel a strong sense of community and support participating with married and divorced couples.

Recruitment and the Referral Process

I market my groups to and receive referrals from school social workers, counselors, psychologists, family physicians, probation officers, psychiatric programs, agencies and community mental health centers, and student mental health centers on college campuses. I find it useful to put together detailed flyers about each of the groups being offered and meeting personally with potential referral sources to further describe the groups and to answer questions they may have about how the group can benefit their clients. It also provides an opportunity to recruit appropriate client participants and screen out those individuals who will not benefit from the group. As mentioned earlier, self-harming needs to be the primary presenting problem.

When recruiting parents for a new Solution-Oriented Parenting Group, I strive to get both parents to agree to participate. I will go to great lengths to engage reluctant fathers, including meeting with them in their homes or some other neutral place. I will let the father know the following: "We can't do it without you, you are the captain of the ship and know your son/daughter better than we do. You and your wife can make a dynamic duo team. Combining your toughness with her emotional sensitivity is just what your son/daughter may need." Most reluctant fathers find comments like these inviting and often appreciate the therapist's outreach efforts. As far as screening out parents goes, I have found that parents with severe cognitive impairment, mental health, and substance abuse problems have grave difficulty mastering and implementing the therapeutic strategies and tools that the parent will be exposed to in the group.

The Stress-Busters' Leadership Group

The Stress-Busters' Leadership Group was first developed in 1999 in response to a local school district's growing epidemic of self-harming students. I also was hearing more and more from mental health and school professionals attending my workshops throughout the United States and abroad that they were seeing a growing number of young adults and adolescents self-harming and engaging in concurrent self-destructive behaviors like bulimia, substance abuse, and risky sexual behaviors. These mental health and school professionals were indicating that they could not find in the psychotherapy literature any specialized skill-based or therapy group approaches for this challenging treatment population. As an attempt to help fill this gap in the treatment delivery system and in the psychotherapy literature, I developed the original Stress-Busters' Leadership Group (Selekman, 2006b). More recently, I have expanded the group to nine sessions and have added some new didactic material and therapeutic strategies and tools to further improve the effectiveness of the group.

The Role of the Group Leaders

At the beginning of a new group, the male-female co-therapy leadership team strives to create a safe, supportive, and upbeat group climate ripe for change. This positive group climate is co-created with the participants by getting to know each group member by their key strengths, intelligence areas, and meaningful flow-state activities. In addition, inviting each group member to share their self-generated pretreatment changes and amplifying and consolidating them, conveys with confidence to them the leaders' belief in their ability to change. Furthermore, we want to elicit from them their treatment expectations of us, and learn about any past negative group experiences they may have had. Conversely, we want to learn from them what they found helpful in past group experiences.

The group leaders in the first few group sessions are quite active at eliciting group members' expertise and successes, amplifying and consolidating their gains, making sure that everyone's voice is heard and respected, providing empathy and validation, normalizing, positive relabeling, and setting limits if necessary. The group leaders use a lot of curiosity regarding soliciting group members' unique stories, expectations of them, and therapeutic questions for eliciting important information about their strengths and resources, for establishing well-formulated treatment, and in co-creating with them compelling future realities. In the latter group sessions, once group members are getting closer to accomplishing their goals and are changing, the leaders are less active and rely more on the group process to carry the group.

In each group session, the leaders present in a clear and concrete manner the group topic didactic presentation and demonstrate how to do both in-session and between-group session experiments. I have found it helpful to type up handouts outlining the concrete steps for performing each of the in-session and between-session therapeutic experiments for the group participants to use while practicing both in the session and at home. This helps increase skill mastery and increases the likelihood of treatment compliance. At the end of the group, each group participant is given a booklet containing all of the in-session and between-session group experiments, as well as descriptions of other tools and strategies they learned in the group. Finally, after a very brief intersession break, the leaders compliment each group member on their strengths and resources, reported pretreatment changes, and hard work in the group. The between-session experiments are then presented. This is followed by the leaders soliciting from group members what they found useful and interesting in the group meeting, what they did not like, and what their best hopes are for future group meetings.

Group Leaders' Rules and Expectations

The group leaders do solicit from participants a list of group rules they think is important for them to respect and live by. Some of the major rules and expectations of the group leaders are:

1. Regarding the importance of client confidentiality, what is discussed in the group stays in the group.
2. Group members are expected to actively participate in meeting discussions, practice in-session experiments, implement assigned experiments between group sessions, and be prepared to share their experiences in the next group meeting.
3. Group members are not allowed to share the graphic details of bloodletting, burning themselves, or whatever other damage they do to their bodies and the methods employed.
4. Group members need to be respectful listeners and honor each other's stories and needs when each member has the floor.
5. There will be no putdowns, other verbal abuse, or any self-inflicted harm or violence directed toward other group members.

The Structure of the Group and Session Topics

Each group session provides its participants with an interesting and upbeat didactic presentation lasting 15–20 minutes, in-session exercises, and one or more therapeutic experiments for the participants to try out and be prepared to discuss in their next group sessions. As the group as a whole begins to get closer to achieving their goals and changing, increasingly longer time intervals between group sessions will be offered as a reward for their hard work and vote of confidence in their skill mastery. The nine session group meetings are called:

1. What Are My Strengths and Protective Shields?
2. Mindfulness Skills
3. Relationship Effectiveness Skills
4. Mood Management Skills
5. Finding Balance and Harmony in Your Life
6. Navigating Family Minefields Successfully

7. Altruism Skills: Reaching Out to Others with Loving-kindness and Compassion
8. Effective Tools for Mastering School Stress
9. Celebrating Change: Congratulations Stress-Busting Experts!

Session 1: What Are My Strengths and Protective Shields?

- The leaders begin the group by establishing rapport with each member.
- The leaders come to know each member by their key strengths, intelligence areas, meaningful flow-state activities, and self-generated pregroup changes.
- The leaders invite the participants to share their expectations of them and the group experience.
- Group rules are established and the leaders share their expectations of the members to be respectful listeners, participate in group discussions, and perform all in-session and between-session therapy experiments.
- The group leaders invite the participants to share their problem stories and the specifics about what led to their referral to or in decision to participate in the group.
- Next, the leaders use the *miracle, presuppositional,* and *scaling questions* (de Shazer, 1988, 1991; Selekman, 2005, 2006b) to establish well-formulated treatment goals with each group participant and begin to co-create with them the kind of compelling future realities they would like to have. The leaders' jobs are to make sure that solvable treatment goals are negotiated.
- The group leaders give a presentation on *Super Kids: Resiliency Protective Factors for Overcoming Adversity.* This consists of listing on a whiteboard or flip chart several resiliency protective factors that have been identified in resiliency research studies with high-risk children and adolescents over the past 40 years. Some of the resiliency factors discussed are the role of adult inspirational others, success in school, maintaining an optimistic explanatory belief system, having strong social skills, and effective and creative problem-solving skills (Anthony & Cohler, 1987; Haggerty, Sherrod, Garmezy, & Rutter, 1994). After the presentation, the leaders invite the group participants to share which of the presented resiliency protective factors they possess, or other coping strategies they have come up with to deal with challenging life situations they have faced and how they used them in the past or use them presently to cope with adverse and stressful life events. This presentation and the subsequent discussion can lead to group members learning new coping strategies they can begin using to cope with or to constructively manage difficult and stressful current life situations.
- Closely related to the resiliency protective factors topic is the recent positive psychology research on the 24 human character strengths and virtues

(Peterson, 2006; Peterson & Seligman, 2004). To help increase the group participants' awareness levels of what their top five signature strengths are and how they can use them in all areas of their lives, the leaders give a brief presentation about the character strengths and virtues and encourages them to go online to www.viastrengths.org to take the VIA (Values in Action) Inventory of Strengths for Youth (see Chapter 2) or the adult version for group participants 19–21 years of age. Once they complete the questionnaire, they are to print out the results and bring them to the next group.

- **In-session experiment:** The participants are asked to perform the *visualizing movies of success* therapeutic experiment. *With your eyes closed, we would like you to picture in your minds a blank movie screen. On that blank movie screen, we would like you to project a movie of some past successful thing you had accomplished or some special place you had visited that was a hit success for you, your family, or friends. Apply all of your senses to the experience, what you see, hear, smell, taste, touch, including color and motion, to really bring the movie to life for you on the movie screen. We will have you do this for 12–15 minutes.* Once the participants do the experiment, the leaders invite them to share their movies of success with one another. Just like the mini-presentation and discussion on resiliency protective factors, this is another wonderful opportunity for participants to learn from one another about how to achieve mastery with different tasks and effective ways to trigger positive emotion. The leaders tap the expertise of the group participants by inviting them to share their useful self-talk and problem-solving actions that helped them to be successful in their movies. They also point out how their movies of success can serve as road maps for future success.

- The group leaders take a short intersession break to come up with compliments for each group member. They are complimented on their resiliencies shared with the group, their strengths, resourcefulness, creativity, and any self-generated pregroup changes they had reported. Next, the between-session therapeutic experiment is offered.

- **Between-session experiments:** The participants are asked to create *victory boxes* over the next week. *Over the next week, we would like you to do two experiments. The first experiment consists of your finding old shoe boxes you can use. Once you have found your shoeboxes, cut slits in the tops of your boxes. On a daily basis, we would like you to keep track of your daily personal victories, write down on slips of papers what they were, what your thinking and actions were to make them happen, and drop them through the slits into your boxes. We would like you to decorate your boxes any way you wish. Please select a few of the slips of your personal victories that were really big for you and bring your boxes in to share with the group at the next meeting. The second experiment involves you taking the online VIA Inventory of Strengths for Youth and bringing your printed-out questionnaire results to the next group meeting to discuss.*

- To close out the group meeting, the leaders will solicit from the group members their feedback about what they liked or disliked about the session, what ideas they found most helpful discussed in the group, and to share with them any recommendations they have for the leaders for future group meeting session content. The participants are given a handout describing the concrete steps for creating and using their victory boxes and how to access and take the VIA Inventory of Strengths for Youth during the next week.

Session 2: Mindfulness Skills

- The leaders begin the second group session amplifying and consolidating any gains reported by the group members.
- The leaders invite group members to read some of their personal victory slips of paper to the group and show everyone their decorated *victory boxes.* For the participants, the information contained in the personal victory slips of paper can serve as future road maps for successful management of challenging life situations or tasks.
- The leaders go over the group members test results from taking the *VIA Inventory of Strengths for Youth* (Peterson, 2006). Group members are invited to share what some of their top five signature strengths are and if they learned anything new about themselves as a result of completing this questionnaire. Often, some of the members make important discoveries about certain signature strengths they did not even know they possessed and begin to think about how they can deploy them in different areas of their lives (see Chapters 2 and 3).
- The group leaders give a presentation on *Buddhist Teachings and Mindfulness Meditation.* They present in a concrete and clear manner the Buddhist teachings of nonattachment, *The Four Noble Truths,* and *The Four Immeasurable Minds* (Hanh, 1997, 1998, 2001). They define for the group what is meant by *mindfulness* and teach them the *sound meditation* and *food meditations.* Handouts are given to the participants outlining the concrete steps of doing both of these meditations. Before having the group members practice the meditations they wish to try, the leaders open up the floor for questions and discussion.
- **In-session experiments:** The group members are to select one of the meditations to practice for 12–15 minutes. The instructions for the *sound meditation* are as follows: *We would like you to get comfortable and relaxed in your chair or you can lie on the floor, whatever feels most comfortable for you. Close your eyes and tune in to the various sounds you hear around you. Simply label in your mind what you hear but don't try to figure out why you are hearing a particular sound, just label it. Try to focus all of your attention on each sound you hear and nothing else. If a thought enters your mind, acknowledge its presence and return your concentration and focus on different sounds you hear*

around you. With the *food meditation,* the leaders like to use a piece of popcorn because most kids like popcorn more than raisins. The instructions for the food meditation are as follows: *We would like you to first get comfortable and relaxed in your chairs. Each step of this meditation must be done very slowly, for 2–3 minutes. After we place a piece of popcorn in your left palm, we would like you to carefully look at its coloring, the shadowing around it, and smell it. Next, we would like you to slowly pick up the piece of popcorn with your right hand and place it in your mouths and roll it around on your teeth and tongues but don't bite down on it yet. The next step is to slowly and finely chew the piece of popcorn but don't swallow it yet. After finely chewing up the piece of popcorn, pay close attention to the bodily sensations you experience as you swallow it and it reaches your stomachs.*

- The group leaders process with the participants what their mindfulness meditation experiences were like and any difficulties they experienced while they were attempting to meditate.
- The group leaders check in with the participants on the steps they had taken to achieve their goals. Every positive step group members took over the week is punctuated with positive accolades and amplifying and consolidating by the leaders.
- After a brief intersession break, the leaders compliment the participants on their great work with the victory boxes and their personal accomplishments over the week. They also compliment them on their patience and desire to develop mindfulness meditation practices.
- **Between-session experiments:** The group members are instructed: *We would like you to pick either the sound meditation or the food meditation to experiment with daily for 15 minutes over the next week. You can do it right after you get up in the morning to chill you out before school, do it right before you go to bed to help relax you so you can sleep better, or use it any time you are stressed out and need to center yourself. All of you have the option of practice using both of these meditations, meditating longer than 15 minutes, or more than once a day, whatever works best for you. We would also like you to experiment over the next week in using your top five signature strengths in novel and creative ways and be prepared to discuss the results of your efforts at our next group meeting* (Peterson, 2006).

Session 3: Relationship-Effectiveness Skills
- The group leaders begin the third meeting exploring with the participants their experiences with practicing the mindfulness meditations. They will normalize for the participants how difficult it is to quiet our minds and keep our focus on the sounds and popcorn. In addition, they point out that intruding bodily sensations, thoughts, and feelings are like the clouds in the sky that are in perpetual motion and will eventually clear out, revealing their beautiful blue sky selves. The participants really identify with and like

this metaphor. The leaders also like to suggest that when meditating, practice the Buddhist principle of *nonattachment*, that is, don't panic or try to avoid intruding negative thoughts or feelings but accept and embrace them like they are welcomed guests in your home (Hanh, 1997, 1998).

- The leaders invite the group members to share some examples of how they used their top five signature strengths in novel ways. They also explore with the group how this experiment had helped expand their horizons and benefited them individually and in their relationships with family members, friends, teachers, and so forth. Often, group participants report that they found this experiment to be helpful and enjoyed doing it.

- The leaders check in with each participant what further progress they were making toward achieving their goals. Scaling questions are most useful for securing a quantitative measurement of their progress. All participants' gains are amplified and consolidated by the leaders.

- For those group members who are not making headway toward achieving their goals, the leaders will use the *coping* or *pessimistic questions* to find out how they have prevented their situations from not getting much worse or what keeps them coming to the group and not giving up (Berg & Miller, 1992; Selekman, 2006b). These questions often produce some helpful client coping strategies and solution-building thoughts that can be consolidated and increased. If these questions are not productive, *conversational questions* can be asked to open up space for the participants to talk about what is keeping them stuck or what they are concerned about (Anderson, 1997). Another option is to go back to basics and negotiate a smaller or new treatment goal.

- The group leaders give a presentation on *The Politics of Gender*. They begin their presentation by showing video clips from popular movies and television shows that blatantly display *patriarchy, sexism, homophobia,* and *racism* in male-female and same-sex relationships. After each video clip, the leaders open up the floor for group reflections and discussion. The leaders provide concrete definitions for each of these important societal issues. The participants also are shown magazine advertisements that blatantly display these negative societal forces in action. It is helpful to explore with the group participants how they are already resisting falling prey to these negative societal forces. Group members can learn from one another how to take a stand and help combat these negative societal forces. In the context of this group discussion, we like to share in the group Malcolm X's famous quote, "If you don't take a stand, you don't stand for anything."

- Since many self-harming clients have difficulties with asserting themselves, or articulating their thoughts and feelings, and have poor conflict-resolution and problem-solving skills, the leaders like to demonstrate how to use assertiveness, communication, and these other skills in relationships by providing role-play demonstrations of how to use them appropriately.

- **In-session experiment:** The instructions for the in-session experiment are as follows: *We would like each of you to pick a partner and take turns role-playing a relationship difficulty you currently have with a family member, a friend, an acquaintance, or someone you would call your enemy. Take turns selecting one or more of the relationship-effectiveness skills to attempt to resolve your relationship difficulty with this person in your role-plays.* After each group member has had a turn practicing the relationship-effectiveness skills in their role-plays, the leaders will open the floor up for questions and discussion.
- After a short intersession break, the leaders compliment the group members on their hard work, thoughtful contributions, and progress toward achieving their goals.
- **Between-session experiments:** The group leaders offer two therapeutic experiments for the participants to try out over the next week. The instructions for the first therapeutic experiment are as follows: *We would like you to daily practice using the relationship-effectiveness skills that you learned in the group. You do not have to use all of them but pick at least two of them to experiment with in any challenging relationship encounter you may experience over the next week.* The instructions for the second therapeutic experiment, *observing oneself high up in a bubble,* are as follows: *We would like you to pretend over the next week that there is a friendly part of you high up above you in a bubble following you around, watching you in every social encounter you have with friends, acquaintances, new peers, family members, or your enemies. This friendly part of you will keep track of what you say or do that helps you establish rapport with new peers, get along with friends and acquaintances, family members, and even your enemies. It also will pay close attention to what you do or say that gets you into trouble with these people and triggers them to distance from, get defensive, and reject you. We are giving you little pocket notebooks to carry around so you can record your observations and reflections after each social encounter. We would like you to bring your pocket notebooks to the next group meeting so we can discuss the important discoveries you made.* The group members are given handouts describing each of the relationship-effectiveness skills, with examples of how to use them, and separate handouts explaining the steps of how to implement the *observing-oneself-high-up-in-a-bubble* experiment.

Session 4: Mood Management Skills
- The group leaders begin by exploring with the participants how their therapeutic experiments went. All participants are encouraged to share examples of how they used their relationship-effectiveness skills effectively and where they might have gotten stuck. The leaders tap the expertise of the group members to generate a list of suggestions on the whiteboard or flip chart, steps their fellow group members can take to resolve their reported

relationship impasses or conflict situations. They also explore with group members what valuable insights they gained from doing the observing-one-self-high-up-in-a-bubble experiment. The leaders can invite other group members to reflect on one another's discoveries, comparing and contrasting their managing and mismanaging social encounters with others."

- The leaders check in with group members about what further progress they are making at achieving their goals. All positive steps and participants' progress is responded to with cheerleading and amplifying and consolidating their gains.

- The group leaders give a presentation on *Changing Your Thoughts and Emotional Patterns*. The leaders teach the participants both the *A-B-C framework* of cognitive therapy (Beck, Rush, & Emery, 1979; Ellis, 1974) and *disputation skills* (Seligman, 2002; Seligman et al., 1995). They illustrate on the whiteboard or flip chart how stressful triggering life events may lead to irrational self-defeating thoughts, unpleasant feelings, and unproductive actions. The disputation skills that are taught are *searching for evidence, searching for alternative explanations, implications,* and *usefulness.* The leaders provide several real-life examples of how to use these skills. After the presentation, the leaders open up the floor for participants' questions and discussion. The leaders also provide handouts explaining both the A-B-C framework of cognitive therapy and the different disputation skills and real-life examples illustrating each skill. There also is ample space provided in the handouts for the group members to practice using these cognitive tools and record their results.

- The leaders also teach the group the *urge surfing* goal-maintenance tool (Marlatt et al., 2008; Marlatt & Kristeller, 1999), which can help the participants stay on track and not cave in to a self-harming episode when they are experiencing emotional distress or they are being pushed around by powerful self-defeating and irrational thoughts. When experiencing negative triggers like unpleasant thoughts and feelings, group members are to visualize in their minds that they are riding a surfboard through big and powerful waves and not wiping out. The big and powerful waves are a metaphor for labeling and accepting the presence of the unpleasant thoughts and feelings that entered their minds. Rather than trying to avoid them or cave in to the urge to self-harm, they keep their main focus and concentration on not losing their balance and surfboards. Urge surfing is an excellent relapse prevention tool.

- **In-session experiment:** The instructions for the in-session experiment are as follows: *We would like you to pick a partner in the group and take turns using the A-B-C framework, presenting how you responded to a recent stressful life event or situation, identifying what your irrational self-defeating thinking was at the time, what your emotional response was, and any unproductive attempted solutions to try to cope with the situation. Next, we would like you to* *pick one or more of the disputation skills you just learned and pretend that you can return to the stressful life event or situation. Which disputation skills would you select and how will you use them to stop your unhelpful thinking and unproductive responses from happening? After each partner takes a turn, he or she is to offer feedback on how well the selected disputation skills were being used or recommendations for what to do differently.*

- After a brief intersession break, the group leaders compliment the participants on their hard work and progress.
- **Between-session experiments:** The instructions for the between-session therapeutic experiment are as follows: *Over the next week, we would like you to practice daily using the A-B-C framework and the disputation skills whenever you are faced with a stressful life event or situation. Please use your handouts to guide you and write down your experiences in the blank spaces of your handouts or on separate sheets of paper. Be prepared to discuss your experiences in the next group meeting. In addition, when the opportunity arises that you are being pushed around by emotional distress or unpleasant thoughts, practice using the urge surfing tool.*

Session 5: Finding Balance and Harmony in Your Life

- The group leaders begin the fifth group session exploring with the participants their experiences experimenting with the A-B-C framework and the different disputation skills. Participants are invited to present stressful situations they encountered and what specific disputation skills they employed to constructively manage these challenging situations. The leaders also explore with the group members experiences using the urge surfing tool to not cave in to self-harming when experiencing emotional distress or unpleasant thoughts.
- The leaders explore with the participants what further progress they have made at achieving their goals. Every positive step they report is responded to with cheerleading and amplification and consolidation of their gains.
- The group leaders give a presentation on *Hozho: Keeping the Mind, Body and Spirit in Balance and Harmony.* The leaders present to the group the important Navajo Indian teaching *hozho* or "walking in beauty" (Arviso-Alvord & Cohen-Van Pelt, 2000). Hozho or "walking in beauty" entails leading a balanced and harmonious life strongly connected to one's cultural identity and values, regularly exercising, maintaining a healthy diet, engaged in meaningful activities, firmly rooted in one's relationships with parents, siblings, grandparents, other extended family members, one's clan, friends, and in one's relationships to animals, nature, the environment, and to the creator. This is a continuous and circular process that we need to honor, respect, and keep in balance. The leaders point out that when all of these dimensions are in balance and regularly attended to, our lives become much more meaningful and fulfilling and we tend to be physically and mentally

stronger. When a combination of these different dimensions of hozho are not balanced or attended to, and we lack a sense of purpose in our lives, we become emotionally and physically vulnerable to developing both psychological and physical difficulties. I like to read to the group the *Blessing Way* Navajo Indian teaching from Lori Arviso-Alvord and Elizabeth Cohen-Van Pelts' book *The Scalpel and the Silver Bear: The First Navajo Woman Surgeon Combines Western Medicine and Traditional Healing* (Arviso-Alvord & Cohen-Van Pelt, 2000):

> *With beauty before me, there may I walk.*
> *With beauty behind me, there may I walk.*
> *With beauty above me, there may I walk.*
> *With beauty below me, there may I walk.*
> *With beauty all around me, there may I walk.*
> *In beauty it is finished.* (p. 157)

After reading the *Blessing Way,* the leaders discuss with the group which of the different dimensions of hozho they feel in balance with and which ones they have neglected or are in unbalanced states. The ensuing discussion is rich in group members' sharing with one another specifics about what they do that helps put them in harmony, such as eating special types of foods, engaging in different types of exercises, engaging in certain meaningful flow-state activities or hobbies, having special conversations with one of their parents or grandparents, and so forth. Next, the leaders will begin the discussion with the group about specific areas of their lives that they feel out of balance with. The leaders expose the group members to the Navajo concept of *lina*, which has to do with the importance of taking care of your body through eating healthy foods, exercising regularly, and refraining from using any chemical substances (smoking, drinking, drug use). The leaders include not self-harming or bingeing and purging as goals to strive for as well. *Lina* also includes viewing one's body in a positive way (Arviso-Alvord & Cohen-Van Pelt, 2000). Finally, the leaders expose the group to the wonderful physical, psychological, and health benefits of *yoga,* which is a holistic way to take care of one's mind, body, and spirit. They demonstrate some useful yogic postures and breathing exercises and have the group participants try them.

- **In-session experiment:** The instructions for the in-session experiment is as follows: *We would like you to pick a partner and take turns sharing with each other what specific and critical dimensions of hozho you think you have neglected and are in need of your immediate attention. Here is a handout with the questions we want you to respond to in this exercise. These important questions can help provide a focus to your dialogue with each another: How well connected am I to my cultural identity and values? What are my personal* values? What do I see as my purpose in life? Do I exercise enough? Do I eat a healthy diet? Do I engage in meaningful activities? Do I feel closely connected to my parents, siblings, grandparents, and extended family? Are there any family members or extended family members that I feel disconnected from that requires my attention? How well connected do I feel to my friends? Are there any friends that I have stopped seeing or I am avoiding who I need to reconcile with? How well connected am I to my pets and animals in general? How much time do I spend out in nature, savoring its beauty? What steps do I take to protect our environment? Do I have a strong spiritual life? What is my relationship with the creator or God?

- After a brief intersession break, the group leaders compliment the participants on sharing their thoughtful reflections on the various dimensions of hozho in their lives, their progress and/or achievement of their personal goals, and reducing or abstaining from self-harming and engaging in other equivalent self-destructive behaviors.

- **Between-session experiment:** The instructions for the between-session experiment are as follows: *Over the next week, we would like each of you to continue to think about and reflect on the questions we gave you. We would like you to pick one or more of the neglected or weak hozho dimension areas to make some positive changes with so as to put them in a more balanced state. Finally, we would like you to either write down on the questions handout or on separate sheets of paper the steps that you took to make the improvements in your selected hozho dimension areas. Be prepared to discuss your successes in the next group meeting.*

Session 6: Navigating Family Minefields Successfully

- The group leaders begin the sixth session exploring with the participants the results of their efforts to achieve more balance and harmony in their lives. Often, group participants find the experiment they were given not only challenging but quite rewarding in helping them improve the quality of their personal lives. They often gain valuable wisdom and insight about themselves, the importance of establishing stronger connections with family, extended family members, and friends, and transcending the boundaries of family to being more connected to nature, the environment, and closely examining their relationships with the creator. Group members compare and contrast their life situations and learn from one another in this rich discussion.

- By this group session, most of the participants have achieved their treatment goals and wish to focus on learning goal-maintenance tools and strategies. The leaders will hand out the *My Positive Trigger Log* for group members to keep track of what they and others do that helps them not cave in to to self-harming or engaging in equivalent self-destructive behaviors. They are asked to bring to the next group their logs for review and for the leaders to see what new ideas they came up with to stay on track and not have slips. All participants' changes are amplified and consolidated.

- The group leaders give a presentation on *Family Politics*. The topics covered in the presentation are family roles, parenting styles, triangles, cross-generational coalitions, problem-maintaining patterns of interactions, family beliefs, intergenerational patterns, and gender power imbalances. Each of these family systems concepts are presented concretely and clearly defined and the leaders provide real-life examples. After presenting each one of these family systems concepts, the leaders open up the floor for questions and discussion. Participants have the opportunity to compare and contrast their families' dynamics and politics. The group members discover that as far as family politics go, they have a lot in common in terms of family stressors they are struggling to cope with. Many group members give examples of emotionally invalidating family interactions, parents clinging to rigid and fixed beliefs about them, serving as parentified children, serving as a confidant for one of the parents, and having parents that have marital and postdivorce conflicts.

- **In-session experiment:** The instructions for the in-session experiment are as follows: *We would like you to take turns doing a family choreography of your family* (Papp, 1983). *This involves selecting group members to serve as your family members and dramatizing how your family looks in motion. When it is your turn, coach your family members on what their facial expressions should look like, where they are positioned in relationship to you in terms of closeness and distance, and how they should be moving around you. Next, we want you to show us ideally how you would like your family to look in motion in relationship to you. After each family choreography performed, we want you to reflect on any new insights you gained about your family and the rest of the group are free to ask questions and give comments. Because of time constraints we will only be able to do two or three family choreographies.*

- After a brief intersession break, the group leaders will compliment the participants on their fine work with the last between-session experiment, the family politics discussion, and their courage and willingness to share their family politics with the group. The leaders also compliment them on other changes they are making in their lives. By this point in the group, members start spontaneously complimenting one another.

- **Between-session experiment:** The instructions for the between-session experiment are as follows: *Over the next week, we would like you to experiment with serving as the agent for change with your families. We would like you to pick a relationship you have with a family member you really would like to change. This family member may yell, nag, blame, lecture, push your buttons, or overburden you too much. So, whenever this family member does anything that upsets you or stresses you out, we would like you to do something different that will really blow his or her mind! It could be something off the wall or* *outrageous or a response that this family member has never experienced from you before. Notice how he or she responds to you when you do something different. Do not tell this family member about the experiment. We will be anxiously waiting to hear about your Academy Award–winning performances in the next group meeting!*

Session 7: Altruism Skills: Reaching Out to Others with Loving-Kindness and Compassion

- The group leaders really look forward to hearing the playful and off-the-wall steps that the participants took to change interactions in certain family relationships. This portion of the group meeting is upbeat, there is a lot of laughter, and some very creative change strategies shared that the participants came up with. In fact, those participants who successfully changed a destructive family interaction or stopped playing a particular family role come to the group more self-confident and proud of their accomplishments. Some group members decide to try out certain strategies with their parents or siblings that they learned from their peers in this group meeting.

- The leaders will review the participants' My Positive Trigger Logs and invite them to share what specifically they were doing to stay on track. To further aid with the goal-maintenance process, the leaders encourage them to use more regularly visualizing movies of success, mindfulness meditation, and their choice disputation skills when faced with stressful and challenging life events. To test the waters, the leaders will ask the group: "What would you have to do to go backward?" When group members can clearly describe what they did that led to their self-harming in the past and what they are doing differently that is improving their life situations, the leaders consider this insight and change. All participants' reported changes are amplified and consolidated.

- The group leaders give a presentation on *Altruism: "Be the Change That You Want in the World."* The leaders begin this presentation by talking about two historic figures that epitomize what altruism is all about, Mahatma Gandhi and Mother Teresa. They share with the group how both of these special human beings were selfless, how they believed that the greatest gift was to give to others, and how they fought for improving the quality of life for the poor, hungry, and marginalized. Gandhi was so committed to fighting for his people's freedom from British rule that he regularly submitted himself to being beaten and jailed by British soldiers and local police. Although they were not Buddhists, they regularly practiced loving-kindness and compassion with not only the people they tried to help but with their harsh critics and enemies as well. The leaders talk about the psychological and health benefits of regularly performing altruistic acts. They invite group participants to share any altruistic acts they performed recently or in the past and what they found most meaningful about their experiences. The leaders open up the floor for questions and discussion.

- **In-session experiment:** The instructions for the in-session experiment are as follows: *We would like you to pick a partner and take turns sharing with each other what would be an altruistic act you would like to perform in your communities that you would find to be most meaningful and why.*

- After a brief intersession break, the group leaders will compliment the participants on their great job with the last between-session experiment and for making good use of their My Positive Trigger Logs for helping them to stay on track or, even after a minor slip, getting back on track quickly. As a vote of confidence, the group members are given a 2-week vacation from the group.

- **Between-session experiment:** The instructions for the between-session experiment are as follows: *Although you will be officially on vacation from the group for 2 weeks, we would like you to pick at least 1 day to perform the altruistic act you discussed with your partner, or another one if it is difficult to arrange. Some good alternative altruistic acts could involve working with handicapped children, homeless people, the elderly, or helping out with an environmental cause. We look forward to hearing about your meaningful experiences. Have a great vacation!*

Session 8: Effective Tools for Mastering School Stress

- The group leaders begin the eighth session exploring with the participants what altruistic acts they performed over the interval break. Many of the participants report feeling good about their service work and for some, they found their experiences so rewarding that they decided to seek ongoing volunteer positions or possible employment with the organizations they did their work for.

- The leaders explore with the group members how they are staying quit from self-harming or engaging in other equivalent self-destructive behaviors. For many participants, the recipe for staying on track and not having slips was a combination of using the My Positive Trigger Log, visualizing movies of success, mindfulness meditation, urge surfing, and staying away from certain people and places. The leaders amplify and consolidate the group members' gains.

- The group leaders give a presentation on *Survival Tips for Managing School Stress*. The leaders present tools and strategies for how to stay on top of one's homework, how to establish cooperative and positive relationships with teachers, and how to constructively handle peer harassment, bullying, and rejection. The leaders strongly recommend that the participants practice using loving-kindness and compassion daily with their teachers and peers, even with students who are attempting to harass or bully them. The leaders share with the group Buddha's strategy of "turning arrows into flowers" in response to being attacked by his enemies and aggressive people (Hanh, 2003; see Chapter 3). They also encourage them to increase the amount of time they are devoting to mindfulness meditation to help them to better cope with school-related stressors. The leaders also will solicit from the group members creative ideas that they have for other participants to help them better cope with school stressors.

- At this point in the group, the leaders test how solid their changes are by asking group members: "What would you have to do to go backward at this point? If you had a minor slip, what steps would you take to quickly get back on track?" When group members can clearly spell out what they used to do that got them into trouble and what they are doing differently now that is helping them stay quit from self-harming and engaging in equivalent self-destructive behaviors, the leaders believe that this reflects their insight and change.

- **In-session experiment:** The instructions for the in-session experiment are as follows: *We would like the group as a whole to decide what stress-busting tools and strategies you think would be most helpful for fourth and fifth graders at a local elementary school to learn. After all of you decide what you would like to teach them, we need to determine who will present what specific tool and strategy. We have arranged for you to give an hour-long stress management prevention workshop for a group of fourth and fifth graders so that you can give back and share the tools and strategies and wisdom that you have gained from participating in the Stress-Busters' Leadership Group. We are very proud of all of you and are quite confident that you will do an excellent job of teaching and helping improve the quality of life for these children. As a vote of confidence to all of you, we are giving you a 3-week vacation from the group, which will officially begin after your scheduled stress-management-prevention workshop at the end of this school week.*

Session 9: Celebrating Change: Congratulations Stress-Busting Experts!

- The leaders begin this meeting congratulating the group members on their excellent stress-management-prevention workshop. In some cases, the buzz will travel throughout a school district and the group will be invited to give the same workshop at other schools. The leaders amplify and consolidate further gains group members made during the 3-week interval break.

- The leaders present the group with a large sheet cake that has written on it: *Congratulations Stress-Busting Experts!* Each group participant is given an achievement award certificate.

- Group members are asked to give speeches reflecting on where they were before the group in terms of their difficulties and where they are now that they turned their situations dramatically around. The leaders will ask questions like: "Let's say that your parents and best friends had joined us for this party. What changes would they report happened with you that they are most pleased about?" "Let's say we had a group reunion meeting 1 year from today. What further changes will each of you share with us that you made happen?" "If we were to invite you to our next Stress-Busters' Leadership Group, what helpful words of wisdom and pointers would you share with the group?" The last question affords the group members the opportunity to share their insights gained from the group experience and underscores their important changes.

- The leaders induct each group member into the *Stress-Busters' Expert Consultants' Association.* Once inducted, they agree to either serve as a guest consultant for future Stress-Busters' Leadership groups or be willing to co-facilitate a group with one of the leaders. Group members often get very excited about doing this future work. Another wonderful opportunity for Stress-Busters' alumni to be involved in is the creation of a *Stress-Busters' Quarterly* publication for their schools that contains valuable stress-management coping strategies and tools and tips for becoming more resilient that they learned in the group. In addition, they can include announcements about interesting and meaningful social action projects they are involved with in their schools and communities and get other students interested in participating in these important causes. In one junior high school, a popular and powerful member of a Stress-Busters' Leadership Group convinced the principal of her school to provide her and some of her group members with a small office to use to provide individual supportive counseling and a small support group for stressed-out students monitored by the school social worker. Finally, some of my Stress-Busters' alumni have gotten involved in doing outreach and peer counseling work in their schools and in other schools in their school districts. They can serve as gatekeepers for identifying and helping at risk students make it to treatment.

- For group members that would like further individual or family therapy with one of the leaders, this option will be made available to them. Group members that have found it difficult to completely abstain from self-harming and engaging in equivalent self-destructive behaviors due to other individual and family difficulties find it to be emotionally uplifting knowing that they can continue to work with one of the group leaders with whom they already have a good relationship. Those group members that may need more intensive work can be offered with their families' participation in the *Pathways to Possibilities Program* (see Chapter 7).

Benefits and Limitations of the Stress-Busters' Leadership Group

Although I have not conducted a scientific evaluation of the effectiveness of the Stress-Busters' Leadership Group, qualitative research has indicated that young adults and adolescents have greatly benefited from participating in this group. Not only have there been consistent reports of significant reduction or elimination of self-harming and equivalent self-destructive behaviors but improvement was reported in all areas of their lives. My colleagues and I have heard the following comments from Stress-Busters' group participants over the years: "The group was awesome!" "I learned a lot about myself and became a better person," "I'm no longer cutting," "School's going better," "I have a better relationship with my parents," "I've dropped my crew and made some new friends," and so forth.

Another benefit of the Stress-Busters' Leadership Group for self-harming adolescents is that upon completing the group, they can be involved in more widespread outreach and prevention work with at-risk kids living in rural and more outlying areas, where there is a lack of mental health services and adequate numbers of professionals. Trained Stress-Busters' Leadership Group graduates are better gatekeepers and more likely to have greater success at engaging at-risk kids for treatment than adults.

In commenting on the limitations of the group, former Stress-Busters participants had to say: "I changed but my parents didn't," "I'm still cutting so it really didn't help," "My parents should be in this group, not me," and "I was still not doing well in school." Comments like these indicate that some of these adolescents may still be in the precontemplative stage of readiness to change (Prochaska et al., 1994), the need for more direct parental involvement, or concurrent family therapy may have contributed to better group treatment outcomes for them. My colleagues and I have learned through group experiences that young adults and adolescents who have progressed into the heavy and severe self-harming practice categories need more than what the Stress-Busters' Leadership Group has to offer. Couples therapy for young adults in intimate relationships and family therapy for young adults and adolescents living at home combined with the Stress-Busters' Leadership Group has been much more effective as a treatment regime with heavy and severe self-harming practice category clients.

Adopting the Stress-Busters' Leadership Group for Self-Harming College Students and Young Adults Living at Home

The Stress-Busters' Leadership Group can be most ideal for college students and young adults living at home. Since many self-harming young adults feel alone or isolated, may have had or continue to have difficulties negotiating the leaving-home-family life-cycle stage, their self-harming and/or concurrent engagement in equivalent self-destructive behaviors has increased, or they have developed other mental health difficulties, this group can help arm them with several tools and strategies to help them to better cope, resolve their difficulties, and provide them with a strong sense of community to help them with this difficult transition period (D'Amore & Lloyd-Richardson, 2008; Haley, 1980).

As far as the structure of the group goes, I have increased the group session presentation time to 30 minutes and each session is an hour and a half in length. By extending this time period, there is much more room for questions and discussion. With session content, I have added material regarding the challenges of the leaving home stage and discussing unfinished family business in the *Family Politics* presentation in the Navigating Family Minefields Successfully group session. With the do-something-different experiment, college group participants can try this out when their parents visit their campuses or when they go home for a holiday or school breaks. I also have young adults take online at www.viastrengths.org the *VIA Inventory of Strengths for Adults* prior to the third group session. The group session topics also can be presented in a more sophisticated and intellectually stimulating way, particularly with college students. Graduates of the Stress-Busters' Leadership groups on college campuses can do outreach and prevention work, serve as future co-facilitators of Stress-Busters' Leadership groups with student mental health center staff, or provide student peer counseling. Some of the college students whom I have worked with were involved in campus-wide campaigns to help reduce binge-drinking problems at their universities.

The Solution-Oriented Parenting Group

The *Solution-Oriented Parenting Group* has been evolving since 1988 (Selekman, 1991, 1999; 2005). The group grew out of my experience running an outpatient adolescent substance-abuse program at a youth service agency. Many of these youths had been in inpatient and residential chemical dependency programs multiple times for their severe substance abuse and equivalent self-destructive behaviors. Following their discharge from these programs, these adolescents quickly relapsed into regular substance abuse, engaging in equivalent self-destructive behaviors, experiencing major family conflicts, and having behavioral problems in school. One of the major reasons why these adolescents relapsed to square one was the fact that while they were institutionalized, nothing significant had changed in their family environments. The parents' fixed and outmoded beliefs about their sons and daughters and emotionally invalidating and other destructive problem-maintaining family interactions had not changed at all. Thus, upon returning home from the inpatient or residential treatment programs, these adolescents were set up for failure because nothing had changed with the family dynamics. To further complicate matters, many of these returning adolescents were refusing to go for family therapy with their parents. These treatment dilemmas led to my creating the Solution-Oriented Parenting Group as a highly effective treatment alternative to family therapy.

Unlike most parenting groups which tend to be heavily problem-focused, where the leaders are the privileged experts, and they bank the change process more on their knowledge bases and insights, the Solution-Oriented Parenting Group places a strong emphasis on the parents' strengths, resourcefulness, creativity, and past successes, and arms them with "hands-on" therapeutic strategies and tools that they can put to immediate use. The parents are viewed as co-collaborators and the lead authors of the kind of solution-determined stories they would like to create with their adolescents. They are the agents of change for their families.

I have found over the years that the Solution-Oriented Parenting Group in combination with the Stress-Busters' Leadership Group for self-harming young adults and adolescents can produce significant changes on both the parental and young adult/adolescent levels and alleviates the need for family therapy. Since many parents are at a loss for how to constructively respond to and manage their young adults' and adolescents' self-harming behavior and may be stuck responding in unproductive ways, the Solution-Oriented Parenting Group can be most helpful to them in teaching "hands-on" therapeutic tools and strategies for how best to respond and for learning more about the territory of self-harm.

The Structure of the Group and Session Topics
The Solution-Oriented Parenting Group consists of eight 90-minute sessions. In each group meeting there is a short presentation and a skill-building exercise offered, which exposes parents to useful tools and strategies they can begin to try out in their relationships with their young adults or teens. After the first hour of the group, the leaders take a short intersession break to come up with compliments for each of the parents regarding their self-generated pretreatment changes, helpful ideas shared with the group, and for being persistent and committed to helping their kids resolve their difficulties and strengthen their relationships with them. The parents are provided with refreshments and some time to get to know one another better while the leaders are meeting alone. Once the leaders reconvene the group, they share their compliments and offer one or more therapeutic experiments to test out in their relationships with their teens. Finally, the first and some of the latter group meetings conclude with the leaders checking in with the parents on their satisfaction with their relationships with the leaders, the educational content, and skills-training components of the group. To help increase treatment compliance and assist parents with how to implement assigned between-session experiments, each session they are given a handout with the experiment concretely described on it. Their valuable feedback can guide the leaders on adjustments they need to make to further strengthen the concerned parents' therapeutic alliances with them and the group experience in general. The eight session group meetings are called:

1. Solution-Oriented Parenting: Empowering Parents to Be the Agents of Change
2. Going for Small Changes
3. Connecting from the Heart: Meaningful Pathways for Further Strengthening Your Relationships with Your Young Adults or Teens
4. If It Works, Don't Fix It
5. If It Doesn't Work, Do Something Different
6. Collaborating for Success: Empowering Your Teens in Larger Systems Mazes

7. Pioneering New Parenting Directions

8. Celebrating Change: Honoring Your Solution-Oriented Parenting Successes

Session 1: Solution-Oriented Parenting: Empowering Parents to Be the Agents of Change

- The leaders begin the first group meeting striving to establish rapport with each parent and coming to know them by their key strengths, talents, past parenting successes, and self-generated pregroup treatment changes.

- The leaders address parent group treatment expectations and preferences they have for them and explore with them their reasons for participating in the group. They also invite parents to share what their past positive and negative treatment experiences were and their best hopes for their group experiences.

- The parents are invited to share which specific parenting behavior they would like to change, such as to stop nagging, blaming, yelling, lecturing, or being too super-responsible with their young adults or teens. Most parents, however, wish to learn how to change their kids' self-harming behaviors or other behaviors that may be of more concern to them. The leaders also want to solicit from the parents what their theories of change are.

- When parents identify a specific behavior of their's they wish to change, the leaders ask the following scaling questions: "If your daughter were sitting right next to you, what specific behavior would she say that you engage in that gets her the most upset with you? On a scale from 1 to 10, with 10 being you rarely yell at her, and 1 all of the time, where would she have rated you a month before coming to this group? How about 2 weeks ago? Are you aware of how you got that to happen? Where would she rate you today? So, what are you going to do over the next week to get up one step higher, to a 5?" The answer to this question may become the parent's initial treatment goal.

- For the educational component of the group, the leaders teach parents about the following: the *eight theoretical assumptions of collaborative strengths-based brief family therapy* as applied to parenting and the parenting guidelines (see Chapter 3); research on the role of *positive emotion* in improving one's psychological, physical, problem-solving, and interpersonal function ing; *learned optimism; key resiliency research findings;* and the *six characteristics of strong families*. The leaders provide important information on why kids self-harm today. They present Fredrickson's research on positive emotion and how as parents they can create a positive climate at home that will help strengthen their relationships with their kids and greatly enhance their creative problem-solving abilities (Fredrickson, 2002, 2003). As part of the presentation on positive emotion, the leaders present both research on *active constructive responding* (Gable et al., 2004) and the important research finding about couples who flourish committing to five compliments for every one complaint made in the relationship (Gottman & Gottman, 2006). The leaders stress that parents should really strive to give their kids daily compliments and acknowledge how much they love them to help inject more positive emotion into their relationships with them.

- Next, the leaders present the key findings from the PENN research project conducted by Seligman et al. (1995) that demonstrated how parents and teachers who respond with optimism and enthusiasm to kids doing both well and poorly on school tests or on other tasks tend to provide a protective function and decrease the likelihood of their developing depression and anxiety difficulties. The leaders perform two role-plays for the parents, first what a pessimistic way of responding looks like when the young adult or adolescent has gotten into trouble or failed a test. Then they will demonstrate how an optimistic parent would respond. The leaders open up the floor for questions and discussion when they are done with the role-plays.

- The leaders present some of the important findings from resiliency studies with at-risk children and youth and how the parents can help their kids become more resilient (Anthony & Cohler, 1987; Haggerty et al., 1994). They point out one of the most important findings regarding parents and key caretakers making themselves available for unconditional emotional support and advice when their kids seek their advice and want to connect with them.

- The important research findings by Stinnett and his colleagues are presented on the six characteristics of strong families: *appreciation, time together, commitment, communication, dealing with crisis in a positive way,* and *spiritual wellness* (Stinnett & O'Donnell, 1996; DeFrain & Stinnett, 1992). The leaders discuss each characteristic and provide concrete examples. Kids need to know that they are loved and appreciated. The leaders point out how today, thanks to high technology, spending time together as a family is becoming increasing less important as a family value and that this formerly cherished family value in past decades is being replaced with unmonitored and lengthy periods of time in front of computer screens. Kids need to know that even when they get into trouble, their parents' commitment and love for them is unconditional. Parents need to keep the lines of communication open with their kids. When they can't talk to one another, kids gravitate toward negative peers who can't talk to their parents and are also disconnected from their parents. Parents need to view crises with their kids or the family as an opportunity to practice teamwork and help one another through tough life situations. Finally, spiritual wellness has not only been found to be a resiliency protective factor, but parents upholding the importance of leading a spiritual life can provide hope and strength.

- Since parents often don't understand why their kids self-harm, it can be of great help to them to understand some of the most common reasons why they engage in this and equivalent self-destructive behaviors (see Chapter

1). The leaders point out that self-harming is a coping strategy for seeking quick relief from emotional distress and it is not suicidal behavior. They point out how a lot of kids who self-harm have difficulties with soothing themselves and how parents can help them with this by being more empathically attuned with them when their kids are experiencing emotional distress and by comforting them. As far as family dynamics go, the leaders share that one common dynamic found in some families of self-harming kids is emotional invalidation. They provide a role-play to illustrate what this looks like. The leaders open up the floor to parents for questions and discussion.

- The leaders teach parents how to *turn negatives into positives* in their minds when they are feeling stuck about how to interpret the meaning of or how to respond to their kids' most challenging behaviors. Some examples the parents are given are: a teen displaying her "attitude problem" is a *dramatic* teen, while a teen who is behaving in an oppositional, defiant way is an *assertive* teen. Parents often find this information and strategy quite useful in helping them respond more constructively to their kids' most challenging behaviors.

- **In-session exercise:** The first skill-building exercise the leaders like to teach parents is *thinking in circles.* The leaders point out how family interactions are circular and how the way we respond to one another affects how they respond to us and so forth. To help provide an example of what this looks like for the parents, the leaders draw a map of a circular problem-maintaining interaction between Barbara and Cynthia (see Figure 6.1). Often, parents find the exercise of thinking in circles newsworthy in that they rarely included themselves as part of the problem when their kids got into trouble, pushed their buttons, or cut themselves. The leaders invite one or two group members to go up to the whiteboard or flip chart and map out one of their circular problem-maintaining interactions and provide all of the details about how it gets set in motion and is perpetuated. Next, the leaders point out to the parents that once they introduce novel and more positive ways of interacting with their kids, this can set in motion a circular solution-maintaining pattern of interaction. They map out on the whiteboard or flip chart an example of a *solution-maintaining pattern of interaction* that Barbara set in motion with her self-harming daughter Cynthia. The leaders underscore that it is these types of patterns of interaction that parents need to keep track of and increase to help reduce and eventually eliminate their kids' problematic behaviors (See Figure 6.2). The leaders open up the floor for questions and discussion.

- The leaders take an intersession break while the parents have their refreshments. They come up with compliments for each parent. As part of their editorial reflection when the group is reconvened, the leaders positively relabel negative behaviors reported by the parents, use normalization, and

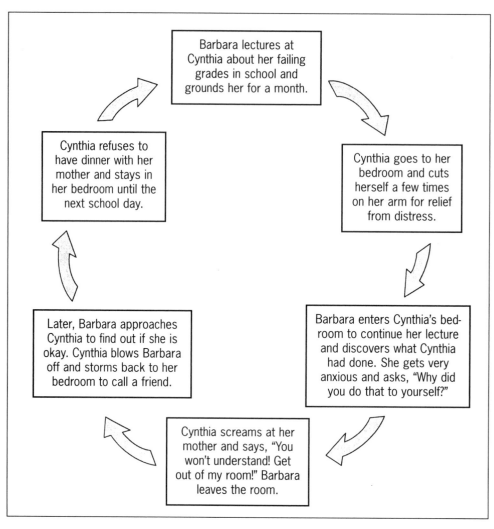

Fig. 6.1 Map of Barbara and Cynthia's Circular
Problem-Maintaining Pattern of Interaction

encourage them to begin to try out some of the parenting tips, tools, and strategies they learned in today's group session. The leaders also solicit from the parents what their perceptions were of the first group session, including the following: what they found helpful, what they want to learn more about, and what concerns they may have that need to be covered in future group meetings.

• **Between-session experiment:** The instructions for the between-session experiment are as follows: *In order for us to get a more complete picture of your kids' self-harming and other challenging behaviors, we would like you to notice on a daily basis what is happening in your relationships with your kids that you would like to continue to have happen. While doing this, we would* *like you to pay close attention to what you are doing that may be contributing to the occurrence of these positive and responsible behaviors happening. Please write those things down and bring your lists to our next group meeting.*

Session 2: Going for Small Changes

• The leaders begin by exploring with the parents the outcome of their exper
  iment. Every positive behavior that is reported is met with cheerleading
  from the group leaders and they amplify and consolidate their gains. With
  each positive step parents report, the leaders ask: "Are you aware of how
  you got that to happen?! Is that different for your daughter to do that? What
  did you tell yourself to pull that off?" Parents often return to this group

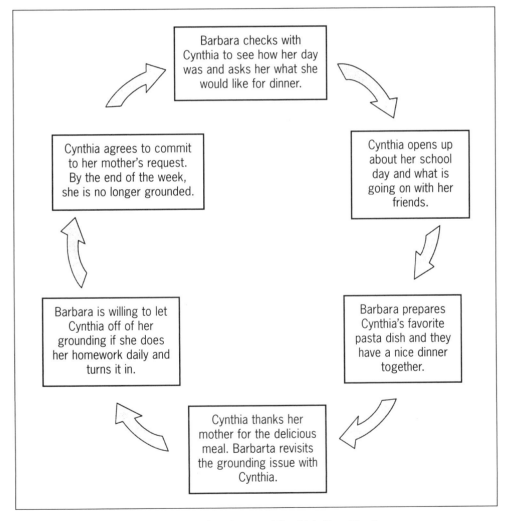

Fig. 6.2 Map of Barbara and Cynthia's New Circular
Solution-Maintaining Pattern of Interaction

session more hopeful and optimistic about their situations.

- After thoroughly processing each parent's results with the between-session experiment, the leaders ask all of the parents to respond to the *miracle question* (de Shazer, 1988). When asked this question parents often smile and enjoy envisioning a future reality minus their problems. The leaders expand the possibilities with each parent regarding the changes they report occurring individually, within the family, with the young adult or teen, at his or her college, high school, or junior high school. Absent family and extended family members are brought into the miracle inquiry as well. Most important, the parents need to speculate what their sons or daughter would say if they were present and what they would want to see changed with them and how they will relate differently with one another when the miracle happened. Finally, the leaders ask the following question to find out about unmentioned pregroup or between-group session changes: "Are any pieces of the miracle happening a little bit now?" The reported pregroup or between-group session mentioned miracle-like changes are amplified and consolidated by the leaders.

- Next, the leaders will further build on the goal-setting process with the parents to get a clearer focus of what specifically they wish to change now about their behavior or their kids'. They ask: "How will you know that you really succeeded in the group? What will be the number one thing that changed that will tell you that you were really glad that you decided to participate in this group?" Once they describe a specific parenting behavior they wish to change or a specific behavior of their kids, the leaders will use *scaling questions* (de Shazer et al., 2007; Selekman, 2005, 2006b) to establish a small behavioral goal with the parents. The leaders ask: "So, on a scale from 0 to 10—where 0 means when you decided to participate in our parents' group and 10 means the day after the miracle—where would you say you are at today? At a 5. What are you going to do over the next week to get one step higher on that scale, to a 6?" The response to this latter question will serve as a parent's initial treatment goal. When parents present lofty or vague goals, the leaders' jobs are to gently and respectfully negotiate small, realistic, and well-formed goals with them. The leaders share with the parents that goals are the beginning of something new and not the end of something and encourage them to enjoy the journey.

- The leaders take their intersession break while the parents have their refreshments. They put together their editorial reflection and compliments for each of the parents. The group is reconvened and they share their editorial reflection and compliments with the parents, particularly underscoring the positive steps the parents took with first group session experiment.

- **Between-session experiment:** The instructions for the between-session experiment are as follows: *Over the next week, we would like you to pick three days to pretend to engage in your kids' miracle behaviors they want to see with you. While you are pretending and trying to get those Academy Awards with your great performances, we would like you to carefully notice how your kids respond. Please write all of your observations on your between-session experiment sheets.*

Session 3: Connecting from the Heart: Meaningful Pathways for Further Strengthening Your Relationships with Your Young Adults or Teens

- The leaders begin the group session by asking the parents: "What further progress have you made?" All parental changes are met with cheerleading from the leaders and they amplify and consolidate their gains. They are asked: "Who earned Academy Awards?" The experiment is processed with the parents. The parents are often pleasantly surprised by the positive behavioral responses they get from their kids when they pretend to engage in their miracle behaviors. In fact, they often report novel, more respectful, and caring responses coming from their kids. In some cases, their kids opened up more to them about their self-harming difficulties and stressors in their lives or they spent quality time doing an activity together.

- The leaders need to check in on the parents' scales and progress they are making toward achieving their goals. Again, they can amplify and consolidate the parents' gains.

- With parents who are feeling stuck or are pessimistic, the group leaders will use the *coping* and *pessimistic questions* (Berg & Miller, 1992; Selekman, 2005, 2006b) to find out what they are doing to prevent things from getting much worse or dropping out of the group. This may lead to pessimistic parents increasing their awareness levels that they are doing some things that seem to prevent their kids' problematic situations from really escalating and getting much worse.

- The leaders also can tap the expertise of the group to brainstorm and list on the whiteboard or flip chart creative ideas they have for the stuck or pessimistic parents to try out.

- Prior to doing the in-session experiment, the leaders give a presentation on the Buddhist principles and practices of *the Four Immeasurable Minds, non-attachment, loving-kindness, compassion,* and *mindfulness meditation* (see Chapter 3; Hanh, 1997, 1998, 2001). The parents are given handouts describing each one of these important Buddhist principles and practices. The leaders teach the parents both the *sound* and *food meditations.* They encourage the parents to first practice using loving-kindness and compassion on themselves and then try it with their kids. In addition, they are asked to pick one of the mindfulness meditations to practice over the next week. The leaders conclude the presentation by pointing out to the parents that getting skilled at using these Buddhist principles and practices will help them to be more present and establish stronger and more meaningful relationships with their kids.

- **In-session exercise:** The instructions for the in-session experiment are as follows: *We would like each of you to pretend that we have sitting over here in the corner of the room an imaginary time machine. Now, if you were to hop into that time machine and take it back in time to a place where you felt strongly connected to your kids and your relationships were in a great place, where back in time would you take the machine? How old are your kids at the time? What are you doing together or talking about? How are you feeling and thinking at the time? Apply all of your senses to the experience, including color and motion. Next, we would like you to think about what aspects, ways of relating, or activities from these meaningful past experiences with your kids you would like to reinstate now in your relationships with them.*
- The leaders take their intersession break while the parents have their refreshments. They construct their editorial reflections and generate a list of compliments for all of the parents. The parents are reconvened for the editorial portion of the session and to receive their between-session experiments.
- **Between-session experiments:** The instructions for the between-session experiments are as follows: *Over the next week, we would like you to pick certain aspects, positive ways of relating, and activities from your imaginary time machine journeys back in time to reinstate in your relationships with your kids between now and the next time we meet. We also would like you to find an old shoe box and cut a slit in the top and create a compliment box. Daily, we would like you and your spouse/partner to write down on slips of paper compliments for your kids and drop them through the slits in your shoe box tops. The compliments can be sharing things that you appreciate they had done for you, achieved, or special qualities you really appreciate about them as people. After dinner or sometime in the evening, we would like you to give the shoe box to your kids to reach in and read their compliments in your company. When asked about why you are doing this, just let them know that you love them and you are trying to make the climate in the household more positive.*

Session 4: If It Works, Don't Fix It

- The leaders begin the group session exploring with the parents the results of their experiments. The parents often report that they found the Buddhist principles and practices helpful, particularly the benefits of approaching their kids with loving-kindness and compassion. They find that meditating after a stressful workday can be quite beneficial for them. In some cases, parents were successfully able to reinstate the best elements from their past time-traveling experiences, which led to them spending some quality time with their kids. Most parents find that the *compliment box* really shocked their kids. In fact, some parents reported that their kids had told them that they did not know that they really appreciated them so much or noticed their good qualities. As a result of this experiment, it helped improve the parents' interactions with their kids.

- The leaders check in with the parents' target goal areas and their progress on their scales. All changes are amplified and consolidated by the leaders. By this time in the group, some parents may have already achieved their initial treatment goal. The leaders ask one or two of these parents to map out on the whiteboard or flip chart some examples of their circular solution-maintaining interactions with their kids. This instills hope with parents in the group who still have not achieved their goals, and they may learn some new ways of trying to interact with their kids.

- For highly pessimistic, stuck, or demoralized parents, the leaders may use the *pessimistic* or *conversational questions* (Anderson, 1997; Berg & Miller, 1992; Selekman, 2006b) to see what keeps the parents coming back to the group and explore with them the *not yet said,* which might be some painful recent loss, a recently diagnosed serious illness, or something that is blocking the change process for the parents. Some examples of conversational questions the leaders might ask are: "Is there something unpleasant or painful going on right now in your life that you have not brought to the group's attention that might be helpful to talk about so you can gain their support? If we could help you to remove one big obstacle that you think is keeping your situation at a standstill right now, what would that obstacle be?"

- The leaders also can tap the expertise of the group and have them brainstorm creative ideas for the pessimistic or stuck parent.

- After the intersession break, the leaders share their editorial reflections and compliments with the parents.

- **Between-session experiments:** The instructions for the between-session experiment are as follows: *Over the next week, we would like you to do two experiments. The first experiment is to complete the My Past and Present Parenting Successes Worksheet* (see Figure 6.3). *Daily, you are to write down on the worksheet any past parenting successful strategies you recently reinstated and any new parenting strategies you come up with that seem to work at gaining your kids' cooperation, respect, or reducing their self-harming or other problematic behaviors you have been concerned about. For those of you on the road to achieving your goals, keep track of what you will do to advance yourself further toward your goals. Remember: DO MORE OF WHAT WORKS!*

Session 5: If It Doesn't Work, Do Something Different

- The leaders begin the fifth group session exploring what further progress the parents are making. Parents are invited to share with the group some of

---

Fig. 6.3 MY PAST AND PRESENT PARENTING SUCCESSES

Instructions: List past and present parenting strategies you have employed to successfully manage your teen's most challenging behaviors.

1.	
2.	
3.	
4.	
5.	
6.	
7.	
8.	
9.	
10.	

---

strategies they just came up with. All parental changes are amplified and consolidated by the leaders. By this stage of the group, parents start spontaneously complimenting one another.

- With parents who just achieved their goals, the leaders will have one or two of these parents map out on the whiteboard or flip chart examples of their circular solution-maintaining patterns of interaction with their kids.
- For parents who continue to feel pessimistic, stuck, or demoralized, the leaders can use *conversational questions* (Anderson, 1997) or *externalize the problem* (White, 1995; White & Epston, 1990). When externalizing a specific problem or pattern, it needs to be based on how the parent describes it or his or her belief about it. For example, if "blaming" is the pattern that has a life all of its own and is getting the best of a parent's relationship with her son, the leaders might ask this parent: "How long has this 'blaming' pattern been getting the best of you and your son? What does the "blaming" pattern

coach you to say or do to him? Have there been any times lately where you outsmarted the 'blaming' pattern and you didn't allow it to push you and your son around?" Questions like these can open up space for the parent to look at the problem as the villain in their family story, not her or her son. Once this shift in thinking occurs, this can lead to new and more positive interactions in their relationship.

- The leaders also can rely on the expertise of the group to generate creative ideas on the whiteboard or flip chart for the pessimistic, stuck, or demoralized parent.
- After the intersession break, the leaders share their editorial reflections and compliments with the parents.
- **Between-session experiments:** The instructions for the between-session experiment are as follows: *Over the next week, we would like you to try a really fun experiment. Whenever your kids try and push your buttons or you are tempted to be too super-responsible with them, that is, robbing them of the opportunity of experiencing the logical consequences of making bad choices or getting into trouble, we want you to experiment with doing something different than your usual course of action* (de Shazer, 1985). *Your actions need to be really different from anything your kids have ever seen before from you, even quite off the wall! Keep track of what works and write them down on your experiment sheets. Have fun!*

Session 6: Collaborating for Success: Empowering Your Teens in Larger Systems Mazes

- The leaders greatly look forward to hearing the creative and off-the-wall ways that parents responded differently to their kids. This is the most fun and upbeat group session. Even the more pessimistic, stuck, and demoralized parents often meet with success using this experiment. Parents spontaneously cheerlead for and compliment each other. The leaders echo the parents' accolades for each other.
- The leaders will have one or two parents who had just achieved their goals map out their circular solution-maintaining patterns of interaction on the whiteboard or flip chart.
- For parents who still may be somewhat stuck, the leaders tap the expertise of the group members to generate some creative ideas for these parents. If externalization of the problem has not been attempted, the leaders may try this at this point to see if it helps.
- The leaders give a brief presentation on the challenges for families involved with adult and juvenile justice, mental health, and school systems, and collaborative tools and strategies they can use to negotiate the help and support they want for their kids. They explore with parents their successes in their workplaces in negotiating things they want with their bosses and colleagues. The parents are encouraged to experiment with the negotiation

skills they already are using successfully in their work roles when attending meetings with these larger-system representatives. The leaders also present how to create a context for a win-win negotiation.

- **In-session exercise:** The instructions for the in-session skill-based experiment are as follows: *We would like you to project yourselves into future important meetings regarding your kids, which may be coming up real soon at your kids' schools or in some other larger systems contexts. We want you to pretend that you already attended this meeting and successfully got what you wanted for your kids. Next, we want you to systematically spell out the steps that you took to make that happen. After you carefully think this through, we would like to hear the steps that you took.*

- This skill-based exercise can empower parents to co-create positive self-fulfilling prophecies. Once successful, the parents' kids will really appreciate their taking a stand for them.

- After the intersession break, the leaders reconvene the group and share their editorial reflections and compliments with the parents.

- **Between-session experiments:** The instructions for the between-session experiment are as follows: *Due to your hard work, great progress, and strong commitment to the group, we want to give you a 2-week vacation as a vote of confidence that you will continue to soar with making individual and relationship changes with your kids. If you feel compelled to do a little work for us on your vacations, we would like you to keep track of what further progress you will make. In addition, if you have any opportunity to try out any of the collaborative tools and strategies or negotiation skills we discussed, let us know how they worked for you.*

Session 7: Pioneering New Parenting Directions

- The leaders begin the seventh session finding out what further progress group members are making. Their changes are amplified and consolidated by the leaders and spontaneously by the other parents.

- Parents who just achieved their goals are asked to map out the whiteboard or flip chart their new circular solution-maintaining interactions with their kids.

- To help cover the back door with the parents, the leaders will ask the following questions: "What would you have to do to go backward at this point? If you have a minor slip, what steps will you take to quickly get back on track?" By this point in the group, most of the parents have achieved their goals and are quite confident that they will not slip back into old patterns and habits.

- After a brief intersession break, the leaders reconvene the group and share their editorial reflections and compliments with them.

- **Between-session experiment:** The instructions for the between-session experiment are as follows: *As a vote of confidence, we decided to give you a*

3-week break from the group to continue to impress yourselves with your great parenting work. While on vacation, when you come up with additional creative parent strategies or pearls of wisdom, please write them down and bring your ideas to our last group meeting. We look forward to hearing what further progress you have made and celebrating you in our last meeting.

Session 8: Celebrating Change: Honoring Your Solution-Oriented Parenting Successes

- The leaders begin the last group meeting with finding out from the parents if they had any new creative parenting strategies or pearls of wisdom they wish to share with everyone.
- The parents' further changes are amplified and consolidated by the leaders. The parents cheer one another on.
- As part of consolidating the parents' gains, the leaders ask the following questions: "Let's say we invited you to our next Solution-Oriented Parenting Group. What helpful pointers and words of wisdom will you share with those parents? Let's say we have a reunion meeting 1 year from today. What further changes that you made will you enthusiastically share with us?"
- The parents are presented with a large sheet cake that has written on it: *Congratulations Solution-Oriented Parents!* The parents are given achievement award certificates and asked to give speeches, reflecting on where they were before the group and where they are at now in terms of all of their changes.
- The parents are inducted into the Solution-Oriented Parenting Alumni Association. As members, they are expected to serve as guest consultants for future parenting groups and may be called upon to co-facilitate a future group with one of the leaders.
- After offering the parents their last editorial reflections and final compliments, the group is concluded.
- Parents who request further individual, couples, or family therapy will be followed up by one of the group leaders.

Benefits and Limitations of the Solution-oriented Parenting Group

Having run the Solution-oriented Parenting Group for the past 20 years with great results, it is my strong belief that the strengths of the group greatly outweigh its limitations. We have had highly conflicted marital and postdivorce couples leave the group much more united as a team and respectful toward each other by the conclusion of the group. Their success in the group as a couple was a positive uplift for their marital or postdivorce relationships. We have had tough gang-involved or kids with multiple self-destructive behaviors who refused family therapy with their parents but contacted me for individual help after the parents had participated in the group. When asked about what made them decide to seek help, they often share that they like the changes their parents made. Finally, I have found that this group can benefit parents of young adults and adolescents who have difficulties with self-harm, substance abuse, eating disorders, attention deficit disorders, and oppositional defiant behavior.

As far as limitations go, some of the parent participants' kids continue to wield their power and are in charge of the family mood; their parents' changes have little effect on dethroning or changing their behavior. The same is true with highly disconnected families where a change in the parents' behaviors does not change the kids' behaviors. With these family situations, the therapist needs to do more direct family work and figure out a way to engage the powerful young adult or adolescent or work with subsystems and establish separate goals and therapeutic work projects.

There are certain couple situations that can preclude or block the change process: (a) the couple has grave difficulty working together as a team in the group and has trouble implementing change strategies at home due to intense conflicts and rage toward each other; (b) the partner who was reluctant to participate in the parenting group despite multiple group leader outreach attempts may undermine or be in coalition with the son or daughter whom the parent group participant is trying to change. In both of these clinical situations, more direct couple therapy is necessary.

Although no formal quantitative study has been conducted on this group to determine its efficacy, follow-up qualitative research interviews with parents at 6 months, 1 year, and 2 years have indicated that they got a lot out of the group, their changes had persisted, and it had improved their relationships with their kids. In the future, I plan to conduct research on the Solution-Oriented Parenting Group that combines both quantitative and qualitative methods.

The Stage Model of Change for Recruiting and Treating Young Adults in Group Therapy

Since research and clinical practice evidence-based experience and wisdom indicates that self-harming clients often do not seek treatment by themselves and are often in the *precontemplative* stage of readiness for change, it makes the most sense to offer specialized groups that match the therapeutic content and treatment strategies and techniques with the unique stage of readiness for change that the members are presently in (Prochaska et al., 1994; Velasquez et al., 2001). Therapists can either run specialized groups for just individuals in specific stages of readiness for change or run a whole group of young adults systematically through all of the stages of readiness for change. Clearly, therapists will have much better group treatment outcomes when the leaders match what they do with the unique stages of readiness for change of each group member. As Prochaska et al. (1994) have discovered through decades of research, helping clients advance to the next stage of readiness for change greatly enhances the likelihood of their future success in treatment.

If the group members are all in the precontemplation stage and do not think they have a problem with self-harm, the leaders need to avoid at all costs putting any pressure on or trying to convince them that they have a problem. Instead, they should use the *two-step tango* strategy of underscoring first how self-harming has benefited them as a coping strategy and its positive neurochemical and psychological effects and the second step of the tango taking the form of planting seeds in their minds and raising their consciousness levels about the benefits of changing (see Chapter 2; Selekman, 2005, 2008, 2008a). This would include the leaders sharing in a relaxed and nonthreatening way with the group some of the potential costs or consequences of continuing to self-harm and engage in equivalent habits (binge drinking, substance abuse, bingeing and purging, risky sexual behavior), such as shame and guilt, low self-esteem, doing serious tissue damage, permanent scarring, loss of friends, doing poorly in school, and so forth. Once the group participants begin to become more keenly aware that the self-harming behavior may be a problem, the leaders can gently and gradually help them advance to the next stage of readiness for change, which is *contemplation*.

In recruiting self-harming young adults for a precontemplators' group, the group flyer or announcement introductory text should be worded as follows:

> We are starting a group for young adults who are benefiting from self-harming and do not wish to quit their self-harming and closely related habits. We are eager to learn from you how specifically self-harming has benefited and been helpful to you in all areas of your life. By agreeing to participate in this group, there will be no pressure put on you to stop self-harming or engaging in closely related habits. We look forward to meeting you.

I have used a similarly worded flyer to engage substance-abusing clients and have met with much success with recruiting group participants. The flyers can be distributed to university student mental health centers and throughout the campus, at local community mental health centers, social service agencies, and psychiatric hospitals.

With *contemplators*, the group leaders can use the *decisional balancing scale* (Prochaska et al., 1994; Velasquez et al., 2001) to help the group members to get unstuck or resolve their ambivalence about the benefits of changing. Once their scales tilt in the direction of change, they can gently and gradually be advanced to the *preparation* stage of readiness for change. The introductory text for a group flyer or announcement for a contemplators' group may read as follows:

> We are starting a group for young adults who have been self-harming and have mixed feelings about it. We are sensitive to the fact that this habit may be benefiting you or serves some other purpose for you but you may have begun to notice certain costs or consequences of maintaining your self-harming habit. Our group is designed to help you feel

less stuck or ambivalent about what to do about your self-harming habit. We look forward to meeting you.

Once the clients are in the preparation stage of readiness for change, they are seeing more clearly some of the major costs or consequences of their self-harming and/or equivalent self-destructive habits and are getting closer to taking some steps to ameliorate these difficulties. However, they often report some very real obstacles that preclude or block the quitting process. The introductory text for a group flyer announcement for a group designed for young adults in the preparation stage would read as follows:

> We are starting a group for young adults who have been self-harming and are thinking about quitting their habits but may be feeling stuck about how to do it or are faced with specific obstacles that get in the way of changing their situations. Our group is specifically designed to provide you with tools and strategies to help you to remove those obstacles and map out your journey for quitting.

Clients who are in the *action* stage of readiness for change are in the starting blocks for conquering their self-harming and possible equivalent self-destructive habits. The group leaders' jobs consist of helping the group members to establish small and realistic behavioral goals and arm them with the tools and strategies to help them achieve them. The introductory text for a group flyer or announcement for a group designed for young adults in the action stage would read as follows:

> We are starting a group for self-harming young adults who are ready to quit their self-harming habits. Our group is specifically designed to help you establish small and realistic goals for yourself and learn effective tools and strategies for conquering your self-harming habits.

Clients in the *maintenance* stage of readiness for change are pleased with their taking steps to conquer their self-harming and equivalent self-destructive habits. However, they may become anxious or worry about backsliding and having slips. Therefore, the main focus of treatment for these individuals is teaching them goal-maintenance tools and strategies to help reduce the likelihood of slips. The group leaders help them to identify both their positive and negative triggers and teach them distress management tools and strategies. The introductory text for a group flyer or announcement for a group designed for young adults in the maintenance stage would read as follows:

> We are starting a group for young adults who have stopped self-harming and have a strong desire to stay quit but have concerns about slip-

ping back into their past self-harming habits Our group is specifically designed to arm you with several tools and strategies to help you to stay quit with confidence.

Finally, young adults in the *termination stage* are completely confident about not slipping back into either self-harming or engaging in former self-destructive behaviors. These individuals make excellent candidates for doing outreach and prevention work on college campuses and in their communities.

Pretreatment Change Group Consultation Meetings with Waiting-List Self-Harming and Other Clients

When outpatient clinics, student mental health centers, or agencies are faced with waiting-list situations, I strongly recommend that a counseling staff member from their clinics, centers, or agencies call these new clients and give them, while they are waiting for their first appointments, the pretreatment change experiment of noticing what they are doing or telling themselves and what intimate others who care about them are doing daily to prevent their situations from getting much worse and even improving their situations (see Chapter 2). They are instructed to write down the positive steps they are taking and bring their lists to a scheduled group meeting at their clinics or agencies in 1 week. One week later, two or three therapists from the clinics, student mental health centers, or agencies can facilitate a one-and-a-half-hour *pretreatment change group consultation meeting* with the new waiting-list clients to have them share with one another what they were doing to prevent their situations from getting much worse and constructive and effective steps they have already taken to improve their situations. The therapist facilitators of the group can ask the waiting-list participants the following questions:

- "Since you first called or walked into our clinic, what have you noticed that has gotten a little bit better with your situations?"
- "While you have been waiting the last 2 weeks for appointments, what steps have you taken to prevent your situations from getting much worse?"
- "What else have you been doing to prevent things from really escalating and getting out of hand?"
- "On a scale of 1 to 10, with 10 being your situation is exactly where you want it to be, and 1 where it is on the road to where things need to be, where would you have rated yourselves when you first called our office on that scale?"
- "How about 1 week ago?"
- "Are you aware of how you did that?!"
- "What other steps did you take to pull that off?!"
- "Where would you rate your situation today?"
- "What are you going to do over the next week to get up one step higher on that scale, to a 5?"

- "What have other members of this group done to successfully manage or resolve the kind of difficulty Margie and her daughter are struggling with right now?"
- "How did that make a difference with your situation?"
- "Steve, you mentioned that you used to have similar difficulties with your son in the past that Walter is currently experiencing with his son. What steps would you recommend that Walter take to resolve this difficulty with his son that really worked for you?"
- "What other sparkling moments and successes do other participants wish to share with the group so we can learn from your expertise?"

The beauty and power in conducting these pretreatment change group consultation meetings is that it further empowers waiting-list clients who are already self-healing, coping well, and productively resolving their own difficulties, and their creativity and resourcefulness have a positive cascading and contagion effect on those waiting-list clients who had not been self-changing at the same pace. Hearing the advanced self-changers' stories and learning what their unique self-generated coping strategies and positive solution-building steps are can instill hope and empower them to further improve their situations. In some cases, after one pretreatment change group consultation meeting, clients take themselves off the waiting list, reporting that their situations had improved to such a degree that they no longer saw the need for counseling. When these clients are asked about how they came to this conclusion, they often state that participating in this one-shot pretreatment change group consultation meeting further enhanced their self-changing capacities, it dissolved the idea that they had a problem, or they had learned some helpful strategies from their fellow group participants that worked with their situations.

Although some new waiting-list clients who have participated in this pretreatment change group consultation meeting choose to remain on the waiting list, I have found that by the time these clients begin seeing a therapist their lengths of stay in treatment are greatly reduced. It appears that this pretreatment single group-session meeting even has a positive effect for these clients as well.

The group makeup can be comprised of individuals, parents, young adults, couples, or families. The numbers on the waiting list will determine the size of the meeting room you will need. If the waiting list is quite large, it is beneficial to run more than one pretreatment change group consultation meeting. The pretreatment change group consultation meeting brief intervention can help eliminate waiting-list problems at outpatient clinics, student mental health centers, and agencies.

CHAPTER SEVEN

The Pathways to Possibilities Program

The *Pathways to Possibilities Program* grew out of my desire to create a family systems-oriented strengths-based intensive outpatient program for at-risk adolescents who have serious and long-standing problems with self-harm, bulimia, substance abuse, and engaging in sexually risky behaviors. I have found that there was a need for an intensive family systems-based aftercare program for at-risk adolescents who had these difficulties and were coming out of residential and inpatient psychiatric treatment programs and returning to virtually unchanged family environments, which sets the stage for prolonged relapse situations. I also wanted to provide a treatment level of care that could better meet the needs of moderate, heavy, and severe self-harming practice adolescent clients. For some moderate, heavy, and severe self-harming practice clients, collaborative strengths-based brief family therapy did not offer enough treatment intensity.

Unlike most intensive outpatient programs for adolescents and their families, the Pathways to Possibilities Program invites clients to be the lead authors of their own treatment plans, which I call *The Blueprint for Change Plan* (see Figure 7.1). The self-harming adolescents and their families not only determine their goals but choose from a menu of treatment modalities and adjunctive services. For each session they can choose from a menu of therapeutic experiments carefully tailored to and in line with their unique theories of change, treatment preferences, expectations, and treatment goals. Although the developers and facilitators of intensive outpatient programs for youths and their families at psychiatric hospitals, community-based agencies, mental health centers, and private practice settings will say that their clients determine their treatment goals and are co-designers of their own treatment plans, this is usually not the case. Over the years, I have worked with many self-harming adolescents and their families that had participated in residen-

Fig. 7.1 THE BLUEPRINT FOR CHANGE PLAN

My/our identified key pretreatment changes

1.

2.

3.

4.

5.

Target behaviors and/or relationship changes desired now

1. Parent's goals

    a.

    b.

    c.

2. Couple's goals:

    a.

    b.

    c.

3. Young adult/teen's goals:

    a.

    b.

    c.

My/our identified and key strengths tapped for goal attainment

1.

2.

3.

4.

5.

6.

Identification of solution-determined system membership and whom to include in future sessions

1.

2.

3.

4.

5.

6.

Treatment modality and adjunct services selection menu

_____Individual therapy

_____Couples therapy

_____Family therapy

_____Solution-Oriented Parenting Group

_____Stress-Buster's Leadership Training Group

_____Collaboration and advocacy with larger systems professionals

_____Mindfulness meditation training

_____Yoga

_____Art therapy

_____Expressive writing therapy

Therapeutic experiment menu

_____ Therapeutic experiment #1

_____ Therapeutic experiment #2

_____ Therapeutic experiment #3

Parents

Name _____ Date _____

Name _____ Date _____

Young Adult/Teen

Name _____ Date _____

Therapist

Name _____ Date _____

---

tial treatment, inpatient, and intensive outpatient treatment programs where not only did they have little input in determining their treatment goals but the treatment program staff they worked with took the lead in deciding which combination of treatment modalities and goals would best meet their needs. When treatment staffs try to become the privileged experts with clients who have had extensive treatment histories, let alone any clients, not only do their difficulties become further perpetuated and more entrenched, but this fuels client demoralization, hopelessness, and despair and can lead to treatment failure.

The Blueprint For Change Plan

When new families are referred to the Pathways to Possibilities Program, my colleagues and I build strong rapport with each family member participating, provide an overview of the program, address family members' concerns and expectations, and co-construct with them their *Blueprint for Change Plan*. After their treatment goals are established, they identify which of their key strengths and self-generated preprogram changes they will use in the goal-attainment process, and who the lead therapist needs to collaborate with from their social networks and larger systems, they can choose from the following menu of treatment modalities and adjunct services that they think can help them succeed at achieving their goals in the most efficacious way:

- Individual therapy
- Couples therapy
- Family therapy
- Solution-Oriented Parenting Group
- Stress-Busters' Leadership Group
- Collaboration and advocacy with larger systems professionals
- Mindfulness meditation training
- Yoga
- Art therapy
- Expressive writing therapy

No matter what type of therapy they select, the clients will have the opportunity to choose from two or more therapeutic experiments to try out between therapy sessions. Empowering clients in this way with having the ultimate say in determining their goals, choosing from a menu of treatment modalities and adjunct services, and session-by-session therapeutic experiments options will greatly reduce client psychological reactance, enhance treatment compliance, help foster a cooperative relationship, and prevent premature dropout situations from occurring.

The Blueprint for Change Plan is flexible and will be reviewed session by session with the therapists and clients to modify or add new treatment goals, add or drop treatment modalities and adjunct services, and determine if helpful and concerned key resource people from the clients' social networks and larger systems professionals should be more actively involved in the treatment process. Therapists and their clients establish a strong partnership with all treatment planning and decision-making. At any given point in the intensive treatment process, therapists and their clients know what is working, what is not helping, and what the next steps are to help them to achieve their goals. Clients are given copies of their Blueprint for Change Plans to take home to regularly review and decide with their families any changes they wish to make with them throughout the treatment process.

Program Treatment Stages

There are three treatment stages of the 9-week Pathways to Possibilities Program: *training, consolidating,* and *giving back.* Each family is unique and may move more quickly or slowly through each of these fluid stages.

The Training Stage

My colleagues and I share with clients that the *training stage* can be viewed as a rite of passage or transition from problems to possibilities for them. As collaborative partners and consultants to clients, we help them identify and utilize their self-generated preprogram changes, key strengths and resources, and past successful coping and problem-solving strategies in their presenting difficulty areas. The adolescents will learn highly effective distress management tools and strategies. Parents will learn what their adolescents' positive and negative triggers and unique needs are and how to strengthen their relationships with them. They also will learn how to tap their own strengths and resources to generate unique solutions for any challenging behaviors they experience with their adolescents. This parental skills training process will occur in the context of either family therapy or a Solution-Oriented Parenting Group or in both places if they choose to do these treatment modalities concurrently.

The Consolidating Stage

In the *consolidating stage*, program participants are making great strides toward achieving their goals. The therapists' job is to help cover the back door with them by teaching them effective goal-maintenance tools and strategies to stay on track and constructively manage inevitable self-harming, bingeing and purging, or substance usage slips. Therapists normalize for families that slips go with the territory of change and offer them valuable wisdom about where they need to tighten up. As part of this stage, we co-construct with families *tribal circles of caring others*, which consist of concerned friends and adult inspirational others of the adolescents, actively involved extended family members, concerned clergy, and involved helping professionals from larger systems, who are all members of the *solution-determined system*. This sacred circle of concerned others will have an opportunity to contribute their expertise and offer added support outside of the therapy office and reflect on the changes they have observed with the adolescents and their families. By actively involving the tribal circle of caring others, therapists can decentralize their roles in the lives of these families and have these important individuals be more central in their lives.

The Giving-Back Stage

In the giving-back stage, we empower adolescents and their parents to share their wisdom and expertise with other adolescents and parents in the community. We make arrangements with area schools and public libraries for adolescents in the program to provide stress management and negative habit prevention workshops for late elementary school–aged and junior high school kids. Parents are invited to provide public prevention presentations on adolescent self-harming behavior or for parents in their community or at school parent-teacher association metings and and serve as guest consultants and co-facilitators of future Solution-oriented Parenting groups if they had participated in this treatment modality in the group. Both adolescents and their families are expected to get involved in social action projects in their communities. Finally, graduates of the Pathways to Possibilities Program are invited to serve as consultants to the program, be part of the orientation process with newcomers to the program, and participate as members of tribal circles of caring others for families that have limited support in their social networks.

Longer Time Intervals between Sessions and Booster Sessions in the Bank

As part of the consolidating and giving-back stages, we give clients increasingly longer time intervals between sessions as a vote of confidence to them. We offer them a choice of the length of time between the session intervals. Once clients achieve their goals and are very satisfied with their treatment outcomes and experiences, they do not have to stay involved with the program for the full 9 weeks. In fact, many of our families finish up well before the final week of the program. They are told that whatever weeks' worth of sessions are leftover will be put in the booster session savings bank if they should need a future tune-up. Families find it reassuring to know that the door is always open to them with the program or with the therapists running it individually.

Adopting the Pathways to Possibilities Program to Self-Harming Young Adults

Although I have included self-harming young adults 18–19 years old and their families in the Pathways to Possibilities Program with adolescents, this tends to work best when they are living at home and are not away at college. It is much more difficult to run a program like this on a college campus without having more direct access to the parents. However, many components of this program and a modified version of it could be implemented on college campuses facilitated by student mental health center staff. If anything, self-harming college students will find the variety of treatment modalities, adjunct services, and the tribal-circle-of-caring-others components of the program most appealing to them.

Program Evaluation

The Pathways to Possibilities Program continues to evolve and my colleagues and I are constantly looking for new ways to improve it. What is lacking is a formalized program evaluation component to provide scientific evidence of its efficacy. Although we have gotten great feedback from past participants of the program, future research is necessary to learn more about what components of the program seemed to be the most beneficial for self-harming clients and their families and posttreatment results in terms of the staying power of their changes over time. The Pathways to Possibilities Program continues to serve as a valuable treatment level of care option with self-harming adolescents and their families who may require more treatment intensity, particularly with adolescents who fall into the heavy to severe self-harming practice categories and have not responded to collaborative strengths-based brief family therapy alone.

CHAPTER EIGHT

The Summit Program

By Kim Johancen-Walt, MA, LPC

"I'm happy." I nearly fell out of my chair as Jennifer spoke these words. Judging by the shocked looks on her parents' faces, I suspect they felt the same way. And then something even more miraculous happened. A huge smile quickly spread across the other faces in the room, including my own. Jennifer had taken the last few steps needed to beat self-harm.

In order for others to fully appreciate this moment, I need to explain a bit about the journey that led to this point. Jennifer, 15 years old, represented one of the most severe cases of self-harming behavior I had worked with in over 10 years. She was referred into our program, *The Summit Program*, due to her self-harming and escalating suicidal behavior. Jennifer reported that her earliest memory of self-harming behavior occurred in the fifth grade when she deliberately threw herself off her bike as she sped down a hill. This incident resulted in Jennifer's breaking both of her wrists.

Jennifer's primary form of self-harm included cutting with occasional incidents of burning herself. Jennifer reported that she was cutting herself up to 50 times a day and was in and out of hospital settings as a result of this behavior. She was finally placed in a residential treatment facility and was again hospitalized after staff found her tearing out her toenails. Jennifer revealed that it was during this final hospitalization that she finally realized her life was in danger. It was here that she began her treatment and dared to take those first few steps that would eventually lead her down a very different path.

I hope everyone working with self-harming adolescents can experience what it is like to watch a client smile the way Jennifer smiled in my office that day. It offers me hope that kids suffering in similar places can find their way out. The Summit Program is a place where many adolescents come to find their smiles.

The Summit Program, a collaborative high school–based program in Durango, Colorado, is funded by La Plata County Human Services, Southwest Colorado Mental Health Center, the Durango School District, and the San Juan Board of Cooperative Educational Services (BOCES). The program is licensed to serve up to 20 students at one time and offers intensive outpatient services to the adolescents and families who participate. Summit staff includes two therapists, a caseworker, a high school teacher, and a classroom aide, and is supervised by the above agencies.

Due to many of the referrals made to the program over the last several years, we have evolved from a traditional day treatment model into one specializing in adolescents who are either self-harming or suicidal. Our referrals come from a variety of sources, including school counselors, teachers, parents, therapists, physicians, and psychiatrists. We are also beginning to see a growing number of both peer and self-referrals to the program. Due to our success in the community, we are seeing more referrals than ever before and we currently have a waiting list for students and families wanting services.

Once accepted into the program, adolescents take the Summit "class" in conjunction with their other regular classes in the high school. They can receive up to five elective credits at the end of a trimester for their voluntary participation. Length of treatment for most students varies between two and four trimesters. While in the program, students receive academic support 2 to 3 days a week and meet with a therapist at least once during the week for individual therapy. Kids also participate in a dialectical behavioral therapy (DBT) skills group twice a week, where they learn and practice various skills that target emotional distress reduction (Linehan, 1993b).

Families are offered both family therapy and DBT parent skills groups. The parent groups are facilitated by Southwest Colorado Mental Health Center therapists and meet weekly. Due to the involvement of Human Services, families can continue to participate in services throughout the summer months that include individual, group, and family therapy. We are now also offering a Summit Graduate Group to adolescents so that graduates can continue receiving support even after completion of the program.

In addition to the above services, therapists are also available to clients for both crisis and on-call support. The adolescents in the program may be in need of support after school hours and are encouraged to seek support as necessary.

Matthew Selekman has greatly influenced the treatment offered to our clients. In his book *Working with Self-Harming Adolescents: A Collaborative, Strengths-Based Therapy Approach*, Selekman offers various techniques and strategies to use with self-harming adolescents and their families. Because of his insight into this treatment population, we have been able to better address the needs of our clients and have seen a tremendous reduction in their symptoms as a result.

Program Data and Treatment Outcomes

Our data is based on the total number of students who participated in the Summit

Program since the fall of 2004. We have served 69 adolescents and have tracked these students both during and after treatment. Specific behaviors discussed here include self-harming and suicidal behaviors, and information about out-of-home placements and school performance is included.

Many of the adolescents who enter our program report multiple self-harming behaviors at the beginning of treatment, including self-mutilation, risky sexual behavior, eating disorders, and substance abuse. Regarding self-mutilation, most students report cutting and burning as their primary forms of self-harm. However, we have worked with other self-mutilation behaviors including hair-pulling and bone-breaking, and we have worked with adolescents who create wounds and do not allow them to heal. Students have reported an 80% average of reduction in self-harming and suicidal behaviors at the conclusion of successful treatment with the Summit Program. In regard to targeting suicidal behavior specifically, several of our students have reported suicide attempts before treatment, and it is therefore important to note that emergency services evaluations have decreased by 72% for students who have participated in the program within the last 3 years (Figure 8.1).

What is equally impressive is that even the students who drop out of treatment prematurely still report a 50% reduction in symptoms related to self-harming and suicidal behaviors. These students are unable to complete treatment for various reasons including legal issues, substance abuse, and/or issues related to poor school performance and school attendance.

In addition to the positive treatment outcomes shown above, the Summit Pro-

Figure 8.1 SUMMIT PROGRAM STATISTICS 2004–2007			
	2004–2005	**2005–2006**	**2006–2007**
Student profile			
Total students served	18	24	28
Total students presenting with history of suicidal ideation/behavior	10	11	13
Total number of students presenting with history of homicidal ideation	1	1	2
Interventions			
Total number of emergency evaluations	14	10	4
Total out-of-home placements and/or hospitalizations	5	3	1

gram has successfully helped prevent out-of-home placements and has also helped keep students from dropping out of high school. Many of the adolescents in our program are at risk for out-of-home placement based on issues including abuse by a parent and/or safety concerns such as an adolescent threatening to commit suicide. Due to the involvement of Human Services, intensive family services, and a swift response from emergency services workers at Southwest Colorado Mental Health Center, most of the adolescents and families we serve receive the support they need to prevent placements.

These preventive efforts help all of the agencies involved with the program to save money that would otherwise be spent on hospitalizations, residential treatment, and foster care. It costs $66,000 per year to keep a child in residential treatment. This cost includes educational, boarding, and treatment costs. The cost of the Summit Program per student is $11,000 per year, resulting in a potential savings of $55,000 per year for every student who does not get placed out of the home. In 3 years, out-of-home placements have decreased by 80% for adolescents who have received treatment in the Summit Program.

Many of our students are at high risk for dropping out of high school for various reasons, such as unhealthy peer groups and little contact with supportive adults. In the 23rd Annual Report to Congress on the Implementation of the Individuals with Disabilities Act, the national rate for students with emotional disturbance who dropped out or moved was 65%. If this rate held true for the Summit Program, then 45 out of 69 students would have dropped out of high school. We have only had 13 Summit students (19%) drop out of high school in 3 years, representing a significant improvement over the national average for this population (see Figure 8.2). Most of the adolescents in our program are receiving the extra academic support they need to meet the increasing pressures of academic standards in today's high schools. They are experiencing academic success and are therefore staying motivated to finish high school and graduate with their peers.

Adolescents are passing 75% of their classes on average when they begin treatment in the program. This number goes up to 80% while they are in the program.

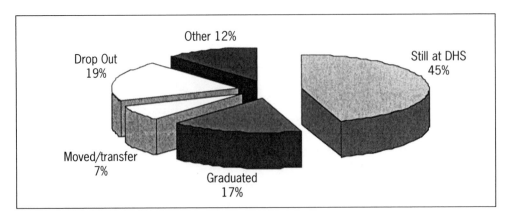

Fig. 8.2 Summit Program Treatment Outcome Results

Students leaving the program are successfully passing 90% of their classes. These numbers indicate that even the kids who drop out of treatment prematurely are getting themselves back on track to graduate from high school.

Case Presentations

Jennifer

After seeing Matthew Selekman present at a conference in Denver 2 years ago, I came back to Durango and immediately began implementing many of his techniques with my clients. Rather than focusing on their problems, I began to focus on their strengths and resiliencies.

After Jennifer returned from residential treatment (still self-harming), she began to consider all the ways she had been able to stay alive despite intense emotional pain. Although I had always challenged her beliefs about self-harm, we now began to discuss all the exceptions to her self-harming behavior. We talked about how she was able to stand up to cutting at least 2 days a week by distracting herself. For example, she listened to soothing music and spent time with her family instead of isolating herself.

Selekman (2006b) discusses the need to celebrate success with clients as a way to capitalize on their progress in treatment. Jennifer celebrated each success she experienced in her efforts to beat self-harm. We had several gatherings, inviting family, friends, Summit staff, and other treatment team providers, including her psychiatrist. As we ate cake, each participant spoke about Jennifer's successes. Jennifer reported feeling like her hard work was acknowledged during these celebrations.

Although Jennifer has effectively beaten self-harm, we continue to applaud her success. For example, she was recently a guest speaker at a therapist consultation meeting where she answered therapists' questions about how to work with adolescents who self-harm. Jennifer's parents and siblings have also offered to talk to other parents and professionals about how their family has been able to overcome many of the struggles they have experienced in their lives.

Michael

Although skeptical, Michael, age 15, and his parents decided to give the Summit Program a try. Michael was referred by a school principal for both self-harming behavior and suicidal thoughts and came to our team after other treatment had been unsuccessful. From the beginning of family therapy, sessions focused on what the family had already done to overcome self-harming behavior. For example, due to their son's dangerous behavior, Michael's parents had begun to look at what they might be doing to contribute to the problems in their family. Historically, Michael's mother had been making most of the parenting decisions and his father had not been part of these decisions.

While participating in family therapy, Michael's parents began to realize their unique strengths as parents, allowing them to focus on solutions instead of the problems in their family. As a result, Michael's father became more confident in his parenting abilities and was able to become a more active participant in Michael's life. Simultaneously, Michael's mother began practicing some of the cognitive-behavioral skills learned in therapy and was able to begin parenting more effectively.

Selekman (2006b) encourages both parents and therapists to regularly check in with adolescents about how their parents are doing with them. When asked this question in one of our family sessions, Michael confirmed that his parents were on the right track. Michael discussed enjoying his father's new involvement in his life and also complimented his mother on allowing him more independence.

Michael has stopped self-harming and is no longer suicidal. He wants to be a psychiatrist and has already begun helping others who have had similar struggles. For example, he recently met with a group of therapists and discussed what he believes to be the essentials of effective treatment with self-harming adolescents. He is an incredible writer and has written several poems on the emotional pain experienced by many teens today. He has allowed me to share many of his poems with other students in the program.

Jade

Jade, age 17, was referred to the program for self-harming behavior and had reported three previous suicide attempts. Jade had a history of sexual abuse and had grown up with both parents abusing drugs and alcohol. Jade was living with her father and her stepmother when she was referred to the program. Jade's father had completed drug rehabilitation and was sober.

Although treatment included giving the family a list of different skills and strategies they could use whenever self-harm threatened Jade, it was the externalization of the behavior that helped create real change for Jade and her family. Selekman (2006b) discusses the effective use of externalization of the problem as a way to help families join forces against the behavior. This skill can be effective for families who otherwise would place blame either on each other or on themselves for their problems. Through the use of this technique, the family was able to work together and stop self-harm from tricking Jade in to engaging in former negative behaviors.

Jade has not cut herself for several months and has not reported feeling suicidal since beginning treatment in the program. She has referred a friend to the program and is currently participating in a sexual abuse survivors group in order to continue standing up to sexual abuse and to build connections with other girls who have also experienced success on similar issues.

Diana

Diana, age 18, was referred by a peer who had already been enrolled in the program. Diana had been accepted into the program due to daily suicidal thoughts. When asked to discuss how her daily thoughts helped her through intense emotional pain, Diana described them as a comforting blanket she could wrap around herself whenever she felt powerless. She stated that, at times, having the choice to take her own life appeared to be the only thing she had control over. Through using a variety of Selekman's cognitive-behavioral skills including asking the adolescent to "play detective" and find proof that irrational thoughts are true, Diana was able to challenge her beliefs that she would be "in control" if she took her own life.

Diana is getting ready to graduate from high school in the spring and wrote a letter discussing her success in Summit Program: "Before (Summit), I woke up every morning just hoping death would show its beautiful face in my mirror. Now I wake up with a smile. . . . I'm almost done with Summit, but I feel as if I've grown a hundred years. I understand so much more. I wish the other kids that have these problems could be in a group like yours."

Charlotte

When Charlotte, age 14, first started the Summit Program, she was cutting at least three times a week and had attempted suicide in middle school where she was discovered by her mother after overdosing on pills found in the family medicine cabinet. Like Jade, Charlotte also had a history of sexual abuse. We discussed how Charlotte had already begun to stand up to her past abuse and to the negative thoughts that rattled around inside her head by being brave enough to enter treatment. We used Selekman's cognitive therapy A-B-C framework in order to further identify various thoughts that pushed her around (Beck, 1995; Selekman, 2006b), celebrated every success made against self-harming behavior, and built connections with other adolescents who had successfully graduated from the Summit Program. She was able to begin focusing on building connections with others, especially her father, Bill, whom she had never talked to about her past sexual abuse.

During an individual session with Charlotte, I assigned the "secret surprise" strategy for her to use with one of her parents (Selekman, 2006b). She decided to clean the house as a way to surprise her mother, Connie. When Charlotte started to clean the house and explained to her father what she was doing, he decided to help her clean. Connie was indeed surprised and, shortly after completing this assignment, Charlotte was not only able to convince both her parents to reintroduce a weekly family game night, but also made efforts to spend more time with her father.

By the time Bill, her father, came to a family therapy session, Charlotte had already begun working toward her goal of building a better relationship with him. In our first session, the family discussed past successes including how the family had made huge strides to move through the damaging effects of Charlotte's earlier sexual abuse. During the session, Charlotte listened to Bill share his anger that Charlotte's perpetrator had never been prosecuted due to inconclusive evidence.

Walls had begun to break down between Bill and Charlotte as Bill went on to discuss how he wanted to be closer to Charlotte but that he did not know how to talk to his teenage daughter. After normalizing that many fathers feel that they do not know how to talk to their teenage daughters, I encouraged Connie to give Bill tips on how to talk to Charlotte due to her obvious success in this area.

I also encouraged Bill to talk to Charlotte about how he had survived his adolescence in order to give her advice on how to navigate her own adolescence. At one point in the session, Bill revealed to Charlotte for the first time that he had also been a cutter when he was younger. I encouraged Charlotte to talk to her father about his experience in beating self-harm in order to get some new ideas on how to stand up to cutting.

In order to help Bill and Charlotte continue building momentum within their relationship, I assigned Charlotte as homework the task of teaching Bill something new at the end of the session. As Selekman (2006b) suggests, I also accentuated the positives by discussing how most of my teenage clients ask me to help get their parents "off their backs" but how Charlotte had asked for me to help her build stronger relationships with her parents. Connie and Bill left my office feeling effective and Charlotte left feeling like she had made progress in building a relationship with her father. Charlotte has reported zero incidents of cutting since this session.

Pharmacological Treatment

In treating self-mutilation, a combination of cognitive-behavioral therapy and pharmacological treatment may need to be considered (Shannon, 2005). Marille Strong, award-winning author of *A Bright Red Scream: Self-Mutilation and the Language of Pain,* suggests that there may be a connection between lower serotonin levels and self-harming behavior (Strong, 1998). Serotonin is a neurotransmitter in the brain that influences mood and aggression, so it makes sense that lower levels of serotonin may fuel impulsive behaviors and other behaviors associated with self-harming behavior (Strong, 1998).

The majority of our students who have not experienced relief in therapy by itself are referred to local psychiatrists for a medication evaluation. It is a myth that all clients who self-harm are suicidal. However, research indicates that if a self-harming client does not experience relief from their symptoms, their symptoms can become exacerbated and they can become suicidal as their sense of hopelessness increases (Shannon, 2005).

Graduate Services

We have begun offering graduate groups to clients who have completed the Summit Program and want additional services. We have modeled this program component after Selekman's *Stress Buster's Leadership-Group* format (Selekman, 2006b). There are currently 7 graduates attending the group and they report that it gives them an opportunity to review skills and stay connected with one another. Group leaders accentuate each member's strengths and offer group members additional skills to help with stress management and emotion regulation. The adolescents also offer one another ideas on how to deal with stress in effective ways without needing to fall back on self-harming and suicidal behaviors.

This group is the result of clients asking for additional support after graduating from the Summit Program. The adolescents are asked to "give back" after completing the group by being available to help Summit therapists teach skills to new students. I have found it particularly useful to pair adolescents who have successfully beaten cutting behavior with Summit students who are actively cutting. The older students can offer skills that they have found particularly useful. For example, Jennifer has talked to both students and therapists about the various skills she has found most helpful in beating self-harm. Jennifer's "Box Skill" has been a favorite among students:

The Box Skill

"Pick a spot to be your safe spot. It can be your bed, a chair, or even a box. Follow these three rules: First, you cannot bring anything into your safe spot that you would use to self-harm. Second, you cannot self-harm in your safe spot. Finally, you cannot leave until you feel safe."

Sexual Abuse Survivors Group

I have also had success in adapting Selekman's Stress Buster's Leadership Group format with a sexual abuse survivors group that serves several students who are either currently in Summit or who have graduated from the program (Selekman, 2006b). Group members identify skills and strategies they have found helpful, and they are also able to discuss their stories in a validating environment.

The girls practice skills both in and out of group sessions. For example, by assigning the "observing oneself-high-up-in-a-bubble" experiment as homework, the girls can observe how they interact in relationships (Selekman, 2006b). This strategy allows adolescents the opportunity to observe how they interact in relationships. This opens up a discussion on how previous abuse may be getting in the way of developing meaningful relationships. Furthermore, by devoting time to the "Politics of Gender" topic, the group is able to discuss how the media perpetuates gender stereotypes that may be damaging to both males and females (Selekman, 2006b).

During our last session, we celebrate each group member's success and discuss how the girls are now considered "experts." Each member is expected to help others who have experienced sexual abuse. For example, group members have talked to SASO (Sexual Assault Services Organization) volunteers at trainings, have individually mentored other girls in the high school, and have come back to talk to current group members about their experiences.

Empowering the Therapist

As a result of shifting to a strengths-based model, our program has seen not only a reduction in symptoms related to self-harming and suicidal behavior, but we have also seen a reduction in other symptoms such as truancy and poor academic performance. Due to our success in the community, we are beginning to see more referrals than ever before, and many are coming from clients themselves.

Selekman's writings are inspirational not only because he offers hope to the families dealing with these issues, but because he also offers hope to the therapist working with them. I have become more positive about the treatment I offer clients after implementing his ideas. I am no longer focusing on the hopelessness that overwhelms many of the families that come to our program. I am able to teach them skills, validate their experiences, and watch them smile as we celebrate their success.

Program data, treatment outcomes, and graphs were provided by Alain Henry, MA.

CHAPTER NINE

Challenging Treatment Dilemmas and Trouble-Shooting Guidelines for Co-Creating Workable Realities

I am frequently asked questions at workshops both in the United States and abroad regarding special treatment dilemmas with more complex and challenging self-harming clients. I present those questions here, along with trouble-shooting guidelines and specific therapeutic pathways that can be pursued to co-create workable realities with challenging self-harming clients and their partners and/or families. I will share my thoughts and clinical experiences regarding what some of the key factors are that can contribute to premature dropout situations and treatment failures occurring with self-harming clients and their intimate partners and/or families. I will conclude the chapter by offering my reflections on future directions needed in the areas of prevention, treatment, and research on self-harming clients and their families.

Challenging Treatment Dilemmas and Therapeutic Recommendations

In this section, seven frequently asked questions by mental health professionals regarding special treatment dilemmas with self-harming clients they have encountered are presented and practical treatment recommendations and trouble-shooting guidelines for how to get unstuck and resolve these challenging clinical situations are offered. The treatment recommendations have grown out of practice-evidenced based experience and wisdom about how to co-create workable realities with these challenging clinical situations with self-harming clients.

Question: *How do you intervene with a self-harming client who frequently symptom-switches back and forth from cutting to bulimia to substance abuse?*

Treatment Recommendations

- The first step is to determine with the clients what meaning they attribute to the constant symptom-switching pattern and how they are benefiting from it. We need to determine if this is a new pattern or a long-standing pattern. If it is a new pattern, we need to explore with the clients the *why now.* Are there any specific new individual. intimate relationship, or family stressors that have not been talked about that are fueling this pattern? Do the clients think by learning some helpful new coping strategies for how to better cope with or removing these stressors will change this pattern?

- With *precontemplators,* we want to use the *two-step tango* strategy of restraint from immediate change and in a relaxed and nonthreatening way begin seeding or planting in their mind the potential costs or consequences physically, psychologically, socially, and with school and/or work for them if this pattern of constant symptom-switching continues (Selekman, 2008). These back-and-forth therapeutic dance steps mirror the clients' pattern and can eventually lead them to begin to entertain the idea that their constant symptom-switching may be presenting a problem for them in their life.

- With *contemplators,* the use of the *decisional balancing scale* can help the clients see visually the advantages and disadvantages of continuing this pattern of constant symptom-switching. By having them rate on a scale from 1 to 4 (1 = slightly important, 2 = moderately important, 3 = very important, and 4 = extremely important), each of the advantages and disadvantages can provide the therapist with valuable information regarding the treatment planning and what therapeutic pathways to pursue (Prochaska et al., 1994; Velasquez et al., 2001).

- If the clients report that they have lost control with the symptom-switching pattern and it has been oppressing them for a long time, one therapeutic option is to externalize it (White, 1995). Together with their intimate partners and/or families they can unify their efforts with the therapist to conquer the symptom-switching pattern.

Question: *What do you do with self-harming clients who are cutting more frequently and much more deeply into their skin tissue?*

Treatment Recommendations

- Similar to the clients who are regularly symptom-switching, we need to determine with them what unique meanings they attribute to the sudden shift in their self-harming practice methods and how it is benefiting them. We need to explore the *why now* with the clients. Are there any specific new individual, intimate relationship, or family stressors that have not been talked about that are fueling this dramatic shift in their self-harming practice methods?

- It also is helpful to determine with the clients if the increase in self-harming episodes and cutting more deeply for them is a form of self-punishment, or have they developed a higher physical tolerance for pain and cutting more often and more deeply into their skin tissue is necessary to get emotional relief or just to feel something.
- If the clients are in a serious intimate relationship or living at home with their family, we need to assess what couple or family problem-maintaining patterns of interactions this behavior is imbedded in and disrupt these unproductive couple and family interactions through the use of pattern intervention strategies (O'Hanlon & Weiner-Davis, 1989; Selekman, 2005).
- The clients may need a more intensive treatment regime combining couple or family therapy with participation in a Stress-Busters' Leadership Group or involvement in the Pathways to Possibilities Program.
- If the clients report that they have lost total control with their cutting behavior, are concerned about their safety, or are cutting around their genitalia, eyes, or other potentially risky bodily areas, I will have them immediately evaluated by a psychiatrist.

Question: *How do you manage self-harming adolescent clients who are deeply entrenched in a negative and powerful peer group?*

Treatment Recommendations:
- This challenging treatment dilemma typically occurs for the following reasons: the parents and adolescents have poor communications and there is little respect for their position of authority, there is emotional disconnection in the parent-adolescent relationship, and the therapists have a weak alliance with the adolescents.
- The therapists need to figure out a way to strengthen their alliance with the adolescents. This can be done by spending a little more session time alone with them to build a relationship and secure more leverage with them by agreeing to change identified parental behaviors that frustrate or aggravate them the most and offering to negotiate with the parents certain privileges they want.
- On the parental level, a *Gandhian nonviolent resistance* parenting approach can be implemented to put the parents back in charge minus the yelling, nagging, lecturing, and so forth (Omer, 2004). They can stage *sit-ins* inside their adolescent's closed bedroom doors and refuse to budge until they come up with some solid and realistic solutions for their self-harming, school failure, substance abuse, or other problematic behaviors. The parents can put together a contract where they agree to stop their yelling, making threats, nagging, and lecturing. Also, in the contract they declare that they will no longer keep a lid on their adolescents' behaviors and will let relatives and close friends know what is going on inside and outside of their

household. Furthermore, they make it clear that they will no longer tolerate their adolescents' self-harming, school failure, and substance abuse. When the adolescents are respectful and responsible, the parents will praise and reward them in a positive way. This strategy will only work if the parents can totally refrain from engaging in any of their former negative behaviors.

- In these clinical situations, it also is helpful to organize a parents' squad of parents whose adolescents regularly hang out together. They can regularly communicate and support one another as a team in busting their adolescents' parties and intervening early to help prevent their adolescents from getting into serious trouble. I have had parents' squads show up at rave parties their adolescents were not supposed to attend.
- With some cases, I have had great success having the self-harming adolescents bring in their crew of friends for me to meet. After establishing good rapport with them, and their seeing me not as a potential threat, they may agree to keep coming back and I can gradually turn this originally negative peer group in a more positive direction.
- Another option is to offer to bring in former adolescent clients who used to have problems with self-harm amd equivalent self-destructive behaviors to serve as temporary peer support group for them until they can make some new friends.

Question: *How do you work with families where both the mother and the daughter have self-harming and bulimia problems?*

Treatment Recommendations:
- When working with families where one of the parents shares the same presenting issues or difficulties as the adolescents, the first step is to help these parents resolve their adolescents' difficulties. We have to believe that the parents possess the strengths and resources to change but may initially feel stuck and may be struggling to cope with stressors unrelated to their sons' or daughters' difficulties. Once we can help the parents get unstuck and help them to better cope with or help eliminate the unrelated stressors, they will be in a better place to resolve their children's difficulties.
- We need to carefully assess at what stage of readiness for change the parents are presently in and match what we do therapeutically with where they are and help them keep advancing through the different stages.
- If the mothers' difficulties with self-harming and bulimia are overshadowing their daughters' problems with these behaviors, adopting a confused and bungling stance could be effective in getting them to help the therapist out. When the mothers begin to see that their behaviors may be having a negative and reinforcing effect on their daughters' problematic behaviors, they will gradually get closer to seeing the need to take action, which in turn will benefit their daughters.

- Another therapeutic option is to externalize the self-harming and bulimia problems that are wreaking havoc in and creating a big wedge of emotional distance in the mother-daughter relationship (White, 1995, Selekman, 2006b). Once they see how they are both being victimized by these two problems, they can join forces as a dynamic duo and conquer them together and establish a more preferred direction with their lives.
- It also can be helpful to use curiosity to open up space to talk about what has not been talked about. There may be painful secrets or other undiscussables that are serving as constraints, hence blocking the change process. The use of conversational questions can help elicit the not-yet-said (Andersen, 1991; Anderson, 1997).
- If they continue to experience difficulties or are a disconnected family, other treatment options would be to see them separately and establish separate treatment goals and therapeutic work projects or have them participate in the Pathways to Possibilities Program to increase the treatment intensity.

Question: *How do you clinically manage a self-harming young adult who had been physically or sexually abused and uses a variety of self-harming methods to get relief from serious flashback and other posttraumatic stress symptoms?*

Treatment Recommendations:
- This is one of the most challenging clinical dilemmas with self-harming clients. The self-harming behavior plays a critical role in helping them to cope. If this behavior is taken away prematurely, without any distress management replacement behaviors that the clients think can help, they may really lose control of their self-harming behavior. In some extreme situations, they may try to take their lives to permanently end the severe emotional pain they are experiencing.
- When working in general with physically or sexually abused clients, I believe that they should take the lead in determining the goals for therapy and what treatment modalities they think can benefit them the best. I have worked with many traumatized clients over the years where their former therapists pushed too hard with their agendas of "working through their traumas," which triggered serious suicide attempts and needless psychiatric hospitalizations.
- When working with physically and sexually abused clients, it is more productive to think clinically in terms of treating the *effects* of their traumas that may still be haunting them today. The clients take the lead in selecting which effect they wish to learn how to better cope with or change. The therapist's job is to negotiate with the clients a small, realistic, and well-formulated treatment goal.
- Some of the distress management tools and strategies I would teach a self-

harming client oppressed by severe posttraumatic symptoms would be *mindfulness meditation* (Hanh, 1997, 1998), *urge surfing* (Marlatt & Kristeller, 1999), *visualizing movies of success* (Selekman, 2006b), and *disputation skills* (Seligman, 2002).

Question: *What do you do therapeutically when the self-harming client is regularly or heavily abusing alcohol and other drugs?*

Treatment Recommendations:

- The first step is to carefully assess at what stage of readiness for change the client presently is in and match what you do therapeutically with where they are at. The *two-step tango* method is a great starting place with clients in the precontemplative stage in that it begins to raise their awareness level that there may be some major costs or consequences for them to simultaneously be engaging in these two very risky behaviors, mainly accidental death! At the clients' pace of self-changing, the therapist should gradually move them through the various stages of readiness for change (Prochaska et al., 1994; Selekman, 2008a; Velasqukez et al., 2001).

- With self-harming adolescents who are regularly or heavily substance-abusing, I have found it to be useful in the context of family therapy to increase the amount of individual session time I have with them to further strengthen my alliances and secure more therapeutic leverage with them. I like to ask adolescents the following three questions: "How can I be helpful to you? What is the number one thing that your parents do that gets you the most upset that you would like me to change? What is the number one privilege you really want from your parents that you want me to fight for you with them?" Often, they had not been asked these questions by previous therapists and they are pleasantly surprised that their new therapists want to be their advocates and are interested in their personal needs and expectations. When therapists succeed as skilled intergenerational labor relations negotiators with their parents, even the most challenging adolescents who are with seriously self-harming and substance-abusing will find it difficult not to attend family therapy sessions when their needs are getting met.

- In clinical situations where I am quite concerned about the adolescents' long history of poor impulse control and impaired judgment due to their heavy substance usage and the risk of accidental death, I will share with them during their individual session time in the first family therapy meeting the following:

> I have been working with kids who have been cutting for the past 25 years and I have never lost anyone and I don't want you to be my first casualty. I know you like to party (use drugs with friends) and you have been doing this for a while, but one of

these days when your (girlfriend/boyfriend/partner/friend(s)) does something to upset you when you are stoned or drunk, you may accidentally sever a vein if you are not paying close attention to what you are doing. So, here are our choices: you can let your parents know what you are doing with the partying, which may be a big step with them for rebuilding trust and getting your freedom back and other privileges that you may desire, which I am happy to fight for with them, or I will have to let them know what you are doing. Which would you prefer?

When working with adolescents and their parents, I honor and respect adolescent clients' confidentiality. However, when it comes to moderate to heavy substance abuse combined with cutting, it is a potentially lethal combination of behaviors. There also are serious professional liability issues in these clinical situations when the therapist knows that the adolescent is engaging in these highly risky behaviors and he or she fails to notify the parents about their sons' or daughters' situation. I have found that when I can successfully connect in a meaningful way with these at-risk adolescents in the very first family session and they have confidence and faith in my ability alter their parents' troublesome behaviors, and to secure the privileges they desire, they often will take this positive risk and responsible step with their parents.

- Many self-harming clients who are also regularly to heavily abusing drugs often are not receptive toward pursuing total abstinence treatment goals. Therefore, the use of a harm-reduction approach may be much more productive in the early stages of treatment with these clients (Denning, Little, & Glickman, 2004; Marlatt, 1998). If in close partnership with them we can reduce some of the consequences of their behavior, this can help them gradually begin to see the advantages of taking these actions in improving the quality of their lives.

Question: *How do you work with a self-harming client who has made multiple suicide attempts in the past?*

Treatment Recommendations:

- Research indicates that clients' past attempts of suicide are the number one risk factor for future attempts (Joiner, 2005; Miller et al., 2007). Therefore, we have to be sensitive to the fact that these unique self-harming clients have faced death multiple times and have a much higher tolerance for pain and fear than most self-harming clients.
- The therapist must strive to establish a strong therapeutic alliance with the clients and tap their expertise as consultants to them, by asking the following questions: "You have seen a lot of therapists before me. What have they overlooked or missed with your situation that is important for me to know

so I can help you in the best way possible?" "What kinds of things could I say or do while we are working together that would really make you upset and possibly lead to you dropping out?" "What is missing in your life or in your relationship with your partner/parents that, if it were present, would make a big difference for you?" "You have shared with me earlier in the session that you had tried to take your life three times. What is your secret about how you were able to conquer these near-death situations?!" "What specifically is happening in your life now that is giving you a glimmer of hope to keep you moving forward with your life?"

- With depressed and pessimistic self-harming clients with suicide-attempt backgrounds, I use *coping* and *pessimistic* category questions to better cooperate with their cooperative response patterns (de Shazer et al., 2007; Selekman, 2006b). The use of *subzero scaling questions* also can be quite useful (Selekman, 2005, 2006b). The client can be asked: "On a scale from –10 to –1, with –10 being that your situation is totally hopeless and irresolvable and –1 that you have a tiny glimmer of hope that your situation may be able to improve just a little bit, where would you have rated your situation a month ago? How about 2 weeks ago? What steps did you take to get up to a –8 from a –10? Are you aware of how you pulled that off? Where would you rate your situation on that scale today? Are you aware of what you did to get up one step higher, to a –7?" The subzero scaling questions can be very empowering for highly pessimistic, demoralized, and suicidal clients in that they help create a therapeutic context for hope and possibilities.

- The use of positive psychology therapeutic experiments like *using my signature strengths in novel ways, planning out my perfect day,* and *you at your best story* (Peterson, 2006) can help trigger positive emotion, which can reduce negative depression and anxiety symptoms and boost these clients' happiness and life satisfaction levels. Also, helping these clients identify their key flow-state activities and spending more time immersing themselves in these pleasurable and meaningful activities can further improve the quality of their lives (Csikszentmihalyi, 1997; Csikszentmihalyi & Csikszentmihalyi, 2006). Similarly, having these clients involved in meaningful service work in the communities can trigger positive emotions for them.

- If couple or family therapy has not been pursued, we need to engage the intimate partner or family and carefully assess what unproductive couple or family interactions the self-harming and suicidal behaviors are fueled by and disrupt them with the use of pattern intervention strategies (O'Hanlon & Weiner-Davis, 1989; Selekman, 2005).

- With some families, they have been riddled with suicide attempts and completions by other members, extended family members, and in previous generations. When working with these families, I have found it helpful to use a family genogram to help family members to see how this powerful family pattern has a life all of its own. I will then externalize the pattern (White, 1995) and get family members fired up to not allow the pattern to claim the life of the client. This effective therapeutic strategy can empower the family to rewrite history and put a stop to the reign of this cruel and devastating family pattern.

- Co-constructing a tribal circle of caring others with clients can provide them with a healing community and a solid support system that can be available to them when experiencing high levels of emotional distress and feeling at risk. It is comforting to know that a safety net of supportive and caring others in their life is firmly in place.

- The clients also may need a more intensive treatment regime that combines individual, couples, family, or group treatment modalities. They can receive all of these treatment modalities in the Pathways to Possibilities Program. Ultimately, the client needs to determine which combination of these treatment modalities best meet their unique needs.

- Finally, it is helpful to have in place good psychiatric backup. I will have the clients evaluated if they are experiencing severe vegetative symptoms, appear to be rapidly deteriorating, or have suicide plans and strong intent to act in spite of taking all of the above therapeutic steps.

Key Factors that Contribute to Clients Prematurely Dropping Out of Treatment and Treatment Failures

Like all therapists, I have lost self-harming clients and their intimate partners and families by inadvertently contributing to their premature exiting from treatment and have experienced my share of treatment failures with these clients as well. We all have our blindspots, make mistakes, fail to connect with clients, and mismanage our clients' situations at one time or another, which may drive them out of our office doors permanently. In some cases, we think we are being very helpful to our clients and making a difference in their lives and a few months or 6 months down the road after we concluded treatment with them, they are calling us to schedule an appointment for the self-harming problem or some other difficulties that were not attended to the first time around.

Self-harming clients, their intimate partners, and/or families can be very difficult to engage and retain in treatment. Working with them can be like being on a roller coaster with lots of twists, turns, steep climbs, and deep drops. When working with these clients, you have to like unpredictability, know how to thrive in chaos, and expect the unexpected happening, even when things are going well (Selekman, 2004).

Over the past 15 years, both in my clinical practice and in consultation with clients and mental health professionals, I have been keeping track of key factors that appear to contribute to self-harming clients and their intimate partners and families prematurely dropping out of treatment and experiencing treatment failure. I will present seven key factors below and briefly reflect on each one. The seven key factors are:

- The therapist's intimidation and anxiety blocks his or her ability to be totally present, genuinely listen, and effectively help the self-harming clients.
- Therapists reinvalidate the self-harming clients by not giving them enough space to share their self-harming stories and how this behavior has benefited them.
- Therapists use an interrogative interviewing style and and/or talk too much in session.
- Therapists mismatch what they try therapeutically with the unique stages of readiness for change the self-harming clients, intimate partner, and family members are presently in.
- The therapists and treatment teams privilege their treatment goals, treatment plans, and expectations for the self-harming clients.
- The therapists and treatment teams have failed to intervene in the multiple levels of the clients' social ecologies.
- The therapists and treatment teams replicate unsuccessful past treatment strategies.

The Therapists Intimidation and Anxiety Blocks His or Her Ability to Be Totally Present, Genuinely Listen, and Effectively Help the Self-Harming Clients

Many therapists report lacking the clinical experience and knowledge base for working with self-harming clients (Whitlock, Eells, et al., 2007). Self-harming clients' provocative, extreme, and perplexing behavior can be very intimidating and can greatly raise the anxiety levels of even the most seasoned of therapists. One of the driving forces that can create emotional distance between therapists and their self-harming clients in their relationships are their own anxieties and fears. Rather than totally being present and genuinely listening to their self-harming clients, they are listening to their own thoughts, like, "I wonder if she is suicidal," "Should I establish a no-suicide contract with her?" "This client really sounds crazy," "I could never do that to myself," or "I wonder if she is a borderline." Therapists who do not have a lot of experience working with this treatment population tend to view the self-harming behavior as a suicidal gesture, assume that the clients have a borderline personality disorder or must have been physically or sexually abused, without even hearing the clients' complete story and having built a relationship with them. Since many self-harming clients often have been in therapy multiple times, they will quickly pick up on their therapists' anxiety and discomfort working with them. If therapists fail to get a handle on their own internal emotional process and catastrophic thinking, they will be ineffectual in helping the self-harming clients improve their situation or they will possibly drop out of therapy. Conversely, when self-harming clients begin to experience from their therapists feeling felt, understood, and empathically embraced, a therapeutic alliance will develop and they are less likely to drop out.

Therapists Reinvalidate the Stories Self-Harming Client by Not Giving Them Enough Space to Share Their Self-Harming Stories and How This Behavior Has Benefited Them

Self-harming clients often have long and painful stories to share about being invalidated, misunderstood, and mismanaged by their parents, older siblings, other significant adults in their lives, and their former therapists and treatment program staffs. As therapists, we need to be careful not to be narrative editors or assume that we understand the unique meanings of the various chapters of the self-harming clients' stories. It is best to use respectful curiosity and interview self-harming clients like cultural anthropologists wanting to learn more details about the chapters of their stories and how their self-harming behavior has been like gifts or resources for them to cope with difficult and stressful life events and emotionally invalidating interactions in their couple and family relationships.

Therapists Use an Interrogative Interviewing Style and/or Talk Too Much

Another way we can invalidate our self-harming clients and set the stage for a premature drop-out situation occurring with them is by bombarding them with too many questions and talking too much. Beyebach and Carranza (1997) have found that therapists who use an interrogative interviewing style and make too many statements greatly contribute to clients dropping out of brief therapy. With self-harming clients who have experienced a great deal of invalidation, we need to adopt a therapeutic stance of reflective curiosity, asking questions from a position of "not-knowing" and giving them plenty of room to respond to each question. The clients' responses should guide the therapists in determining what questions to ask next.

We should never be working harder than our clients. As the great hypnotist Milton H. Erickson put it best, "It is the patient who does the therapy. The therapist only furnishes the climate, the weather. That is all. The patient has to do all of the work." (Havens, 2003, p. 110). Some self-harming clients have had so many past negative treatment experiences and have been let down by their parents and other significant adults so often in their lives that they may be untrusting of their new therapists and talk very little in the beginning of treatment. For some therapists who are eager to help and get to know their new self-harming clients better, their long stretches of silence or short responses to their questions make them anxious, which leads to them talking too much and working too hard. The truth of the matter is that our taciturn and silent self-harming clients are not passive recipients of what we ask and try with them in sessions but are active participants. The wheels are turning in their heads and they are sizing us up about whether or not they can trust us and safely share their painful and difficult self-harming stories with us. It is important to remember, particularly with self-harming clients, that we need to be patient and that self-harming clients change at their own unique pace.

Therapists Mismatch What They Try Therapeutically with the Unique Stages of Readiness for Change the Self-Harming Clients, Intimate Partners, and Family Members Are Presently In

As Prochaska et al. (1994) have repeatedly demonstrated, therapists and treatment program staff need to carefully match what they do with the unique stages of readiness the clients, their partners, and family members are presently in. With any given family, each member may be at a different stage of readiness for change. However, which is so often the case, therapists and treatment program staff often use treatment strategies and approaches that are geared for clients in the action stage of readiness for change. Prochaska et al (1994) have found that only 20% of the clients seen by outpatient therapists or in treatment programs are in the action stage upon entering treatment. When the other 80% of the clients fail to adhere to the treatment goals, plans, and expectations of their therapists or treatment program staff, they are labeled "resistant" and "noncompliant." I have worked with many young adult and adolescent self-harming clients who were asked to leave programs due to their "noncompliance issues." The ironic thing about these clients is that they all had wanted help with their difficult situations but they felt misunderstood, "not listened to or respected," and mismanaged.

The Therapists and Treatment Teams Privileges Their Treatment Goals, Treatment Plans, and Expectations for the Self-Harming Clients

When the therapist and treatment program staff privilege their treatment goals, plans, and expectations for the clients, their partners, and/or family, it can trigger high psychological reactance and client noncompliance, which can set in motion a premature dropout situation occurring or possibly their experiencing another treatment failure. In order for self-harming clients to be the lead authors of their new more preferred solution-determined stories, they need to determine their treatment goals and choose which treatment modalities and therapeutic experiments they think can best benefit them. This is how best to co-create cooperative partnerships with self-harming clients and/or their partners and families.

The Therapists and Treatment Teams Have Failed to Intervene in the Multiple Levels of the Self-Harming Clients' Social Ecologies

Similar to substance abuse, self-harming behavior is multifaceted and there are multiple reasons why our clients engage in this behavior. Often, self-harming clients attract concerned family members, relatives, friends, and involved helping professionals like a magnet. Out of love and concern, these individuals will persist in certain actions, even unproductive ones, to try to stop the self-harming persons from hurting themselves. Surprisingly, most therapists have a tendency to treat self-harming clients individually rather than in a couple or family therapy context and do not actively collaborate with key members from their social networks and involved helping professionals from larger systems. Unless we intervene with self-harming clients' intimate partners, their families, concerned key members from their social networks, and the involved helping professionals, therapeutic gains can unravel if these individuals are stuck engaging in the same unproductive attempted solutions and clinging to fixed beliefs about the self-harming clients. It is my contention that successful treatment with self-harming clients must target interventions at the individual, family, peer group, social network, and larger-systems levels.

The Therapists and Treatment Teams Replicate Unsuccessful Past Treatment Strategies

Most of the self-harming young adults and adolescents I have worked with had already experienced multiple treatment failures in both outpatient and inpatient settings. Some of the major reasons for this were that they kept on receiving in the past the same types of treatment approaches and modalities and their goals were not driving the treatment. I have heard frequently from parents of self-harming adolescents that they had been excluded from their sons' or daughters' treatment in the past and were in the dark about how best to respond to their self-harming episodes. This is why it is critical with self-harming clients and their families that have had multiple treatment experiences to take the time in the very first session to find out the details about what has not worked treatment-wise in the past. Neglecting to do this can set the clients up for another demoralizing treatment failure and further perpetuate their hopelessness and despair.

As far as the treatment of self-harming young adults and adolescents living at home goes, family therapy should be the treatment of choice unless there are specific extenuating circumstances for not doing this, such as in the case of disconnected families or when this treatment modality has been employed repeatedly in the past and had only exacerbated the self-harming clients' difficulties. However, it may be that the treatment preference is to be seen individually. We need to honor our clients' treatment preferences to help foster cooperative relationships with them. When working with older self-harming adolescents and young adults involved in serious intimate relationships, it often is more therapeutically effective to see the couple together than to see the self-harming partners alone. If this is therapeutically contraindicated, I may see the partners separately, particularly if one or both of the partners wish to be seen individually because of safety issues or they think it will be more beneficial for them. I will still maintain a relational focus and will intervene in such a way to benefit both the individual partners and the couple relationship.

Future Directions for Prevention, Treatment, and Research for Self-Harming Young Adults and Adolescents

Although we have learned a lot more about young adult and adolescent self-harm, there is a great deal of further work that needs to be done in the areas of prevention, treatment, and research with this challenging treatment population. I will present important themes and lessons learned from clinical practice with self-harming clients and their intimate partners and/or families. Outlined below are some of my recommendations for future work that needs to be done in the areas of prevention, treatment, and research.

Prevention

- On a macro level, broader scale educational initiatives need to be implemented on college, secondary, and primary school campuses for school personnel regarding the nature of student self-harming behavior. Constructive and effective staff response protocols need to be in place, so that these at-risk students can get the support and the help they need if they open up to school staff, or are identified as being at-risk by other students. Since children as young as 9 are beginning to surface who are self-harming and engaging in equivalent self-destructive behaviors, it is important that education and prevention efforts be initiated with 4th, 5th, and 6th grade teachers and nurses working in elementary schools. Parent-Teacher Association meetings, on both the primary and secondary school levels, are another important context for providing education and prevention information. When school personnel and parents better understand the nature of self-harming behavior and how best to constructively respond, they can help prevent self-harming epidemics from occurring in their schools and communities.

- Since self-harming individuals rarely seek counseling (let alone medical treatment) even after seriously hurting themselves, and are often isolated and lonely, it may be beneficial to tap the support and expertise of former self-harming clients or Stress-Busters' group alumni. They may do outreach work, identifying at-risk self-harming students, and getting them to treatment. This type of macro-level prevention initiative could be of great benefit on junior high, high school, and college campuses. Former self-harming clients or Stress-Busters' group alumni who wish to get involved can work closely with the campus student mental health center and counseling staff to receive supervision and back-up in identifying and engaging at-risk self-harming students.

- Both the Stress-Busters' Leadership and Solution-Oriented Parenting groups are secondary prevention interventions that can be used at the senior and junior high school levels, where student self-harming behavior has been identified as a growing problem.

Treatment

- Engaging self-harming individuals for treatment can be quite challenging. Most of these individuals are precontemplators, and not even window-shoppers for counseling. Since self-harming is a hidden practice, individuals engaging in this behavior often perceive going for couple or family therapy as a threat to their cherished habit and coping strategy that has worked for them. In addition, many self-harming clients report being plagued by painful and overwhelming depressed and anxious moods and self-defeating thoughts that paralyze them and leave them at a loss as to what to do. Therefore, we need to use therapeutic approaches that are non-threatening and strengths-based, and that make it inviting for self-harming individuals to want to get help for themselves and determine their goals, the frequency of visits, and change at their own unique pace. Treatment approaches that combine the best elements of solution-focused brief therapy (de Shazer et al., 2007), positive psychology (Peterson, 2006; Seligman, 2002; Snyder & Lopez, 2007), and motivational- enhancement therapy (Arkowitz et al., 2008; Miller & Rollnick, 2002) can provide this. All of these approaches can reduce clients' depressed and anxious moods, psychological reactance, defensiveness, noncompliance, alter self-defeating thinking, raise their hope and optimism levels, and trigger positive emotion. Collaborative strengths-based brief therapy combines the best elements of all of the above approaches and more.

- Treatment with self-harming clients and their intimate partners and/or families needs to be flexible and integrative. Some self-harming clients' situations can be quite complex and may require combining therapeutic tools and strategies from both individual and family therapy approaches.

- In partnership with the self-harming client and their intimate partners and/or families, we can determine with them at what systems levels to target interventions. The self-harming behavior may be influenced and maintained by a combination of individual, couple, family, extended family, peer group, school/occupational, other larger systems, and community factors.

Research

- What is greatly needed are well-controlled treatment outcome studies that combine quantitative and qualitative methods, a random sampling procedure, and a large heterogeneous sample that is diverse in terms of gender, culture, and socioeconomic levels. Multiple measures should be used to accurately assess individual, couple, or family changes as a result of the treatment received. Two or more treatment control groups can be compared to the experimental treatment group's results. Separate studies need to be conducted with young adult and adolescent self-harming individuals, rather than combining these age groups. Treatment outcome follow-up should be at 6 months, 1 year, and 2 years to assess the staying power of the treatment approaches used in the study.

- Since dialectical behavior therapy and cognitive-behavioral therapy are the most commonly used treatment methods for self-harming clients, it would be interesting to do a treatment outcome study comparing these two treatment approaches with collaborative strengths-based brief therapy in separate studies with young adults and adolescents. The studies would offer valuable insights about the strengths and limitations of each treatment approach with each age group, and help professionals determine what sets of therapeutic tools and strategies seem to be of the most therapeutic benefit to self-harming clients.

• Qualitative research should be conducted with identified self-changing self-harming individuals who never received treatment and former self-harming clients who are both flourishing in the world and avoiding this and equivalent self-destructive behaviors such as bulimia, substance abuse, and sexual promiscuity. Research interviews can tap their expertise and wisdom about what their secrets are for how they kicked their self-harming habits and equivalent self-destructive behaviors, and their recommendations for self-harming individuals and therapists who treat them about what works and greatly benefited them, such as: different types of quitting styles, useful self-talk, self-generated coping and problem-solving strategies, and how best to cope with toxic people and places. This valuable information can be useful for developing new therapeutic tools and strategies to share with our self-harming clients and their intimate partners and/or their families.

Final Reflections

This treatment manual is an attempt to offer both new and seasoned therapists a comprehensive overview of the most up-to-date research on young adult and adolescent self-harm and a variety of treatment modalities that have shown great clinical results with this treatment population. It is my hope that readers will be inspired by the therapeutic ideas discussed in this treatment manual to further expand on these ideas and different treatment modalities, and that clinical researchers will explore new treatment outcome research territory by conducting well-controlled and designed studies on collaborative strengths-based brief therapy with individuals, couples, families, and groups.

REFERENCES

Ainsworth, M. (1978). Patterns of attachment: A psychological study of the strange situation. Hillsdale, NJ: Erlbaum.

Alexander, J.F., Pugh, C., & Parsons, B. (1998). *Blueprints for violence prevention: Vol. 3. Functional family therapy*. Boulder, CO: Center for the Study and Prevention of Violence.

Allgood, S.M., Parham, K.B., Salts, C.J., & Smith, T.A. (1995). The association between pretreatment change and unplanned termination in family therapy. *American Journal of Family Therapy, 23,* 195–202.

American Psychiatric Association. (1994). *Diagnostic and statistical manual of mental disorders* (4th ed.). Washington, DC: Author.

Andersen, T. (1991). *The reflecting team: Dialogues and dialogues about the dialogues*. New York: Norton.

Anderson, C.B., & Bulik, C.M. (2002). Self-harm and suicide attempts in bulimia nervosa. *Eating Disorders: The Journal of Treatment and Prevention, 10,* 227–243.

Anderson, H. (1997). *Conversation, language, and possibilities: A post-modern approach to therapy*. New York: Basic Books.

Anderson, H., & Gehart, D. (Eds.) (2007). *Collaborative therapy: Relationships and conversations that make a difference*. New York: Routledge.

Anthony, E.J. & Cohler, B.J. (Eds.) (1987). *The invulnerable child*. New York: Guilford Press.

Ariely, D. (2008). *Predictably irrational: The hidden forces that shape our decisions*. New York: HarperCollins.

Arkowitz, H., Westra, H.A., Miller, W.R., & Rollnick, S. (2007). *Motivational interviewing in the treatment of psychological problems*. New York: Guilford Press.

Arviso-Alvord, L. (2008, July). *Creating healthy environments: Wisdom from Native American ceremonies*. Workshop presented at the Suicide: Breaking the Silence Conference, Window Rock, AZ.

Arviso-Alvord, L., & Cohen-Van Pelt, E. (2000). *The scalpel and the silver bear: The first Navajo woman surgeon combines western medicine and traditional healing*. New York: Bantam Books.

Assay, T.P., & Lambert, M. (1999). The empirical case for common factors in therapy: Quantitative findings. In M.A. Hubble, B.L. Duncan, & S.D. Miller (Eds.), *The heart and soul of change: What works in therapy* (pp. 33–57). Washington, DC: American Psychological Association.

Beck, A. (1995). Cognitive therapy with personality disorders. In P. Salkovskis (Ed.), *Frontiers in cognitive therapy* (pp. 165–181). New York: Guilford Press.

Beck, A., Rush, A., & Emery, G. (1979). *Cognitive therapy of depression*. New York: Guilford Press.

Bennett, J. (2007, December 17). What you don't know can hurt you. *Newsweek, 10.*

Bennett-Goleman, T. (2001). *Emotional alchemy: How the mind can heal the heart*. New York: Harmony Books.

Benton, S.A., Robertson, J.M., Tseng, W., Newton, F.B., & Benton, S.L. (2003). Changes in counseling center client problems across 13 years. *Professional Psychology: Research and Practice, 34*(1), 66–72.

Berg, I.K. & Miller, S.D. (1992). *Working with the problem drinker: A solution-focused approach*. New York: Norton.

Beyebach, M., & Carranza, V.E. (1997). Therapeutic interaction and drop-out: Measuring relational communication in solution-focused therapy. *Journal of Family Therapy, 19*(2), 173–213.

Birchler, G.R., Fals-Stewart, W., & O'Farrell, T.J. (2005). Couples therapy for alcoholism and drug abuse. In J.L. Lebow (Ed.), *Handbook of clinical family therapy* (pp. 251–281). New York: Wiley.

Birchler, G.R., Fals-Stewart, W., & O'Farrell, T.J. (2008). Couple therapy for alcoholism and drug abuse. In A.S. Gurman (Ed.), *Clinical handbook of couple therapy* (pp. 523–545). New York: Guilford Press.

Blakeslee, S., & Blakeslee, M. (2007). *The body has a mind of its own: How body maps in your brain help you do almost everything better.* New York: Random House.

Bohus, M., Limberger, M., Ebner, U., Glocker, F.X., Schwarz, B., Wernz, M., et al. (2000). Pain perception during self-reported distress and calmness in patients with borderline personality disorder and self-mutilating behavior. *Psychiatry Research, 95,* 251–260.

Boscolo, L., Cecchin, G., Hoffman, L., & Penn, P. (1987). *Milan systemic family therapy: Conversations in therapy and practice.* New York: Basic Books.

Bowen, S., Witkiewitz, K., Dillworth, T.M., & Marlatt, G.A. (2007). The role of thought suppression in the relationship between mindfulness meditation and substance use. *Addictive Behaviors, 32*(10), 2324–2328.

Bowlby, J. (1979). The making and breaking of affectional bonds. London, UK: Tavistock.

Bowlby, J. (1988). The secure base: Clinical applications of attachment theory. London, UK: Routledge.

Brown, M.Z., Courtois, K.A., & Linehan, M.M. (2002). Reasons for suicide attempts and non-suicidal self-injury in women with borderline personality disorder. *Journal of Abnormal Psychology, 111,* 198–202.

Campbell, R.S., & Pennebaker, J.W. (2003). The secret life of pronouns: Flexibility in writing style and physical health. *Pschology Science, 14,* 60–65.

Carter, R. (2008). *Multiplicity: The new science of personality, identity, and the self.* New York: Little, Brown.

Carter, B., & McGoldrick, M. (Eds.) (1989). *The changing family life cycle: A framework for family therapy.* New York: Gardner Press.

Chamberlain, P., & Rosicky, J.G. (1995). The effectiveness of family therapy in the treatment of adolescents with conduct disorders and delinquency. *Journal of Marital and Family Therapy, 21,* 441–459.

Claes, L., Vandereycken, W., & Vertommen, H. (2004). Self-injurious behaviors in eating disordered patients. *Eating Behaviors, 2/3,* 263–272.

Connors, G.J., Donovan, D.M., & DiClemente, C.C. (2001). *Substance abuse treatment and the stages of change: Selecting and planning interventions.* New York: Guilford Press.

Conterio, K., & Lader, W. (1998). *Bodily harm: The breakthrough healing program for self-injurers.* New York: Hyperion.

Crow, D.M. (2000). *Physiological and health effects of writing about stress.* Unpublished doctoral dissertation, Southern Methodist University, Dallas, TX.

Csikszentimahalyi, M. (1990). *Flow.* New York: Harper & Row.

Csikszentimahalyi, M. (1997). *Finding flow.* New York: Basic Books.

Csikszentimahalyi, M., & Csikszentmihalyi, I.S. (Eds.) (2006). *A life worth living: Contributions to positive psychology.* New York: Oxford University Press.

D'Amore, K., & Lloyd-Richardson, E. (2008, June). *Non-suicidal self-injury among college students: Integrating qualitative and quantitative findings.* Paper presented at the International Society for the Study of Self-Injury, Harvard University, Cambridge, MA.

Davidson, R.J. (2003). Affective neuroscience and psychophysiology: Toward a synthesis. *Psychophysiology, 40,* 655–665.

DeFrain, J., & Stinnett, N. (1992). Building on inherent strengths of families: A positive approach for family psychologists and counselors. *Topics in Family Psychology and Counseling, 1*(1), 15–26.

Denning, P., Little, J., & Glickman, A. (2004). *Over the influence: The harm reduction guide for managing drugs and alcohol.* New York: Guilford Press.

De Shazer, S. (1985). *Keys to solutions in brief therapy.* New York: Norton.

De Shazer, S. (1988). *Clues: Investigating solutions in brief therapy*. New York: Norton.

De Shazer, S. (1991). *Putting difference to work*. New York: Norton.

De Shazer, S., Dolan, Y., Korman, H., Trepper, T., McCollum, E., & Berg, I. K. (2007). *More than miracles: The state of the art of solution-focused brief therapy.* Binghamton, NY: Haworth Press.

Diener, E., & Biswas-Diener, R. (2008). Happiness: Unlocking the mysteries of psychological wealth. Malden, MA: Blackwell.

Dimeff, L. A., Baer, J. S., Kivlahan, D. R., & Marlatt, G. A. (1999). *Brief alcohol screening and intervention for college students: A harm reduction approach*. New York: Guilford Press.

Dohm, F. A., Striegel-Moore, R. H., Wilfrey, D. E., Pike, K. M., Hook, J., & Fairburn, C. G. (2002). Self-harm and substance abuse in a community sample of Black and White women with binge eating disorder or bulimia nervosa. *International Journal of Eating Disorders, 32,* 389–400.

D'Onofrio, A. A. (2007). *Adolescent self-injury: A comprehensive guide for counselors and health care professionals*. New York: Springer.

Duncan, B. L., Hubble, M. A., & Miller, S. D. (1997). *Psychotherapy with "impossible cases": The efficient treatment of therapy veterans*. New York: Norton.

Duncan, B. L., & Miller, S. D. (2000). *The heroic client: Doing client-directed, outcome-informed therapy*. San Francisco: Jossey-Bass.

Durrant, M., & Coles, D. (1991). The Michael White approach. In T. C. Todd & M. D. Selekman (Eds.), *Family therapy approaches with adolescent substance abusers* (pp. 135–175). Needham Heights, MA: Allyn & Bacon.

Dweck, C. S. (2006). *Mindset: The new psychology of success*. New York: Random House.

Ellis, A. (1974). *Techniques for disputing irrational beliefs*. New York: Institute for Rational Living.

Emmons, R. A. (2007). *Thanks! How the new science of gratitude can make you happier*. Boston: Houghton-Mifflin.

Emmons, R. A. & McCullough, M. E. (2004). *The psychology of gratitude*. New York: Oxford University Press.

Epston, D. (2000, May). *Crafting questions in narrative therapy practice*. Workshop presented at the Evanston Family Therapy Center, Evanston, IL.

Epston, D. (1998). *Catching up with David Epston: Collection of narrative-based Papers 1991–1996*. Adelaide, South Australia: Dulwich Centre Publications.

Eskin, M. (1995). Suicidal behavior as related to social support and assertiveness among Swedish and Turkish high school students: A cross-cultural investigation. *Journal of Clinical Psychology, 51,* 158-172.

Evans, K., Tyrer, P., Catalan, J., Schmidt, U., Davidson, K., & Dent, J. (1999). Manual-assisted cognitive-behavior therapy (MACT): A randomized controlled trial of a brief intervention with bibliotherapy in the treatment of recurrent deliberate self-harm. *Psychological Medicine, 29,* 19–25.

Favaro, A., Ferrara, S., & Santonastaso, P. (2004). Impulsive and compulsive self-injurious behavior and eating disorders: An epidemiological study. In J. L. Levitt, R. A. Sansone, & L. Cohn (Eds.), *Self-harm behavior and eating disorders: Dynamics, assessment, and treatment* (pp. 31–45). New York: Brunner-Routledge.

Favazza, A. R. (1998). *Bodies under siege: Self-mutilation and body modification in culture and psychiatry*. Baltimore: Johns Hopkins.

Favazza, A. R., & Selekman, M. D. (2003, April). *Self-injury in adolescents*. Annual Spring Conference of the Child and Adolescent Centre, Department of Psychiatry, University of Western Canada, London, Ontario, Canada.

Fisch, R., & Schlanger, K. (1999). *Brief therapy with intimidating cases: Changing the unchangeable*. San Francisco: Jossey-Bass.

Fisch, R., Weakland, J., & Segal, L. (1982). *The tactics of change*. San Francisco: Jossey-Bass.

Fredrickson, B. L. (2002). Positive emotion. In C. R. Snyder & S. J. Lopez (Eds.), *Handbook of positive psychology* (pp. 120–135). New York: Oxford University Press.

Fredrickson, B. L. (2003, July/August). The value of positive emotions. *American Scientist, 91,* 330–335.

Freeman, J., Epston, D., & Lobovits, D. (1997). *Playful approaches to serious problems: Narrative therapy with children and their families.* New York: Norton.

Friedlander, M. L., Escudero, V., & Heatherington, L. (2006). *Therapeutic alliances in couple and family therapy: An empirically informed guide to practice.* Washington, DC: American Psychological Association.

Friedman, S. (Ed.). (1995). *The reflecting team in action: Collaborative practice in family therapy.* New York: Guilford Press.

Gable, S. L., Reis, H. T., Impett, E. A., & Asher, E. R. (2004). Capitalizing on daily positive events. *Journal of Personality and Social Psychology, 87,* 228–245.

Gallagher, R. P., Zhang, B., & Taylor, R. (2003). *National survey of counseling directors, 2003.* Alexandria, VA: International Association of Counseling Centers, Inc.

Gardner, H. (1993). *Multiple intelligences: The theory in practice.* New York: Basic Books.

Gardner, H. (1999). *Intelligence reframed: Multiple intelligences for the 21st century.* New York: Basic Books.

Gardner, H. (2004). *Changing minds: The art and science of changing our own and other people's minds.* Boston: Harvard Business School Press.

Garofalo, R., Wolf, R. C., Wissow, L., Woods, E. R., & Goodman, E. (1999). Sexual orientation and risk of suicide attempts among a representative sample of youth. *Archives of Pediatrics and Adolescent Medicine, 153,* 487–493.

George, E., Iveson, C., & Ratner, H. (1999). *Problem to solution: Brief therapy with individuals and families.* London: Brief Therapy Press.

Gergen, K., & Gergen, M. (2007, March). *Multiplicity.* Workshop presented at the Annual Psychotherapy Networker Conference, Washington, DC.

Gladwell, M. (2002). *The tipping point: How little things can make a big difference.* New York: Back Bay Books.

Goleman, D. (2003). *Destructive emotions: How we can overcome them.* New York: Bantam Books.

Goolishian, H., & Anderson, H. (1988, November). *The therapeutic conversation.* A three-day intensive training sponsored by the Institute of Systemic Therapy, Chicago.

Gottman, J. M., & Gottman, J. S. (2006). *10 lessons to transform your marriage: America's love lab experts share their strategies for strengthening your relationship.* New York: Crown.

Gottman, J. M., & Gottman, J. S. (2008). Gottman method couple therapy. In A. S. Gurman (Ed.), *Clinical handbook of couple therapy* (pp. 138–167). New York: Guilford Press.

Gratz, K. L. (2006). Risk factors for deliberate self-harming among female college students: The role of interaction of childhood maltreatment, emotional inexpressivity, and affect intensity/reactivity. *American Journal of Orthopsychiatry, 76,* 238–250.

Gratz, K. (2001). Measure of deliberate self-harm: Preliminary data on the deliberate self-harm inventory. *Journal of Psychopathology and Behavioral Assessment, 23,* 253–263.

Gratz, K., Conrad, S., & Roemer, L. (2002). Risk factors for deliberate self-harm among college students. *American Journal of Orthopsychiatry, 72,* 128–140.

Groopman, J. (2007). *How doctors think.* Boston: Houghton Mifflin.

Gross, E. F. (2004). Adolescent internet use: What we expect, what teens report. *Journal of Applied Developmental Psychology, 25,* 633–649.

Haggerty, R. J., Sherrod, L. R., Garmezy, N., & Rutter, M. (1994). *Stress, risk, and resilience in children and adolescents: Processes, mechanisms, and interventions.* Cambridge, UK: Cambridge University Press.

Haley, J. (1980). *Leaving home: The therapy of disturbed young people.* New York: McGraw-Hill.

Hanh, T. N. (1991). *Peace is every step: The path of mindfulness in Everyday life.* New York: Bantam Books

Hanh, T. N. (1997). *Teachings on love.* Berkeley, CA: Parallax Press.

Hanh, T. N. (1998). *The heart of Buddha's teachings: Transforming suffering into peace, joy, and liberation*. Berkeley, CA: Parallax Press.

Hanh, T. N. (2001). *Anger: Wisdom for cooling the flames*. New York: Riverhead Books.

Hanh, T. N. (2003). *Creating true peace: Ending violence in yourself, your family, your community, and the world*. New York: Free Press.

Hanh, T. N. (2007). *The art of power*. New York: HarperOne.

Harrington, R., Kerfoot, M., Dyer, E., McNiven, F., Gill, J., & Harrington, V. (1998). Randomized trial of home-based family intervention for children who have deliberately poisoned themselves. *Journal of the American Academy of Child and Adolescent Psychiatry, 37,* 512–518.

Hartman-McGilley, B. (2004). Feminist perspectives on self-harm behavior and eating disorders. In J. L. Levitt, R. A. Sansone, & L. Cohn (Eds.), *Self-harm behavior and eating disorders: Dynamics, assessment, and treatment* (pp. 75–93). New York: Brunner-Routledge.

Hauser, S. T., Allen, J. P., & Golden, E. (2006). *Out of the woods: Tales of resilient teens.* Cambridge, MA: Harvard University Press.

Havens, R. A. (2003). *The wisdom of Milton H. Erickson: The complete volume*. Williston, CT: Crown House.

Hawton, K., & Rodham, K. (2006). *By their own young hand: Deliberate self-harm and suicidal ideas in adolescents*. London: Jessica Kingsley.

Hawton, K., Townsend, E., Avensman, E., Gunnel, D., Hazell, P., House, A. (2006). Psychosocial and pharmocological treatments for deliberate self-harm. *Cochrane Library, 3,* 1–61.

Heath, N. L., Toste, J. R., Nedecheva, T., & Charlebois, A. (2008). An examination of non-suicidal self-injury among college students. *Journal of Mental Health Counseling, 30*(2), 1–20.

Heath, N. L., Schaub, K., Holly, S., & Nixon, M. K., (2008). Self-Injury today: Review of population and clinical studies in adolescents. In M. K. Nixon & N. L. Heath (Eds.), *Self-injury in youth: The essential guide to assessment and intervention* (pp. 9–27). New York: Routledge.

Hilt, L., & Nolen-Hoeksema, S. (2008, June). *Functions of non-suicidal self-injury in young adolescent girls*. Paper presented at the International Society for the Study of Self-Injury Conference, Harvard University, Cambridge, MA.

Hoffman, L. (1988). A constructivist position for family therapy. *Irish Journal of Psychology, 9,* 110–129.

Hoffman, L. (2002). *Family therapy: An intimate history*. New York: Norton.

Hollander, M. (2008). *Helping teens who cut: Understanding and ending self-injury*. New York: Guilford Press.

Hubble, M. A., Duncan, B. L., & Miller, S. D. (Eds.) (1999). *The heart and soul of change: What works in therapy*. Washington, DC: American Psychological Association.

Iacoboni, M. (2008). *Mirroring people: The new science of how we connect with others*. New York: Farrar, Straus, & Giroux.

Jim, H. (2008, July). *The origin of suicide from a Dine perspective*. Workshop presented at the Suicide: Breaking the Silence Conference, Window Rock, AZ.

Joiner, T. E. (2005). *Why people die by suicide*. Cambridge, MA: Harvard University Press.

Joiner, T. E., Pettit, J. W., Walker, R. L., Voelz, Z. R., Cruz, J., Rudd, M. D., et al. (2002). Perceived burdensomeness and suicidality: Two studies on the suicide notes of those attempting and those completing suicide. *Journal of Social and Clinical Psychology, 21,* 531–545.

Kabat-Zinn, J. (1990). *Full catastrophe living*. New York: Delacort Press.

Kabat-Zinn, J. (1995). *Wherever you go there you are: Mindfulness meditation in everyday life*. New York: Hyperion.

Kegan, R., & Lahey, L. L. (2001). *How the way we talk can change the way we work*. San Francisco: Jossey-Bass.

Kemperman, I., Russ, M. J., & Shearin, E. (1997). Self-injurious behavior and mood regulation in borderline patients. *Journal of Personality Disorders*, 11, 146–157.

Kessler, R.C., Costello, E.J., Merikangas, K.R., & Ustun, T.B. (2001). Psychiatric epidemiology: Recent advances and future directions. In R.W. Manderrscheid & M.J. Henderson (Eds.), *Mental health, United States, 2000* (pp 000–000). Washington, DC: U.S. Government Printing Office.

Keyes, L.M., & Haidt, J. (Eds.) (2003). *Flourishing: Positive psychology and a life well-lived.* Washington, DC: American Psychological Association.

Kissin, B., Platz, A., & Su, W.H. (1971). Selective factors in treatment choice and outcome in alcoholics. In N.K. Mello & J.H. Mendelson (Eds.), *Recent advances in studies of alcoholism*. Washington, DC: Government Printing Office.

Klein, K., & Boals, A. (2001). Expressive writing can increase working memory capacity. *Journal of Experimental Psychology*, 130, 520–533.

Klonsky, E.D. (2007). The functions of deliberate self-injury: A review of evidence. *Clinical Psychology Review*, 27, 226–239.

Klonsky, E.D., Oltmanns, T.F., & Turkheimer, E. (2003). Deliberate self-harm in a non-clinical population: Prevalence and psychological correlates. *American Journal of Psychiatry, 160*, 1501–1508.

Kraut, R., Patterson, M., Lundmark, V., Kiesler, S., Mukophadhyay, T., & Scherlis, W. (1998). Internet paradox: A social technology that reduces social involvement and psychological well-being? *American Psychologist, 53*, 1017-1031.

Krystal, H. (1982). Alexithymia and the effectiveness of psychoanalytic treatment. *International Journal of Psychoanalytic Psychotherapy, 9*, 353-388.

Lambert, K.G. (2006). Rising rates of depression in today's society: Consideration for the roles of effort-based rewards and enhanced resilience in day-to-day functioning. *Neuroscience and Behavioral Reviews, 30*(40), 497–510.

Lambert, M., & Bergin, A.E. (1994). The effectiveness of psychotherapy. In A.E. Bergin & S.L. Garfield (Eds.), *Handbook of psychotherapy and behavior change* (4th ed., pp. 143–189). New York: Wiley.

Langbein, D.R., & Pfohl, B. (1993). Clinical correlates of self-mutilation among psychiatric inpatients. *Annals of Clinical Psychiatry, 5*, 45–51.

Lay-Gindhu, A., & Schonert-Reichel, K.A. (2005). Non-suicidal self-harm among community adolescents: Understanding the "whats" and "whys" of self-harm. *Journal of Youth and Adolescence, 34*(5), 447–457.

Lenhart, A., Madden, M., & Hitlin, P. (2005). Teens and technology: Youth are leading the transition to a fully wired and mobile nation. *Pew Internet and American Life Project: Teens and Technology*, 1–48.

Lepore, S.J. (1997). Expressive writing moderates the relation between intrusive thoughts and depressive symptoms. *Journal of Personality and Social Psychology, 73*, 1030–1037.

Lepore, S.J. & Smyth, J.M. (2002). *The writing cure: How expressive writing promotes health and emotional well-being*. Washington, DC: American Psychological Association.

Levine, M. (2006). *The price of privilege: How parental pressure and material advantage are creating a generation of disconnected and unhappy kids*. New York: HarperCollins.

Lewinsohn, P.M., Rohde, P., & Seeley, J.R. (1996). Adolescent suicidal ideation and attempts: Prevalence, risk factors, and clinical implications. *Clinical Psychology Science and Practice, 3*, 25–46.

Liddle, H.A., Rowe, C., Diamond, G.M., Sessa, F.M., Schmidt, S., & Ettinger, D. (2000). Toward a developmental family therapy: The clinical utility of research on adolescence. *Journal of Marital and Family Therapy, 26*, 485–500.

Linehan, M.M. (1993a). *Cognitive-behavioral treatment in borderline personality disorder*. New York: Guilford Press.

Linehan, M.M. (1993b). *Skills training manual for treating borderline personality disorder*. New York: Guilford Press.

Linehan, M.M. (2000). Behavioral treatments of suicidal behaviors: Definitional obfuscation and treatment outcomes. In R.W. Maris, S.S. Cannetto, J.L. Mcintosh, &

M.M. Silverman (Eds.), *Review of suicidology* (pp. 84–111). New York: Guilford Press.

Linehan, M.M., Heard, H.L., & Armstrong, H.E. (1993). Naturalistic follow-up of a behavioral treatment for chronically parasuicidal borderline patients. *Archives of General Psychiatry, 50,* 971–974.

Lloyd-Richardson, E.E., Perrine, N., Dierker, L., Kelley, M.L. (2207). Characteristics and functions of non-suicidal self-injury in a community sample. *Psychological Medicine, 37*(8), 1183–1192.

Lofthouse, N. (2008, June). *Adolescent non-suicidal self-injury on an inpatient unit.* Paper presented at the International Society for the Study of Self-Injury Conference, Harvard University, Cambridge, MA.

Lofthouse, N., Muelenkamp, J.J., & Adler, R. (2008). Non-suicidal self-injury and co-occurrence. In M.K. Nixon & N.L. Heath (Eds.), Self-injury in youth: The essential guide to assessment and intervention (pp. 59–78). New York: Routledge.

Lowenstein, T. (2005). *Buddhist inspirations: Essential philosophy, truth, and enlightenment.* London: Duncan Baird.

Lutz, A., Greischar, L., Rawlings, N., Ricard, M., & Davidson, R. (2004). Long-term mediators self-induce high amplitude gamma synchrony during mental practice. *Proceedings of the National Academy of the Sciences, 101,* 16369–16373.

Lyubomirsky, S. (2007). *The how of happiness: A scientific approach to getting the life you want.* New York: Penguin Books.

Maisel, R., Epston, D., & Borden, A. (2004). *Biting the hand that starves you: Inspiring resistance to anorexia/bulimia.* New York: Norton.

Malchiodic, C.A. (Ed.). Creative inverventions with tramuatized children. New York: Guilford Press.

Malchiodi, C.A. (Ed.) (2003). *Handbook of art therapy.* New York: Guilford Press.

Marlatt, G.A. (Ed.) (1998). *Harm reduction: Pragmatic strategies for managing high risk behaviors.* New York: Guilford Press.

Marlatt, G.A., Bowen, S., Chawla, N., & Witkiewitz, K. (2008). Mindfulness-based relapse prevention for substance abusers: Therapist training and therapeutic relationships. In S.F. Hick & T. Bien (Eds.), *Mindfulness and the therapeutic relationship* (pp. 107–122). New York: Guilford Press.

Marlatt, G.A., & Kristeller, J. (1999). Mindfulness and meditation. In W.R. Miller (Ed.), *Integrating spirituality in treatment: Resources for practitioners* (pp. 67–84). Washington, DC: American Psychological Association.

McDermott, D., & Snyder, C.R. (1999). *Making hope happen: A workbook for turning possibilities into reality.* Oakland, CA: New Harbinger.

McKeel, A.J. (1999). A selected review of research of solution-focused brief therapy. Retrieved April 10, 1999, from http://www.enabling.org/ia/sft

McVey-Noble, M., Khemlani-Patel, S., & Neziroglu, F. (2006). *When your child is cutting: A parent's guide to helping children overcome self-injury.* Oakland, CA: New Harbinger.

Michel, B., & Nock, M. (2008, June). *The pain paradox: Understanding pain analgesia in NSSI.* Paper presented at the International Society for the Study of Self-Injury Conference, Harvard University, Cambridge, MA.

Miller, A.L., Rathus, J.H., & Linehan, M.M. (2007). *Dialectical behavior therapy with suicidal adolescents.* New York: Guilford Press.

Miller, D. (2005). *Women who hurt themselves: A book of hope and understanding.* New York: Basic Books.

Miller, W.R., & Carroll, K. (2006). *Rethinking substance abuse: What the science shows and what we should do about it.* New York: Guilford Press.

Miller, W.R., & Rollnick, S. (2002). *Motivational interviewing: Preparing people for change* (2nd ed.). New York: Guilford Press.

Minuchin, S. (1974). *Families and family therapy.* Cambridge, MA: Harvard University Press.

Minuchin, S. & Fishman, H.C. (1981). *Family therapy techniques.* Cambridge, MA: Harvard University Press.

Moos, R. (1979). *Evaluation of educational environments: Procedures, measures, findings, and policy implications*. San Francisco: Jossey-Bass.

Muelenlkamp, J. (2006). Empirically supported treatments and general therapy guidelines for non-suicidal self-injury. *Journal of Mental Health Counseling, 28,* 166–185.

Muehlenkamp, J., & Guitierrez, P.M. (2004). An investigation of differences between self-injurious behavior and suicide attempts in a sample of adolescents. *Suicide and Life-Threatening Behavior, 34,* 12–24.

Muehlenkamp, J., & Guitierrez, P.M. (2007). Risk for suicide attempts among adolescents who engage in non-suicide self-injury. *Archives at Suicidal Research, 11,* 69–82.

Muehlenamp, J., Yates, B., & Alberts, A. (2004, April). *Gender and racial differences in self-injury*. Paper presented at the Annual American Association of Suicidology Conference, Miami, FL.

Murray, C.D., & Fox, J. (2006). So internet self-harm discussion groups alleviate or exacerbate self-harming behavior? *Australian E-Journal for the Advancement of Mental Health, 5.* Retrieved March 23, 2008, from http//www.auseinet.com/journal/vol5iss3/murray.pdf

Nardone, G., & Salvini, A. (2007). *The strategic dialogue: Rendering the diagnostic interview a real therapeutic intervention*. London: Karnac.

Nardone, G. & Watzlawick, P. (2005). *Brief strategic therapy: Philosophy, techniques, and research*. London: Karnac.

Nasser, M. (1997). *Culture and weight consciousness*. London, Brunner-Routledge.

Nasser, M. (2004). Dying to live: Eating disorders and self-harm behavior in a cultural context. In J.L. Levitt, R.A. Sansone, & Cohn, L. (Eds.), *Self-harm behavior and eating disorders: Dynamics, assessment, and treatment* (pp.15–31). New York: Brunner-Routledge.

Neret, G. (1994). *Salvador Dali 1904–1989*. Berlin, Germany: Benedict Taschen.

Nock, M.K., Joiner, T.E., Gordon, K.H., Lloyd-Richardson, E., & Prinstein, M.J. (2006). Non-suicidal self-injury among adolescents: Diagnostic correlates and relation to suicide attempts. *Psychiatry Research, 144*(1), 65–72.

Nock, M., & Prinstein, M.J. (2004). A functional approach to the assessment of self-mutilative behavior. *Journal of Consulting and Clinical Psychology, 72*(5), 885–890.

Nock, M., & Prinstein, M.J. (2005). Contextual features and behavioral functions of self-mutilation among adolescents. *Journal of Abnormal Pyschology, 114*(1), 140–146.

Norcross, J.C. (2008, December). Psychotherapy relationships that work: Tailoring the relationship to the individual client. Workshop presented at the Milton H. Erickson Brief Therapy Conference, San Diego, CA.

O'Connor, R.C., Sheehy, N.P., & O'Connor, D.B. (2000). Fifty cases of general hospital parasuicide. *British Journal of Health Psychology, 5,* 83–95.

O'Hanlon, W.H. (1987). *Taproots: Underlying principles of Milton H. Erickson's therapy and hypnosis*. New York: Norton.

O'Hanlon, W.H., & Weiner-Davis, M. (1989). *In search of solutions: A new direction in psychotherapy*. New York: Norton.

Omer, H. (2004). *Nonviolent resistance: A new approach to violent and self-destructive children*. Cambridge, UK: Cambridge University Press.

Osuch, E.A., & Payne, G.W. (2008). Neurobiological perspectives on self-injury. In M.K. Nixon and N.L. Heath (Eds.), Self-injury in youth: An essential guide to assessment and intervention (pp. 79–110). Nw York: Routledge.

Papp, P. (1983). *The process of change*. New York: Guilford Press.

Parker, M.W., Winstead, D.K., & Willi, F.T. (1979). Patient autonomy in alcohol rehabilitation: I. Literature review. *International Journal of Addictions, 14,* 1015–1022.

Patterson, G.R., Reid, J.B., & Dishion, T.J. (1992). *Antisocial boys*. Eugene, OR: Castalia.

Paul, T., Schroeter, K., Dahme, B., & Nutzinger, D. (2002). Self-injurious behavior in women with eating disorders. *American Journal of Psychiatry, 159,* 408–411.

Pennebaker, J.W. (2004). *Writing to heal: A guided journal for recovering from trauma and emotional upheaval*. Oakland, CA: New Harbinger.

Pennebaker, J. W. (1997). *Opening up: The healing power of expressisng emotions.* New York: Guilford Press.

Pennebaker, J. W. & Graybeal, A. (2001). Patterns of natural language use: Disclosure, personality, and social integration. *Current Directions in Psychological Science, 10,* 90–93.

Pennebaker, J. W., & Susman, J. R. (1988). Disclosure of traumas and psychosomatic processes. *Social Science and Medicine, 26,* 327–332.

Peterson, C. (2006). *A primer in positive psychology.* New York: Oxford University Press.

Peterson, C., & Seligman, M. E. P. (2004). *Character strengths and virtues: A handbook and classification.* New York: Oxford University Press.

Piran, N. (1998). Prevention of eating disorders: The struggle to chart new territories. *Eating Disorders: The Journal of Treatment and Prevention, 6,* 365–371.

Piran, N. (2001). Re-inhabiting the body. *Feminism and Psychology, 11,* 172–176.

Plante, L. G. (2007). *Bleeding to ease the pain: Cutting, self-injury, and the adolescent search for self.* Westport, CT: Praeger.

Pope, D. (2001). *Doing school: How we are creating a generation of stressed out, materialistic, and mis-educated students.* New Haven, CT: Yale University Press.

Pope, D., & Simon, R. (2005). Help for stressed students. *Educational Leadership, 62,* 33–37.

Post, S., & Neimark, J. (2007). *Why good things happen to good people: The exciting new research that proves the link between doing good and living a longer, healthier, happier life.* New York: Broadway Books.

Prochaska, J. O., Norcross, J. C., & DiClemente, C. C. (1994). *Changing for good: The revolutionary program that explains the six stages of change and teaches you how to free yourself from bad habits.* New York: Morrow.

Reinhurz, H. Z., Giaconia, R. M., & Silverman, A. B. (1995). Early psycho-social risks for adolescent suicidal ideation and attempts. *Journal of the American Academy of Child and Adolescent Psychiatry, 34,* 599–611.

Remafedi, G., French, S., Story, M., Resnick, M. D., & Blum, R. (1998). The relationship between suicide risk and sexual orientation: Results of a population-based study. *American Journal of Public Health,* 88(1), 57–60.

Rey Gex, C. R., Narring, F., Ferron, C., & Michaud, P. A. (1998). Suicide attempts among adolescents in Switzerland: Prevalence, associated factors and comorbidity. *Acta Psychiatrica Scandinavia, 98,* 28–33.

Roberts, D. F., Foehr, U. G., & Rideout, V. (2005). *Generation M: Media in the lives of 8–18 year-olds.* Washington, DC: Kaiser Family Foundation.

Rollnick, S., Mason, P., & Butler, C. (1999). *Health behavior change: A guide for practitioners.* Edinburgh, UK: Churchill-Livingstone.

Rollnick, S., Miller, W. R., & Butler, C. (2008). *Motivational interviewing in health care: Helping patients change behavior.* New York: Guilford Press.

Rosenkrantz, M., Jackson, K., Dalton, I., Dolski, C., Ryff, B., Singer, D., et al. (2003). Affective style and vivo immune response: Neurobehavioral mechanisms. *Proceedings of the National Academy of Sciences, 100,* 11148–11152.

Ross, S., & Heath, N. (2002). A study of the frequency of self-mutilation in a community sample of adolescents. *Journal of Youth and Adolescence, 31,* 67–77.

Sachsse, U., Von Der Heyde, S., & Huether, G. (2002). Stress regulation and self-mutilation. *American Journal of Psychiatry,* 159(4), 672.

Sansone, R. A., Levitt, J. L., & Sansone, L. A. (2004). Psychotropic medications, self-harm behavior, and eating disorders. In J. L. Levitt, R. A. Sansone, & L. Cohn (Eds.), *Self-harm behavior and eating disorders: Dynamics, assessment, and treatment* (pp. 245–259). New York: Brunner-Routledge.

Santisteban, D. A., Muir, J., Mena, M. P., & Mitrani, V. B. (2003). Integrative borderline adolescent family therapy: Meeting the challenges of treating adolescents with borderline personality disorder. *Psychotherapy: Theory, Research, Practice, & Training,* 40(4), 251–264.

Santisteban, D. A., Coatsworth, J. D., Perez-Vidal, A., Kurtines, W. M., Schwartz, S. J., Laperriere, A., et al. (2003). Efficacy of brief strategic family therapy in modifying Hispanic adolescent behavior problems and substance use. *Journal of Family Psychology, 17,* 121–133.

Schroeder, S. R., Oster-Granite, M.L., & Thompson, T. (2002). Self-injurious behavior: Gene, brain, behavior relationships. *Research in Developmental Disabilities, 23*(5), 367–368.

Selekman, M. D. (1991). The solution-oriented parenting group: A treatment alternative that works. *Journal of Strategic and Systemic Therapies, 10*(1), 36–49.

Selekman, M. D. (1995). Rap with wisdom: Peer reflecting teams with tough adolescents. In S. Friedman (Ed.), *The reflecting team in action: Collaborative practice in family therapy* (pp. 205–223). New York: Guilford Press.

Selekman, M. D. (1997). *Solution-focused therapy with children: Harnessing family strengths for systemic change.* New York: Guilford Press.

Selekman, M. D. (1999). The solution-oriented parenting group revisited. *Journal of Systemic Therapies, 18*(1), 5–24.

Selekman, M. D. (2004, January/February). Working with self-harming teens can be an unpredictable roller-coaster ride. *Psychotherapy Networker, xx,* 77–85.

Selekman, M. D. (2005). *Pathways to change: Brief therapy with difficult adolescents* (2nd ed.). New York: Guilford Press.

Selekman, M. D. (2006a, October). Co-authoring solution-determined stories with self-harming adolescents. *Context: The Magazine for Family Therapy and Systemic Practice,* 87, 34–40.

Selekman, M. D. (2006b). *Working with self-harming adolescents: A collaborative strengths-based therapy approach.* New York: Norton.

Selekman, M. D. (2008a, January/February). Mission possible: The art of engaging tough teens. *Psychotherapy Networker, xx,* 23–24.

Selekman, M. D. (2008b). Adventures in time traveling: Co-creating compelling future realities with families. *Journal of Brief Therapy,* 5(2), 89–103.

Selekman, M. D. & Schulem, H. (2007). *The self-harming adolescents and their families expert consultants project: A qualitative study.* Unpublished manuscript.

Selekman, M. D. & Todd, T. C. (1991). Crucial issues in the treatment of adolescent substance abusers and their families. In T. C.. Todd & M. D. Selekman (Eds.), *Family therapy approaches with adolescent substance abusers* (pp. 3–28). Needham Heights, MA: Allyn & Bacon.

Seligman, M. E. P. (2002). *Authentic happiness.* New York: Free Press.

Seligman, M. E. P. (2003). *Nine-month vanguard master class in authentic happiness coaching and positive psychology,* Bethesda, MD.

Seligman, M. E. P., Reivich, K., Jaycox, L., & Gillham, J. (1995). *The optimistic child: A revolutionary program that safeguards children against depression and builds lifelong resilience.* Boston: Houghton Mifflin.

Shannon, J. (2005). *Self-mutilation behavior in youth and adults: Causes, treatment, and prevention.* Denver, CO: Cross Country.

Sharples, T. (2008). Teens' latest self-injury fad: Self-embedding. *Time* Magazine Archive, retrieved December 17, 2008, from http://www.time.com/time/printout/ 0,8816,1865995,00.html.

Shearin, E.N. & Linehan, M.M. (1994). Dialectical behavior therapy for borderline personality disorder: Theoretical and empirical foundations. *Acta Psychiatrica Scandinavia, 89,* 58–61.

Shneidman, E.S. (1985). *Definition of suicide.* New York: Wiley.

Siegel, L. (2008). *Against the machine: Being human in the age of the electronic mob.* New York: Spiegel & Grau.

Simmons, R. (2002). *Odd girl out: The hidden culture of aggression in girls.* New York: Harcourt.

Skegg, K. (2005). Self-harm. *Lancet, 366,* 1471–1483.

Skegg, K., Nada-Raja, S., Dickson, N., Paul, C., & Williams, S. (2003). Sexual orientation and self-harm in men and women. *American Journal of Psychiatry, 160*(3), 541–546.

Snyder, C. R., Michael, S. T., & Cheavens, J. S. (1999). Hope as a psychotherapeutic foundation of common factors, placebos, and expectancies. In M. A. Hubble, B. L. Duncan, & S. D. Miller (Eds.), *The heart and soul of change: What works in therapy* (pp.179–201). Washington, DC: American Psychological Association.

Snyder, C. R. & Lopez, S. J. (Eds.) (2007). *Positive psychology: The scientific and practical explorations of human strengths*. Thousand Oaks, CA: Sage.

Souvander, A., Avomaa, A., Pihlakoski, P., Haavista, A., Rautava, P., Helenius, H. (2006). Early predictors of deliberate self-harm among adolescents: A prospective follow-up study from age 3 to age 15. *Journal of Affective Disorders, 93,* 87–96.

Stinnett, N., & O'Donnell, M. (1996). *Good kids: How you and your kids can successfully navigate the teen years*. New York: Doubleday.

Stone, J. (2008, July). *Integrating post-colonial model of historical trauma for suicide with Native American youth*. Workshop presented at the Suicide: Breaking the Silence Conference, Window Rock, AZ.

Strong, M. (1998). *A bright red scream: Self-mutilation and the language of pain*. New York: Penguin Books.

Surya Das, L. (2007). *The big questions: How to find your own answers to life's essential mysteries*. New York: Rodale.

Szapocznik, J., Hervis, O., & Schwartz, S. (2003). Brief strategic family therapy for adolescent drug abuse. *Therapy manuals for drug addiction*, Manual 5. Bethesda, MD: U.S Department of Health and Human Services, National Institutes of Health.

Szapocznik, J., & Kurtines, W. M. (1989). *Breakthroughs in family therapy with drug-abusing and problem youth*. New York: Springer.

Szapocznik, J., & Williams, R. A. (2000). Brief strategic family therapy: Twenty-five years of interplay among theory, research, and practice in adolescent behavior problems and drug abuse. *Clinical Child and Family Psychology Review, 3*(2), 117–134.

Talmon, M. (1990). *Single session therapy: Maximizing the effect of the first (and often only) therapeutic encounter*. San Francisco: Jossey-Bass.

Thomas, T., & Watzman, A. (1999). *Carnegie Mellon study reveals negative potential of heavy internet use on emotional well-being* (press release). Retrieved March 23, 2008, from http://ncii.cs.cmv.edu/progress/pressrel.html

Tulloch, A. L., Whitlock, L. B., Hoyt, D. R., Johnson, J. D. (1997). Adolescent-parent communicationand self-harm. *Journal of Adolescent Health, 21,* 267–275.

Van der Kolk, B. A., Roth, S., Pelcovitz, D., Sunday, S., & Spinazzola, J. (2005). Dis-orders of extreme stress: The empirical foundation of complex trauma adaptation. *Journal of Traumatic Stress, 18,* 389–399.

Velasquez, M. M., Maurer, G. G., Crouch, C., & DiClemente, C. C. (2001). *Group treatment for substance abuse: A stages-of-change therapy manual*. New York: Guilford Press.

Wagner, B. M., Aiken, C., Mullaley, P. M., & Tobin, J. J. (2000). Parents' reactions to adolescents' suicide attempts. *Journal of the American Academy of Child and Adolescent Psychiatry, 39,* 429–436.

Wagner, B. M., Cole, R. E., & Schwartzman, P. (1995). Psychosocial correlates of suicide attempts among junior and senior high school youth. *Suicide and Life-Threatening Behavior, 25,* 358–372.

Walsh, B. W. (2006). *Treating self-injury: A practical guide*. New York: Guilford Press.

Wampold, B. (2001). *The great psychotherapy debate: Models, methods, and findings*. Mahwah, NJ: Erlbaum.

Watkins, P. C., Scheer, J., Ovnicek, M., & Kolts, R. (2006). The debt of gratitude: Dissociating gratitude and indebtedness. *Cognition and Emotion, 20*(2), 217–241.

Watzlawick, P., Weakland, J., & Fisch, R. (1974). *Change: Principles of problem formation and problem resolution*. New York: Norton.

Weiner-Davis, M., De Shazer, S., & Gingerich, W. (1987). Building on pretreatment change to construct the therapeutic solution: An exploratory study. *Journal of Marital and Family Therapy, 13*(4), 359–363.

White, K. (2008, July). *Navajo cultural identity and depression*. Workshop presented at the Suicide: Breaking the Silence Conference, Window Rock, AZ.

White, M. (1986). Negative explanation, restraint, and double description: A template for family therapy. *Family Process, 25*(2), 169–184.

White, M. (1988). Anorexia nervosa: A cybernetic perspective. In J.C. Hansen and J.E. Harkaway (Eds.), *Eating disorders* (pp. 117–129). Rockville, MD: Aspen.

White, M. (1995). *Re-authoring lives: Interviews and essays*. Adelaide, South Australia: Dulwich Centre Publications.

White, M. (2007). *Maps in narrative practice*. New York: Norton.

White, M. & Epston, D. (1990). *Narrative means to therapeutic ends*. New York: Norton.

Whitfield, S., (1992). *Magritte*. Brussels, Belgium: Ludion.

Whitlock, J. (2008, March). Non-suicidal injury and recovery: What students say about why they started, how they stopped, and what they learned along the way. Workshop presented at the Creating Healthy Community Conference, University of Michigan, Ann Arbor. MI.

Whitlock, J., Eckenrode, J., & Silverman, D. (2006). Self-injurious behavior in a college population. *Pediatrics, 117,* 6.

Whitlock, J., Eells, G., Cummings, N., & Purington, A. (2007). *Non-suicidal self-injury in college populations: Mental health provider assessment of prevalence and need.* Unpublished manuscript.

Whitlock, J., & Knox, K. (2007). The relationship between suicide and self-injury in a young adult population. *Archives of Pediatrics and Adolescent Medicine, 161*(7), 634–640.

Whitlock, J., Lader, W., & Conterio, K. (2007). The internet and self-injury: What psychotherapists should know. *Journal of Clinical Psychology: In Session, 63,* 1135–1143.

Whitlock, J., Muehlenkamp, J., & Eckenrode, J. (2008). Variation in non-suicidal self-injury: Identification and features of latent classes in a college population in emerging adults. *Journal of Clinical Child and Adolescent Psychology, 37*(4), 725–735.

Whitlock, J., Powers, J., & Eckenrode, J. (2006). The virtual cutting edge: Adolescent self-injury and the internet. *Developmental Psychology, 42*(3), 407–417.

Whitlock, J., Purington, A., & Gershkovich, M. (2009). Influence of the media on self-injurious behavior. In M. Nock (Ed.), *Understanding non-suicidal self-injury: current science and practice.* Washington, DC: American Psychological Association.

Yates, T.M. (2004). The developmental psychopathology of self-injurious behavior: Compensatory regulation in post-traumatic adaptation. *Clinical Psychology Review, 24,* 35–74.

INDEX

protective shields, of self-harmer, in Stress-Busters' Leadership Group, 235–37
Prozac, for self-harming behavior, 30
psychiatric medications, for self-harming behavior, 30
psychoeducational therapy, traditional group therapy vs., 230–31
psychological issues, in self-harming behavior, 12–14
Purington, A., 1, 20–24

question(s)
    assessment, for self-harmers, 69–70
    best hopes, 87
    consolidating, in staying on track, 174–75
    conversational, 108–9, 262-63
    coping, 259, 294
    coping sequence, 106–7
    covering-the-back-door, 88–89
    in establishing well-formulated treatment goals, 86–88
    externalizing, 110–11
    future-oriented, 27
    goal-setting clarification, 105–6
    miracle, 27, 258
    percentage, 110, 111
    pessimistic, 259, 294
    pessimistic sequence, 107–8
    presuppositional, 86–88
    reversal, 109–10
    scaling, 27, 88, 258
        subzero, 54, 294
    well-formulated treatment goals-related, 86–88

race, in self-harming behavior, 11–12
readiness for change, stages of, of self-harmers, 55–58, 57f
reflection, therapeutic, 93
reinforcement, narrative, 23
Reinhurz, H.Z., 19
"rejection pattern," empowering couple to conquer long-standing, case example, 203–9
relationship(s)
    changes in, desired by self-harmers, 86–89
    peer, of self-harmers, 78–81
relationship-effectiveness skills, in Stress-Busters' Leadership Group, 238–40
relative(s), lost, say "hello" in order to say "good-bye" to, 144
resiliency protective factors, of self-harmers, 41–42
resources
    inner, of self-harmers, 39–41
    self-harming difficulties as, 47–48
responding
    active constructive, 112
    passive constructive, 112
reversal questions, 109–10
reward(s), effort-driven, 130
rigid views, clinging to, implications and usefulness of, 129–30
ritual(s), family connection-building, 135–70. see also family connection-building rituals
Rodham, K., 12, 13, 19, 23

Roemar, L., 10
Rohde, P., 144
Ross, S., 12
ruminating about negative life events, implications and usefulness of, 129–30
Russ, M.J., 8–9

Sachsse, U., 6
Salts, C.J., 39
Salvini, A., 100
San Juan Board of Cooperative Educational Services (BOCES), in The Summit Program funding, 278
Santisteban, D.A., 24, 25, 29
SASO (Sexual Assault Services Organization), 285
say "hello" in order to say "good-bye" to lost parents, siblings, or close relatives, 144
scaling questions, 27, 88, 258
    subzero, 54, 294
Scheer, J., 132
Scherlis, W., 24
Schmidt, U., 24
school
    self-harmers functioning at, 81–82
    stress related to, tools for mastering, 247–48
searching for evidence disputation skill, 128
searching for narrative explanations, 128–29
secret surprise experiment, 164–65
Seeley, J.R., 144
selective serotonin reuptake inhibitors (SSRIs), for self-harming behavior, 30
Selekman, M.D., 5–6, 9, 14, 17, 20, 21, 25–26, 29, 39, 278, 281–86
self-destructive behavior couples, 202–3
self-embedding, 3
self-harm. see also self-harmers; self-harming behavior
    high tolerance for bodily pain and, 6–7
    methods of, 4–5
    symptoms switching in, 5–6
self-harmers
    alcoholic, recommendations for, 292–93
    artwork of, cautionary note about responding to, 164
    assessment questions to ask, 69–70
    attempted solutions for, 70–72
    body-scanning by, 127
    brief therapy with, 214–28. see also brief therapy, with self-harming young adults and adolescents
    bring close friend to first couples therapy session, 198
    Buddhist principles and healing practices for, 121–124
    candle meditation for, 119–20
    challenges with, 34–35
    chilling-out room for, 116–18
    cloud shape watching for, 120
    confidence of, 52–55
    deeply entrenched in negative peer groups, 289–90
    disputation skills of, 127–28
    drug abuse by, recommendations for, 292–93
    embracing dragon to release princess/prince for, 124–25

therapeutic alliance building, 49–50
therapeutic experiments, 135–70
    choreographing new life, 168–69
    compliment box, 155–56
    do something different, 165–67
    drawing out oppressive thoughts, mood states, and habits, 160–62, 161f
    experiencing future selves to establish new parent-young adult/adolescent relationships in the now, 139–41
    famous guest consultants experiment, 147–48
    gratitude letter and visit, 155
    imaginary feelings X-ray machine, 156–58, 157f
    imaginary time machine, 135–37
    invisible family interventions, 145–47
    looking back/looking forward, 167–68
    my documentary about me, 168
    my extraordinary newspaper headline, 151
    my family story mural, 158–160, 159f
    my favorite author re-writes my story, 150–51
    observing-oneself-up-high-in-a-bubble, 79, 150
    planning out your perfect day, 153–54
    pretend miracle happened, 167
    resolving past conflicts and traumatic events, 137–39
    secret surprise experiment, 164–65
    soul collages, 162
    taking imaginary time machine anywhere in time, 144–45
    three good things, 152–53
    using your top signature strengths in novel ways, 154–55
    working with disconnected families, 169–70
    you at your best story, 151–52
therapeutic experiment selection menu, for self-harmers, 93
therapeutic reflection, 93
therapeutic relationship factors, 28
The Scalpel and the Silver Bear: The First Navajo Woman Surgeon Combines Western Medicine and Traditional Healing, 243
The Summit Program, 277–86
    box skill, 285
    case examples, 281–84
    data from, 278–81, 279f
    DBT in, 278
    empowering therapist in, 285–86
    funding of, 278
    graduate services, 284–85
    pharmacological treatment in, 284
    treatment outcomes, 278–81, 280f
thinking
    agency, 53, 152
    pathway, 53, 152
Thirteen, 9, 20, 21
Thomas, T., 24
thought(s), oppressive, drawing out, 160-62, 161f
three good things, 152–53
thrill-seekers, self-harming behavior by, 2–3
tools for mastering school stress, in Stress-Busters' Leadership Group, 247–48
Toste, J.R., 11
Townsend, E., 30
traditional group therapy, psychoeducational therapy vs., 230–31

training stage, in Pathways to Possibilities Program, 275
traumatic events, past, resolving of, 137–39
treatment considerations, in readiness for change, 58
treatment drop-outs
    factors contributing to, 295–99
    letters to, 59–60
treatment failures, factors contributing to, 295–99
treatment goals, well-formulated, questions related to, 86–88
tribal circle of caring others
    co-constructing of, 215–28
        case example, 216–28
            initial consultation session, 217–18, 223–25
            post-therapy case reflections, 221–22, 228
            referral process, 216–17, 222–23
            second session, 218–20, 225–26
            telephone follow-up, 221, 227
            third session, 220, 226–27
        last session, 220–21, 227
triggers, of self-harmers, positive and negative, 77–78, 78f
Turkheimer, E., 30
turning arrows into flowers, 123–24
23rd Annual Report to Congress, on Implementation of the Individuals with Disabilities Act, 280
two-step tango strategy, 55–56, 267, 288, 292
Tyrer, P., 24

urge(s), overcoming of, in self-harmers' management, 127
urge surfing, in self-harmers' management, 121
using your top signature strengths in novel ways, 154–55

Values-in Action Classification of Character Strengths and Virtues, 44
Values-in Action Inventory of Strengths, 44
Vandereycken, W., 19
Vertommen, H., 19
VIA Inventory of Strengths for Adults, 251
VIA Inventory of Strengths for Youth, 44, 237
VIA Inventory of Strengths Questionnaire, 44
virtue categories, 44
visit(s), gratitude, 155
visualization, 27, 124
    of movies of success, in self-harmers' management, 125–27
visualization experiments, in self-harmers' management, 124
visual-spatial intelligence area, 158–62, 159f, 161f
Von Der Heyde, S., 6

"Walking in Beauty," 97
walk-ins, pretreatment experiments for, 38–39
Walsh, B.W., 31
Wampold, B., 100
warning signs, early identification of, in staying on track, 176–77
Watkins, P.C., 132